From Rail-Splitter to Icon

From

LINCOLN'S IMAGE

IN ILLUSTRATED PERIODICALS, 1860–1865

to Icon

GARY L. BUNKER

THE KENT STATE UNIVERSITY PRESS · KENT & LONDON

© 2001 by The Kent State University Press,
Kent, Ohio 44242
Library of Congress Catalog Card Number 2001029859
ISBN 0-87338-701-5
Manufactured in the United States of America

08 07 06 05 04 03 02 01   5 4 3 2 1

Chapter 8 first appeared in the *Journal of the Abraham Lincoln
Association* 17.1 (1996): 53–87. This slightly revised version
appears here courtesy of the *Journal of the Abraham Lincoln
Association* and the Board of Trustees at the University of
Illinois, Urbana-Champaign.

Library of Congress Cataloging-in-Publication Data
Bunker, Gary L., 1934–
From rail-splitter to icon : Lincoln's image in illustrated
periodicals, 1860–1865 / Gary L. Bunker.
    p.   cm.
Includes bibliographical references (p.) and index.
ISBN 0-87338-701-5 (alk. paper)
1. Lincoln, Abraham, 1809–1865—Caricatures and cartoons.
2. Lincoln, Abraham, 1809–1865—Pictorial works.
3. Lincoln, Abraham, 1809–1865—Relations with journalists.
4. Illustrated periodicals—United States—History—19th
century. 5. Press and politics—United States—History—
19th century. 6. United States—Politics and government—
1861–1865—Journalists. 8. United States—History—Civil
War, 1861–1865—Press coverage. I. Title.
E457.63.B86 2001
973.7'092—dc21

                                          2001029859

British Library Cataloging-in-Publication data are available.

To Carol

Contents

Acknowledgments

$\mathcal{G}$enerous research funding from the College of Family, Home, and Social Sciences at Brigham Young University supported the acquisition of photographs, the payment of permission fees, and two professional development leaves in 1990 and 1996 to access diverse archival repositories, which included the American Antiquarian Society; Boston Atheneum; the McLellan Lincoln Collection at the John Hay Library, Brown University; Buffalo and Erie County Public Library; Chicago Historical Society; Special Collections, Gettysburg College; Huntington Library; Illinois State Historical Society; Lilly Library, Indiana University at Bloomington; Library of Congress; Library of Virginia; Lincoln Memorial University, Harrogate, Tennessee; the Lincoln Museum, Fort Wayne, Indiana; Newberry Library; New-York Historical Society; New York Public Library; New York State Library; Ohio State Historical Society; Pennsylvania State Historical Society; Princeton University; Special Collections, Providence Public Library; Department of Special Collections, the University of Chicago Library; Rare Book and Special Collections Library, University of Illinois at Urbana-Champaign; University of Minnesota; Western Reserve Historical Society, and Wisconsin Historical Society.

To several individuals I owe a special debt. Draper Hill, cartoonist for the *Detroit Free Press* and a specialist on Thomas Nast, kindly informed me about the Nineteenth-Century Political Cartoon Scrapbook in Special Collections at Gettysburg College. David Hedrick, Special Collections librarian at Gettysburg College, gave competent assistance with that resource. Jennifer B. Lee, former curator of printed Books at the John Hay Library at Brown University, provided valuable help with the library's Lincoln collection. Mark E. Neely Jr., Lincoln scholar and former director of the Lincoln Museum, shared his knowledge of the pictorial and textual domain and identified important iconography. Philip J. Weimerskirch, Special Collections librarian at the Providence Public Library, helped me navigate through the relevant visual materials in the fine C. Fiske Harris Collection on the American Civil War and Slavery. Richard Samuel West, author, collector, dealer, and specialist in antiquarian periodicals, generously shared his private Lincoln collection and expertise. Georgia B. Barnhill, Andrew W. Mellon Curator of Graphic Arts at the American Antiquarian Society, introduced me to two invaluable graphic resources from the Civil War period: the William A. Smith and Samuel B. Woodward Cartoon Collections. Access to the visual arts collection at the Boston Atheneum was graciously provided by its curator, Sally Pierce. William H. Loos, curator of the Rare Book Room at the Buffalo and Erie County Public Library, provided photographs from their collection of *Frank Leslie's Budget of Fun* and the *Comic Monthly*.

After reading an early version of the manuscript, Michael Burlingame, professor of history at Connecticut College, New London, encouraged publication. James A. Rawley, Carl Adolph Happold Professor Emeritus at the University of Nebraska, reviewed the complete manuscript; his encouragement and suggestions were invaluable. Special appreciation must be extended to Thomas F. Schwartz, Illinois State historian and editor of the *Journal of the Abraham Lincoln Association*. His patient support and competent advice via telephone and letter went the second mile. He read the manuscript as it unfolded, introduced it to other Lincoln scholars, and reviewed it for The Kent State University Press. John T. Hubbell, Director Emeritus of The Kent State University Press, aggressively pursued and committed his press to the project in uncommon, expeditious fashion. Joanna Hildebrand Craig, editor-in-chief; Erin L. Holman, managing editor; Will Underwood, interim director; and the entire Kent State University Press staff have rendered valuable assistance and substantially improved the finished manuscript. Finally, Carol B. Bunker, my devoted companion of many years, to whom this volume is dedicated, not only spent tireless hours assisting me with the basic research in libraries across the land, but also has been the central source for the quality of my life. To all these and others I am ever indebted for whatever may be praiseworthy in this volume, yet I am solely responsible for any defects or oversights that remain.

One

Introduction

*B*y almost any measure in the popular culture, Abraham Lincoln was more publicly visible than any prior president in American history. This disparity was not a simple matter of differential popularity. Indeed, Lincoln was beset with criticism at home and abroad throughout the duration of his administration. What, then, was the origin of this increased visibility? In America, innovation in popular art, photography, and journalism coincided with the eruption of unparalleled social and political fermentation that thrust Lincoln's image into magazines, mass-produced separately published prints, cartes de visite, song sheet covers, campaign papers, patriotic envelopes, broadsides, books and pamphlets, and newspapers.[1] The products of developing technology, expanding media outlets, a growing cultural appetite for illustration, and the existence of skilled artists, engravers, and photographers felicitously converged with the Lincoln presidency. Citing a contemporary art journal, historian Frank Mott described this burgeoning cultural phenomenon as the "illustration mania." "Nothing but illustrated works are profitable to publishers, while the illustrated magazines and newspapers are vastly popular."[2]

In the visual arts, the continuous maturation of printmaking from primitive woodcuts to sophisticated engravings on wood, metal, and stone enhanced the quality and increased the quantity of all forms of illustration.[3] The technology of photography was also coming of age.[4] During the Civil War, Mathew Brady and Alexander Gardner, among others, photographed their way into professional fame, and the Lincoln portraits advertised and encouraged the craft's growth.[5] Separately published prints in fine and popular art were at the peak of public regard; this was also true of political caricature in that medium. Neither the image of James Buchanan, Lincoln's presidential predecessor, nor that of Ulysses S. Grant, the 1868 president-elect, was as frequently featured in this medium as that of Abraham Lincoln. Thus humor, too, was enthroned in the visual medium as in no other previous period.[6] Like it or not, Lincoln was in the limelight for the duration of his administration.

Nowhere in the domain of popular culture was the explosion of imagery more apparent than in the medium of the illustrated magazine. About 1850, American pictorial journalism was born, but a decade passed before it matured. Its two major forms—the comic pictorial and the illustrated news weekly—were patterned after the proven British model of *Punch* and the *Illustrated London News*.

In the humor medium, *Yankee Notions* (1852–75) was the first American magazine to establish any degree of longevity, but before long it was joined by a spate of worthy competitors. With the exception of *Yankee Notions* and *Nick Nax* (1856–75), which were relatively lean on Lincoln caricature, most new illustrated periodicals were not even around for James Buchanan's election. However, for good or ill, the *Comic Monthly* (1859–81), *Frank Leslie's Budget of Fun* (1859–78), *Phunny Phellow* (1859–76), *Vanity Fair* (1859–63), *Momus* (1860), *Merryman's Monthly* (1863–75), *Southern Punch* (1863–65), and *Funniest of Phun* (1864–67) all molded Lincoln's image. Adding the British veteran *Punch* (1841–1992, 1996–) and its newly born comic sisters *Fun* (1861–65) and the *Comic News/Bubble* (1863–65), the comic genre produced more than 250 Lincoln cartoons.

These copiously illustrated comic magazines also stocked their supply of political ammunition with doggerel and satire. These two imposters, doggerel and satire, were close relatives of caricature, and with impunity they embellished Lincoln's profile with their own unique brand of creativity. Skillfully using the artifices of exaggeration, incongruity, surprise, irony, and distortion, these linguistic tools either enhanced or diminished Lincoln's credibility. For example, Artemus Ward's version of playful satire simply added color to Lincoln's early image. Although the satirist's Lincoln was far removed from the dignified and urbane stature of the presidency, that fact did not always blemish Lincoln's character; sometimes his backwoods roots and projected lack of sophistication endeared him to the common people. It was that kind of logic that inspired the "rail-splitter" image to promote Lincoln's initial campaign for the presidency.

In the Union's illustrated news medium, *Frank Leslie's Illustrated Newspaper* (1855–1922) and *Harper's Weekly* (1857–1916) were the flagships. Before the war, *Frank Leslie's Illustrated Newspaper* had already attained a circulation of 164,000, and it had not yet reached its full stride. Leslie's younger competitor, *Harper's Weekly*, surged "to 120,000 by the end of 1861," even before Thomas Nast's art cultivated and charmed a devoted audience of admirers.[7] So popular were these magazines that the informal distribution system extended to the Civil War battlefield. In 1859, the *New York Illustrated News* (1859–64) fearlessly cast its lot with the formidable competition already waged by *Frank Leslie's Illustrated Newspaper* and *Harper's Weekly*. In the South, the *Southern Illustrated News* (1862–65) advocated the Confederate perspective. Although distant from the national centers of popular art and engraving and operating from a modest economic base, it did its best to emulate British and American predecessors. Although its illustrations could not match the quantity or quality of its Northern antagonists, it was not one whit behind its rivals in zeal; Lincoln did not escape its satirical sting.

As with their counterparts in comic publications, illustrations in the news medium held center stage. A full-page front-cover drawing, a double-page center masterpiece (or two full, single-page images), a back-page cartoon (sometimes more), and a sprinkling of smaller graphics throughout an issue kept graphic art and photography in the foreground. Nevertheless, the visual arts were not the only source of Lincoln imagery; lively editorial commentary and informative news articles were also vital forces in shaping public attitudes toward Lincoln.

To humor and entertain subscribers, even the illustrated news periodicals reserved space for social and political caricature. Popular artists that published in these periodicals were among the best nineteenth-century America had to offer. In the early 1860s, the *New York Illustrated News* boasted artist Thomas Nast until *Harper's Weekly* shrewdly lured him away. Yet he was not the only draw; Frank Bellew, William Newman, Henry L. Stephens, J. H. Howard, John McLenan, and a host of others amused, beguiled, and provoked their devotees with the caustic wit of caricature.

Other forces at work also honed Lincoln's public image. Never before had the nation been so fragmented politically. When the irrepressible conflict over slavery and secession exploded into the Civil War, it engaged deep, seething emotions. For Southerners, Lincoln personified the source of their struggle. Consequently, there was little ambiguity in the Southern press over Lincoln's nefarious identity. Furthermore, the gravity of the political turmoil and the interdependent economic ties between America and England propelled the strife beyond national boundaries, and when the British comic press sided with the Confederate cause, Lincoln became the natural scapegoat. For the duration of the war, many British writers and artists mauled Lincoln's public persona. In fact, England's image makers were the primary sculptors of his pejorative international reputation.

In the North, it was a given that Lincoln would be vigorously opposed by the Democratic Party, especially the Copperhead wing. However, Lincoln could not have anticipated that he would be caught so often in the crossfire of criticism within his own political party. Typically, his moderate political posture courted the wrath of both conservatives and radicals. Yet it was the radical abolitionist segment that assailed his leadership, questioned his competence, and strove to topple him from the presidency. Ironically, this internal threat marshaled the most damaging domestic assault on Lincoln's presidential image.

Yet Lincoln contended with more than political fragmentation. Underlying and aggravating the division in the land was a more fundamental social problem: the malaise of prejudice. To be sure, it was a good sign that the national conscience was wrestling with the question of human liberty, but that cause was not undertaken without considerable national ambivalence. The disease of human condescension was pervasive in the world, and America was not immune to the epidemic. Although racial intolerance toward African Americans was the current focal point, that particular kind of intolerance was only symptomatic of a much larger social issue. Nativist apprehensions and fears motivated antipathy toward foreigners. Animosity toward the Irish was the most prominent ethnic theme in contemporary cartoons from eastern periodicals, but in California the Chinese were perceived as the growing nemesis. Many American Indians had been already dispossessed of their lands under the rationale of "manifest destiny," and others were just a few years away from the onset of major wars with the federal government. On the religious front, Catholics, Jews, and Mormons suffered from the limits of American pluralism. Finally, women had been denied fundamental human rights, including the right to vote, but they were decades away from that goal. Because of this entrenched and intractable pattern of behaviors and attitudes, the prognosis for social change on the issue of slavery was problematic. To say the least, Lincoln's role in facilitating meaningful change was daunting and the personal costs to his public image potentially devastating. These social and political factors materially affected the ultimate construction of Lincoln's public profile.

Given the extant staple of publications on the Lincoln image, what justification is there for yet another volume? Albert Shaw's pioneering cartoon history ended prematurely with the year of Lincoln's 1860 election and left a void for students of the cartoon genre.[8] More recently, the excellent work *The Lincoln Image* focuses on the rich and varied materials from an outstanding exhibit it represented. *The Lincoln Image* specializes in works of fine and popular art in separately published prints. It features the portrait genre from art and photography, and modestly exhibits a few works from the domain of political caricature. Like all good research, it is circumscribed by a set of sensible parameters that define its own scope and identity. Nevertheless, it deliberately excludes magazine illustrations and bypasses the verbal dimension of Lincoln image making.[9] Closest in spirit to my study is Rufus Rockwell Wilson's fine *Lincoln in Caricature*. Wilson elected to sample a broader domain of separately published prints, campaign papers, and illustrated magazines. However, within the illustrated periodical domain, he thoroughly investigated only three domestic magazines: *Vanity Fair*, *Frank Leslie's Illustrated Newspaper*, and *Harper's Weekly*. As for publications from abroad, he confined his study to *Punch* and *Fun*. Wilson ignored verbal characterizations of Lincoln in the periodicals he studied. Thus, he relinquished the vast majority of the illustrated periodical genre for other scholars to study.[10] In 1984, Harold Holzer, Gabor S. Boritt, and Mark E. Neely Jr. noted that the pictorial dimension had been neglected and that their volume, *The Lincoln Image*, was just "making a beginning."[11] *From Rail-Splitter to Icon* builds on the graphic foundation others have laid, and it aspires to blend the pictorial and verbal traditions in the magazine genre, which molded Lincoln's reputation.

Historically, Lincoln scholars have devoted most of their attention to illustrations in periodicals such as *Frank Leslie's Illustrated Newspaper*, *Harper's Weekly*, *Vanity Fair*, and England's *Punch* and *Fun*. This study includes such traditional sources, but it also examines the full array of contemporary illustrated magazines. Although *Vanity Fair* is a laudable exemplar of the comic genre, it scarcely represents the rich, though obscure, legacy of the *Comic Monthly*, *Frank Leslie's Budget of Fun*, *Funniest of Phun*,

Mr. Merryman's Monthly, Momus, Nick Nax, Phunny Phellow, Southern Punch, and *Yankee Notions*. Moreover, when the *Illustrated London News*, the rare *Comic News*, and its short-lived successor, the *Bubble*, are added to *Punch* and *Fun*, our understanding of the British magazine tradition is enhanced. Likewise, inclusion of the *New York Illustrated News* and the *Southern Illustrated News* in the illustrated news genre enriches and complements impressions gleaned from *Harper's Weekly* and *Frank Leslie's Illustrated Newspaper*.

From *Rail-Splitter to Icon* also intends to illuminate such traditional sources as *Harper's Weekly, Frank Leslie's Illustrated Newspaper, Vanity Fair, Punch*, and *Fun*. In part, new insights come from comparative analyses of magazine content from the same and different genres (comic and news), different geographical regions (North, South, and England), and between magazines that held radically different philosophical positions on Lincoln (for example, the *New York Illustrated News* and *Harper's Weekly* during the summer of 1864). Moreover, specific analyses of individual magazines, like *Harper's Weekly*'s central role as a Lincoln loyalist and significant orchestrator and advocate of his 1864 political campaign, enhance our knowledge of both the magazine and the president.

Failure in the past to tap the lavish content of the rarest magazines was as much a problem of accessibility as neglect. Even now, complete files for *Frank Leslie's Budget of Fun*, the *Comic Monthly, Phunny Phellow*, and *Funniest of Phun* during the Civil War are nonexistent in libraries. Nevertheless, the vast majority of Lincoln illustrations from these obscure sources is now available. Isolated issues or prints can be located at scattered libraries from the Huntington Library in the West to the Library of Congress in the East, in a few private print collections, in Civil War scrapbook and cartoon collections, and from paper ephemera and print dealers. The quest is painstaking, but the reward psychologically compensatory. Unfortunately, some of these Lincoln images, especially loose prints, are not identified as to source, date, and page. Moreover, artists sometimes failed to sign their work. However, a dogged pursuit of contextual clues can solve many puzzles. For example, *Frank Leslie's Illustrated Newspaper*, in its advertisement section, luckily describes the major contents of caricature for several specific forthcoming issues of *Frank Leslie's Budget of Fun*. As a rule, it also lists prominent contributing artists. Such clues confirm the source and date of publication for many of the magazine's detached illustrations, and when the cartoon is unsigned, give plausible leads to identify some of the artists. In some instances, the identification of certain artists helps to identify the source of the publication. For example, Thomas Nast's work in *Phunny Phellow* is rarely signed, but his distinctive artistic style betrays him and the source of his work. Also of help at times was the subject of the image, which occasionally delineated a narrow time frame that helped identify the date of publication by process of elimination. Generally, when all else failed, the print could be identified as part of a collection at a specific archival repository.

Several research benefits accrue from reliance upon the larger universe of magazines. The quantity and quality of pictorial and lexical Lincoln images are substantially increased. Not only is the number of artists augmented, but the extent of Lincoln portfolios is also amplified for several individual artists, namely, William North, William Newman, Thomas Nast, Matt Morgan, Frank Bellew, J. H. Howard, Henry L. Stephens, and John McLenan, among others. For example, without the *Comic News* and the *Bubble,* a significant portion of Matt Morgan's Lincoln caricature would be lost. These two magazines extend coverage for Morgan's Civil War and Lincoln drawings from September 1864 to March 28, 1865. Furthermore, the same two periodicals identify a few images from British artists other than Morgan. In the case of Thomas Nast, his work in the *New York Illustrated News* and *Phunny Phellow* materially augments his Lincoln repertoire. Overall, the expanded universe of magazines also enlarges the geographical and temporal dimensions of Lincoln prints. To illustrate, two magazines—*Southern Punch* and the *Southern Illustrated News*—represent the South, and, whereas *Vanity Fair* ceased publication in July 1863, several other rare magazines from the comic genre fill this image gap to the end of the Civil War. In fact, the *Comic Monthly, Frank Leslie's Budget of Fun, Nick Nax, Phunny Phellow,* and *Yankee Notions* more than span the Civil War period. In effect, the additional content from a baker's dozen of rare magazines enhances our knowledge of Lincoln's image, the image makers, the temporal and geographic representation of the imagery, and the periodical sources of those images.

In addition, a comparative analysis across magazines reveals the outlines of larger patterns. For example, during the Civil War a running journalistic battle developed between Northern comic magazines and Britain's *Punch, Fun,* and the *Comic News.*[12] From England's shores, John Tenniel, Matt Morgan, and their artistic peers created a steady stream of anti-Union illustration, largely directed at Abe Lincoln or the mythical Jonathan, Britain's version of Uncle Sam. An equally formidable corps of artists from America returned the favor with their own caricature aimed at Lord John Russell, Prime Minister Henry John Temple Palmerston, the fictional John Bull, and the symbolic French icon, Napoleon. This war of words and graphic images attacked foes with the armament of amusement, condescension, and gratuitous nationalism. The spirited exchange debated the merits of neutrality or intervention, the blockade and its economic ramifications, the rationality or irrationality of war, the relative stature of national leadership in the two countries, and anything else that piqued the cartoonist's or satirist's whim or fancy.

In general, this study traces the development of the Lincoln image in illustrated periodicals from 1860 to 1865. Its principal focus is on graphic images, but relevant magazine content from editorial essays, satire, doggerel, and news articles is also woven into the narrative to help the reader better understand the substance of Lincoln's changing public profile.[13] Thus, contemporary magazine content constitutes the primary source. Instead of analyzing isolated images, however, this investigation seeks thematic patterns and chronologically organizes chapters around topical motifs that span the interval from Lincoln's ascent to the presidency to his assassination. For example, the 1860 and 1864 elections, the evolution of emancipation, and Lincoln's role in the vicissitudes of the Civil War are examined via the vehicle of visual and verbal magazine imagery.

Despite the vast panorama of characters who played major roles in the illustrated periodical version of the Civil War (Jefferson Davis, Robert E. Lee, Ulysses S. Grant, Horace Greeley, James Gordon Bennett, Stephen A. Douglas, George McClellan, John C. Frémont, John Bull, Napoleon, Uncle Sam, and numerous others), Abraham Lincoln obviously occupied center stage. From his exhilarating political victory in 1860 through the trials of administration and war to final Union conquest, we see him as magazine illustrators and journalists in the North, South, and England saw him: a collage of caricature, satire, doggerel, editorial essay, and descriptive news accounts—an enigmatic mosaic of misrepresentation and reality. Our view is filtered through the veneer of humor, diverse motives, the respective lenses of his political opponents and advocates, the prism of the Southern perspective, the angular nuances of friends and foes in the North, and through a glass darkly from distant England. It is shaped by numerous, sometimes incongruous, bipolar images: the ignominious defeat at Fredericksburg and glorious victory at Atlanta; the vision that he was too soft on slavery and yet was its implacable foe; the villain and champion of civil liberties; an embarrassment to the King's English as well as an eloquent craftsman of words; the inveterate joker and melancholy figure; a tyrant and a gentle man "with malice toward none, and charity for all"; and a rough-hewn backwoods politician and statesman comparable to George Washington. Finally, we perceive Lincoln through the perspective of zealous advocates of presidential violence as well as those who honor him as worthy of wearing the martyr's crown.

Two

The Development
of Lincoln's Image
in Periodicals

here may be odd pieces of history left lying around to be discerned," wrote Norman Cousins, "pieces that, when put together, may change the contours of an event, or at least our understanding of it."[1] For the most part, the "odd pieces" in this research consist of rare prints in obscure illustrated periodicals. By combining these esoteric pieces with the familiar corpus of Lincoln graphics from contemporary magazines and supplementing this expanded collection of prints with editorial commentary, news reports, satire, and doggerel, this study has reconstituted a set of raw materials that facilitate the rethinking, revising, and reconstructing of Lincoln's illustrated image in periodicals. Given the larger universe of pieces to create a new version of the Lincoln puzzle, the contours of this revamped image have, indeed, taken on new configurations and invested our understanding with new meanings and interpretations.

Alfred Bush, curator of Western Americana at Princeton University, once told me that one of the most effective ways to preserve antique prints is to publish them anew. Naturally, this novel process of historical restoration revivifies and animates more than the prints. The artists who created them, the magazines that embodied them, and the era that spawned them are also revisited and reawakened. Moreover, as new meanings from these images are conceived and imputed to Abraham Lincoln and his period, historians preserve the national memory from the dementia of unwritten history. Furthermore, as new colors, shadings, and modest illumination are dabbed on the canvas of history, some deflected light also subtly falls on the transformation of national character, exposing blemishes (such as ethnic condescension) and revealing strengths (such as a resilient capacity for social change). Yet while the imagery of this collection of prints and its journalistic companions (satire, doggerel, editorial opinion, and descriptive news) enriches our understanding of the national watershed of civil war, its principal illumination focuses squarely on Abraham Lincoln. This chapter summarizes the salient dimensions of the Lincoln profile and traces the evolution of his multifarious image in periodicals.

In 1860, Lincoln's tentative, untested, and unrefined image emerged from the nominating convention of the Republican Party and was successively thrust into the heat of political battle, the glowing embers of presidential responsibility, and the searing fire of civil war. Diverse image blacksmiths of the popular culture in the North, South, and England molded, hammered, shaped, twisted, and honed unique constructions of the malleable public Lincoln. Again and again, these artisans of imagery pulled him in and out of the flames, alternately heating and cooling, to make finely nuanced revisions. Out of that creative process, these media smithies wrought not just one but many versions of Lincoln. The images are as variegated as the creators who forged them. Many Lincoln specimens resembled the philosophical orientation that motivated and shaped his creation. For example, the pro-Lincoln "rail-splitter" and "Wide Awake" images were specifically honed to promote his 1860 candidacy. At the same time, the anti-Lincoln "Black Republicanism" shibboleth sought to disparage his slavery policy of containment. Although none of these catchwords retained their potency for long in the political jargon and symbolic visual repertoire, Abraham Lincoln was, nevertheless, about to become the most visually conspicuous political figure in the history of the republic. With an unprecedented surge of synergy, popular art commenced to create and recreate Lincoln's public persona.

In general, the developmental pattern of the Lincoln profile was not linear; it contained both peaks and troughs. These highs and lows roughly paralleled the irregular, undulating patterns of politics and the Civil War. If the Union army's humiliation at Fredericksburg, Lincoln's frustration in finding competent generals, and political disillusionment with Lincoln in the summer of 1864 symbolized the deepest troughs, victories at Gettysburg, Vicksburg, Atlanta; Lincoln's election to a second term; the Thirteenth Amendment to the Constitution; and the surrender of Gen. Robert E. Lee at Appomattox scaled the highest peaks. To be sure, Lincoln's subordinates in the cabinet and generals in the field absorbed some of the media punishment and deservedly shared whatever accolades were accorded the Lincoln administration, but the president neither would nor could dodge the bullets of accountability. Fortunately for Lincoln, the depths of discouragement in August 1864, when Lincoln realistically despaired winning the election, were rapidly drained by Sherman's triumph at Atlanta. This event immediately altered the political complexion, giving Lincoln a smashing victory over Gen. George McClellan in this pivotal presidential election. From this high-water mark, Lincoln's dynamic national image began to acquire an increasingly settled, favorable social consensus. But it was in the convergence of the Lincoln landslide with tangible evidence that the national objectives of full emancipation, imminent reunion, the end of the war, and lasting peace were about to be achieved that directly conferred a more stable civic persona. The trauma and tragedy of assassination accelerated the process of constructing and cementing a relatively enduring "consensual" Lincoln image. The speed with which the assassination transformed and sanctified the memory of the fallen president is vividly chronicled by the rapid, wholesale reconstruction of Lincoln's image in England's comic press and among his staunchest American critics.

Throughout the duration of the Civil War there were significant exceptions to this conception of a vacillating Lincoln image. For example, except for an initial period of tentative testing and appraisal, *Harper's Weekly*'s staid editorial image was consistently favorable in the face of the transient storms of political controversy. Although *Harper's Weekly*'s editorial staff acknowledged perplexing problems, it typically lauded Lincoln's leadership and repeatedly defended him from his critics. Moreover, the magazine medium in general, with few exceptions, tended to understate Lincoln's problems more than did certain newspaper sources. By the same token, England's comic press and the South's illustrated media were as constantly unfavorable toward Lincoln as *Harper's Weekly* was supportive. Only the passage of time solidified and validated these polarized, entrenched opinions for their respective ideological camps.

Nevertheless, what was true of *Harper's Weekly*'s single-minded editorial commitment to Lincoln was not quite as valid in the realm of political caricature. The inherently playful, impersonal, and condescending nature of this artistic medium exposed Lincoln's human foibles and exploited his idiosyncrasies. How else could cartoonists perform their functions as critics and entertainers? Still, when Lincoln was juxtaposed to the usual spate of conventional antagonists—Jefferson Davis, John Bull, Napoleon III, Copperheads, and Democrats—the Northern periodical press tended to cast him in the more favorable light. Furthermore, when the stakes were very high, caricature could also be subservient to political orthodoxy. For example, Thomas Nast's and Frank Bellew's *Harper's Weekly* drawings during the campaign for the 1864 presidential election strictly endorsed the Republican Party line.

The construction of the public Lincoln in the Union media was also selective; some opinions mattered more than others. For example, although Horace Greeley materially affected Lincoln's early image by helping him seize the 1860 presidential nomination, Greeley's scathing rebuke of the president and his cabinet backfired in the wake of First Bull Run. Moreover, the *New York Tribune* editor's persistent penchant for second-guessing the president typically damaged Greeley's reputation more than Lincoln's. In fact, when Lincoln seemed to be heeding Greeley's advice, the president's credibility was questioned by cartoonists more than when he repudiated it. That Greeley was often stereotyped as an aggravating, officious, intrusive busybody and political pest tended to diminish the force of his political clout.

Almost as often, Lincoln was at odds with the *New York Herald*'s James Gordon Bennett. Both Bennett and Greeley had a knack for drawing attention to themselves in presidential confrontations, but neither managed for long to boost his own stock or current pet peeve at Lincoln's political expense. Likewise, at least in illustrated periodicals, the Copperhead critique from Fernando and Ben Wood, Horatio Seymour, Clement Vallandigham, and the like also failed to galvanize significant opposition. In late 1864, even the Democratic campaign for the presidency miscarried in its effort to capture the fancy of this medium. To be sure, Bennett, Greeley, the Copperheads, and Republican and Democratic foes alike assaulted the bastion of Lincoln's defense, but the illustrated periodical genre, in the main, tended to be less receptive to wholesale criticism than did its newspaper counterpart.

What, then, were the chief forces that, from Lincoln's 1860 nomination to his assassination, wrought the differential Lincoln configurations in the illustrated press? Judgment of Lincoln's presidential stature revolved around four questions:

1. How sound is Lincoln's national vision on the vital issues (slavery, union, and war)?
2. What is the probability that his policies and executive decisions (emancipation, selection of generals, and reconstruction) will solve the nation's problems?
3. Are Lincoln's personal attributes (competence, character, personality, and so forth) equal to the taxing demands of the presidency?
4. Do the current results of Lincoln's policies (battlefield performance, liberation of slaves) justify national confidence?

At any given time during Lincoln's administration, answers to these questions defined Lincoln's ephemeral credibility. By reducing the first two questions to ideological and public policy concerns, three major factors, apart from the singular power of Lincoln's assassination, were crucial in shaping his image: the appraisal of Lincoln's political ideology, public policy, and executive decisions; the personal attributes ascribed to Lincoln—especially those that implicated his competence; and the perceived outcomes of his policies in achieving the nation's aspirations pertaining to union, slavery, and war.

Of course these variables were not independent. For example, an artist might denigrate Lincoln's policy on slavery, ridicule his executive ability, and argue that the policy hampered successful prosecution of the war. Certain broad policies, like the Emancipation Proclamation, might also be appraised on multiple levels (for instance, as a military necessity to end the war, a political instrument to facilitate union, and a humane decree to improve the condition of black Americans). Furthermore, the forces that affected Lincoln's image were differentially screened by the geographical locus (North or South, British or American), the prevailing political bias (favorable or unfavorable), and a magazine's general purpose: comic (caricature, satire, or doggerel) or serious (news or editorial). In addition, artistic competence (style, substance, technical ability, and reputation) also contributed to the effectiveness of an image.

By dint of Lincoln's ideological position on slavery, union, and war, the South's aversion toward him at the lower levels of policy, personal characteristics, and outcome were relatively fixed. In effect, he had become the quintessential Confederate scapegoat. To the degree that England's comic press adopted a sympathetic position toward the Confederacy, Lincoln's fate was also sealed as a recipient of relatively uniform, stinging political satire. Thus, the greater the disparity of ideological agreement at the level of national vision, the less tolerance for accommodation at the lower levels. Of course, a corollary mirror image principle operated when there was high ideological correspondence between Lincoln's vision and particular constituencies. For example, *Harper's Weekly*'s consistent loyalty to Lincoln on slavery, union, and war dictated a pattern of patience with the president's new policies, general approbation of his leadership, and a tolerant interpretation of criteria that defined concrete outcomes. Somewhere between these defining continua fell the Copperheads, disenchanted Republicans of radical or conservative labels, and Democrats or any other partially alienated political entity. The greater the political alienation at the level of national objectives, the more critical the evaluation of policy, leadership, and outcomes. Conversely, the more Lincoln's policy, personal characteristics, and palpable political results were judged to lack goodness of fit with national goals, the higher the probability of political disparagement.

Naturally, the process of judgment was not simply a series of rational decisions among perceptions of vision, policy, personal characteristics, and outcomes; irrational forces were also at work. Artists liberally used ad hominem logic to vilify Lincoln or his adversaries. Regardless of political affiliation, negative political campaigning also partook of mindless irrationality. Finally, the license to misrepresent, distort, and disparage, inherent in the crafts of satire and political caricature, also stretched the limits of reason. In 1876, abolitionist Frederick Douglass reflected on the intense castigation hurled at Lincoln from diverse sources, which included the "house of his friends": "Few great public men have ever been the victims of fiercer denunciation than Abraham Lincoln was during his administration. He was often wounded in the house of his friends. Reproaches came thick and fast upon him from within and from without, and from opposite quarters. He was assailed by abolitionists; he was assailed by slaveholders; he was assailed by the men who were for peace at any price; he was assailed by those who were for a more vigorous prosecution of the war; he was assailed for not making the war an abolition war; and he was most bitterly assailed for making the war an abolition war."[2]

POLITICAL IDEOLOGY, PUBLIC POLICY, AND IMAGE

Inasmuch as Lincoln was at the cutting edge of any domestic or international controversy, whenever his political agenda clashed with popular or official views, something about his illustrated periodical image had to give; publicly, he was either defended, impugned, or attacked. Among the prominent ideological variables that affected attitudes toward Lincoln were the containment of slavery versus popular sovereignty, emancipation versus slavery, union versus secession, executive versus legislative reconstruction, war versus peace, international neutrality versus intervention, involuntary versus voluntary military service, and the suspension of civil liberties versus their preservation. Lincoln's position on these issues circumscribed the polemical turf over which he and his political adversaries fought.

For illustrative purposes, two of the policies listed above are examined for their connection with the development of Lincoln's image in conjunction with the 1860 and 1864 presidential elections. The first, what Lincoln's detractors called "Black Republicanism," distorted and radicalized Lincoln's early slavery policy of containment. The second, emancipation, continually evolved between 1861 and 1865. Ironically, Lincoln's emancipation policy was accused of being both too radical and too conservative, but it was also the policy that earned him worldwide recognition. The strident reaction from the South (and even England's comic periodicals) against the preliminary emancipation and the Emancipation Proclamation was expected, but no one could have predicted the bruising political cartoons from General Frémont's political camp during the 1864 presidential campaign that maligned Lincoln for being soft on slavery and slow on emancipation. These were the public image hazards Lincoln risked by sticking his neck out on important policy issues in the volatile political environment of the Civil War. Let us briefly trace the connection of these two policies to the evolution of his image.

In the 1860 presidential campaign Lincoln's immediate, limited objective was to underscore his commitment to contain, not abolish, slavery. Lincoln was appalled by Stephen A. Douglas's doctrine of popular sovereignty, which opened the door to slavery in territories by lubricating the hinge of electoral self-determination. Compared to the confrontational politics of the abolitionists, checking slavery's expansion beyond its traditional boundaries was rather a moderate goal, which Lincoln hoped would diminish Southern fears and dampen the momentum for secession. However, the act of reaffirming his fidelity to the Constitution, which then protected slavery, was offset by his effort to preclude the extension of slavery and expose its moral contradictions. His position was unambiguous: "If, then, we of the Republican party who think slavery is a wrong, and would mould public opinion to the fact that it is a wrong, should get the control of the general government, I do not say we would or should meddle with it where it exists, but we could inaugurate a policy which would treat it as a wrong, and prevent its extension."[3]

This liberal feature of Lincoln's argument, his slavery policy of containment, endangered a vulnerable flank. To besmirch his views with a radical image, his antagonists used guilt by association to inflame political passions, appeal to sectional paranoia, and exacerbate fears of social change. The gist of the opposition's message was that Lincoln's Black Republicanism flirted with miscegenation and touted abolition. It was this convoluted image, which appeared in magazines during and shortly after the 1860 presidential campaign, that his opponents conveyed via cartoon, satire, doggerel, and editorial commentary. Whatever the appeal of Lincoln's so-called Black Republicanism to specific voters, it was one of the early dominant media themes used by campaign strategists to taint his political ideology in order to soil his public image.

In the summer of 1864, Lincoln's other political flank was exposed. At that time, the radical wing of the Republican Party was disillusioned with the president. What was the origin of this festering discontent? In part, it was political opportunism and ambition, compounded by the frustrations incident to a protracted, distressing war.

However, intraparty division also involved a struggle over leadership style and political philosophy. Lincoln, a moderate, was being assailed by a more aggressive political agenda. When the president pocket vetoed the Wade-Davis Bill, a legislative initiative on reconstruction that stipulated emancipation for individual states, he incensed his radical colleagues. Specifically, they were upset by what they perceived as Lincoln's slow pace of emancipation but the Radical Republicans had not, as yet, been able to find a candidate to run against Lincoln. Consequently, General Frémont's radical independent party strategists took the initiative to publish a series of vindictive anti-Lincoln cartoons on reconstruction and emancipation themes. These images vigorously challenged Lincoln's leadership. The cartoons pictured the president as unprincipled, expedient, and incompetent, and indecisive on slavery. Never before had he been so unfairly defamed by a political rival on ideological grounds, but negative campaigning was common at the time.

Leadership style, more than any other variable, differentiated Lincoln from Frémont and other Radical Republicans. Lincoln was astute enough to figure out that any policy that embraced revolutionary social change, especially one as deeply ingrained in tradition as slavery, required a sensitive, rational, and deliberate modus operandi to alter public attitudes. Lincoln's preference for a gradual, persuasion-based style was inherent in an early document he wrote about change within individuals:

> When the conduct of men is designed to be influenced, persuasion, kind, unassuming persuasion, should ever be adopted. It is an old and a true maxim, that a "drop of honey catches more flies than a gallon of gall." So with men. If you would win a man to your cause, first convince him that you are his sincere friend. Therein is a drop of honey that catches his heart, which, say what he will, is the great high road to his reason, and which, when once gained, you will find but little trouble in convincing his judgment of the justice of your cause, if indeed that cause really be a just one. On the contrary, assume to dictate to his judgment, or to command his action, or to mark him as one to be shunned and despised, and he will retreat within himself, close all the avenues to his head and his heart; and tho' your cause be naked truth itself, transformed to the heaviest lance, harder than steel, and sharper than steel can be made, and tho' you throw it with more than Herculean force and precision, you shall no more be able to pierce him, than to penetrate the hard shell of a tortoise with a rye straw.[4]

However, the task of persuading a nation to change its fundamental institutional values so deeply rooted in economic interest, constitutional and judicial precedent, cultural tradition, and the seductive doctrine of racial superiority was the most formidable and arduous ideological challenge the country had faced since its birth during the Revolution. To Lincoln's credit, when the chilling reality of a bitter and bloody civil war and mounting political pressure influenced the president to consider emancipation, he did not abandon this ideal of persuasion. Would it work at this level of executive diplomacy? He thought so. When General Frémont and Gen. David Hunter attempted to usurp authority in the field by prematurely imposing involuntary emancipation, Lincoln rightly repudiated their brazen, if naive, boldness. But he also reserved the right to propose emancipation in his own inimitable way—with a "drop of honey" rather than a "gallon of gall." Unlike Generals Frémont and Hunter, Lincoln was sensitive to what an emancipation policy might mean to the fragile psychological morale of border-state loyalty. Furthermore, lacing his initial emancipation overture with softer gradual, voluntary, and compensatory features, Lincoln laid important foundations for justifying the Emancipation Proclamation as a military necessity. Initially, this steady, stepwise tactic tended to defuse the fears of conservative sceptics and reassure border-state residents that the president was not going too fast. It even temporarily bridled the tendency for impatient impulsiveness on the part of his radical colleagues and abolitionist critics.

When it became clear that the South would not take the bait of gradual, voluntary, and compensatory emancipation, Lincoln effectively acted the part of a firm political pragmatist painfully schooled by the realism of war, political pressure, and the intransigence of Confederate conviction. Still, Lincoln did not abandon the carrot entirely for the stick. Even the preliminary emancipation offered a window of opportunity and fair warning for Confederate leaders to reconsider the implications of the next step. Finally, when the full-blown Emancipation Proclamation confined itself to the liberation of slaves within the recalcitrant Confederate lines, Lincoln had again adopted the moderate path. What Lincoln objected to in the Wade-Davis Bill was the proposition that the federal government could impose emancipation on individual states by simple legislative fiat. Moreover, his vision of Southern reconstruction, consistent with his record of moderation, offered a milder version than that proposed by Congress. On the whole, the public sentiment seemed to value Lincoln's centrist style, which eventually paved the way for the adoption of the Thirteenth Amendment to the Constitution and finally effaced the blot of slavery from the national escutcheon. Eventually, even some abolitionists conceded the wisdom of Lincoln's gradualist emancipation policy:

> His great mission was to accomplish two things: first, to save his country from dismemberment and ruin; and second, to free his country from the great crime of slavery. To do one or the other, or both, he must have the earnest sympathy and the powerful cooperation of his loyal fellow countrymen. Without this primary and essential condition to success, his efforts must have been vain and utterly fruitless. Had he put the abolition of slavery before the salvation of the Union, he would have inevitably driven from him a powerful class of the American people and rendered resistance to rebellion impossible. Viewed from the genuine abolition ground, Mr. Lincoln seemed tardy, cold, dull, and indifferent, but measuring him by the sentiment of his country, a sentiment he was bound as a statesman to consult, he was swift, zealous, radical, and determined.[5]

No policy conceived by Lincoln held greater import than the Emancipation Proc-lamation—for the nation, for his developing and enduring public persona, or for his personal satisfaction. Although Lincoln's emancipation policy embroiled him in con-troversy throughout most of the Civil War, it eventually elevated him to singular political esteem in the eyes of the world. In the end, no ideological foundation was more important to his enduring political stature.

PERSONAL ATTRIBUTES AND IMAGE

Lincoln's public identity also revolved around several personal dimensions that in-volved his competence, character, personality, background, and physical appearance. An assessment of Lincoln's leadership might involve a collage of all these attributes. Humor, though an integral part of Lincoln's personality, was also linked to evalua-tions of his competence and character. Because his humor both endeared him to and repelled him from others, cartoonists and satirists could use it to serve either end. Physically, on the one hand, Lincoln's imposing size lent itself to portrayals of pow-er, decisiveness, and leadership. On the other hand, size could be easily transformed into negative press. Associative cues (such as a rail, log cabin, spittoon, or back-woods' dialect) called forth Lincoln's frontier background. Artists extracted the ef-fect they desired from circumstances at hand. Inventive captions and guilt by associ-ation (Lincoln as an ape) imputed additional meaning. Initially, because Lincoln did not bear any of the liabilities or assets of political incumbency, these distinctive per-sonal characteristics were important early markers in defining his national identity.

It was not long before satirists and political cartoonists transformed and reduced these personal features into easily recognized stereotypic symbols through the stan-dard processes of distortion, exaggeration, and simplification. Artists contrived their own inimitable image of Lincoln, which they used for the sake of entertainment or to convey some semblance of "truth." Whether they aimed to ridicule, denigrate, promote, or celebrate this quasi-artificial Lincoln, they knew how to ply their craft. Although none of Lincoln's presidential predecessors had entirely escaped this form of public examination, Lincoln arrived on the political scene precisely at the histori-cal apogee of its application. For almost five years, with equanimity, he tasted the bittersweet fruits of political caricature.

The Frontier Image

In 1860, when Lincoln's political backers chose to feature their candidate as the "rail-splitter," they hoped to link him to the venerable saga of the American dream. This frontier image was associated with an aura of innocence, rugged individualism, self-made Americans, manifest destiny, persevering pioneers, down-to-earth common people, and the work ethic. The nicknames "Old Abe" and "Father Abraham," with their homey ring of familiarity, dovetailed nicely with the "rail-splitter" imagery. Although this familiar moniker did not last long after Lincoln's election, except for an occasional encore, the backwoods theme lingered throughout his administration.[6] At the same time, his critics got almost as much mileage as his admirers out of his humble origins. For Lincoln's adversaries, the frontier imagery conjured up an entirely different set of qualities: awkwardness, uncouthness, naivete, incompetence, lack of sophistication and proper breeding, inexperience, and want of education. Indeed, compared to William Seward in his own party, or Stephen A. Douglas in the Democratic Party, Lincoln's experience and preparation for the presidency seemed, on the surface, abysmally lacking.

"To all outward appearances he was less prepared to be President of the United States than any other man who had run for that high office. Without family tradition or wealth, he had received only the briefest of formal schooling. Now fifty years old, he had no administrative experience of any sort; he had never been governor of his state or even mayor of Springfield. . . . He had served only a single, less than successful term in the House of Representatives and for the past ten years had held no public office. . . . To be sure, his debates with Douglas had brought him national attention, but he had lost the senatorial election both in 1855 and in 1859."[7] Critics easily fused the reality of Lincoln's apparent inadequacies and inexperience to his frontier reputation. It was this unpolished, ill-prepared image that Lincoln's detractors often invoked to question his competence and overall suitability for the presidency. With alacrity, cartoonists liberally used this motif to entertain, if not always to denounce.

The Joker Image

Some scholars have argued that Lincoln's humor was "never a real asset in sober Victorian America,"[8] but this is a difficult thesis to defend. The soil of the Victorian era germinated an impressive and unprecedented spate of humor periodicals, and it produced the golden age of cartooning. But what about the specific effect of Lincoln's drollery? Good evidence affirms that Lincoln's wit had broad appeal. The edited transcripts of Lincoln's part in the Lincoln-Douglas debates are generously sprinkled with allusions to "laughter," "cheers and laughter," "renewed laughter," "laughter and applause," and "roars of laughter."[9] Lincoln's native talent evolved early in his political and social life, and his repertoire included jokes, stories, and word plays. His neighbors attested to his ability to convulse an audience in laughter and win them over.[10] But did this gift transfer to the inner sanctum of the presidency? With few exceptions, at least for Lincoln's admirers, his humor seemed to be an asset. "He could afford to joke," wrote David H. Donald, "because he generally made a favorable impression."[11]

In truth, from the cartoonist's perspective, Lincoln's penchant for humor elicited a bipolar reaction. At one pole, his wit was viewed as shallow, insensitive, and coarse. The reproach typically came from his political enemies. In fact, an analysis of the twenty cartoons in domestic magazines that explicitly alluded to Lincoln's jocular temperament reveals that the overwhelming pejorative image came from four hostile sources: *Southern Illustrated News, Southern Punch, New York Illustrated News,* and *Funniest of Phun.*[12] The negative cartoons from the last two magazines were produced on behalf of General Frémont's attempt to topple Lincoln from the presidency in 1864. In fact, most of the cartoons that denounced Lincoln's purported poor taste in humor came from these four typically critical sources. Some other negative images were prompted by the infamous and embarrassing Union loss at the Battle at Fredericksburg. One of the most notable rebukes came from *Harper's Weekly;* it reprimanded Lincoln by juxtaposing his reputation for joking with the loss of "15,000 sons."

At the opposite end of the spectrum, Lincoln's appreciation for and own expression of humor was often deemed delightful, discerning, and endearing. When the fable of Miles O'Reilly was published, the humane presidential pardon for this fictional, witty character was attributed in a front, full-page *Comic Monthly* cartoon to the fact that "Honest Old Abe . . . dearly loves a joke." The entrepreneurial spirit produced "*Old Abe's Jokes*"; whether the jokes were apocryphal did not seem to matter, and *Harper's Weekly* advertised the availability of the little volume just off the press. A cartoonist for *Frank Leslie's Budget of Fun* claimed, tongue-in-cheek in a double-page spread, that "*Old Abe's Jokes*" could be purchased at Sanitary Fairs, which raised funds for the comfort and care of soldiers and their families. For his part, Frank Bellew took advantage of Lincoln's well-known jocularity to make fun of Gen. George McClellan's 1864 candidacy for the presidency. Lincoln held a miniature McClellan in his hand and impishly remarked, "This reminds me of a little joke."[13]

Still, no comic magazine outdid *Yankee Notions* in celebrating Lincoln's humor. *Yankee Notions* spotlighted the latest Lincoln yarn as "Old Abe's Last" and respectfully published several humorous stories attributed to Lincoln.[14] Even well before Lincoln's election as president, the magazine relished Lincoln humor. During his administration, a series of prefatory and valedictory statements in *Yankee Notions* approvingly emphasized Lincoln's comic reputation. In 1861, it facetiously claimed to have "engaged Abe Lincoln, who will contribute a variety of Presidential Jokes." In 1862, the valedictory satire gratuitously ascribed the president's humor to his purported habit of reading the magazine: "Jonathan admits that President Lincoln is something of a joker, having been a constant reader of the *Notions,* but, with due respect to the Commander-in-Chief of the Army, Jonathan suggests that even Presidential jokes lose quality by coming to the people second-hand. Jonathan therefore congratulates the nation that there will be hereafter a National Bureau of Funny Affairs, established for the better regulation of current jokes."[15]

In 1863, the preface of *Yankee Notions* issued its own version of "General Order No. 1":

In view of the requirements of the times, to save the country and preserve the Constitution in the very best of spirits, Jonathan puts on his war-paint, converts his writing-desk into a battery, turns his inkstand into a projectile, and changes his goose quill into a shot-gun, and in this way assumes command of the Federal jokers, and Confederated punsters.

I. President Abraham Lincoln, having ineffectually cracked his fund of jokes, without splitting any of the many sides of the Confederacy, and "nobody being hurt," is hereby relieved from chief command of our funny boys, and is formally discharged as a wit of too small a calibre to make an impression on thick-headed Southern jokers, with orders to report all further sallies, in that direction, to his superior, at these headquarters.[16]

In its valedictory for 1863, *Yankee Notions* perpetuated the tradition by another friendly reference to its "Joking President": "A celebrated . . . beauty said that a woman who could joke was far from a goner; and a nation wherein *Yankee Notions* is published—so say nothing of its having a Joking President, will come out 'right side up' against any odds—Copperheadism, John Bullism, and Louis Napoleonism into the bargain. . . . There is cause enough around us for melancholy, and of course so much the greater need for jollity. Jonathan will rise equal to the occasion, and will make the year 1864 memorable, as the great JOKISS ANNIBUS, Honest Old Abe (God bless him), has promised to contribute."[17] Finally, a December 1864 proclamation put the capstone on these annual allusions to the joker "Abram Linkon":

Know ye, that I, Abram Linkon, Prince of Jokers, and Fun Maker General to the Universal Yankee Nation, do hereby proclaim, enuciate, and pronunciate, that our trusty servant, Jonathan, is truly loyal, patriotic, and plucky; and furthermore declare, that the *Yankee Notions* is our chief organ for the publication of all our best jokes, little and otherwise, and that in the checkered scenes through which our beloved country has passed, and is passing, his *Notions* has done good service, cheering the despondent, elevating the depressed, and sustaining the weak. I therefore proclaim Jonathan our Joker-in-Chief, and hereby appoint the First of January, 1865, as a grand day of HA! HA! HA! throughout the United States and therefore call upon all loyal citizens to subscribe—and pay for the *Notions*, believing that nothing will so much conduce to the general good of all Creation, and this Nation in particular, as cheerfulness, good humor, fun, and laughter.

In order that the good results looked for, may be the more surely secured, I do hereby promise to tell on that day, through the *Yankee Notions*, one or more of those "little stories" of which I am so often "reminded," choosing the *Notions* as my medium, for the reason that it is the best, and because Jonathan having been long on the track, has proved himself to be of good bottom, and in crossing the stream of time, I see no reason why I or the people should swop horses.[18]

Of course, there was more to Lincoln's humor than these bipolar extremes indicated: "Most stories he recounted simply because he thought they were funny. Laughing along with his visitors helped break the ice. But he also knew how to use story-telling to deflect criticism, to avoid giving an answer to a difficult question, and to get rid of a persistent interviewer. . . . Lincoln used this technique throughout his presidency, to the bafflement of those who had no sense of humor and the rage of those who failed to get a straight answer from him."[19]

But humor was not just a device to "break the ice," "deflect criticism," "avoid giving an answer to a difficult question," or "get rid of a persistent interviewer"; nor was it just an escape hatch for comic relief from the intense pressures of high office. It did all of these and more. One could no more separate the mature Lincoln from integrity or the slogan "malice toward none and charity for all" than from his inclination to joviality. This was an integral part of his core personality—a fascinating, if ironic, counterpoint to his melancholy. According to Danish philosopher Søren Kierkegaard, "The melancholy have the best sense of the comic."[20] In any case, Lincoln endeared friends, won over fence-sitters, and disarmed or offended his foes with the power of his wit, and one thing is certain—this was not an affectation.

The Image of Integrity

The substance of Lincoln's character was also contested. Although most images commended "Honest Old Abe" for his integrity, his most vociferous detractors compared him to the Roman Empire's Nero and Herod.[21] Furthermore, thinkers in that category classified him as bellicose, expedient, tyrannical, vengeful, weak, bloodthirsty, and intolerant. However, in the Union media, Lincoln's reputation for integrity was one of his most stable images; it was easier to assail his competence and leadership.

The Leadership Image

Among Lincoln's attributes, the question of leadership assumed highest priority among his critics and advocates. In the final analysis, the substance of virtually all evaluations revolved around this theme. Questions of vision, policy, and results all rotated on the axis of political competence. If most critics were willing to concede Lincoln's fundamental integrity, they were unwilling to grant him, carte blanche, any concession on leadership. Repeatedly, he would have to prove himself. Every policy, decision, and outcome was subjected to spirited public analysis. Did Lincoln possess the native intellect, rhetorical power, leadership, vision, experience, financial sagacity, knowledge, diplomacy, military instincts, and wisdom to govern a nation in crisis? For a while, even *Harper's Weekly* wondered whether he was equal to the imposing task. Within the dark side of the frontier and jokester images lurked this interrogative about Lincoln's qualifications for leadership. No matter what the is-sue—union, secession, slavery, emancipation, reconstruction, peace or war, inter-national diplomacy, the economy, the suspension of civil liberties, selecting military leadership, the draft—the more fundamental question asked whether or not Lincoln had the required qualities. This query of presidential capabilities dogged him through-out his administration. It was the sum and substance of many versions of the Lincoln image.

The Physical Image

Artists and wordsmiths also used Lincoln's ample physique, unique countenance, and other physical attributes to convey distinctive imagery. His lanky limbs, enor-mous hands and feet, and imposing size were conspicuous candidates for pictorial and verbal satire. Because his natural form towered over most contemporaries, it was easy enough to exaggerate or contrast these differences for humorous or disdainful effect. Numerous cartoons featured images of size, strength, or power: "Gulliver Abe," the "rail-splitter," "Abe the Giant Killer," "A Galvanized Split Rail," "Honest Old Abe and the Little Boy" (Stephen A. Douglas), the "Western Cincinnatus," "Gates-by Lincoln," that "Big Fellow," "Sinbad Lincoln," "Big Lincoln Horner," "Long Abraham Lincoln, a Little Longer," "Long Abe," and the "Tallest Ruler on the Globe." However, at the whim of the image maker, Lincoln's size could also make him appear clumsy, inept, awkward, foolish, and gangling—or as a buffoon. His countenance, hair, beard, and dress were equally versatile tools to create various impressions: handsome or homely, neat or unkempt, happy or melancholy, dignified or indisposed. Whether to praise, ridicule, or just entertain, these images effectively fulfilled the intended purpose of their artistic creators.

The Image that Justified National Confidence

Another set of images evaluated the ostensible, tangible results of Lincoln policies in terms of the accomplishment of national goals. What was the present prognosis of the war, slavery, and union? On balance, was the Lincoln administration facilitating or hampering national objectives? The most obvious indicator used to gauge closure on achievement of the country's major aspirations was battlefield progress. Obvi-ously, there could be no union or full emancipation without an end to the war. Be-tween Fort Sumter and Appomattox, the war was, indeed, the single most riveting theme. In general, as the war effort progressed or faltered, so Lincoln's public profile soared or plummeted. On the one hand, with the ignominious defeat at Fredericks-burg, Lincoln's stock plunged. Vicariously, he suffered from the lethargy and ineffec-tiveness of the Army of the Potomac and the military crisis brought upon the nation by incompetent generals. At sea, the *Alabama* terrorized shipping lanes and damaged impressions of Lincoln's competence as commander in chief. The psychological costs of prolonged war wearied the nation and tested the mettle of national endurance. Such frustrations created the need for a national draft, threatened international intervention, spawned peace initiatives, and encouraged the Copperhead movement and the suppression of civil liberties. These war-instigated policies varied in popularity, and Lincoln felt the pressure generated by political necessity.

On the other hand, the encouraging triumph at Antietam enabled the president to announce the timetable for the Emancipation Proclamation. Although neither the benign military effects nor the profound moral and political ramifications of the proclamation were immediate, its powerful influence was ultimately one of the most compelling factors in restoring the Union and forging an enduring, positive image. The almost simultaneous series of victories at Gettysburg, Vicksburg, and Port Hudson reinvigorated the national will and delivered the country out of military doldrums at a crucial point in the war. Yet no military victory was more timely or pivotal than Sherman's capture of Atlanta. Atlanta launched the final phase of the war, delivered a crushing psychological blow to the Confederacy, and bolstered, if not ultimately secured, Lincoln's reelection. Finally, after four difficult years, Lincoln had garnered a decisive mandate from the people and earned a level of popularity previously unknown to him. Indeed, the events of war helped sculpture Lincoln's ephemeral public identity.

Meanwhile, Lincoln was sorely criticized by war-weary political factions for not pursuing peace more aggressively. On this count, Horace Greeley was a frequent irritation, but the Copperheads and Peace Democrats did more than pester Lincoln; they launched a major pacification program. Indeed, the principal issue between the Republican and Democratic Parties in the 1864 election was the question of peace or war. Had Sherman not conquered Atlanta, the matter might have evolved into an epic struggle. But General Sherman's victory defused the potentially explosive issue, and magazines throughout the country mounted an impressive assault on the peace proponents' platform. Mercilessly, cartoonists and editorial writers attacked a policy of pacification, and Lincoln benefitted from the propaganda. Ironically, the impressive mandate for war granted to Lincoln in the presidential election put him in a commanding position to either negotiate for peace or pursue a policy of unconditional surrender. Vindicating Lincoln, the opposition's peace policy backfired and significantly enhanced Lincoln's ultimate stature.

Next to the war, slavery preoccupied the press. The drive toward secession, the concomitant 1860 election, and the threat of war were all about slavery. After emancipation became an integral part of Lincoln's war policy, the nation's progress toward that objective also became a measure of its confidence in Lincoln's leadership. However, as noted earlier, Frémont and other Radical Republicans failed to persuade the public that Lincoln's slavery policy was not in the best interests of the nation. In the end, victory at war, full emancipation for the slaves, and the nation's reunification sealed Lincoln's place in history.

By ranking each illustration on a three-point scale—positive (3), neutral (2), and negative (1)—a useful, though crude, index of "popularity" has been constructed. The measure is useful because it provides a standard basis for comparing presidential popularity as shown in contemporary magazines for a particular month, set of months, or year. In addition, it facilitates temporal contrasts and comparisons, suggests what events or issues may have precipitated Lincoln's censure or praise, assesses the importance of geographic locus (England, Confederacy, or Union) on evaluation, and provides data on the relative impact of specific magazines and artists. For example, to the degree that the measure is sensitive, we can determine Lincoln's relative popularity after a battle like Fredericksburg, during an election campaign, in the eyes of a particular artist (for example, Thomas Nast), in the overall estimation of any magazine *(Phunny Phellow*, for instance), in England, the South, or the North, or on visible public policies (like emancipation). With the aid of the index, we can examine various patterns of public opinion or even impute ostensible causal linkages or interpretations based on data extracted from the contemporary popular culture.

Indeed, there are also clear limitations to this rough methodology.[22] Obviously, these ratings do not meet the conventional standards of scientific rigor. The judgments are subjectively made by one rater (the author). Hence, there are no estimates of reliability or validity. Moreover, the publication of prints lagged behind historical events (from Europe the lag time was naturally greater), so that prints that carried scores on the Battle of Fredericksburg were published a few weeks after the fact. Although the disaster at Fredericksburg occurred in December 1862, the associated prints did not appear until January or February 1863. Thus, if annual public opinion scores are compared, this event of 1862 is actually calculated for 1863, when the prints appeared. Furthermore, the occurrence of nearly simultaneous events, such as the effective date of the Emancipation Proclamation's implementation (January 1863) and the media response to Fredericksburg (January 1863), may diminish the public reaction to one or both occurrences. In the case of Fredericksburg and issuance of the Emancipation Proclamation, Fredericksburg tended to upstage emancipation. In addition, the "popularity" score for a magazine excludes editorial and other nonvisual indicators. Finally, unless explicit Lincoln content was present in the print (Lincoln's physical presence or allusions to Lincoln in the captions), scores were not calculated. Thus, potential implicit criticism or praise of Lincoln was always ignored.

Despite the inherent flaws in the measurement, the advantages of its use outweigh the disadvantages. I am willing to live with a pragmatic convention in order to yield some "systematic" sense of public opinion patterns. Individual readers must judge for themselves the utility and justification of this analytic tool. For purposes of clarity, I examined the annual patterns of public opinion in the illustrated magazine genre.

Public Opinion as Seen in Periodicals during 1860

For various reasons, this was a singular year in Lincoln graphics. First, the prints were preoccupied with one topic: the presidential election. Naturally, the political atmosphere was charged with polemical excitement. Cartoonists argued for or against particular candidates and sometimes, to generate humor, ridiculed them all. Second, by a wide margin, Northern comic magazines overwhelmingly (72 percent) surpassed the news weeklies (27 percent) in graphic output. In fact, just two comic periodicals, *Frank Leslie's Budget of Fun* and *Vanity Fair*, created more than half (54 percent) of the total array of prints, and each magazine either matched or eclipsed the combined productivity from *Frank Leslie's Illustrated Newspaper, Harper's Weekly,* and the *New York Illustrated News*. After 1860, this striking disparity between the news and comic genres vanished.

Third, in virtually every magazine the preponderance of Lincoln prints portrayed a positive impression. This same generalization could not be made for Lincoln's rivals John Bell, John C. Breckinridge, and Douglas. To be sure, Lincoln was reproached for his Black Republicanism and inexperience. Nevertheless, throughout the duration of the campaign, public opinion viewed him favorably. For all magazines, he averaged 2.5 on a three-point scale. His image in the illustrated news weeklies (*Frank Leslie's Illustrated Newspaper, Harper's Weekly,* and the *New York Illustrated News*) was 2.8. Even in the irreverent comic genre he received a respectable 2.4. Furthermore, Lincoln's popularity gained momentum as the campaign progressed. For the first five months (May–September), Lincoln's approval index averaged a modest 2.4. However, during the crucial months of October and November the score markedly improved to 2.8, and in December it concluded with the positive score of 2.6. Of course, Lincoln's popularity was partially an artifact of the desperate division within the Democratic Party, as well as the tepid response to Bell's candidacy.

Fourth, the frequency of Lincoln prints steadily gathered momentum over the course of the campaign. Although Lincoln's election images were spread out between May and December, 63 percent appeared between October and December. October and November eclipsed all months in productivity because of the election's approaching climax. Given the data on media popularity, any increase in public exposure for Lincoln proved politically fortuitous. Finally, contrary to the American pattern, the 1860 election did not arouse the British cartoonists to spirited action; they behaved like disinterested spectators rather than partisan critics.[23]

Public Opinion as Seen in Periodicals during 1861

Aside from lingering plaudits that Lincoln continued to receive from his electoral victory and a spate of political caricature on the distribution of spoils of office, three major themes monopolized this year's visual repertoire: (1) the ceremonial journey from Springfield to Washington, D.C.; (2) the inauguration; and (3) the tragic sequence of secession, Fort Sumter, and the Civil War. Each of these three motifs shares two obvious common features. First, the events are marked either by formality and official ritual, or by the somber realities of grave conflict. This serious tone lent itself to coverage by the three illustrated news weeklies. Thus, whereas the comic genre and political caricature had dominated popular art in the 1860s, the illustrated news weeklies assumed the chief burden of responsibility for 1861. As a result, *Harper's Weekly, Frank Leslie's Illustrated Newspaper,* and the *New York Illustrated News* combined to create 56 percent of the prints, the comic genre contributed 43 percent, and England's *Punch* brought up the rear with the final 1 percent. As yet, Lincoln had not become embroiled in enough controversy to attract either the full-blown wrath or humor of *Punch.* Still there was ample opportunity for wit from the Northern comic magazines. Like *Harper's Weekly* in the news genre, *Frank Leslie's Budget of Fun* (37 percent) led the comic medium in numbers of prints, followed by *Phunny Phellow* (24 percent) and *Vanity Fair* (20 percent). Thus, just three magazines almost monopolized comic production (81 percent).[24] *Yankee Notions* (13 percent) and the *Comic Monthly* (6 percent) accounted for the residue.

Second, because the Lincoln journey, the inauguration, and the outbreak of the war occurred early in the year, so did the bulk of imagery. In 1860, magazine illustrations naturally revolved around the November election. In 1861, the peak of popular art occurred in the month of March. In fact, no other single month between 1860 and 1865 (not even the assassination) generated more visual Lincoln content. Several factors contributed to this media phenomenon: tension that surrounded the evolving national crisis was high, the mystique of a newly elected president piqued the public interest, and the ritual of inauguration was a seasonal highlight. Lincoln's surreptitious train ride from Harrisburg, Pennsylvania, to Washington, D.C., injected a comic element into this instantaneous national conversation piece, and artists and photographers were poised to exercise their crafts to a degree unprecedented in American history. However, the image explosion did not end in March. The finality of secession and disunion, the firing on Fort Sumter, and war drove the media onward. Almost 70 percent of the Lincoln prints for this year were published between the first of March and the end of May. No three-month period between Lincoln's 1860 campaign for the presidency and his assassination came close to matching this proliferation of Lincoln images.

The principal portion of Lincoln's whirlwind journey from Springfield to Washington, D.C., featured formal receptions to honor the president elect in major cities along the way. Without exception, these ritual whistle stops brought Lincoln consistently good press in the three illustrated weeklies. However, when Lincoln abruptly changed his itinerary to avoid harm's way, the comic press, aided by media hype, temporarily seized the reins. Lincoln probably could not have avoided the public relations fiasco associated with his midnight flight, but the adverse publicity receded quickly in the euphoria of inauguration. To be sure, bypassing Baltimore brought an occasional reprise of the affair either for good humor or to question the president's suitability for office. Nevertheless, in the main, these prologues to Lincoln's presidency bolstered or sustained public opinion; Northern confidence, if wary, still surged more than it sub-sided. Despite the usual tensions and misgivings associated with the transfer of pow-er and the threat of sectional unrest, this brief hiatus created opportunities to consol-idate hard-won political gains.

What tangible evidence from the magazine medium supports this sanguine view of public opinion? What about the war? Did attitudes toward Lincoln rapidly decline as the nation faced secession? If Lincoln's evolving image is taken as a rough index of public support, then it appears that Union solidarity for a neophyte president held firm in the face of this wrenching national trial. From the perspective of visual imag-ery, 1861 was a banner year for Lincoln's public relations. Based on over one hundred illustrations, his graphic index for popularity was a robust 2.6. Sixty-seven percent of the illustrations were assigned a positive rating, 28 percent neutral, and just 5 percent negative. As expected, the comic magazine perspective (2.5) was slightly less favorable than that of the illustrated news weeklies (2.7). Nevertheless, even the comic medium gave the president-elect a refreshing, positive interlude.

If we plot public opinion on specific issues in numerical order, the five most fre-quently treated print themes were (1) secession, Fort Sumter, and the Civil War; (2) the journey from Springfield to Washington, D.C.; (3) the inauguration; (4) the spoils of office; and (5) Lincoln's first presidential election. In terms of graphic illustra-tions, there is no evidence that Lincoln's popularity declined as a function of esca-lating conflict. As a matter of fact, none of these themes ranked below 2.5, and the inauguration led at 2.9. The last portion of Lincoln's trip to the capital garnered un-favorable publicity (1.8), but the overall ranking for the journey was still 2.5. If indi-vidual magazines are examined, none dips below the critical threshold of 2.0 (actual-ly this rank is unreliable because it is based on only one image), and the majority (70 percent) exceed 2.5. *Harper's Weekly* (twenty-six prints), the *New York Illustrated News* (twenty prints), and *Frank Leslie's Illustrated Newspaper* (nineteen prints) were the most prolific producers of Lincoln visual images, but numerically *Frank Leslie's Budget of Fun* (seventeen prints) from the comic genre was barely edged by its seri-ous counterparts. In short, the testament from the visual dimension of contemporary periodicals shows little evidence of the erosion of Lincoln's public standing.

When the early Union military accomplishments were hardly stellar, why didn't Lincoln's reputation as commander in chief suffer? For one thing, burgeoning sec-tional pride and patriotism, instigated by Northern indignation over secession, Fort Sumter, and the Civil War, granted Lincoln a generous, if circumscribed, period of patience and pardon. For example, a large segment of the press (Horace Greeley to the contrary) was willing to consider the defeat at Bull Run a military anomaly. In addition, the growing threat of interventionist reprisal from England, because of international provocations like the blockade and the Trent Affair, was blunted by a nationalistic united front. Third, throughout the Civil War the philosophical orien-tation of most illustrated periodicals was biased toward the Republican Party. Final-ly, in the beginning, blame was easily transferred to such scapegoats below the first tier of national leadership as generals or cabinet officers. Nevertheless, Lincoln's reservoir of public goodwill was exhaustible.

Public Opinion as Seen in Periodicals during 1862

Because there were no public relations events in 1862 quite like those of 1861 (Lincoln's trip to the White House, the inauguration, and the eruption of the Civil War), the number of Lincoln prints in the Northern press declined to its lowest wartime level. In 1861, there were more than five times more Lincoln images in the illustrated news than in 1862, and nearly twice as many in the comic medium. Lincoln's war image retained its status as the principal theme. Two patterns are noteworthy. First, in comparison to 1861 (2.5), Lincoln's popular war persona remained stable (2.6). What is remarkable about the stability is that it continued despite the sensational resurgence of Confederate military prowess in the second half of the year. Not until the bitter defeat at Fredericksburg did Lincoln lose much of his popularity. Although that agonizing defeat occurred at the end of 1862, the disillusion it generated was not reflected in the press until January 1863.

Next to the war, emancipation was most important to the American public. Because abolitionists had not swayed the American people to their way of thinking, Lincoln's moderate alternative of voluntary, gradual, and compensated emancipation within the parameters of the Constitution had greater, if still incomplete, public appeal. Popular artists in the illustrated periodical press portrayed Lincoln's emancipation philosophy in an astonishingly positive light (2.8). By contrast, the abolitionist doctrine paled in popularity. Nevertheless, for many Northerners, emancipation was still a radical idea, and it was greeted with scepticism and revulsion as one traveled south. Still, from the magazine artist's perspective, as the Army of the Potomac marched toward Fredericksburg, Lincoln had not yet fallen from public grace.

Meanwhile, across the Atlantic, contrary to the Union pattern, verbal and visual anti-Lincoln imagery was prominent in England's comic press. For the first time in the Civil War, *Punch* and *Fun* competed cartoon for cartoon with American comic magazines on the Lincoln theme. In political caricature, *Punch*'s John Tenniel and *Fun*'s Matt Morgan became leading anti-Lincoln cartoonists. The intensity of feeling was not too far removed from the pejorative rhetoric that soon began to appear in the *Southern Illustrated News*.[25] However, the ideological rigidity that characterized popular portrayals of Lincoln, Secretary of State Seward, and Jonathan (Uncle Sam) in Great Britain's comic press tended to be matched in nationalistic zeal by American cartoonists' caricatures of Prime Minister Palmerston, Foreign Minister Russell, and John Bull. American and British cartoonists alike consistently reveled in condescending, contemptuous, and comic portraits of each other's leaders and their policies.

However, there were rare exceptions to this rule. In the spring of 1862, Union forces scored a series of impressive victories. Both *Punch* and *Fun* grudgingly recognized Lincoln for these military feats. Notwithstanding these two aberrations,

Lincoln's average war score for 1862 was a mere 1.4. His cumulative ranking on emancipation was worse (1.2). In English and Confederate political caricature, Lincoln's typical rank throughout the war was the lowest possible score. Accordingly, the only Confederate print in the *Southern Illustrated News* heartily condemned Lincoln. To be sure, Thomas J. "Stonewall" Jackson punished the Union army in the second half of the year. Nevertheless, Union cartoonists saw the war (2.6) and emancipation (2.8) in a favorable light; the Confederate and British cartoonists begged to differ with that view. After the Battle of Fredericksburg, Union pictorial satire about the war took a turn for the worse, conveniently forgetting the considerable Confederate liabilities.

Public Opinion as Seen in Periodicals during 1863

Judged by print artifacts, the Battle of Fredericksburg was Abraham Lincoln's public relations Waterloo. Public opinion plunged! The defeat symbolized something deeply and fundamentally amiss with the Union's military capability. In its immediate, spontaneous analysis, the illustrated media spared no level of leadership from caustic condemnation. In a series of testy January cartoons, *Harper's Weekly*'s illustrators orchestrated a critique against Lincoln, Edwin M. Stanton, Gideon Welles, Henry W. Halleck, Ambrose Burnside, and others. Obviously, *Harper's Weekly* was not the sole participant: *Frank Leslie's Budget of Fun, Frank Leslie's Illustrated Newspaper,* the *New York Illustrated News,* and *Phunny Phellow* shared the indignation. Arguably, Fredericksburg can be seen as the most important military action of the Civil War. It led to the reconvening of the Joint Committee on the Conduct of the War, stirred the Copperheads, animated a peace initiative, encouraged a thorough administrative review of generals in the field, raised grave questions about the competence of each link in the chain of command, and even upstaged the issuance of the Emancipation Proclamation.[26]

The print scores reveal divergent patterns between illustrations in Union periodicals and those in British and Confederate publications. In Northern periodicals, during the first half of the year, Lincoln's popularity declined to its lowest level in his entire administration. On the war, if print scores in January (1.5) and February (1.2) were dismal, by June the cumulative score was not much better (1.5). Even so, the battles of Gettysburg, Vicksburg, and Port Hudson strengthened the national morale, and the year ended on a positive note (2.4). Lincoln's highest marks were given in conjunction with Copperhead antipathy (3.0) and the threat of international intervention (2.7). *Vanity Fair,* though only in business through July, praised Lincoln more than any other comic or news magazine (2.6). Quite to the contrary in the Deep South and in England, passionate hostility was directed squarely at Lincoln. Bemused and bolstered by Fredericksburg and the crisis of Union military leadership, but sustained and hardened by ideological conviction, *Punch* (1.3), *Fun* (1.0), the *Southern*

Illustrated News (1.0), and *Southern Punch* (1.0) merrily maligned Lincoln, their arch-enemy, throughout the year.

Public Opinion as Seen in Periodicals during 1864

In 1864, the traditional media sources that opposed Lincoln in England and the South remained constant. However, a dramatic change occurred in the North. When certain elements in the radical wing of Lincoln's own political party launched a serious threat to Lincoln's quest for another four years in the White House, the Republican defectors shrewdly galvanized political support from two illustrated periodicals, the *New York Illustrated News* and a new comic magazine, *Funniest of Phun,* that began publication in June 1864. Since 1860, the *New York Illustrated News* had been fairly loyal to Lincoln, but the change toward a more liberal philosophy in June was as decisive as it was abrupt. This strategy gave the radical movement modest political leverage in both the news and the comic genres. Although the radical challenge to Lincoln's race for the White House failed miserably during September 1864, it lasted long enough to deposit a vivid record of anti-Lincoln political caricature, mainly by Frank Bellew, in the *New York Illustrated News* and *Funniest of Phun.*

At first, the visual and verbal political attacks on Lincoln were generic because Radical Republicans had not settled on their own candidate. Initially, Salmon P. Chase, Ulysses S. Grant, and John C. Frémont appeared in cartoons as viable candidates for the disillusioned radical faction. However, when John C. Frémont bolted from his radical colleagues, to establish an independent third party, the *New York Illustrated News* and *Funniest of Phun,* in the absence of any other radical alternative, shifted their allegiance to Frémont. Soon Lincoln was vilified in cartoons and verbal rhetoric by the Frémont campaign with hostility comparable to that of the treatment he received in the Confederate and British comic press.

Since 1861, the vagaries of war more than any other theme had asserted the greatest impact on the Lincoln image. However, the 1864 presidential election re-enthroned politics as the central motif. Election polemics polarized the various magazines into three distinct ideological camps. As usual, the Confederate (1.0) and English (1.2) comic periodicals were adamantly opposed to Lincoln; they sympathized with the peace platform of the Democratic Party. Although pacifist Democrats were disappointed with George McClellan's public disavowal of peace, he was their only political hope. Championing General Frémont's candidacy, the *New York Illustrated News* (1.3) and *Funniest of Fun* (1.0) also bitterly repudiated Lincoln. However, when Frémont's political aspirations collapsed, opposition to Lincoln from these two magazines dissolved. In the end, the remaining news and comic magazines closed ranks behind Lincoln. Cumulative print scores for this set of periodicals for any single year between 1860 and 1864 had never been higher. On the comic side, the combined score for all themes in *Frank Leslie's Budget of Fun, Comic Monthly, Merryman's*

Monthly, Phunny Phellow, and *Yankee Notions* attained 2.8. The cumulative score for *Harper's Weekly* and *Frank Leslie's Illustrated Newspaper* reached 2.7. If only the election images are calculated, the scores soar higher. In effect, whereas some print scores reflected greater total opposition to Lincoln's second-term candidacy, others demonstrated extraordinary loyalty and unity. Furthermore, as the year wore on the frequency and favorability of scores increased for periodicals that supported the president. The last quarter of the year produced more prints than any prior quarter and ended with an average overall score of 2.9. By the end of 1864, all principal national goals were nearing closure: victory at war, a constitutionally mandated emancipation, and reunion. Suddenly, Abraham Lincoln's standing with the American people had never been better.

Public Opinion as Seen in Periodicals during 1865

Excluding the assassination prints, which were overwhelmingly positive, Lincoln's popularity solidified even further before his death. The cumulative print scores for *Frank Leslie's Budget of Fun, Comic Monthly, Frank Leslie's Illustrated Newspaper, Harper's Weekly, Phunny Phellow,* and *Yankee Notions* maintained a 2.9 average. Although the *Southern Illustrated News* and *Southern Punch* had only two March issues in 1865, no Lincoln visual images appeared in any of their four numbers. In Great Britain, the *Comic News/Bubble* persistently denounced Lincoln until its demise at the end of March 1865 (1.0), but *Punch's* enthusiasm for anti-Lincoln caricature precipitously declined and *Fun's* energy was spent even earlier after Matt Morgan left in 1864 to work for the *Comic News.* In comparison to 1863 and 1864, Lincoln had almost token opposition in Britain's press.

The assassination consolidated and accelerated the rapid development of favorable public opinion, energized a healing process in the land, and transformed, refined, and narrowed the parameters for the final evolution of Lincoln's image to the status of international icon.

The Comic Press
and Lincoln's Rise
to the Presidency

In the 1860 presidential campaign, the American political landscape was permanently changed. The emergence of the American illustrated magazine had galvanized a revolution in illustration.[1] For the first time in an American presidential election, an array of cartoons and caricature appeared in comic periodicals such as *Momus*, *Frank Leslie's Budget of Fun*, *Vanity Fair*, *Comic Monthly*, and *Phunny Phellow*. On the whole, this new watershed of political caricature was fortuitous for Abraham Lincoln, for it helped to transform his status from dark horse candidate to president of the United States. Augmenting the venerable tradition of separately published prints and the advent of illustrated political campaign papers, the new media produced an unprecedented volume of political caricature. Truly, this was a historic development in the depiction of American politics through graphic illustrations.

To be sure, on the more serious side illustrated magazines like *Harper's Weekly*, *Frank Leslies Illustrated Newspaper*, and the *New York Illustrated News* also depicted important features of the 1860 election visually. Portraits of the candidates and of political parades like Lincoln's Wide Awake processions also graced the pages of these news weeklies. However, during Lincoln's initial bid for the presidency political caricature in these magazines was only incidental. Thus, this study traces the development of the visual image of Lincoln's candidacy almost exclusively in the comic periodical.

In 1860, among the most conspicuous comic artists for these New York–based magazines were Frank Bellew, William Newman, Henry L. Stephens, J. H. Howard, and William North. All these artists drew for multiple comic periodicals. Whatever their own political preferences, the artists alternately praised and condemned Lincoln, Douglas, Breckinridge, and Bell. The nature of the illustration depended on a variety of factors: the neutral or partisan philosophy of the magazine, the appearance and behavioral eccentricities of the candidates, the political nuances of events, the momentous issues of the day, the opportunities for humor, the relative perceived success of the candidates, and the individual whims, moods, or political predilections of the artist. On the whole, only the very finest illustrators were selected to create feature cartoons and caricature.

Before his nomination, Lincoln did not appear in any political caricatures in the comic press. However, after he surmounted the formidable barrier of nomination he was as popular a political target as any candidate. Both Lincoln and Douglas, leading contenders in the North, shared the limelight in illustrated periodicals significantly more often than either Bell or Breckinridge; hence, in this chapter, the former pair receive greater attention than the latter. Because of Lincoln and Douglas's political prominence, they became fair game for the popular artist's full repertoire of weaponry. There was something inherently comic about each candidate. Lincoln's spindly body, bony features, homely countenance, disposition to spin yarns, and possession of titles such as "the rail-splitter" and "Old Abe" defined him as a colorful personality and candidate. The artists thrived on Stephen A. Douglas, as well. Rotund, full jowled, and short, the popular and controversial "Little Giant" was a perfect foil for this political rivalry. The two major candidates had easily exploitable physical features, traits, reputations, and political ideologies that cartoonists contrasted as often as possible. Furthermore, because most comic magazines were published weekly or monthly, the illustrators had time to design and provide details for double-, single-, and half-page comic exhibitions. These were not simple line drawings; they were fine, painstaking creations, the products of finely honed craftsmanship cut into wood by skilled engravers for the final printing. Such masterpieces of the period were cherished and treasured by their readers and savored by collectors of nineteenth-century paper ephemera. Likewise, Lincoln and Douglas themselves also left indelible impressions on voters, and a lasting imprint on the history of a nation.

THE COMIC REACTION TO LINCOLN'S NOMINATION

On April 29, 1860, Lincoln admitted to Lyman Trumbull, "The taste is in my mouth a little" for the nomination.[2] However, Lincoln was also philosophical about his chances. For many months, Stephen A. Douglas and William Seward had been the front-runners. Their images appeared with frequency on the pages of American periodicals as if the parties had already chosen their nominees.[3] Yet the volatile debate over slavery and the turbulent atmosphere of secessionist agitation produced political instability that should have warned any candidate not to be overconfident. Ironically, a dialogue between Douglas and Seward in a cartoon caption just a month before their own nominating conventions predicted political disaster for both. The setting was "the impending crisis at Charleston." "Douglas—'Well Billy, what are you driving at now?' Seward—'Why I'm peddling books—anything to get a living! Shall I put you down for the impending crisis?' Douglas—'No thankee Billy, the impending crisis will put us both down, I reckon.'"[4] Indeed, the volatile political climate eventually removed Seward from the Republican race, ultimately relegated Douglas to political oblivion, and opened the door for Lincoln's historic election to high office. Consistent with his unique philosophy of fatalism (the doctrine of necessity), Lincoln's own postelection appraisal of himself as an "accidental instrument" acknowledged his own indebtedness to such external events.[5]

On May 12, 1860, *Harper's Weekly* published the photographs, engraved on wood, of the "Prominent Candidates for the Republican Presidential Nomination at Chicago."[6] Seward, *Harper's Weekly*'s favorite son, was featured with a significantly larger picture, embellished with decorative art, in the center of the double-page illustration. Appropriately, Lincoln and the other nine dark horse candidates were given subordinate billing. At the Chicago convention, however, Lincoln defied the odds and was nominated on the third ballot.

On May 23, *Momus* scooped all of its journalistic peers by more than two weeks when it announced the results of the Republican convention with a full-page drawing by William North entitled "A Link on (A. Lincoln) the Light-House at Chicago."[7] Judging from accompanying sarcasm, *Momus* regretted Seward's astonishing defeat at the hands of the upstart Lincoln. "Instead of nominating one of their able party leaders, whom they were instructed by their constituents to nominate," lamented a satirical editorial, "they have had the good sense to put up the name of Old Uncle Abe, whose great claim upon the sympathies of the people rests upon the statesmanlike qualification of having gone bare-foot when a boy and split rails for his father."[8] However, *Momus* was not the only illustrated periodical with misgivings about Lincoln's ascendancy to the head of the party. *Vanity Fair* described his nomination as "The Republican Fizzle." "He is a characterless candidate, supported by an aimless party," observed the comic paper. Among his liabilities, "which, if there is any power in newspaper fun, will go far toward defeating him" were the following:

> First, he is known by the tenderly-affectionate soubriquet of "Old Uncle Abe"—a good title for the Chief Magistrate of the United States of North America. Further, he is a longitudinal person, with a shambling gait. . . . If he ever gets clear of the name of "Two-Shilling Candidate" it will be very singular. He was defeated in a political contest by Douglas—a significant fact, should the Little Giant be nominated at Baltimore. He opposed the Mexican War, thereby showing a sort of contempt for the Spirit of '76, the Bird, and other Fourth of July deities. . . . He has a thin, almost nasal voice, and his grammar is not so far above suspicion as Caesar's wife is reported to have been. These are about all the things that are known of him, good, bad, or indifferent, so far as the great voting mass goes.[9]

Reading between the lines, these observations were not just comic hyperbole, but an early, genuine expression of concern for the suitability of the Republican standard-bearer to meet the lofty demands, expectations, and standards of the presidency. For some, it would take time to accept Lincoln as a bona fide candidate and eventual president; for others, he would never measure up.

A WESTERN LUMINARY.

A LINK ON (A. LINCOLN) THE L'GHT-HOUSE AT CHICAGO.

"A Link on (A. Lincoln) the Light-House at Chicago," *Momus*, May 23, 1860, 3. Reproduced from the Collections of the Library of Congress.

Initially, this skeptical tone persisted in *Vanity Fair*'s assessment of the new nominee. The popular description of Lincoln as "the two-shilling candidate" was exploited by *Vanity Fair*. In the next issue, one of Henry L. Stephens's cartoons poked fun at "Another Two Shilling Candidate." In the cartoon dialogue, a black gentleman named Abe reported his intention to give up whitewashing for rail splitting. "1st Colored

Person.—'Abe, is yese gwine to guv up de wite washin' perfession, eh?' 2d Colored Person.—'Yes, 'deed I is—gwine to split rails now—Bobbolitionists make um President—p'raps—Yah! Yah!'" The guilt by association was not lost on the subscribers to *Vanity Fair*. Of course the denunciation cut both ways; both Lincoln and African Americans were maligned.[10]

On June 2, 1860, Frank Bellew pictured "Honest Old Abe" with maul and wedge splitting the "Democratic Party." Ironically, when Douglas had defeated Lincoln for

"The Last Rail Split by 'Honest Old Abe,'" *Momus*, June 2, 1860, 61. Reproduced from the Collections of the Library of Congress.

the Senate in 1858, Lincoln had confided with intimate friends that Douglas's doctrine of popular sovereignty would come back to haunt him. "The fight must go on. The cause of civil liberty must not be surrendered at the end of one, or even, one hundred defeats. Douglas had the ingenuity to be supported in the late contest both as the best means to break down, and to uphold the Slave interest. No ingenuity can keep those antagonistic elements in harmony long. Another explosion will soon come." Lincoln was even more explicit and prophetic about the political ramifications of the explosion: "There will be another blow-up in the so-called democratic party before long."[11] For him, it could not have come at a more propitious time. In some political circles, Lincoln's articulate exposition of the slavery issue in the Lincoln-Douglas debates had hurt Douglas. Nevertheless, the Democrats ultimately needed no assistance from the Republicans to become divided. The irreconcilable Buchanan-Douglas rift and an irreparable North-South sectional fissure over slavery virtually sealed the national fate of the party for 1860.

Momus portrayed the division editorially, in doggerel and caricature. "The Northern and Southern Democrats . . . will separate bodies or they will be nobodies. We confess that we incline to the latter opinion," admitted the *Momus* editorial.[12] In comic verse, *Momus* mocked the antipathy between Buchanan and Douglas in a piece titled "There Was a Convention at Charleston":

> This is the Buck, with spreading horn,
> That hates the Giant shaven and shorn,
> Beloved of the men that won't own the corn,
> Of splitting the party, distracted and torn,
> That elected the chairman full of scorn,
> Who rejected our Mayor all forlorn,
> Who went in for wool and came out shorn,
> At the Convention at Charleston.[13]

Finally, *Momus* caricatured the effects of the internal schism for Stephen A. Douglas. It depicted the "Little Giant" as a bursting helium balloon at "Charleston, May 3, 1860." Of course, *Momus* was not alone. Later, complete with a funeral procession, *Frank Leslie's Budget of Fun* prematurely proclaimed the death of the Democratic Party.[14]

However, there were also tensions within the Republican Party. When Horace Greeley turned his back on the candidacy of William Seward, the press criticized Greeley for his disloyalty. For two reasons, the emotional fallout from the affair held negative repercussions for Lincoln. First, because Greeley facilitated Lincoln's win, one interpretation construed Lincoln as someone who was hostage to the editor of the *New York Tribune*. In other words, Lincoln was just a pawn pushed around by Greeley's powerful influence. This image plagued Lincoln well into his presidency. Second, inasmuch as Lincoln was a direct beneficiary of Greeley's actions, any political enemies of the *New York Tribune*'s editor might more easily generalize and impute some degree of blame to Lincoln in an alleged conspiracy to defeat Seward.

Momus entered this debate early. As if the democratic process had been bypassed, William North depicted the *Tribune*'s editor "offering the Chief Magistracy to the Western Cincinnatus"—Lincoln. Tongue-in-cheek, *Momus* announced the creation of "a thoroughly new and indisputably original drama in five acts" entitled "The Long-Hoarded Revenge of a Disappointed Office-Seeker." According to the message of the play, an embittered Greeley, "the snake in the grass," wreaked vengeance on Seward for his failure to pay off prior political debts.[15] By implication, Lincoln was now the debtor.

Vanity Fair caricatured Greeley as "The New Brutus, and Seward as the fallen Caesar."[16] In the full-page cartoon, "Et Tu, Greeley?" the illustrator literally diminishes the normally gangly Lincoln into the puny, black image of Pompey. Seward dies at the feet of Lincoln, as Greeley, Frank Blair, and Henry Raymond make their escape. "Great Caesar Seward has fallen at the feet of Pompey Lincoln's statue, in the Wigwam of Chicago. His erstwhile friends turned Greeley, the rough and unkempt orator, for fourteen years his right-hand man, inflicted the fatal wound, like his prototype of old, with the sharp and searching steel-pen. It was through this wound that Caesar Seward's political life ebbed forth. So, gathering his robes about him, the mighty demagogue went down, to bite the dust upon the Wigwam floor— politically dead beyond resuscitation. There let him rest, but if remorse can find a

"The Tribune Offering the Chief Magistracy to the Western Cincinnatus," *Momus*, June 9, 1860, 73. Reproduced from the Collections of the Library of Congress.

MARK ANTONY RAYMOND.
CÆSAR SEWARD.

CASCA BLAIR.
BRUTUS GREELEY.

"ET TU, GREELEY?"

"Et Tu, Greeley?"
Vanity Fair, June 2,
1860, 361. Author's
Collection.

place in Brutus Greeley's heart, must he not shudder when, in darkness and alone, he hears the echo of those last sad words, 'Et Tu, Brute?'" None of this discussion enhanced the stature of Lincoln.

The comic papers explored every angle of the Seward-Greeley connection and used multiple modes of communication to satisfy the lighthearted appetites of subscribers. In doggerel, *Vanity Fair* let Greeley speak for himself. What follows is just a verse of rhyme from a much larger universe of comic doggerel on the same theme:

I have nipped him at Chicago,
I have made my Seward wail,
I've ordained that Uncle Abram
Shall be ridden on the rail.[17]

Any incipient power this alleged unholy alliance between Greeley and Lincoln may have had to damage Lincoln's credibility was nullified by Seward's forthright campaigning for Lincoln.

The nominating process had been full of bombshells: Lincoln's stunning upset of Seward; the division of the Democratic Party into Northern (Stephen A. Douglas) and Southern (John C. Breckinridge) factions; and the emergence of John Bell's Constitutional Union Party. The vicissitudes of the two major parties were aptly summarized in a *Vanity Fair* illustration patterned after a popular nursery rhyme, "The Story of Five Little Pigs." In this case, the five little pigs were, respectively, Stephen A. Douglas, Horace Greeley, Abraham Lincoln, William Seward, and President James Buchanan. "This little pig, named Stephen, went to market (Charleston Market), but was not disposed of; this little pig, named Horace, (should have) stayed at home; this little pig, named Abe, got a piece of roast beef; and this little pig, named William, got none; and this little pig, named James, cried Wee! Wee! Wee! I can't get over the (Coyode) investigation."[18] Thus the nominations were in place, and the final race for the White House began.

LINCOLN'S CANDIDACY FOR THE WHITE HOUSE

On the basis of a cartoon by H. L. Stephens that appeared in *Vanity* Fair, Lincoln's prospects for the presidency were "Shaky." Modeled after a famous tightrope walker's bold traverse of Niagara Falls, Stephens's cartoon shows "Mr. Abraham Blondin De Lave Lincoln" in his own "daring transit" across some undefined chasm while the White House looms in the distant background. However, instead of walking a tightrope, Lincoln attempts the feat on a rotten, "perilous rail." Presumably, the intent of this imagery was to conjure up the weakness of a candidacy that, in part, relied on political gimmicks such as Lincoln's notoriety as a common "rail-splitter." Yet the cartoon also carries a more compelling critical message. The perilous exploit is compounded by Lincoln carrying an African American in a carpet bag. Orchestrating the event from the edge of the precipice, the omnipresent Horace Greeley remonstrates, "Don't drop the carpet bag."[19] This image of the advocacy of black American interests had earned Lincoln's party the sobriquet "Black Republicanism," a stereotype Stephen A. Douglas had used to defame Lincoln in their memorable debates.

The Republican platform of 1860 tested the apprehensions of American voters in regard to social distance between black and white Americans, and some opponents of the Republicans did everything they could to evoke racial fears. For example, the

SHAKY.

DARING TRANSIT ON THE PERILOUS RAIL, · · · · Mr. Abraham Blondin De Lave Lincoln.

"Shaky," *Vanity Fair*,
June 9, 1860, 377.
Author's Collection.

Democratic Expositor and National Crisis, a Douglas campaign paper, challenged the "Wide Awakes [to] get the Republican editors to print in large letters the following from a western paper: 'He (Lincoln) believes the negro is human—he has a soul—he has intellect—and in so far as the rights of suffrage or any other rights of citizenship is concerned, he should be placed on an equality with the rest of mankind.'" Because of substantial racism in the land, the charge—that Lincoln might endorse these more humanitarian beliefs—was made to damage his political credibility. By 1860, Lincoln was accustomed to being smeared as a "Black Republican." Consequently, he was amply prepared with an astute rejoinder that defined the concept in his own terms: "I am what they call, as I understand it, a 'Black Republican.' (Applause and laughter) I think slavery is wrong, morally and politically. I desire that it should be no further spread in these United States, and I should not object if it should gradually terminate in the whole Union."[20] Obviously, Lincoln's Black Republicanism made some voters nervous, and the Douglas camp's tactics capitalized on the presence of vulnerable emotions.

In July, *Momus* struck a positive blow in support of Lincoln. A William North cartoon displayed a far more formidable Republican candidate in "Abe, the Giant Killer." As a result of the final split in the Democratic Party, the giant evolved into a two-headed specimen: Douglas and Breckinridge. In this cartoon, Lincoln takes on the heroic aura of the underdog David slaying the divided, Democratic Goliath. In this image, Lincoln is clearly in command.[21]

Vanity Fair contrasted the commencement of the political battles among Lincoln, Douglas, Breckinridge, and Bell with a more "innocent" era of George Washington, John Adams, and Thomas Jefferson in the wake of the Revolutionary War. In "Serene above Them All," Henry L. Stephens pictures the four candidates in full battle gear, swinging their swords at opponents and defending themselves with shields. Columbia observes the ugly fray from the lofty perspective of the "Father of the Country" and his two illustrious successors, Adams and Jefferson.[22] The argument implicit in the cartoon: the founding fathers were above such mundane political antics of this world.

"Abe, the Giant Killer," *Momus*, July 21, 1860, 120. Reproduced from the Collections of the Library of Congress.

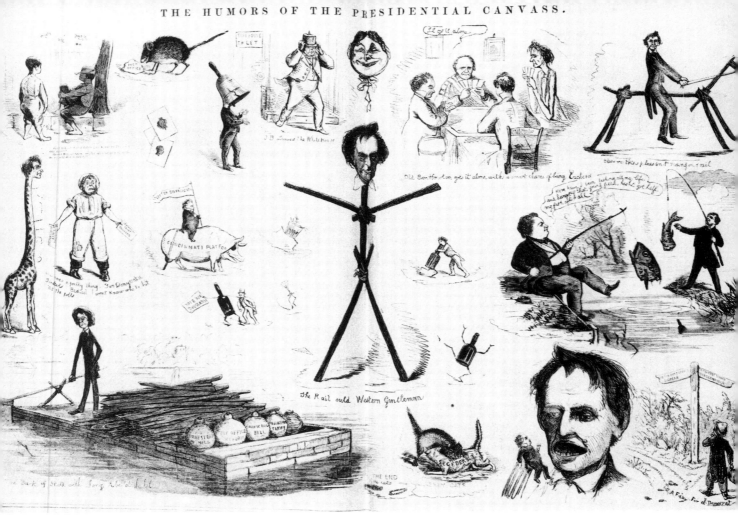

By the end of July, *Momus* was dead, a victim of competitive economic struggle in the world of comic periodicals. However, in August, the *Comic Monthly, Frank Leslie's Budget of Fun,* and *Phunny Phellow* filled the void. For *Comic Monthly,* Frank Bellew created a serial cartoon that featured "The Humors of the Presidential Canvass."[23] Although all four presidential candidates were included in the print, Lincoln clearly received preeminent publicity. In the middle of the double-page illustration, Lincoln is featured as "The Rail ould Western gentleman." In the upper right-hand corner, Lincoln rides a hobby horse made, naturally, of rails. "Bless me," he says, "this is pleasant riding on a rail." At the far left of the middle row, his head rests on the body of a giraffe, a symbol of his novel, elongated stature. At the lower left portion of the cartoon, Lincoln's modest notoriety as a flatboat pilot is amplified with the caption "The Bark of State with Long Abe at the helm." Prominently displayed at the front of the flatboat are major planks in his party's platform: "Homestead Bill, Post Office Reform, Pacific Rail Bill, and Protective Tariff." In the lower right, Lincoln opens his mouth as if to consume a greatly reduced "Little Giant." And in the middle right, Lincoln's tall presence towers over his three competitors in a symbolic card game. In effect, the arrangement of the Lincoln image surrounds the other candidates, and is also at the focal point in the center.

In contrast, Lincoln's opponents are given short shrift. Aside from his appearance in the card game image, Bell is conspicuous only because of his obscurity. His presence is confined to a solitary image of a bell (for his head) on a very small body. Likewise, the Democratic Party is noted unfavorably. President Buchanan is shown leaving "The White House," to which is attached a sign that reads, "This House to Let." Stephen A. Douglas rides a lame pig, labeled "Cincinnati Platform," and carries a sign, "Squatter Sovereignty." A "Vote for Douglas" label is attached to a whiskey bottle. The other three images that focus on Douglas and Breckinridge show (1) a confused Irishman who holds ballots for both and exclaims, "I won't know who to hit at the polls"; (2) "A Fix for a Democrat" who does not know which way to turn at a crossroads that points to either Breckinridge or Douglas; and (3) Breckinridge and Douglas angling at the same fishing hole, only to find that each can only catch one-half of the Democratic Party fish. Again, this particular illustration was partial to Lincoln, but others were not.

Also in August, in a half-page cartoon, Lincoln and Hamlin were unceremoniously dismissed by Columbia because of their Black Republicanism. To an ailing Columbia, Uncle Sam remarks, "Columby, dear, I've brought in Drs. Lincoln and

"Black Draught," *Frank Leslie's Budget of Fun,* August 1, 1860, 9. Courtesy of the American Antiquarian Society.

UNCLE SAM — " *Columby, dear, I've brought in Drs. Lincoln and Hamlin—maybe they can do you some good?*"
COLUMBIA — " *Oh, dear, do take them away! I can't bear those black draughts ; they—heh—they—heh—kill me !*"

Hamlin—maybe they can do you some good?" As the lead doctor, Lincoln bears a huge bottled prescription—"Black Draught." But Columbia is in no mood for that kind of medicine. To Uncle Sam she brusquely replies, "Oh, dear, do take them away! I can't bear those black draughts; they—heh—they—heh—kill me!"[24] This image epitomizes the anxiety elicited in some quarters by Black Republicanism.

However, the message from Columbia in the bottom half-page cartoon of the same date, entitled "Columbia and Her Suitors," though wary, was not so abrupt. In this version, Columbia will wait until November to pick her suitor. Uncle Sam is her intermediary. "Well, gentlemen, Miss Columbia will think over your proposals, and she'll give you an answer next November. I have no doubt your intentions are honorable and your affections disinterested. Live in hope, gentlemen."[25] This image was more tentative; it claimed that the national jury was still out.

Phunny Phellow's entry in August highlighted Stephen A. Douglas's fix "in a tight place." "Douglas, (in great perplexity)—Which horn of the dilemma shall I take?"

"Columbia and Her Suitors," *Frank Leslie's Budget of Fun*, August 1, 1860, 9. Courtesy of the American Antiquarian Society.

UNCLE SAM– *"Well, gentlemen, Miss Columbia will think over your proposals, and she'll give you an answer next November. I have no doubt your intentions are honorable and your affections disinterested. Live in hope, gentlemen."*

(A fierce Brahman bull with "North" and "South" as the horns of the dilemma stands between Douglas and the White House). "I don't believe it will make any difference; I'm sure to be thrown, anyhow!" In the same issue, a small Thomas Butler Gunn cartoon depicts a "German Politician" trying to persuade his friends to vote for Lincoln. "I tell you, mine frients, Lincoln's ter man. He goes for lager beer and Switzer kaise all der time! Yah!" "Enthusiastic Democrat—Dry up—Old puddin' Head! What are yer torkin' about? Ain't Horace Greeley and the other Black Republicans tryin' to stop free trade on Sundays, s-a-y?" With respect to impact, this was a relatively insignificant image. Nevertheless, it reflects the spirited political dialogue in the European ethnic community, and the concomitant concern for the candidates' stance on ethnicity. After all, the Republicans were dogged with suspicions of a nativist bias and alleged connections to a Know-Nothing past. Such images symbolized the political relevance of ethnicity.[26]

As the political campaign became more heated—and the potential for secession more vivid—illustrators became more enervated. On September 1, 1860, William North's front-page cartoon in *Frank Leslie's Budget of Fun* linked the specter of disunion with the contest for the presidency. "That Horrid Darkey Who Won't Let Folks Sleep," a graphic, if insensitive, metaphor of secession, was shown banging on

"That Horrid Darkey Who Won't Let Folks Sleep," *Frank Leslie's Budget of Fun*, September 1, 1860, front page. Courtesy of the American Antiquarian Society.

SCENE ON BOARD THE UNITED STATES STEAMER—PASSENGERS, STEVE DOUGLAS, BELL, LINCOLN, BRECKINRIDGE, AND OTHERS. SAMBO—*Gentlemen passengers for Salt River will please to git ready.— [Aside] Wonder who dat passenger is who 'spects to git out at de Wite House?*

the dissonant drum of disunion. In the foreground, judging from his facial expression, the noise of secession appears to rattle President Buchanan. According to the caption, the "scene[is] on board [the] United States steamer—passengers, Steve Douglas, Bell, Lincoln, Breckinridge, and others." After getting the attention of the passengers with the instrument of percussion, "Sambo" warns the "gentleman passengers for Salt River," that ominous symbol of defeat, "will please to git ready—[Aside] 'Wonder who dat passenger is who 'spects to git out at de Wite House?'"[27] Now, Lincoln's chances for the White House looked better than ever, but no one was conceding anything. More than sixty days remained before the election, and anything could happen.

On September 1, 1860, a clever cartoon by Henry L. Stephens used "Uncle Sam's" pawnshop as a way to illustrate the threatening obstacles still in Lincoln's way. The customary sign outside the business is inscribed with the names of three claimants to ownership of the national enterprise: Douglas, Breckinridge, and Bell. In effect, Lincoln cannot enter Uncle Sam's pawnshop without overcoming his competitors' claims. Still, the lead caption, "Three to One You Don't Get It," was only true in the numerical sense. Because Lincoln was now the established favorite, his odds were much better. (Of course, there was always the possibility and open speculation that someone would strike a political deal, or, in the vernacular of the time, fusion, but political difference and personal ambition conspired against such an arrangement.) The dog Buchanan, current occupant of the shop, barks at Lincoln's approach, but Buchanan's size and apparent trepidation mark him more as a nuisance than a threat. Continuing the conjecture, the log cabin in the background signifies the distance between the backwoods reputation of Lincoln and the sophistication of the Capitol. And although Lincoln, axe in hand, seems to approach the pawnshop with confidence, the rails he strives to pawn—"Chicago Platform," "Tribune," "Sambo," and "Stock in Trade"—were often conceived as liabilities rather than assets, rails not easily split with finesse or sheer power. Nevertheless, Lincoln does all in his might to pawn his controversial wares, and as he approaches the shop he is an imposing figure.[28]

Also in September, *Phunny Phellow* caricatured Lincoln as "A Galvanized Split Rail." The caption and the animated caricature promoted the impression that Lincoln's campaign was in high gear. In *Frank Leslie's Budget of Fun*, William North depicted the presidential sweepstakes as a swimming race. Boxing, sprinting, and horse racing were all used to compare the relative position of candidates in the presidential campaigns of 1860 and 1864. This was a first for swimming. Lincoln led the pack, Douglas was a close second, Breckinridge lagged behind, and Bell was literally out of the picture. North entitled the cartoon the "Great Swimming Match to Come Off on the Fourth of November. Stakes—the White House, and $100,000,000 of Patronage." The imaginary conversation among Lincoln, Douglas, and Breckinridge revealed the vigorous nature of the campaign: "Uncle Abe—'Where's your strength now, Steve? You've got nothing to squat on!' Steve—'I wouldn't squat on your rail if I could, Abe! I swim to win a Free Soil and not a Black Republic! Make Way!' Breck—

"THREE TO ONE YOU DON'T GET IT."

[VARIATION ON THE POPULAR INTERPRETATION OF THE MEANING OF THE PAWNBROKER'S SIGN.]

"Three to One You Don't Get It," *Vanity Fair*, September 1, 1860, 117. Author's Collection.

'I'm coming, boys! The race is not always to the swift nor the battle to the strong!' [Left swimming]."[29] The race was not over, political ambivalence was still acute, but Lincoln was ahead.

In late September, Henry L. Stephens's feature cartoon in *Vanity Fair* took a portion of one of Stephen A. Douglas's recent stump speeches as its theme. Douglas had predicted Lincoln's political collapse: "'My friends, there is no patriotic duty on earth more gratifying to my feelings than to make a speech over Mr. Lincoln's political

UNCLE ABE— *"Where's your strength now, Steve? You've got nothing to squat on!"*

STEVE—*I wouldn't squat on your rail if I could, Abe! I swim to win a Free Soil and not a Black Republic! Make way!"*

BRECK— *"I'm coming, boys! The race is not always to the swift nor the battle to the strong!"* [Left swimming.]

grave. [Loud cheers] I do not make this remark out of any unkindness to Mr. Lincoln, but I believe that the good of his own country requires it." Stephens pictured Douglas as a pious, hypocritical Quaker preacher, "Aminidab Sleek," solemnly pronouncing Lincoln's misfortune.[30] Although Douglas's remarks seemed to exude confidence, his decision to tour the country on the "stump" was a calculated risk and an act of quiet desperation.

In 1860, it was considered in poor taste and bad form for a presidential candidate to go on the road and speak on his own behalf. Whatever advantage accrued to Douglas by taking his case directly to the public may have been more than offset by ill will that this violation of traditional convention generated. Soon a deluge of bad press, not the least of which was a stream of cartoons, engulfed his campaign. Of these images, the most popular was a rejoinder to the humorous notion that Douglas was just on the way to visit his mother. In another vein, *Phunny Phellow* upbraided Douglas for violating the stump speech norm of political propriety. The caption, "Honest Old Abe and the Little Boy in Search of His Mother—A Sensation Story," introduced a contrived dialogue between Lincoln and Douglas. "Lincoln—'What's the matter, my poor little boy?' Douglas—'Boo-hoo-hoo! I've lost my mother! I enquired for her at that white house yonder, but they told me she wasn't there, and wasn't likely ever to be there!' Lincoln—'Never mind, bubby—you come along with me, and I'll learn you to split rails, and you may live to be a President yet, who knows?'"[31]

On September 29, H. L. Stephens, acting on a telegraphic dispatch out of Washington D.C., caricatured rumors allegedly circulated among Breckinridge supporters that Douglas was almost ready to give his support to Lincoln. Exploiting a common stereotype, the artist dressed up James Buchanan and William Yancey as gossip-mongering women. A "Scan.[dal] Mag.[azine] at Washington" is the humorous foil for the purported source of the conversation between "Miss J. B." [James Buchanan] and "Nancy [William Yancey] of Alabama." "Yes, my dear, and they do say, Steve Douglas is going to sell out to Old Abe, and Old Abe's to give him ever so much money and quicksilver, besides the whole town of Chicago. But I wouldn't mention it for anything."[32]

In early October, the pageantry of Lincoln's political organization, the Wide Awakes, turned the attention of some cartoonists to the Wide Awake image. In "Sensations of the Month," the *Comic Monthly* combined the animated activity of the

"Honest Old Abe and the Little Boy in Search of His Mother—A Sensation Story." *Phunny Phellow*, November 1860, front page. Reproduced through permission of the Rare Book and Special Collections Library, University of Illinois at Urbana-Champaign.

Wide Awakes with the visit to the United States of the Prince of Wales, which produced a grand double-page caricature, "The Prince of Wales and the Wide Awakes." In the process, the cartoon also outlined the duties of the Wide Awake organization: "(a) To confirm the [convert]; (b) to animate the dilatory; (c) to instruct the inquiring; and (d) to reason with the wavering"—all in the interest of a "vote for Lincoln."[33]

When William Seward went on the stump on behalf of Lincoln's cause, *Vanity Fair* could not resist the temptation to caricature him in a complete Wide Awake costume: "Seward's Grand Starring Tour—King Richard III—up with my Wigwam! Here will I lie tonight." Moreover, when the Lincoln campaign tried to enlist James Gordon Bennett and the *New York Herald* to its cause, a cartoon by Henry L. Stephens showed two comely Wide Awake women offering to exchange Bennett's tattered personal coat for a "Wide Awake" coat from Pennsylvania and a hat from "Indiana." "What Will He Do With It?" asks the caption. "Miss Pennsylvania" said, "'Now, friend Bennett, don't thee think it's most time for thee to change thee garment for a better one?' In Scottish brogue Bennett replies, 'Deed Lassies—it's a bonnie braw coatie—and this auld Buchanan thing is gettin' unco ragged. Weel—weel—I dinna ken [Well, well, I don't know].'"[34] The Wide Awake campaign seemed to be making a difference.

Phunny Phellow's cartoon fare for presidential candidates was meager in October. Although all four candidates were present in "Old Buck's Shaving Saloon," the cartoonist simply used the occasion to deprecate Buchanan's administration.[35] However, the October 1 menu of illustrations in *Frank Leslie's Budget of Fun* provided a novel change of pace; one of the cartoons depicted three of the candidates' spouses (those of Breckinridge, Douglas, and Lincoln) holding forth on a politically sensitive religious issue: "The religious issue was injected into the campaign when the Chicago press and *Tribune* asserted that Douglas's chief strength lay in his Roman Catholic support. Douglas had married a Catholic, Adele Cutts, and his children were brought up in that faith; the Republicans alleged that the Little Giant had become converted to Catholicism."[36] A subtle undercurrent of anti-Catholic prejudice pervaded the cartoon. Broaching the delicate ecclesiastical domain, a priest stirs the brew of "Catholic influence" and polls the spouses for ingredients they would add to the political pot. "Now then my lasses, in order to make this pot-pie palatable, we must have the right sort of ingredients—so let's see what you have to offer?" asks the priest. "Miss Douglas (who was originally a cabinet-maker) offers a first-class cabinet Ministership and sundry other promises of places, which promises she will keep— politically speaking. Miss Breckinridge proposes to flavor the pie by a fine Savoying Foreign Mission, and will protect the Church's interest, and promises to *carry out* the *Bulls* emanating from the Church—which doubtless she will do. Miss Lincoln, a strappin' gal from out West, offers free farms for all the offices at home and abroad for the Church people—and some think she'll be likely to keep her promises."[37] Although all three spouses make concessions to religious organizations, the two Democratic spouses' political overtures were more specific; they were direct appeals for ecclesiastical support. Inasmuch as *Frank Leslie's Budget of Fun* was a Republican organ, linking the two Democratic Party candidates to religious favoritism was a political ploy to appeal to anti-Catholic prejudice. What began as an attack on Douglas's purported Catholic connections also included Breckinridge. The cartoon used classic guilt by association and blatantly appealed to religious intolerance.

THE PRESIDENTIAL POT-PIE.

"The Presidential Pot-Pie," *Frank Leslie's Budget of Fun,* October 1, 1860. Courtesy of the American Antiquarian Society.

AN ILLUSTRIOUS COOK INSTRUCTING SOME OF HIS MOST INTERESTING PUPILS, MISSES LINCOLN, DOUGLAS, AND BRECKINRIDGE.

ILLUSTRIOUS COOK— *"Now, then, my lasses, in order to make this pot-pie palatable, we must have the right sort of ingredients—so let's see what you have to offer?"*

MISS DOUGLAS (who was originally a cabinet-maker) offers a first-class cabinet Ministership and sundry other promises of places, which promises she will keep—politically speaking.

MISS BRECKENRIDGE proposes to flavor the pie by a fine Savoying Foreign Mission, and will protect the Church's interest, and promises to *carry out* the *Bulls* emanating from the Church—which doubtless she will do.

MISS LINCOLN, a strappin' gal from out West, offers free farms for all the offices at home and abroad for the Church people—and some think she'll be likely to keep her promises.

On October 15, *Frank Leslie's Budget of Fun* returned with a more conventional rail-splitting image. In "The Perilous Voyage to the White House," the artist depicted Lincoln and a generic African American astride a rail that extends across "Salt River" to the "White House." Looking at Breckinridge, Bell, and Douglas, the African American exclaims, "Guy Massa Lincoln ef dey get us off I spose you know whar we am gwine to." (Answer: the Salt River.) The caption notes, "Uncle Abe, attacked by Squatter-Sovereign Douglas, Nix-com-arouse Breckinridge and Old-Fogy-Union-

THE PERILOUS VOYAGE TO THE WHITE HOUSE.

"The Perilous Voyage to the White House," *Frank Leslie's Budget of Fun*, October 15, 1860, 8–9. Courtesy of the American Antiquarian Society.

Uncle Abe, attacked by Squatter-Sovereign Douglas, Nix-com-arouse Breckinridge and Old-Fogy-Union-Womanism Bell-and-Everett, dares the perils of the Salt River, expecting to win the White House in the distance. P'rhaps he will get it—p'rhaps he won't. The intelligent reader will perceive J. B. in the distance preparing to absquatulate.

Womanism Bell-and-Everett, dares the perils of Salt River, expecting to win the White House in the distance. P'rhaps he will get it—p'rhaps he won't. The intelligent reader will perceive J. B. in the distance preparing to absquatulate." If only on a perilous rail over the foreboding Salt River, the Black Republican Lincoln, nevertheless, expects "to win the White House."[38]

October was a rich month for significant Lincoln graphics. Closing the month was a fine Henry L. Stephens caricature of Lincoln, Douglas, and Breckinridge that appeared in *Vanity Fair*. In "Sich a Gittin Up Stairs," the three political rivals appear as black-faced minstrels. Condescending minstrel dialect, apparently from the voice of Breckinridge, describes the event: "Miss Douglas beller out. Den she jump between us. But I guess she no forgit de day wen Abra'm show his genus! Sich a Gittin Up Stairs I neber did see." Early in the campaign, the hopeless struggle to gain control of the considerable potential for votes within the Democratic Party had preoccupied Douglas and Breckinridge. Yet any opportunity for Douglas to gain the support of Southern Democrats or for Breckinridge to get that of Northern party members was obviously slipping away. Meanwhile, Lincoln seized the political initiative, a dismaying development for the Democratic camp that led to an astonished admission in minstrel vernacular that Lincoln's shooting star was rising—"Sich a Gittin Up Stairs I Neber Did See." A bellows on the floor, inscribed *Tribune,* symbolized Horace Greeley's facilitating role in Lincoln's candidacy. The parrot's utterance from the bird cage, "Brecky's Got a Cracker," let it be known that not only Douglas, but also Breckinridge, had his hands full.[40]

On the eve of the election the *Comic Monthly* did not venture any bold political forecasts. Resigned to await the verdict of the people on November 6, it was content to offer pictorial satire in a double-page cartoon that encompassed all of the candidates. The artist, J. H. Howard, included a dozen campaign scenes in the cartoon. Nevertheless, Lincoln, the consensus choice to win, was still the focal point. For example, Douglas and Breckinridge were getting splinters from the Lincoln rail. The three-headed fusion candidate of Bell, Breckinridge, and Douglas implied that the only chance for upsetting Lincoln was for his adversaries to combine forces. Indeed, in "The Battle in New York," the artist spuriously linked Bell, Breckinridge, and Douglas as a united front against Lincoln. In "The State of the Case," the "Spirit of Disunion" was unable to ignite the tinder of Bell, Breckinridge, and Douglas to burn "The Original Rail"—Lincoln—at the stake. Why? Because he was "wide awake." Finally, "The Heads of the Breckinridge Party" were committed to "haul old Abe over the coals."[40] Later in the campaign, such obsession with Lincoln underscored the identity of the leading candidate.

In confident anticipation of Lincoln's victory, Henry L. Stephens portrayed "Dr. Lincoln" holding the sword of authority, vox populi, about to separate the political Siamese twins, James Gordon Bennett and President James Buchanan. Before performing the "wonderful surgical operation" to sever the critical connection between the two—"the secret service fund"—Lincoln informed the political patients "Chang"

"Sich a Gittin Up Stairs," *Vanity Fair*, October 27, 1860, 213. Author's Collection.

"SICH A GITTIN UP STAIRS."

"MISS DOUGLAS BELLER OUT. DEN SHE JUMP BETWEEN US. BUT I GUESS SHE NO FORGIT DE DAY WEN ABRA'M SHOW HIS GENUS! SICH A GITTIN UP STAIRS I NEBER DID SEE. SICH A GITTIN UP STAIRS I NEBER DID SEE!"

and "Eng" what to expect. "Don't be scared, my boys, 'tis as easy as lying."[41] The message? It was only a matter of time until Lincoln was empowered to rectify any residue of graft and corruption in the Buchanan administration.

If the *Comic Monthly* and *Vanity Fair* only implicitly intimated Lincoln's virtual lock on the presidency, the partisan *Wide Awake Pictorial* was utterly unrestrained in predicting the outcome. Supremely self-assured, a front-page graphic image unabashedly displayed "Honest Old Abe Marching Forth to the White House."[42]

After the *New York Herald* and *Express* forecast gloom and doom from Lincoln's stunning win, *Vanity Fair* made light of its pessimism. In the "deplorable result of Lincoln's election as depicted by the *Herald* and *Express*," the artist visually summarized the sad state of national affairs. The long caption described his humorous parody. "On the house-top Horace Greeley is, of course, seen fiddling over the ruins of our beloved country. To the left you behold the pure-minded and upright J. G. B. [James Gordon Bennett] shutting up shop, preparatory to returning to his native land. Cows graze in Fulton street. Desolation everywhere, and the world done for generally."[43] Clothed in wit, the cartoon was potent ridicule of a bleak prognosis for the Lincoln administration.

To judge from the cartoons, the black community saw Lincoln differently. Slaves saw "a good time coming. . . . 'I say, Dinah, de wite folks rudder 'spec dat Massa Lincoln is a-gwine to gib a monster clam bake nex March to all de cullud pussons in Washington!'" Another cartoon offered hope as a "result of the election. 'I hab de felicity ob dancin de next set wid you, Miss Angeline?' 'Oh, yes, Augustus. Since you have assisted in the election of Honest Old Abe, I can refuse you nothing!'"[44] Such images disclosed thinly veiled elements of ethnic paternalism and condescension, but they were better than other popular blatantly racist cartoon fare. Nevertheless, in such trying times with an untested president not many cartoonists were inclined to sketch utopian dreams about the new regime.

London's *Punch* broke its silence on the election with a small illustration of a slave showing his master a headline that announced the results. In this initial, sanguine impression of Lincoln, *Punch*'s caption also satirically censured South Carolina in the periodical's own matchless, amusing way:

> In consequence of the election of Abraham Lincoln as President of the United States (bravo, hooray, O my brothers!), it is announced that South Carolina, in an ecstacy of slave owner's rage, has ordered a solemn day of humiliation, on which all the slaves in the State are to be flogged, and all the copies of the Scriptures burned. Moreover, she calls a Convention, and declares that she is going to separate from the Union, and be an independent State, and have representatives of her own at the Courts of Europe. We hear that her first demands on England are, that to show our sympathy in her hate of the President, Lincoln Cathedral be pulled down, the County of Lincoln be re-christened and called Breckinridge County, that all Lincoln and Bennett hats be immediately smashed in, that Lord Lincoln be transported, and that when Falstaff in the play speaks of "thieves in Lincoln green," he be ordered to say "President Lincoln's black thieves." Anything to please the lovely Carolina.[45]

Plainly, this cartoon represented a short-lived honeymoon for Lincoln and the English comic press. It was only a matter of time before he would become the major target of Britain's comic artists.

(Overleaf) "The Political Sensation," *Comic Monthly,* November 1860, 8–9. Courtesy of the American Antiquarian Society.

THE FUSION CANDIDATE. | HEADS OF THE BRECKINRIDGE PARTY. | THE DIVING BELL. | DEMOCRAT ON THE FENCE. | THE BELLE (Everett) OF THE SEASON. | THE STATE OF THE CASE.

SENSATION.

THE GROWTH OF THE BELL.

POOR LITTLE DUG.

THE BATTLE IN NEW YORK.
LINCOLN.—[loq.] " Three to one ain't fair exactly, but come on boys."

THE NEWSBOYS.
HORACE [to RAYMOND.] I say, Hank who's that 'ere Jim Bennett hurrahin' for now? Wasn't he a hollerin' fur Lincoln a little while ago?
HANK.—Yaas—but he'es allus a makin' a muss of some kind, darn him, you can never tell who he is hollerin' for."

ENGAGED.
OF THE PRESIDENTIAL CANDIDATES. [Take your choice, reader]—I have heard, sir, that the House will be vacant on the 4th of March. I should like to have a lease of it for four years. SAM. I am afraid, sir, that it is already engaged, but if not let by the middle of November, you might call again. Good day.

MARCH FORTH.

THE GROWTH OF THE BELL. │ POOR LITTLE DUG. │ THE BATTLE OF NEW YORK. │ THE NEWSBOYS. │
ENGAGED. │ MARCH FORTH.

"Wonderful Surgical
Operation," *Vanity
Fair*, November 3, 1860,
225. Author's
Collection.

WONDERFUL SURGICAL OPERATION,
PERFORMED BY DOCT. LINCOLN ON THE POLITICAL CHANG AND ENG.
POLITICAL CHANG, J. B——N.
POLITICAL ENG, J. G. B——TT.

Even a reluctant Columbia made an uneasy peace with Lincoln's ideological reputation as a Black Republican: "Miss Columbia–'Good gracious, Abraham Lincoln!
how did you manage to get the situation of overseer of my farm?' Old Abe—'Why,
you see, Miss Columby, it was a sort of a free fight among the other fellows, and so
while they were busy wrangling the other boys kinder put me right through.' Miss
Columbia—'Oh, Abe, how could they—and things so mixed up as they are? Well
(she sighs), and what are you going to do?' Old Abe—'Why, Miss Columby, I'm

going to act on the squar, and do what's best for the interests of the hull farm if they'll only give me a chance. I'll take care that our blessed bird loses none of its feathers.' Miss Columbia—'Why, then, perhaps, after all, you are not so Black as you are painted.'"[46] These apprehensions of change were inevitable. The political instability of a divided nation, the specter of secession, even war, and the tradition of racial disdain stoked the embers of unrest.

However, the comic press was interested in more than the political reverberations of Lincoln's election. It also offered humorous explanations of how Lincoln had won. *Frank Leslie's Budget of Fun* resorted to Shakespeare's *Richard III* to explain "The Smothering of the Democratic Princes." Two explanations of the illustration were presented. The caption gave a short version in prose: "Enter two Assassins (vide

"Good Gracious, Abraham Lincoln!" *Frank Leslie's Budget of Fun,* January 1861, 16. Reproduced from the Collections of the Library of Congress.

Shakespeare). Catesby Lincoln and Ratcliff Sanders steal surreptitiously into the Apartment of the Sleeping Princes, Bell and Breckinridge, and smother them with the Pil(lar)low of Squatter Sovereignty."[47] The longer poetic account was more detailed and witty:

Richard III.—Act the Best, Scene the Worst

[The Philadelphia Curtin[48] rises, and discloses Bell and Breckinridge, the
Democratic twin Princes, on their Patent Fusion Platform.]
Prince Bell—Good-night, sweet Breckinridge! Oh, Marcy Sakes,
We've been too long, dear Breck, the Wide-Awakes!
Prince Breck—a fair goodnight—indeed, a more than fair,
If we're not troubled by Fernando the nightmare. [They Sleep]
[Enter Abe Lincoln in armor, and George Sanders disguised as a Wide-A-
Wake.]
Abe Lincoln—Thus far into the bowels of the land
We've crept, friend George—but you understand,
Without my going over the whole scene.
Hold up the light and give to me the bolster,
With which I'll smother them before a soul stir.
Come, Little Giant, squatter sovereign height,

"The Smothering of the Democratic Princes," *Frank Leslie's Budget of Fun*, November 15, 1860, front page. Courtesy of the Department of Special Collections, the University of Chicago Library.

I'll make you do a power of good tonight!
For I, without your cushion could not squeeze
The light out of such sturdy chaps as these.
I hope that Bell has read old Everett's last
Paper in Bonner's, and that Buck has passed.
His fourteenth toddy; for 'twixt you and I,
Such potions make it very sweet to die.
Wide-Awake George—Cease your philosophy—it's rather stale—
Smother the twins—my light begins to pale.
Abe Lincoln—Here goes!
And thus I douse the squatter sovereign—[Smother them]
Thus do I send them o'er the river Styx.
Called the Salt River in our politics. [Curtin falls][49]

Thus were Douglas, Bell, and Breckinridge abruptly dispatched down Salt River, Buchanan dismissed, and Abe Lincoln left to savor the fruits of victory.

One cartoonist, W. T. Crane, attempted to summarize some of the factors responsible for Lincoln's political success. Crane put the president-elect in the background of a picture with representatives of his supporters (including Horace Greeley); then Lincoln brings them to a pile of discarded election artifacts. Pointing, he says, "My friends, you are the workmen, and there are the tools which have done it!" Dancing on an old kerosene oil drum is "The Great Original Wide-Awake" (an obvious jab at Black Republicanism), who wears the cap and cape of the organization, holds a kerosene lantern in one hand and "Old Uncle Abe's Original Rail" in the other, and is surrounded by miscellaneous paraphernalia such as a maul, axe, cannon, rockets, "Dupont's Best" (gun powder), musical instruments for a band, flags, the patriotic eagle symbol, whiskey, and a host of such signs as "Old Abe is going to do it," "Republican Nomination," "Rita goes for Lincoln and Hamlin," "A Home for Every Nigger," "Honesty is the best policy," "Wide-Awake," "Rail Splitter," and "On to victory."[50] To be sure, the cartoon asserts that the shibboleths of the 1860 Republican Party, the organized hoopla, the signs, symbols, uniforms, bands, parades, and the like helped him win the election, but the cartoon also symbolized elements of national anxiety over Lincoln's Black Republicanism.

Finally, one belated comic analysis of Lincoln's elevation to the presidency credited loyal voters from a cross section of ethnic America for their vital part in his election. The quotation in the caption is attributed to Lincoln. Although not found in the *Collected Works*, it bears the stamp of Lincoln's eloquence and grace. "My dear friends and adopted fellow-citizens, I cannot express to you in words how deeply I am obliged to you for your generous votes. They have made me what I am. Without you, I should have remained what I was—nothing. My emotions overpower me, as you can easily perceive. Be assured that I will do for you whatever LIES IN MY POWER!" Compared to the serious remarks of appreciation ascribed to Lincoln, the graphic image is incongruously comic. Speaking to his ethnic benefactors, Lincoln sits astride

"The Great Original
Wide-Awake," *Frank
Leslie's Budget of Fun,*
December 15, 1860.
Courtesy of the
American Antiquarian
Society.

THE GREAT ORIGINAL WIDE-AWAKE.

a huge eagle. Flanking the president on his right is William Seward, and on Lincoln's left is Uncle Sam. In one hand, Uncle Sam holds a Wide Awake lantern, and in the other certificates of "appointment for all offices," including some to "Prussia" and "Sardinia." Apparently, Seward grasps within his hands the list of appointees. Carl Schurz stands in the foreground, a beer mug hanging from his neck and an elaborate pipe from the Old Country sits in his right hand, both of which symbols establish his German ethnicity. He listens intensely in anticipation, perhaps for his presidential appointment. Meanwhile, an Italian organ grinder, a stoic pipe-smoking German, and a shillelagh-waving, jig-dancing Irishman responds to the president's entreaties in accordance with ethnic stereotypes that prevailed at that time. An African American, the ubiquitous symbol of Black Republicanism, stands in the background.[51]

A few comic analyses of the postelection scene attended to the candidates' personal lives. A William Newman cartoon speculated on the breakfast experience of "the successful and unsuccessful candidates . . . the morning after" in the homes of

Douglas and Lincoln. The dialogue tells the story. "Mrs. L.—'D'ye take your tea sweet, Abra'm?' Mr. L.—'any how, my dear—I'm satisfied.' Mrs. D.—'D'ye take coffee, judge?' Mr. D.—'Yes, strong as—poison!'"[52]

In the same vein, a clever, humorous depiction of Lincoln's changing countenance as a function of adversity or success was exhibited in "A Phenomenon of Portraiture." The artist wanted to show "how the chances of success affect the features of a presidential candidate in the eyes of his friends." Of course, the caricature validated the hypothesis with the artist's own self-fulfilling prophecy about Lincoln's portraits across time in May, August, and November. In May, "His first [portrait] looks hideous—cadaverous—repulsive." In August, "As his chances improve so do his looks. He is now tolerable." And finally in November, "Being chosen, he grows quite handsome—even angelic."[53] The habit of assessing Lincoln's emotional state from his countenance was a popular pastime. "The appearance of Mr. Lincoln has somewhat changed for the worse within the last week," wrote one *New York Herald*

"Old Abe and His Electors," *Frank Leslie's Budget of Fun*, April 15, 1861, 8. McLellan Lincoln Collection, Brown University Library.

OLD ABE AND HIS ELECTORS.

OLD ABE— *"My dear friends and adopted fellow-citizens. I cannot express to you in words how deeply I am obliged to you for your generous votes. They have made me what I am. Without you I should have remained what I was—nothing. My emotions overpower me, as you can easily perceive. Be assured that I will do for you whatever* LIES IN MY POWER!*"*

THE SUCCESSFUL AND UNSUCCESSFUL CANDIDATES AT BREAKFAST THE MORNING AFTER (NOV. 7). 1860

Mrs. L.—" D'ye take your tea sweet, Abra'm ?"
Mr. L.—" Any how, my dear—I'm satisfied."

Mrs. D.—" D'ye take coffee, judge ?"
Mr. D.—" Yes, strong as—poison !"

A. LINCOLN'S PORTRAITS IN MAY IN AUGUST AND IN NOVEMBER. 1860

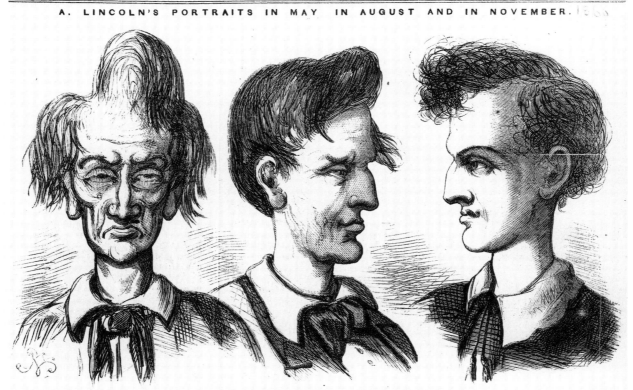

A PHENOMENON OF PORTRAITURE,

SHOWING HOW THE CHANCES OF SUCCESS AFFECT THE FEATURES OF A PRESIDENTIAL CANDIDATE IN THE EYES OF HIS FRIENDS.

1.
His first looks hideous—cadaverous—repulsive.

2.
As his chances improve so do his looks. He is now tolerable.

3.
Being chosen, he grows quite handsome—even angelic.

journalist. "He ... looks more pale and careworn. ... But ... the vigor of his mind and steadiness of his humorous disposition are obviously unimpaired." From a comparison of photographs over time, one of Lincoln's major biographers drew a similar, if more serious, conclusion: "Lincoln's face began to reveal his inner torment as lines of travail etched his features. One need not imagine the soul-torture of this man of peaceful disposition as he launched the nation on a brothers' war; his countenance depicts his suffering. Successive photographs of Lincoln, taken throughout the war, reveal his heartache."[54]

In the aggregate, images from the comic press entertained the public, identified Lincoln and Douglas as the major protagonists for Northern voters, defined the candidates' major obstacles, and shaped and reflected the realities of the race. The cumulative Lincoln image contrived by the comic press, though mixed, seems on balance to have benefitted Lincoln more than Douglas.

From the outset, the images of Bell and Breckinridge were significantly less frequent and prominent than those of Lincoln or Douglas. Neither Bell nor Breckinridge was ignored, but each was on the periphery of the contest. Of course, the popular vote in the North ultimately validated that perception. Even in the electoral vote, where Douglas was almost shut out, Breckinridge and Bell earned the bulk of their support from the Deep South and the border states. For all intents and purposes, the match in the comic press was between Lincoln and Douglas.

The shocking outcomes of the Republican and Democratic conventions set the tone for the early imagery. In the Republican Party, the Seward faction was deeply disappointed and hurt by the sudden turn of events. The comic press captured these emotions. Such imagery raised questions about Lincoln's suitability. Did he have the experience, political sagacity, independence, astute philosophy, and leadership to lead the nation? Could he overcome these hurdles? Initially, Lincoln would have to emerge from the shadow of Seward's popularity, heal any intraparty wounds inflicted in the struggle for the nomination, overcome the perception that he was beholden to Horace Greeley or anyone else, and establish his worthiness as a viable candidate. The Republicans could not win with a "two-shilling candidate" or even a common "railsplitter." Or could they? With unwitting help from a desperately divided Democratic Party, a qualified candidate who was perceived as marginally qualified might still win. Under those circumstances, even a convincing victory would not add up to unqualified public confidence or a clear mandate from the people. And, in fact, that is what happened. When the euphoria of political triumph dissipated, Lincoln had virtually no constituency in the South and only a fragile mandate in the North.

Judging from the cartoons, the campaign's most formidable challenge was to persuade the electorate that Lincoln's leadership and his brand of Black Republicanism was appropriate medicine for an unhealthy nation—no mean task for a former dark horse candidate. Only superficially did Lincoln end up winning this battle even in the

(*Opposite above*)
"The Successful and Unsuccessful Candidates at Breakfast the Morning After," *Frank Leslie's Budget of Fun*, December 15, 1860. Courtesy of the American Antiquarian Society.

(*Opposite below*)
"A Phenomenon of Portraiture," *Frank Leslie's Budget of Fun*, December 15, 1860. Courtesy of the American Antiquarian Society.

North. The question of Lincoln's leadership and anxiety over his policy toward slavery lingered throughout much of his administration. In cartoons, qualms expressed over Lincoln's Black Republicanism were harbingers of just how excruciatingly difficult this presidency would be. The national division was not just sectional. Soon enough, Lincoln would feel intense discomfort because of this divisive issue from both the right and left flanks of political opinion above the Mason-Dixon line, even within his own party.

Coming out of the Charleston and Baltimore conventions, Douglas was bruised and scarred by political infighting. Compared to his preconvention image, his political persona was disfigured.[55] Afterward, he was skirmishing on too many fronts—against Buchanan and Breckinridge (and his Southern minions) within his own party, and with Lincoln and Bell outside. The Democratic machine, as Buchanan had known it in his victory of 1856, was no longer operational. For Douglas, the sectional schism and the quarrel with Buchanan were monumental barriers. Beyond that, Douglas still had to persuade the electorate that popular sovereignty was the best policy.

The extent to which the comic press shaped or reflected the realities of the presidential election are always difficult to unravel. To a degree, the comic press probably did both. Shaping implies persuasive intervention in the outcome. On the surface, reflection stresses the description of events and conditions, but it is not divested of influence. For example, the intent of political polling is to reflect current realities, but the very nature of that information may galvanize political action. Whatever their underlying motives—to shape or reflect reality—comic images often depicted an embattled Douglas hemmed in by the powers of division. He was rarely ruled out of the race, but generally presented as the underdog. On the other hand, there were images of Lincoln capturing the initiative, moving forward, building momentum, and standing in the forefront. Not only was the relative quality of the content more positive, but it also appeared more frequently. Thus, on the whole, the comic press did not hinder Lincoln's chances for victory. Indeed, it may have enhanced them.

On the matter of entertainment, the verdict is less ambiguous. The comic artists and writers definitely brought humor to a nation besieged by conflict and hungry for laughter and lighter moments, but the duration of emotional relief was as ephemeral as the reader's fleeting glance at the image.

From Springfield
to the Battlefield

or Abraham Lincoln, the peaks of victory and inauguration were adjacent to valleys of responsibility and crisis. All presidents face the burdens of organizing an administrative team, setting a legislative agenda, and articulating a national vision, but this president was abruptly confronted with secession and catastrophic war. Even before voting, the nation tottered perilously near the edge of calamity, but Lincoln's election moved the forces of separation closer to the brink of fatal and final decision. Furthermore, between the election and inauguration, President Buchanan had not been able to calm the storm. Not since the Revolution had the survival of the American dream been at such risk; nor were political passions so inflamed, the powers of restraint so taxed, and reason so clouded. Only a miracle on a grand scale could have preserved and strengthened the frayed fibers of national unity and trust. The petitions for that miracle to divine and mortal powers were not granted; civil war was imminent.

THE PRESIDENT-ELECT AT SPRINGFIELD

In the wake of exhilaration from the election, the volume of political caricature declined. Instead, portraits of Lincoln and his family appeared in the domestic and foreign news media with pictures of the Lincolns' Springfield residence, the president and vice president, and other human interest illustrations. Meanwhile, Henry L. Stephens treated his followers to a fascinating satirical cartoon in *Vanity Fair* at the expense of President Buchanan and president-elect Lincoln. In "Dogberry's Last Charge," Stephens used the characters Dogberry (President James Buchanan), Verges (James Gordon Bennett), and Seacoal (Abraham Lincoln) from Shakespeare's *Much Ado about Nothing* to create a parody of the forthcoming presidential transition, as only a cartoonist can see it, from one so-called inept leader to the next. Even the title of the play hints that, for the sake of a good laugh, Stephens intended to have some fun of his own. In the roster of dramatis personae, Shakespeare describes Dogberry

"Dogberry's Last Charge," *Vanity Fair,* December 15, 1860, 297. Author's Collection.

Dogberry - - - - - - - - - J. B——n.

Seacoal - - - - - - - - - A. L——n.

Verges—A good old man–but who will be Talking - J. G. B——tt

DOGBERRY—*Come hither, neighbor Seacoal. Well, for your favor sir, why give God thanks, and make no boast of it; and for your writing and reading, let that appear when there is no need of such vanity. You are thought here to be the most senseless and fit man for the constable of the watch; therefore bear you the lantern: this is your charge! you shall comprehend all vagrom men! You are to bid any man stand, in the prince's name.*

SEACOAL—*How, if he will not stand?*

DOGBERRY—*Why then, take no note of him, but let him go.*—SHAKESPEARE.

and Verges as "two foolish officers." What about the role of Lincoln? As Seacoal, he is sincerely thought by Dogberry (Buchanan) "to be the most senseless and fit man for the constable of the watch." The juxtaposition of the oxymoron "senseless and fit" is a commentary on Buchanan's alleged incompetence, but the phrase hardly compliments Lincoln. The dialogue gives credit to Seacoal for knowing how to read and write, but not much else. Seacoal is a lowly commoner whose modest charge, given by Dogberry, is simply to comprehend "vagrom [vagrant] men." According to the dubious application of the Shakespearian theme, even after receiving his commission as constable, Lincoln/Seacoal has trouble understanding what he is to do, and Buchanan/Dogberry is equally incapable of giving an adequate orientation to Seacoal's job. Thus the whole affair of transition in leadership is really "much ado about nothing."[1]

In general, though, the anxieties of secession became the temporary obsession of comic illustrators. For example, Henry L. Stephens depicted Lincoln bargaining with Southern firebrand William Yancey. "Lincoln.—'I say Yancey—if you'll let me have these [White House] stables in peace for the next four years, I'll give you some of the best stalls and see that your nag [Fugitive Slave Law] is well taken care of.'"[2]

Contrary to this activist image, Lincoln's behavior was actually subdued. From his nomination to his election, in accordance with contemporary political convention, Lincoln did not speak publically about the tense contemporary issues, except through the surrogate voices of his advocates. What irked some members of the press was Lincoln's decision to remain silent between the election and the inauguration, a period when the nation seemed to slide inexorably toward separation and confrontation. What was needed, argued James Gordon Bennett, outspoken editor of the *New York Herald*, was unequivocal, decisive reassurance from the president-elect. In a cartoon entitled "Badgering Him," Henry L. Stephens pictured a feisty dog, James Gordon Bennett, attempting to flush out the taciturn Lincoln. "Come out, Mr. Lincoln," barked a frustrated Bennett, but to no avail.[3]

Lincoln justified his silence on three grounds: first, he contended that his position on slavery was a matter of public record; second, further exposition of his views was futile, because they were often distorted by the press; and third, "I should wait, see the developments, and get all the light I can, so that when I do speak authoritatively, I may be as near right as possible." On his way to Washington, he explained, "I have not kept silent since the Presidential election from any party wantonness, or from any indifference to the anxiety that pervades the minds of men about the aspect of the political affairs of this country. . . . When the time does come I shall then take the ground that I think is right . . . for the North, for the South, for the East, for the West, for the whole country."[4] However, Lincoln's diplomacy of deferral neither arrested the momentum for secession nor quieted a discontented press. Notwithstanding, Lincoln would not end his official silence until the inaugural address.

In response to Lincoln's inaction, *Vanity Fair* took refuge in a satirical article, "Mr. Lincoln Has Spoken":

In response to the persuasive calls of the N.Y. *Herald,* and moved by the convincing logic thereof, Mr. Lincoln has responded. He has spoken and forwarded to *Vanity Fair* proofsheets of his words, copies of which will be sent to every paper in the United States, and likewise to South Carolina. . . . "Fellow citizens, I appear before you to-night in consequence of the urgent calls made upon me by that whole-souled Benit (his name means blessed you know). . . . Gentlemen, I respect Mr. B., and commit every copy of his paper to memory. His words are engraven upon my shoulder-blades like the marks of the descending thong upon his. How could I refuse to speak when so called upon? Gentlemen, I am speaking. Now what do you want me to say? I suppose you want to know about my Cabinet, my policy, my appointments, my administration . . . in advance. I will tell you. (At this stage the most intense silence prevailed. You could have heard a needle stick into a pin-cushion). . . . I mean to have Cabinet pictures in my house, the best I can get, and Cabinet champaigne, the best that I can buy, and any other necessary Cabinet that may be required. . . . As to my policy, or policies . . . I will have my two Life policies in two good companies for $5000, each in favor of Mrs. Abe. Insurance policies upon my personal property in several staunch associations. Lottery policies I am opposed to. The best policy, Honesty, I am in favor of. . . . Now as to my appointments, like my habit they will be costly as my purse can buy, though not expressed in fancy. Mr. Greeley I shall not employ for my tailor. As to my administration, I shall spank my children, and kiss my wife, and go to meeting as often as I please, and I shall pay all my bills as I go along, and exhort everybody else to do the same."[5]

So much for Mr. Lincoln's so-called Springfield speech, and his end to the policy of silence.

TO THE VICTOR BELONG THE SPOILS

Following Lincoln's election to the presidency, the comic press satirized the distribution of spoils of office. At the cabinet level, Lincoln's top administrative priority, cartoonists were preoccupied with poking fun at the processes of political influence. Who has access to the president? they asked. This question revolved around the political axes of Horace Greeley and William Seward. Which of these two would win the approval of the president? The imagery's underlying motivation was not concerned only with the potential influence of this decision on Abraham Lincoln, but also with the quality of the cabinet candidates. Of particular concern was the possible appointment of Simon Cameron.

However, there was also humor generated by appointments at the bureaucratic level—of deputies, clerks, postmasters, ministers, and ambassadors. As the Democratic Party left office, the door to federal patronage swung open. And Lincoln's generous, if unwise, open-door policy added opportunities for humor. Neglecting to delegate sufficient responsibility, the president-elect spent hours with bureaucratic aspirants. Like vultures at their prey, office seekers descended upon Lincoln in Springfield and Washington D.C., bringing with them their credentials in hopes of personal audiences with the president and a slice of the patronage. For the president, this "necessary evil" of filling vacancies in the vast bureaucracy was onerous, time-consuming, and frustrating. In addition, the task distracted him from weightier matters of the presidency. For him, this whole process was no laughing matter, but to the illustrated media it was another golden opportunity to peddle comic wares.

THE COMIC PRESS AND THE CABINET

At least in the eyes of the comic press, the political battle between Horace Greeley and William Seward at the nominating convention for the Republican Party at Chicago resumed in an effort to influence Lincoln's formation of a new cabinet. In December 1860, Henry L. Stephens's cartoon in *Frank Leslie's Budget of Fun* assumed that Greeley had gained the upper hand, and that Seward, standing in front of his political ally and confidant Thurlow Weed, was no longer under consideration for a cabinet slot. "Horace (the serving man, in his Lincoln livery)—'Sorry for you, Mr. Seward, but we can't find you a place in the White House—so many of our customers don't like you! Go away, and let that gentleman from the South come in. The boss wants to see him.'" This premature speculation assailed "The Ingratitude of the Republic-ans" for the purported oversight. But Seward, of course, had not been overlooked. As seen in Horace Greeley's relative importance vis-à-vis Vice President Hannibal Hamlin (the small dog on the porch) and Greeley's powerful position in the cartoon as the supposed presidential liaison over cabinet appointments, Stephens also suggested that Greeley possessed a disproportionate amount of input in the process of selecting a cabinet.[6] These apprehensions had no substantial foundations.

In fact, three months later the popular artist Henry L. Stephens reversed his position. Now, William Seward and Thurlow Weed hold "The Inside Track" with the president, and Horace Greeley is locked out. "Trust to my friend Seward—trust to us," says Thurlow Weed to Lincoln. "We'll compromise this little difficulty for you. But trust to US. Gentlemen from the country are often egregiously swindled by unprincipled sharpers [an allusion to Horace Greeley, who is barred from entering the door]. (Impressively) TRUST TO US!"[7] Implicit in the cartoon is a subtle undercurrent suggesting that Lincoln is a naive newcomer from the country who needs sophisticated advice from astute politicians William Seward and Thurlow Weed.

In reality, neither Seward nor Greeley had the inside track. Lincoln consulted widely on cabinet appointments, and his advisors included Vice President Hannibal Hamlin. The president-elect sought individuals of integrity, experience, talent, and good judgment. Although he did not want to be "committed to any man, clique, or faction," he was a political realist.[8] Even though the managers of his presidential campaign, against his better judgment, made unauthorized overtures in exchange for

THE INGRATITUDE OF THE REPUBLIC-ANS.

ACE (the serving man, in his Lincoln livery) — " *Sorry for you, Mr. Seward, but we can't find you a place in the White House — so many of our customers don't like you! Go away, an
gentleman from the South come in. The boss wants to see him.*"

"The Ingratitude of the
Republic-ans," *Frank
Leslie's Budget of Fun*,
December 15, 1860.
Courtesy of the
American Antiquarian
Society.

political support, Lincoln felt bound to honor those commitments. Nevertheless, prior commitment was not the sole criterion in any case. To be sure, the president was under enormous political pressure from many directions, and when he had no first-hand knowledge of a prospective appointee, he was obliged to weigh the judgment of others. However, to accede to persuasion deemed tenable is rational behavior for anyone. Thus, it is not the presence of political influence that is problematic, but the nature of the response. Rationally or irrationally, the president-elect accepted the advice of some and rejected that of others. Among those whose counsel he rejected to one degree or another were powerful personalities, including Horace Greeley and

William Seward. Lincoln did not acquiesce to Seward's opposition to Salmon P. Chase and Gideon Welles, nor did he accede to the wishes of Horace Greeley to reject Simon Cameron. Only with respect to Cameron and Caleb Smith did Lincoln reluctantly allow the factor of political support to weigh more heavily in the many-faceted calculus of decision making. Although he was personally unenthusiastic about Smith and Cameron, he hoped they would not disappoint him. Pure and simple, the realities of political influence notwithstanding, this was primarily a Lincoln cabinet.

The Seward-Greeley polarity can be seen in another Henry L. Stephens cartoon. Stephens depicted Lincoln awarding the "Grand Distribution of Government Pap"

"The Inside Track," *Vanity Fair*, March 2, 1861, 103. Author's Collection.

THE INSIDE TRACK.

THURLOW WEED TO PRESIDENT ELECT.—"Trust to my friend Seward—trust to US. We'll compromise this little difficulty for you. But trust to US. Gentlemen from the country are often egregiously swindled by unprincipled sharpers. (Impressively) TRUST TO US!"

to several office seekers. First in line for the "U. S. Pap" is Horace Greeley, but William Seward unobtrusively whispers in Lincoln's ear, "Don't give him much, Aunt Abey, b'caus he only help't you to spite me." Edward Bates, Lincoln's eventual choice for attorney general, and others hold out their plates for the spoils of office. To the group of starved applicants "Aunty Abe" says, "Why, boys, how hungry you do seem! You look as though you could eat me!" Horace Greeley retorts, "So you'd be hungry, aunty, if you'd not tasted pap for eight years!"[9] That Greeley did not receive any of the perks of office ran counter to the popular belief that Lincoln was somehow politically beholden to him.

Another variation of eating the spoils of office, "The 'Ins' and the 'Outs,'" pictures rats with the heads of Lincoln, Cameron, and Bates contentedly sitting on a gigantic ball of nibbled cheese. Obviously, they were the "Ins." Also depicted as rats, James Gordon Bennett, Horace Greeley, Henry Raymond, and other prominent editors of New York newspapers, the "Outs" come for their share, but are ungra-

"Grand Distribution of Government Pap," *Frank Leslie's Budget of Fun*, April 1, 1861. Courtesy of the American Antiquarian Society.

GRAND DISTRIBUTION OF GOVERNMENT PAP.

AUNTY ABE— *"Why, boys, how hungry you do seem! You look as though you could eat me!"*
MASTER GREELEY— *"So you'd be hungry, aunty, if you'd not tasted pap for eight years!"*

Old Abe

"Come clear out, ye
Varmints!
none of your

THE "INS" AND THE "OUTS."

" your sly nibbles at our cheese. There's nothing for you here ; there's not half enough for us— the Southern rats have carried off so much
we shan't be able to make it last our time !"

Budget of Fun Apl 15 1861

ciously turned away by "Old Abe." "Come clear out, ye Varmints! None of your sly nibbles at our cheese. There's nothing for you here; there's not half enough for us— the Southern rats have carried off so much, we shan't be able to make it last our time!"[10]

Although Seward was publicized more than any other government appointee before the Senate ratified the cabinet, Simon Cameron, nominee for the post of secretary of war, received more negative press. Lincoln felt most uneasy about his selection. Lincoln's ideal standard of cabinet integrity was high. "Gentleman, in the formation of my cabinet, I shall aim as nearly as possible at perfection. Any man whom I may appoint to such a position, must be, as far as possible, like Caesar's wife, pure and above suspicion, of unblemished reputation, and undoubted integrity. I have already appointed Senator Seward and Mr. Bates, of Missouri, and they are

"The 'Ins' and the 'Outs,'" *Frank Leslie's Budget of Fun*, April 15, 1861. McLellan Lincoln Collection, Brown University Library.

men whose characters I think the breath of calumny cannot impeach. . . . I will not have any man associated with me whose character is impeached."[11]

Nevertheless, Lincoln could not dispel his own suspicion about Cameron's fundamental integrity, nor could others. Henry L. Stephens felicitously captured Cameron's want of public confidence and Lincoln's personal misgivings in the "Alarming Appearance of the Winnebago Chief—Cameron at Springfield."[12] Invoking guilt by association, Stephens's cartoon reminded his readers that Cameron's reputation had already been tarnished by allegations that he defrauded the Winnebago Indians of a substantial sum of money. The caption expressed Cameron's sense that Lincoln had mixed feelings about the appointment. "Cameron.—'You've sent for me, and I've come. If you don't want me, I'll go back to my wigwam.'" After Lincoln notified Cameron of his intention to ask him to serve, the president-elect, changing his mind, asked him to gracefully decline. Unfortunately, the suggestion was not followed. Lincoln regretted Cameron's appointment to the cabinet. Within the year, *Vanity Fair* was objecting to the secretary of war's conduct and scolding Lincoln for not replacing him.

> Old Simon the Seller-er has a fat berth,
> As every one plainly may see,
> And he's not the man to say what it is worth,
> For a wary old soul is he;
> For a wary old soul is he.
> In contracts and jobs he never doth fail,
> And he's hoodwinked the man, once a splitter of rail;
> Yet he never raileth, he quaintly doth say,
> As he pockets his hundreds and thousands per day:
> But Ho! Ho! Ho! Old Simon doth know,
> How plenty of money will make the mare go.
>
> So Abraham reclines in his high-backed chair,
> And wishing, yet fearing to say
> That Simon had better no longer be there,
> But go back to Penn-syl-va-ni-a,
> But go back to Penn-syl-va-ni-a.
> But Simon says No, I have battled too long
> For this placer, to give it up now for a song.
> So the people must rise and to Abraham must go
> Saying, this Joker's played out, give us a new Joe.
> While Ho! Ho! Ho! The contracts still flow,
> For Simon says, money will make the mare go.[13]

Simon Cameron was ultimately replaced by Edwin M. Stanton.

Little more than a month after Lincoln's election, humorist Artemus Ward framed his satirical "Visit to Old Abe Lincoln" around the patronage theme. "There4, hevin no politics, I made bold to visit Old Abe at his humstid in Springfield. I found the old feller in his parler, surrounded by a perfeck swarm of orifice seekers. . . . Jest at this pint of the conversation another swarm of orifice seekers arrove & cum pilin into the parler. Sum wanted post orifices, sum wanted collectorships, sum wanted furrin missions, and all wanted sumthin. I thought Old Abe would go crazy. He hadn't more than had time to shake hands with 'em, before another trmenjis crowd cum porein onto his premises. His house and dooryard was now perfeckly overflowed with orifice seekers, all clameruss for a immejit interview with Old Abe."[14] Granting a potent dose of comic exaggeration, Ward's classic masterpiece was not entirely devoid of truth, awarding political patronage was an arduous, exhausting presidential obligation. However, given Lincoln's partiality for wit, this is precisely the kind of satire that would have given the president some comic relief from such official duties.

The visual analogue of Artemus Ward's humorous parody of "orifice seekers" was entitled "Gulliver Abe, in the White House, Attacked by the Lilliputian Office-Seekers." Whispering recommendations in Gulliver Abe's ears are—who else?— Horace Greeley and William Seward. Meanwhile, in pursuit of patronage, the army of applicants hangs from Lincoln's coat, scales his arms, frolics in his pockets, dangles from his coattails, scampers up one leg, slides down the other, straddles his fingers, nestles snugly in his vest, balances precariously on his elbow, waves to friends below, and swings on a rope from his hand. The bedlam on the ground is just as frantic. The horde of office seekers hoists ladders and ropes to aid their climb upon the giant dispenser of political favors. Some, impatiently waiting their turn, wave Wide Awake flags or smoking lanterns, whereas others ascend the rungs of the ladders to enhance their chances for positions. In the tumult, some have fallen to the ground, others are running, and all seem to be in perpetual motion. The artist, Henry L. Stephens, showed the beleaguered and besieged Gulliver Abe lamenting, "Well, this is orful! Who'd a' ever believed such diminutivorous varmints could have had such impudence! Why, they're creeping all over me! I feel a kinder goosefleshy. Scratch himself couldn't get rid of 'em!"[15]

Artemus Ward's burlesque in words was also a scene of one tumultuous uproar, a virtual beehive of activity.

"Good [heavens]!" Cride Old Abe, "they cum upon me from the skize down the chimneys, and from the bowels of the yearth!" He hadn't more'n got them words out of his delikit mouth before two fat offiss-seekers from Wisconsin, in endeverin to crawl atween his legs for the purpuss of applyin for the tollgateship at Milwawky, upsot the President eleck & he would hev gone sprawlin into the fire-place if I hadn't caught him in these arms. But I hadn't more'n stood him up strate, before

"Gulliver Abe, in the White House, Attacked by the Lilliputian Office-Seekers," *Frank Leslie's Budget of Fun*, March 15, 1861, front page. Courtesy of the American Antiquarian Society.

GULLIVER ABE— *"Well, this is orful! Who'd a' ever believed such diminutivorous varmints could have had such impudence! Why, they're creeping all over me! I feel a kinder goosefleshy. Scratch himself couldn't get rid of 'em!"*

another man cum crashin down the chimney, his head strikin me vilently agin the inards and prostratin my voluptoous form onto the floor. "Mr. Linkin," shoutid the infatooated being, "my papers is signed by every clergyman in our town, and likewise the skoolmaster!"

Fortunately, Artemus Ward single-handedly rescued Lincoln.

"What air you here for?" I continnered, warmin up considerable, "can't you giv Abe a minit's peace? . . . Go home, you miserable men, . . . git a clerkship on sum respectable manure cart. . . . Ef in five minits from this time a single sole of you remains on these here premises, I'll go out to my cage near by, and let my Boy Constructor loose!" . . . You ought to hev seen them scamper. . . . They run orf as tho Satun hisself was arter them with a red hot ten pronged pitchfork. In five minits the premises was clear. . . . "How kin I ever repay you, Mr. Ward, for your kindness?" sed Old Abe. . . . "By poerin' ile upon the troubled waters, North and South! . . . And then if any State wants to secede, let 'em Secesh!" . . . "How 'bout my Cabnit Ministre, Ward?" sed Abe. "Fill it up with Showmen, Sir! Showmen is devoid of politics. They hain't got a darn principle!" . . . He shook me cordyully by the hand—we exchanged picters, so we could gaze upon each others' liniments when far away from one another—he at the hellum of the ship of State, and I at the hellum of the show bizniss—admittance only 15 cents.[16]

What reasonably objective historian could improve on these droll verbal and visual descriptions of President Lincoln's predicament in the face of office seekers?

According to the creative concoctions of popular illustrators, the president was not entirely defenseless in these situations. He had his own devices to deplete the ranks of office seekers. Of course, the most satisfying was to give offices to deserving recipients. In "Old Abe and His Electors," Seward read the list of appointees, Uncle Sam held the certificates of "appointment for all offices," and Abraham Lincoln offered his personal commendation (in this case to Carl Schurz). However, the decision to reject an applicant must have been painful to the potential giver and receiver, and cartoonists contrived more elaborate, novel, useful, and witty ways to dispatch the legion of supplicants. After the Civil War started, "the ingenious manner in which President Lincoln receives those who apply for an office" depicted him using a kind of creative conscription. Lincoln armed the office seekers with weapons and sent them off to combat.[17]

In *Phunny Phellow*, the artist conceived an embattled Lincoln resorting to divine intervention. Reptiles symbolically wrap themselves around his arms and legs, their fangs flicking out the sign "office." Raising his hands to the heavens, "Old Abe invokes the spirit of St. Patrick to rid him of the reptiles that destroy his peace." Apparently, his axe and maul, lying on the floor, were no match for the reptiles—the lowly, but tenacious, office seekers.[18]

The prolific cartoonist Henry L. Stephens invented a scheme that would enable Lincoln to placate applicants without having to fill official positions. The subterfuge was embodied in the following caption:

Seward.—"Abe, here's old Botheram just passed the window. We shall have to give him a mission. He worked hard for us, and he'll just worry our lives out till he's served." Old Abe.—"Yes, he deserves something good and he shall have it." [Whispers to Billy] Seward.—"My dear friend Botheram, I'm delighted to inform you that, as a slight acknowledgment of your services in the late campaign, I am requested by his Excellency to hand you the mission to San Juan de Loando, a charming location on the coast of Africa. To be sure, the last four Ministers have died there of the coast fever; but your robust constitution can laugh at such trifling ailments—and, should the worst happen, you will have the glorious satisfaction of dying for your native land!"[19]

The name "Botheram" implicitly describes the aggravating irritations of the president's obligation. Another variation on this theme used the parallel name, "Botherby," changed the appointment to Fiji, and discouraged the office seeker with the specter of cannibalism. Parenthetically, the five spitoons that surround Lincoln's desk in these cartoons disdainfully dig at Lincoln's backwoods' reputation.[20]

Popular artists and journalists also assumed the perspective of the office seeker, humorously exploring their motives, strategies, hopes, disappointments, and fears. Many of former President Buchanan's political appointees stood to lose their jobs. A few verses of doggerel in the humor periodical *Nick Nax* aptly expressed the anxieties of a wholesale, political transition.

> Abrahm, spare this head,
> Touch not a single hair
> Of its official life,
> For "Old Buck" placed it there!

"Old Abe Invokes the Spirit of St. Patrick," *Phunny Phellow,* May 1861, 16. Reproduced through permission of the Rare Book and Special Collections Library, University of Illinois at Urbana-Champaign.

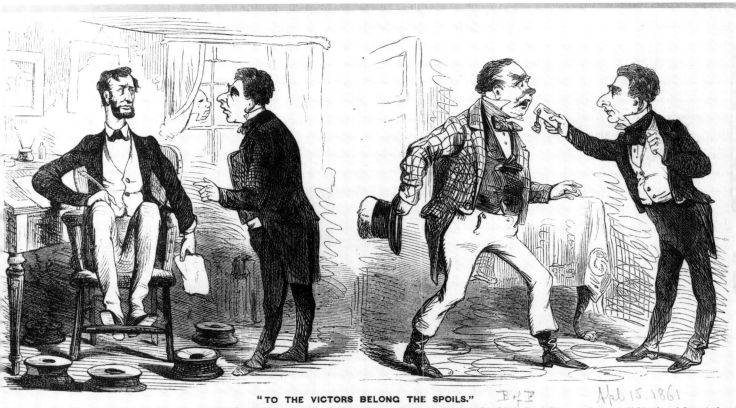

"TO THE VICTORS BELONG THE SPOILS."

ᴇᴡᴀʀᴅ—" *Abe, here's old Botheram just passed the window. We shall have to give* n a mission. He worked hard for us, and he'll just worry our lives out till he's ʋed."

ʟᴅ ᴀʙᴇ—" *Yes, he deserves something good, and he shall have it.*"

[Whispers to Billy.]

Sᴇᴡᴀʀᴅ—" *My dear friend Botheram, I'm delighted to inform you that, as a slight acknowledgment of you services in the late campaign, I am requested by his Excellency to hand you the mission to San Juan de Loande a charming location on the coast of Africa. To be sure, the last four Ministers have died there of the coa fever; but your robust constitution can laugh at such trifling ailments—and, should the worst happen, you wi have the glorious satisfaction of dying for your native land!*"

If victims you must have,
Strike at my friend Jo Yard,
Josephus Shaun and Speer—
Dear Abrahm, hit 'em!

But spare this head of mine,
And it will never fail
To bless, that same old Coon
A sittin on a rail![21]

In contrast to the bleak picture sketched in the doggerel, "Mr. Whippletrot's Plum Pudding," a cartoon in *Comic Monthly,* reflected high hopes and a precise, calculated strategy for achieving a presidential appointment. This gigantic culinary gift would surely secure Mr. Whippletrot a prize plum of an office. Unfortunately, his expectations were dashed. The artist E. F. Mullen used twelve panels in his serial cartoon (forerunner of the comic strip) to spell out the inspiration for the origin of the idea, the complicated execution of the plan, and the disappointing result. The president gets the pudding, but Mr. Whippletrot does not get the job.

"To the Victors Belong the Spoils," *Frank Leslie's Budget of Fun,* April 15, 1861. McLellan Lincoln Collection, Brown University Library.

(*Overleaf*)
"Mr. Whippletrot's Plum Pudding," *Comic Monthly,* January 1861, foldout. Courtesy of the American Antiquarian Society.

Mr. Whippletrot explains to Mrs. W. sharer of his joys, and partner of his woes that in order to pave the way to that berth in the Custom House, it will be necessary to send something nice to long Abe at Christmas. Now, what shall it be?

Can't think, and so resolves to sleep on it.

And a donkey engine engaged to perform the severe labors.

[Hooray!—'tis done.]

Arrives at Springfield, is transferred to a wagon. The Lincoln mansion, from the graphic pencil of Mr. Lincoln, jr., can be seen in the left hand corner.

Mr. L., Mrs. L. and all the little L.'s look with amazement on the wonderful construction.

In the silent watches of the night, it comes upon him. It must, it shall be a pum pudding of most magnificent dimensions.

Cooks are engaged to superintend the construction thereof.

But what next? Mrs. W. in the most unfeeling manner derides him and his pudding, imagining that it will prove too large to move.

But genius conquers all things, and Whipplerot gets his pudding on a car at last

Mr. L. proceeds to carve it in a characteristic manner.

Takes a little of the pudding cold March 5th, 1861, just after being extremely sorry, that nothing could be done just now for Mr. Whippletrot.

(1) Mr. Whippletrot explains to Mrs. W., sharer of his joys, and partner of his woes, that in order to pave the way to that berth in the Custom House, it will be necessary to send something nice to long Abe at Christmas. Now, what shall it be? (2) Can't think, and so resolves to sleep on it. (3) In the silent watches of the night, it comes upon him. It must, it shall be a plum pudding of most magnificent dimensions. (4) Cooks are engaged to superintend the construction thereof. (5) And a donkey engine engaged to perform the severe labors. (6) Hooray 'tis done. (7) But what next? Mrs. W. in the most unfeeling manner derides him and his pudding, imagining that it will prove too large to move. (8) But genius conquers all things, and Whippletrot gets his pudding on a [railroad] car at last. (9) Arrives at Springfield, is transferred to a wagon. The Lincoln mansion, from the graphic pencil of Mr. Lincoln, jr., can be seen in the left hand corner. (10) Mr. L., Mrs. L., and all the little L.'s look with amazement on the wonderful construction. (11) Mr. Lincoln proceeds to carve it in a characteristic manner [with maul and wedge]. (12) Takes a little of the pudding cold, March 5th, 1861, just after being extremely sorry, that nothing could be done just now for Mr. Whippletrot.[22]

In a similar *Phunny Phellow* serial cartoon, "Mr. Longlank" organizes a petition drive to persuade the president. The petition is so large that it requires an extra railroad car to transport it, and security guards to protect it from covetous competitors. Alas, Mr. Longlank is no more successful than Mr. Whippletrot; he is betrayed by a so-called friend.

(1) Mr. Longlank resolves to apply for the collectorship of Tad-pole Island. (2) Draws up a petition. (3) He is endorsed copiously. (4) Highly elated, he starts for the depot. (5) Is obliged to take an extra car for his petition. (6) Arrives at Willard's. (7) Is put in the Concert rooms, fearing he will loose [sic] his petition. (8) He takes it to the office to deposit in the safe. (9) Finding no room at the office, engages two policemen to guard it, and seeks a private lodging. (10) Runs across his old friend Jones from his native town. (11) Jones agrees to take charge of his petition and present it to the President for him. (12) Jones uses his friend's petition to further his own interests. (13) Has seen the President. Sure thing! No mistake! Longlank elated. (14) Satisfied, he finds a vacant hook in the market house and sleeps. (15) Resolves to thank the President in person. President never heard of him. (16) Astounded, he rushes to see his friend Jones. Jones thinks it strange. (17) Jones receives the appointment. (18) Longlank sees in the paper that Jones is appointed and collapses.[23]

Thus the sad saga for the collectorship of Tad-pole Island is resolved to the benefit of the deceptive Mr. Jones, and to the detriment of the naive Mr. Longlank. In this comic episode, neither competence nor character is served or celebrated in the bestowal of office. It is unadulterated raillery.

Some images ostensibly about patronage and Lincoln were really designed to make fun of African Americans. This was an era of blatant ethnic insensitivity, and to entertain the humor periodicals thrived on disdain. In a before-after cartoon sequence, "A Political Wire Puller" (in the current vernacular—one who pulls strings) who seeks the spoils of office "Visits Old Abe." "He had no sooner heard the [election] 'returns,' than packing up his extra shirt and collar, he started for Springfield to see Old Abe. Imagine his delight on beholding that great man (six feet four in his stockings), not above his old occupation by which he had made his way in the world, actually axe in hand, splitting rails by the thousand. What a sight! exclaimed Squibb. O that the world could see him thus in his unaffected Democracy." In the sequel panel, the enthusiastic office seeker realizes he has mistaken Lincoln for a tall, black rail-splitter. The element of surprise in the mistaken identity, the incongruity of the idealized expectation and mundane fulfillment, creates the obtuse amusement.[24]

This patronizing, racist theme took on a different configuration in "A Model Minister." In this illustration, a "facetious Southerner" mocks the abilities of "Sambo." "'Here, Abe, if the Liberia Mission is not yet disposed of, is a gentleman I can conscientiously recommend for that highly important position!' Sambo—'Yah, Yah, sah! I can talk de langwidge ob de court I am gwine to—dat's more dan Massa Dayton can!'"[25] The colloquial dialect and spelling in the caption only fed the fire of derision. This image, like its companions, had nothing to do with patronage. It was motivated by racial prejudice, and discussion of the spoils of office afforded an opportunity for the blatant derogation of black Americans.

If one compares imagery devoted to the cabinet and the bureaucracy, the former contained more serious content than the latter. When Henry L. Stephens thought that Seward had been ignored as a candidate for the cabinet, his art expressed concern. When Stephens ascribed Seward's neglect to Horace Greeley, the illustration also seemed to send up a warning flag. But when Thurlow Weed and William Seward had "the inside track" over Greeley, there was less obvious discomfort. In comparison, Stephens's critical caricature of Simon Cameron, who was favored by Seward but anathema to Greeley, was more compatible with Greeley's politics. Thus, although there was some ambiguity about the philosophical position of the artist or his sponsors, there was no question about passion for the quality of the cabinet or the existence of apprehensions about unwise political influence. Implicit in these admittedly few images was also the question of how decisive Lincoln would be. Naturally, the necessity of new officials to demonstrate their ability to govern confronts all national leaders. In this manner, cabinet-related images expressed anxiety over the process and outcome of appointments.

Imagery that focused on the bureaucracy, except for that fueled by conspicuous racial forebodings inherent in the period, was lighthearted and geared to entertain. The caricature "Gulliver Abe" and Artemus Ward's delightful satire on the victimization of the president by duties imposed by the spoils system were pure enjoyment. If the images subtly suggested the need for reform, they did so with endearing wit.

The president-elect was accorded a degree of empathy for his willingness to assume the stresses and strains of office. During a period of incomparable uncertainty, political conflict, and crisis the humorous diversion was good therapy for the country.

FROM SPRINGFIELD TO WASHINGTON, D.C.

Illustrations that covered the period between Lincoln's farewell remarks at Springfield to his arrival in Harrisburg, Pennsylvania, were almost exclusively serious and descriptive. They were published in the three popular illustrated news weeklies. Artists who accompanied Lincoln on the journey sketched the president's receptions at Cleveland, Buffalo, Columbus, and New York, scenes along the way, and the hoisting of the flag at Philadelphia.[26] Reporters recorded the brief, guarded, extemporaneous remarks of the president, and discussed associated activities at the major cities on the route.

Notable as a comic exception to illustrations of the overall journey was an eighteen-panel, serial cartoon from *Phunny Phellow* entitled "Progress Of 'Honest Old Abe' on His Way to the White House." For the most part, the captions explain themselves.

1. "Mr. Lincoln packs his baggage." Lincoln holds open the lid of a trunk, which contains cannons, balls, swords, and other weapons. Under Lincoln's arm is the Constitution, an axe, and a rifle.
2. "Takes an affectionate farewell of his family."
3. "Takes with him some axes to grind." The axes are marked "fraud," "treason," "secession," and "robbery."
4. "And another much neglected and useful institution [hemp] to splice Mason and Dixon's line with." A long coil of hemp with a noose at the end rests against a sign that shows a body swinging from a gallows, along with the following text: "New Duties on hemp, not particularly specified in the Tariff Bill, recommended to the Executive Committee. . . . Resolved, that all traitors be hereby suspended!"
5. "Takes a Homeopathic case of remedies for the Constitution." The "remedies" include "U. S. Bullets" and "U. S. Powder."
6. "Takes also an instrument for 'dry cupping,' [a twelve-inch mortar] to be applied to Constitutional 'weak backs' South or North of the line."
7. "Makes a Speech to the suckers" (his farewell remarks in Springfield).
8. "What everybody expects." A form letter to office seekers from the "White House," says, "Dear Sir, You are hereby appointed to any position you may desire under my administration. I would resign in your favor, but I can't constitutionally. Yours, A. Lincoln."
9. "Cincinnati goes whole hog for the Union." Only hogs show up to greet Lincoln in Cincinnati.

10. "Better a dinner of 'herbs,' etc., than a stalled ox."

11. "The Legislature."

12. "Or the Governor therewith."

13. "He makes some delicate allusions to a ship of state whilst in New York City."

14. At Barnum's museum for oddities, Lincoln "goes to see What Is It?—has heard of him frequently"—a slave.

15. "Hears the Star Spangled Banner 'done' by a heavy peanut woman in the chorus at the Academy."

16. "Peace-loving James [Buchanan] gives some advice: Thee'd better not fight about this gay colored bunting, Abraham, don't!"

17. "The fight—'scotched, not killed.'"

18. "The instrument of in-auger-ation"—a corkscrew.[27]

Panel seventeen, "the fight—'scotched, not killed,'" refers to the most sensational leg of the trip, the secret, cloak-and-dagger phase from Harrisburg to Washington, D.C. This segment transformed a dignified presidential journey to a parody. Counseled by federal officers that the president's life may be in jeopardy, Lincoln reluctantly consented to extreme security measures. Humorists in the illustrated press would not have addressed the incident except for the extraordinary circumstances. Rumors of Lincoln's purported disguise in an article written by Joseph Howard in the *New York Times* stirred the imagination, and caricaturists—not known for constraint—took over from there.

The earliest comic rendition in *Frank Leslie's Budget of Fun* was also the most singular. Not only did it ignore Howard's report of Lincoln's purported Scotch clothing, but it also beat its comic competitors, *Vanity Fair, Phunny Phellow,* and the *Comic Monthly,* on three fronts. First, Frank Leslie's artists scooped the field by more than a week. Second, the conspicuously displayed front-page cartoon gave primary salience to the event. Third, in originality, no other comic piece could compare, though others were very good.

In the cartoon, a wary Abraham Lincoln still sits in Herring's safe—the mock, impenetrable shield of security for his harrowing experience. Aiding and abetting the humorous effect, Lincoln carries his patented axe for protection. The safe door has just been flung open by Horace Greeley, masquerading, of course, as the chief of federal security. Wearing his rumpled hat, the *New York Tribune* editor is armed with a revolver in his belt and a sword poised to ward off any traitor. A dialogue between Buchanan and Lincoln further promotes the travesty. "President Buchanan.—'So you are here at last, Abe! I am glad to see you in so SAFE a conveyance.' Old Abe.—'Yes, I'm all right. Wouldn't you like to borrow this safe for your Indian Bonds?'" And who constitutes the cadre of security forces? Lincoln's Wide Awakes! They brandish the unlikely combination of politically symbolic, oil-burning lanterns and militant, fixed bayonets. Loaded with incongruities, the caricature effectively solves the problem of "How Abe Lincoln Escaped the Fire-Eaters of the South and the Flames of Secession."[28]

(*Overleaf*)
"Progress of 'Honest Old Abe' on His Way to the White House," *Phunny Phellow*, April 1861, 8–9. Courtesy of the American Antiquarian Society.

1. Mr. Lincoln packs his baggage.

2. Takes an affectionate farewell of his family.

3. Takes with him some axes to grind.

7. Makes a speech to the suckers.

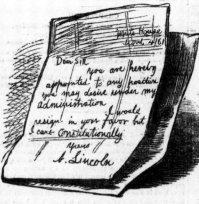

8. What everybody expects.

9. Cincinnati goes the whole hog for the Union.

13. He makes some delicate allusions to a ship of state whilst in New York City.

14. Goes to see What Is It?—has heard of him frequently.

15. Hears the Star Spangled Banner "done" by a heavy pea and woman in the chorus at the Academy.

4. And another much neglected and useful institution to splice Mason & Dixon's line with.

5. Takes a Homœpathic case of remedies for the Constitution.

6. Takes also an instrument for "dry cupping," to be applied to Constitutional "weak backs," South or North of the line.

10. "Better a dinner of herbs," etc., than a stalled ox.

11. The Legislature.

12. Or the Governor therewith.

16. Peace-loving James gives some advice.

17. The flight—"Scotched, not killed."

18. The instrument of in-auger-ation.

"How Abe Lincoln Escaped the Fire-Eaters of the South and the Flames of Secession," *Frank Leslie's Budget of Fun*, March 1, 1861, front page. Courtesy of the Buffalo and Erie County Public Library.

PRESIDENT BUCHANAN— *"So you are here at last, Abe! I am glad to see you in so* SAFE *a conveyance."*
OLD ABE— *"Yes, I'm all right. Wouldn't you like to borrow this safe for your Indian Bonds?"*

Harper's Weekly also joined the fun at the expense of the president-elect. "The Flight of Abraham" was apparently drawn by John McLenan; he signed one of the four serial panels. The panels were divided sequentially into segments of the experience: "The Alarm," "The Council," "The Special Train," and "The Old Complaint." The text was appropriated from "a modern daily paper," but the captions in the body of the cartoon were conceived by the artist. In the first panel, "The Alarm," the newspaper version calmly describes the origin of the crisis. "On Thursday night, after he had retired, Mr. Lincoln was aroused, and informed that a stranger desired to see him on a matter of life and death. A conversation elicited the fact that an organized body of men had determined that Mr. Lincoln should never leave the City of Baltimore alive. Statesmen laid the plan, Bankers endorsed it, and Adventurers were to carry it into effect." However, the shorthand cartoon caption does not mince words; it goes straight to the heart of the matter. "Run Abe for your life—the blood tubs are after yer." In "The Council," the journalist explains, "Mr. Lincoln did not want to yield, and his friends cried with indignation. But they insisted and he left." Similarly, the cartoon depicts a determined, undaunted, and intractable Lincoln reacting to the alarm: "Run—no never—let 'em shoot," while his weeping wife implores, "Do go, do." Out of deference to family and friends, discretion overrides valor and he departs. There is no caption in the third panel, "The Special Train," but, corresponding to the newspaper description, Lincoln is verily in flight. "He wore a Scotch plaid Cap, and a very long military Cloak, so that he was entirely unrecognizable." Taking his cue from the newspaper, the cartoonist dressed the president accordingly and set Lincoln in animated motion. Finally, in "The Old Complaint," the journalist simply notes, "Mr. Lincoln, accompanied by Mr. Seward, paid his respects to President Buchanan, spending a few minutes in general conversation." In this case, however, the cartoonist exercised the full liberties of the craft. He depicted Lincoln shaking uncontrollably and Seward endeavoring to save face for Lincoln by ascribing his tremors to "the old complaint," "Only a little attack of Ague, your excellency."[29] Although humor is to be taken with a grain of salt, these images did not necessarily inspire confidence in the president-elect.

Also borrowing the Scottish theme, young Thomas Nast of the *New York Illustrated News* joined the crowd of cartoonists who could not restrain the impulse to exploit inherent comic elements. In the "Arrival of Mr. Lincoln at the Camden Station, Baltimore," Nast, like many of his artistic peers, transformed a mundane scene of Lincoln transferring trains by dressing the president-elect in the simple disguise of a jaunty Scottish cap and long cloak. A more dramatic unsigned cartoon shows Lincoln emerging out of nowhere from a cloud of dust to the "Awful Consternation of the Old Party at the White House, and Sudden Appearance of Lincoln (Chief

"Awful Consternation of the Old Party at the White House, and Sudden Appearance of Lincoln—(Chief Magician, Mr. Seward)," *New York Illustrated News*, March 9, 1861, 288. Courtesy of the New York State Library.

Magician, Mr. Seward)." Seward waves his magic wand, instantly producing for a stunned, if impressed, President Buchanan the physical presence of the president-elect, straight from Camden Station. Although the incident at Baltimore generated good humor, some people interpreted it as demeaning to Lincoln and the presidency. However, the *New York Illustrated News* disagreed. "It was a great pity for Baltimore," lamented the magazine, "but under the circumstances it could not be helped."[30]

Vanity Fair blamed Lincoln's advisors for miscalculating the degree of danger that the president-elect faced. "By the advice of weak men, who should straddle through life in petticoats instead of disgracing such manly garments as pantaloons and coats, the President elect disguises himself after the manner of the heroes of two-shilling novels, and rides secretly, the deep night, from Harrisburg to Washington. . . . Thus Mr. Lincoln is made, by his ill-advisers, to exhibit fears of trusting himself among the people of Baltimore—Baltimore which is true to the Union—Baltimore which is the metropolis of the Union-loving State of Maryland." Hence, the impression was fostered that a "two-shilling president" acted the part of a "two-shilling novel." Two caricatures from *Vanity Fair* were consistent with this imagery of frivolity. The first, "The MacLincoln Harrisburg," pictured the president in kilts lightheartedly dancing the highland fling. The second, "The New President of the U.S.," showed him traveling incognito by virtue of a heavy disguise after the fashion of Scotland.[31] Apparently, this popular burlesque imagery did not dignify the president's arrival.

Like *Phunny Phellow*, the *Comic Monthly* reacted belatedly to Lincoln's abrupt change in itinerary, and it did so with a clever, double-page cartoon, "Incidents in the Career of President Lincoln." Lincoln was pictured in five of the cartoon's eight panels, two of which William Newman signed and six of which were unsigned. The panels were arranged sequentially.

1. "On his way to Washington, his Illinois friends, fearing danger, surround him and conceal him from his enemies." Although Lincoln's associates actually do encircle him, he is not concealed; his top hat and face tower above all, as if he is alone.

2. "The devoted plug-ugly who endeavored to throw off the train by placing an obstruction [himself] on the track." The dull, stereotypical behavior and the countenance and pipe betray the Irish identity of the "obstruction."

3. "Rumors of plots abounding, his friends suggest a disguise." The proposed disguise is a woman's bonnet, cape, dress, purse, scarf, and umbrella.

4. However, "The disguise finally adopted" is the Scotch apparel, described above by a New York journalist.

5. "A New York detective in Baltimore, DISGUISED, has found the infernal machine with which the President is to be blown up."

6. "Another enthusiastic policeman detects a villain endeavoring to take Lincoln off and suppresses him." The alleged villain is an innocent photographer taking a picture of Lincoln's train.

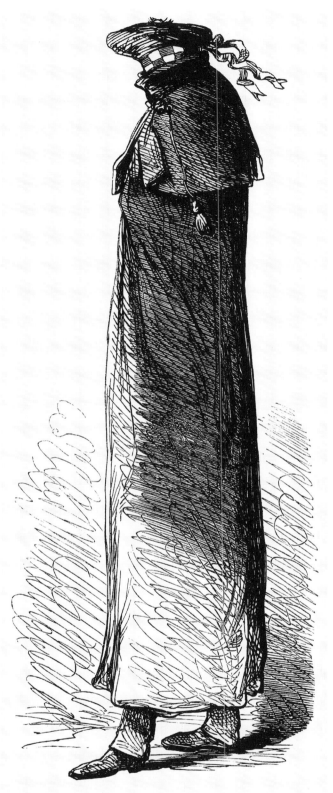

"The New President of the United States," *Vanity Fair*, March 9, 1861, 114. Author's Collection.

THE NEW PRESIDENT OF THE UNITED STATES.
FROM A FUGITIVE SKETCH.

"Incidents in the Career of President Lincoln," *Comic Monthly*, April 1861, 8–9. Courtesy of the American Antiquarian Society.

7. The "Supposed amusement of Mr. Seward in the Cabinet" involves a Lincoln marionette who can be manipulated at the whims of the secretary of state.

8. But the "Real State of things in Washington at the present time of writing" is "Greeley and Seward contesting the possession of the President." Horace Greeley and William Seward are shown in a tug of war for Lincoln's allegiance—a cleverly conceived and executed raillery.[32]

Although the Baltimore affair quickly faded from the pages of illustrated magazines, it was not easily forgotten. Lincoln's partisans used memory of the incident to validate his actions. It was no surprise to find doggerel in the generally pro-Lincoln *Yankee Notions* that idealized Lincoln's passage through Baltimore almost one full year after his famed flight through the city.

> Here is Old Abe, whom the Southerners swore,
> They'd murder if ever he touched Baltimore;
> 'Twas a year ago, though, since they hatched up this plot
> And since then they've been touched in a very sore spot;
> In New York he imprisoned their F. F. V. Traitors,
> And fed them on bread, water, fish and potatoes,

Rumors of plots abounding, his friends suggest a disguise.

The disguise finally adopted.

Supposed amusement of Mr. Seward in the Cabinet.

Real State of things in Washington at the present time of writing. Greeley and Seward contesting the possession of the President.

DAY

> And although so reviled at, 'twas his willing hand
> That brought Baltimore back to a real merry land.[33]

In comparison, one of Lincoln's political detractors, the British *Comic News*, belatedly used the president's trip through Baltimore as a pretext to denigrate American manners.[34]

THE CHANGING OF THE GUARD

When Lincoln arrived in Washington, D.C., he knew it would take time to establish himself as a credible leader. Even the preinaugural cartoons in the Republican-smitten *Harper's Weekly* held the president-elect at arm's length. In one cartoon, "Our Presidential Merryman," John McLenan used as his caption lines from a local newspaper: "The Presidential party was engaged in a lively exchange of wit and humor. The President Elect was the merriest among the merry, and kept those around him in a continual roar." In the background, however, the cartoonist drew a funeral procession of the "Union Constitution." Juxtaposing these contradictory elements, humorous and serious, McLenan accomplished two objectives. On the one hand, incongruity spawns the conditions on which humor depends. Comedy thrives on surprise and on the incompatibility of disparate ideas; thus, McLenan fulfilled his intent to entertain. On the other hand, McLenan broached the issue of Lincoln's presidential decorum and dignity. He questioned the appropriateness of Lincoln's propensity for laughter against the backdrop of the nation's serious condition.[35] Such are the hazzards of the conjunction of a sense of humor and a solemn, official responsibility.

A companion cartoon in the March 1861 issue of *Harper's Weekly* addressed Lincoln's ideological suitability for the presidency. The artist, M. Nevin, contrasted the established legend, George Washington, with the untested neophyte, Lincoln. While Washington kneels at the church altar preparing for communion, a pious, praying Lincoln waits his turn. Ironically, George Washington is deemed unworthy for there is "No Communion with Slaveholders." "Stand aside, you Old Sinner! We are Holier than thou!" claims the clergyman. Apparently, Lincoln also fails to pass the test because of his alleged self-righteous views on slavery. Of course, *Harper's Weekly* was not initially hostile to the president, nor was it ready to embrace him. Like the media in general, it wondered "if Abraham Lincoln is equal to the position he fills."[36] Only time would tell.

On March 4, 1861, Lincoln took the oath of office from Chief Justice Roger Taney. *Vanity Fair* marked the transition of presidents with an illustration that depicted the rising sun of Lincoln "melting away" the "Great Iceberg" Buchanan.[37] However, the pomp and ceremony of the inauguration was not, in the main, grist for comic fare. Appropriately, the three news weeklies sent their staff artists with sketch pads to record the major events, but it took time to get illustrations from the drawing board to wood engravings to press. Hence, the inauguration as illustrated in print form was not celebrated in the news weeklies until March 16 and 23. Readers were treated to a dazzling display of retrospective pageantry, and all three periodicals reserved a double-page or foldout spread for the inaugural address. Thomas Nast's now rare centerpiece in the *New York Illustrated News* attended to every detail: the inaugural procession, Lincoln's arrival at the capitol, the oath of office, the inaugural address, Lincoln's visits to the Senate and House of Representatives, and the grand ball. However, Thomas Nast's singular cartoon in the *New York Illustrated News* may have conveyed as much truth as the capsulized descriptions of inauguration activities. Assuming the sectional perspectives of both the North and South, Nast caricatured Lincoln as he surmised the typical ideologue from each section might receive the message of his inaugural address. To the North, Nast's Lincoln was the personification of peace; to the South, he was the epitome of bellicosity, the essence of the enemy.[38] Wittily and profoundly, Nast captured the enormous gap of sectional misunderstanding.

Although the comic press generally ignored the inauguration, it did not ignore Lincoln himself. According to *Frank Leslie's Budget of Fun*, "Old Abe's First Night in the White House" was a rip-roaring affair. In the first panel of the cartoon, "Old Abe takes his family to ascertain how Old Buck has left the cupboards supplied with eatables and drinkables." When Lincoln opens the pantry door, he finds a gun rack, guns, and "Dupont's powder." The next scene shows "Young Bob" warning, "Pa, don't touch the supper! The cook must have been a Secessionist—he's put pepper in the tea!" In the "Grand expulsion of the old servants from the White House," Lincoln, his spouse, and children personally chase the servants away. They are apparently replaced by the "Arrival of very Wide-Awake attendants, with certificates of astonishing character!" Again, the artist uses the occasion to demean black Americans. Finally, "the happy family" are "all right at last."[39]

Lincoln's new beard was a spectacle. Incredibly, "His New Facial" was the topic of a front-page article in the *New York Illustrated News*. Taking advantage of Lincoln's nascent fame, entrepreneurs advertised products to stimulate the growth of beards and cartoonists caricatured the commercial craze to mimic the president. For example, at one drugstore the "Delusive Druggist" shows clients a wax likeness of the president and his beard, and offers huge jars of "Lincoln's Whiskeropherous." "There's 'is Heffigy in wax, sir, wiskers and all," says the druggist, from the Old Country. "Try one of them pots, and in three weeks you'll be as 'airy and 'ansom as 'im."[40]

Miscellaneous cartoons and caricatures depicted Lincoln in a variety of poses and circumstances. One pictured his right arm unnaturally elongated from the ordeal of handshaking, whereas another showed a theater manager cancelling performances out of deference to curiousity about Lincoln. Lincoln's Black Republicanism, a dominant and pervasive theme at the outset of his administration, was also mocked by a kiss from "A Black Republican Damsel." Other cartoons assumed a more serious posture. For example, in "Consulting the Oracle," Lincoln receives counsel from Columbia: "President Lincoln.—'And what next?' Columbia.—'First be sure you're

THE PRESIDENT'S INAUGURAL.

This is the way the North receives it.   And   This is the way the South receives it

"The President's Inaugural," *New York Illustrated News*, March 23, 1861, 320. Author's Collection.

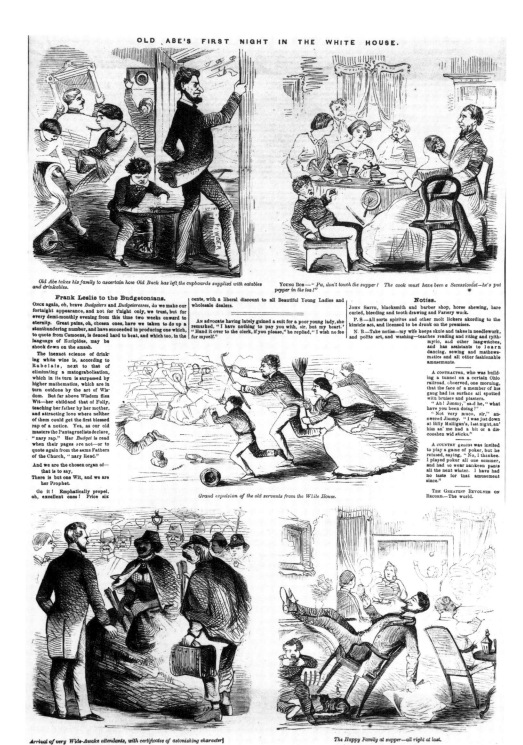

"Old Abe's First Night in the White House," *Frank Leslie's Budget of Fun*, April 1, 1861, 9. Courtesy of the American Antiquarian Society.

right, then go ahead.'" A second exchange between Lincoln and Columbia represents Dr. Lincoln proposing his "Homeopathic Treatment" to "Miss Columbia." "Now, Miss Columbia, if you will follow my prescriptions, which are of an extremely mild character, but which your old nurse, Mrs. Buchanan, seems to have been so averse to, I have no doubt but what the Union will be restored to position, health, and vigor."[41]

SECESSION AND FORT SUMTER

On the evening Lincoln returned to the White House from the inaugural ball he was handed a letter from Maj. Robert Anderson at Fort Sumter informing the president "that their [federal troop's] provisions would be exhausted before an expedition could be sent to their relief." This letter marked the commencement of the long crisis that plagued all of Lincoln's first term and diminished only slightly before his assassination. Despairing over Buchanan's administration of the approaching conflict, the North looked to Lincoln for hope. In December, Lincoln had conveyed to an emissary of President Buchanan expression of his desire that the South "suspend all action for

"Agency for the Lincoln Whiskeropherous," *Vanity Fair*, March 16, 1861, 126. Author's Collection.

Delusive Druggist.—THERE'S 'IS HEFFIGY IN WAX, SIR, WISKERS AND ALL. TRY ONE OF THEM POTS, AND IN THREE WEEKS YOU'LL BE AS 'AIRY AND 'ANSOM AS 'IM.

dismemberment of the Union, at least, until some act, deemed to be violative of [Southern] rights, shall be done by the incoming administration." In Ohio, while on his way to Washington, Lincoln had reaffirmed his hope of "living in peace and harmony one with another" and declared, "We shall again be brethren."[42] However, in spite of these hopes, sentiment in favor of secession mounted.

Cartoons also reflected the gravity of the situation. Mending the severe break with "Union Glue" was definitely "a job for the new cabinet-maker." Lincoln was also shown trying to unravel the tangled yarn of secession left by the Buchanan administration. Under the general heading "The Theory of Coercion," two cartoons in *Frank Leslie's Budget of Fun* cast Lincoln into the uncomfortable role of the presidential enforcer. In both images, he balances precariously on the point of bayonets. In the cartoon on the left side of the page, Gen. John E. Wool lifts Lincoln with his bayonet into the lofty presidential chair while Lincoln carries his reliable axe. "General Wool.—'Now, Uncle Abe, I'll give you a shove, and keep you there when I get you there.' Uncle Abe.—'Thank you, General—it is a great comfort to me to hear you say so.'" The other cartoon depicts Lincoln perched on a stack of bayonets. "Old Abe.—'Oh, it's all well enough to say that I must support by force the dignity of the high office you have elevated me to—but it's darned uncomfortable sitting, I can tell yer!'"[43] Collectively, these images anticipated the personal stresses and strains that befell the president.

Dealing with the fact of secession was painful enough, but Lincoln and his political ideology were sometimes charged with causing it. Certain popular images reinforced this assertion. An example of this appeared in *Frank Leslie's Budget of Fun*.

"A Black Republican Damsel," *Phunny Phellow*, April 1861, front page. Reproduced through permission of the Rare Book and Special Collections Library, University of Illinois at Urbana-Champaign.

A "BLACK REPUBLICAN DAMSEL FOLLOWING THE EXAMPLE OF THE OTHER PRETTY GIRL WHO KISSED HONEST OLD ABE.

GENERAL WOOL.—" Now, Uncle Abe, I'll give you a shove, and keep you there when I get you there."
UNCLE ABE—" Thank you, General—it is a great comfort to me to hear you say so."

OLD ABE—" Oh, it's all well enough to say that I must support by force the dignity of the high office you have elevated me to—but it's darned uncomfortable sitting, I can tell yer!"

Here the rail-splitter swings the maul of the "Chicago Platform" at the wedge, William Seward, and together Lincoln, Seward, and the Republican Party's Chicago platform divide the North from the South. Such logic had assailed Lincoln in the Senate campaign of 1858, when he expressed intense displeasure with the argument: "Myself, and those with whom I act have been constantly accused of a purpose to destroy the union; and bespattered with every imaginable odious epithet."[44] Now, when he was president, impeachment of his integrity on such flimsy charges hurt even more. In Lincoln's hierarchy of values preserving the Union ranked even higher than the abolition of slavery. Notwithstanding Lincoln's last-ditch effort to breathe new life into the Union, it was too late.

After the inauguration, the beginning of the Civil War needed only a triggering device, and Fort Sumter provided the mechanism. On March 15, Lincoln convened his newly formed cabinet to seek its counsel. *Frank Leslie's Illustrated Newspaper* pictured the cabinet in deliberation, and the caption announced its verdict: "the evacuation of Fort Sumter." However, Lincoln rejected its initial advice for another course. Instead of evacuation, he would inform the governor of South Carolina in advance that he would resupply the garrison at Fort Sumter without any attempt to bolster its forces. This decision required delicate diplomacy. Henry L. Stephens brilliantly

"The Theory of Coercion," *Frank Leslie's Budget of Fun,* March 15, 1861, 13. Courtesy of the General Research Division, New York Public Library Astor, Lenox, and Tilden Foundations.

OLD ABE—" *Hurt you, Uncle Bill?*"
BILL S——D—" *Hurts like the very d—d—d—deuce, but I won't squeal!*"

"Hurt You, Uncle Bill?" *Frank Leslie's Budget of Fun*, March 1, 1861, 8. Courtesy of the Buffalo and Erie County Public Library.

characterized the fragile situation at Fort Sumter in the cartoon entitled "Prof. Lincoln in His Great Feat of Balancing." In the circus ring, Lincoln balances on his forehead the dove of peace on one side of the bar and Fort Sumter on the other, while Seward, the clown, points approvingly to his performance. Naturally, Horace Greeley, tracking the president's every move, carefully monitors the spectacle from the front row.[45]

A few weeks later, Henry L. Stephens mixed his Fort Sumter metaphors in a cartoon published in *Frank Leslie's Budget of Fun*. Stephens replicated the juggler metaphor in the caption "Great and astonishing trick of Old Abe, the Western Juggler," but drew Lincoln as the circus sword swallower.[46] This, too, was a clever metaphor. The artist left interpretation of the caricature to the reader, but one such interpretation might have been: Out of deference for peace, Lincoln strives earnestly to swallow the sword of war; ultimately, however, it is an impossible task. Likewise it was futile for Lincoln to juggle or swallow the Sumter crisis without dire national repercussions.

Cognizant of earlier recommendations to evacuate Fort Sumter, *Frank Leslie's Budget of Fun* also tried to justify that possibility. "Take your castle [Fort Sumter], Davis," says Lincoln—"it is not worth one drop of brothers' blood!" However, shielded behind Lincoln's back is the trump card, Fort Pickens. Implicitly, the cartoon suggests that the loss of Fort Sumter was still a relatively easy solution.[47]

Characteristic of the comic medium, *Phunny Phellow*'s solution to the Fort Sumter crisis was also somewhat simplistic. Cartoonist J. A. Read pictured a weak, indulgent, vacillating Buchanan vis-à-vis a more bold, firm, and resolute Lincoln. The

Great and astonishing trick of Old Abe, the Western juggler.

"Great and Astonishing Trick of Old Abe, the Western Juggler," *Frank Leslie's Budget of Fun*, April 15, 1861. McLellan Lincoln Collection, Brown University Library.

"Prof. Lincoln in His Great Feat of Balancing," *Vanity Fair*, March 23, 1861, 139. Author's Collection.

PROF. LINCOLN IN HIS GREAT FEAT OF BALANCING.

"The Generous
Rivals," *Frank Leslie's
Budget of Fun,* April 15,
1861. McLellan Lincoln
Collection, Brown
University Library.

"An Anxious Mamma
and a Fractious Child,"
Phunny Phellow, April
1861, 16. Reproduced
through permission of
the Rare Book and
Special Collections
Library, University of
Illinois at Urbana-
Champaign.

fractious child, "The Infant Southern Republic," says to her "Anxious Mama," Buchanan, "Boo hoo-hoo! I want Fort Sumter!" "Mrs. Buchanan" replies, "Now, Baby, you can't have it. You've got two or three forts and a number of ships and arsenals already; and you won't be allowed to keep even them, for here comes Honest Old Abe to take them all away from you!" Literally carrying a big stick, Lincoln strides emphatically in the door to retrieve the national possessions, but the cartoonist underestimated the tenacity, perseverance, and will of the South.[48]

After Major Anderson surrendered to Gen. Pierre Gustave Toutant Beauregard's South Carolina troops, Frank Bellew showed a resigned Lincoln swallowing the Fort Sumter pill. "Granny Seward—'Now, Abe, take your physic like a man! The Sumter Pill you must swallow right away; the Pickens one you needn't for a day or two.'"[49] So began the war as envisioned by a core of artists that the illustrated press had commissioned to humorously editorialize and describe the crucial role of Fort Sumter.

TAKING THE PILL.

"Taking the Pill," *Phunny Phellow,* May 1, 1861. Courtesy of the American Antiquarian Society.

The shelling and fall of Fort Sumter aroused patriotic, retaliatory, and bellicose impulses, and artists in the North inflamed the passions of Union loyalty for a war that many did not want but in good conscience could not avoid. Ascribing the blame to Jefferson Davis, these early images rationalized, idealized, and justified the war with palatable euphemisms of street fighting and boxing matches. Perhaps charitably, the terrors and untold tragedies of war were initially concealed from naive, impressionable youth.

One of the earliest such illustrations from the portfolio of Henry L. Stephens portrays Lincoln and Gen. Winfield Scott bearing rifles. When Uncle Sam asks them what their militant appearance means, "Master Lincoln" explains, "Why this here Jeff Davis and his fellers' been a crowin' over us long enough, and now there's a goin' to be a row." "Well, now! If you're goin' to fight, mind you," replies Uncle Sam, "fight like your father—go!" Lincoln's father, of course, is the father of his country—George Washington. Predictably, Stephens's next cartoon compared the situation soon after Fort Sumter's surrender to the Revolutionary War. The artist also displayed Lincoln with the same zeal—the "Spirit of 76"—as his renowned predecessor. Columbia and Lincoln are shown together nurturing their new crop of troops, "the Hardy Bunker Hill Flower, the Seventh Regiment Pink, the Fireboy Tulip," and other plants." After Columbia asks "Old Abe" what the gallows is doing among the crops, the president replies, "That is rare in this country—it will bloom shortly and bear the Jeffersonia Davisiana."[50] Again, the anticipation of the gallows blooming "shortly" promotes the expectation of a relatively brief conflict. The idealization of war as a solution to political problems appeals to readers to overlook the grave consequences of warlike behavior.

In May, cartoons at home and abroad used the benign, deceivingly harmless, boxing match euphemism for war. Lincoln and Davis were the contestants. An illustrated broadside advertisement, which promoted the sale of the May issue of *Phunny Phellow*, pitted Lincoln against Davis in the "Great Fight for the Championship between the Southern Filibuster and the Western Railsplitter."[51] O. Morse was the artist. To be sure, gladiator and boxing metaphors contained hostile and aggressive elements, but in comparison with war, they were thoroughly sanitized.

This particular broadside also illustrated another type of public pressure the president experienced. Prodding Lincoln from the sidelines was Horace Greeley. "'Why don't you go in Abe? What's the use o' waitin' for an openin' any longer?' Abe.— 'Keep cool and let yer hair grow Horace! I know wot I'm about. I want to tire him out!'" Greeley's post–Fort Sumter editorials did not shrink from counseling the president. "He would raise the President's call [for recruits] from 75,000 to a 'Half Million' at once; he would make a 'patriotic loan' of $100,000,000 and send to Europe, for delivery within thirty days, for 100,000 firearms." Soon Greeley would also announce his own six-point strategy.[52] To Lincoln, the constant barrage of second-guessing was an occupational hazard, and Horace Greeley was a sharp, painful, and persistent thorn in the president's side.

OLD ABE.—Aint there a nice crop? There's the hardy Bunker Hill flower, the Seventh Regiment Pink, the Fireboy Tulip—That tricolored flower grows near Independence Hall—the Western Blossoms and Prairie Flowers will soon begin to shoot.

COLUMBIA.—What charming plant is this?

OLD ABE.—That is rare in this country—it will bloom shortly and bear the Jeffersonia Davisiana.

"Old Abe—Ain't There a Nice Crop?" *Vanity Fair*, May 4, 1861, 211. Author's Collection.

The atmosphere in the immediate aftermath of Fort Sumter raised the legitimate question of foreign neutrality. Would the European powers intervene in any way? Would they attempt to mediate the conflict, or recognize the Confederacy as an independent political entity? What were the implications of war for the divided country? A Lincoln caricature in *Frank Leslie's Budget of Fun*, "The Old Woman in Trouble," implies that Lincoln, the symbol of national identity, was experiencing an identity crisis—the "Old Woman" did not know whether she was one or two nations. The accompanying doggerel explicated the meaning of the illustration.

"Great Fight for the Championship," broadside advertisement for *Phunny Phellow*, May 1861. McLellan Lincoln Collection, Brown University Library.

There was an old woman as I have heard tell,
She went to Washington her wooden nutmegs to sell;
But in going to market, as I have heard say,
She fell into a dose upon market-day.

There came a sly pedlar, Jeff Davis the stout,
He cut her Southern skirts all round about—

He cut off her petticoats up to her knees,
Until the poor lady began for to freeze.
And when this poor lady began to awake,
She found Southern Shiverly had made her shake;
Her knees 'gan to tremble, and she 'gan to cry,
"Marcy sakes! Uncle Sammy, this cannot be I."

"If it be not I, as I suppose it to be,
There's John Bull, the dog, and he knows me—
And there's a fine rooster, the Gallic Shanghai—
I'll go to those creatures," said she with a sigh.

"And if it be I—dog will waggle its tail,
But if it be not I, he will bark without fail;
And the fine Gallic Shanghai will crow with delight,
If I should be I—but if not, he will fight."

THE OLD WOMAN IN TROUBLE.

"The Old Woman in Trouble," *Frank Leslie's Budget of Fun*, May 1, 1861. Courtesy of the American Antiquarian Society.

Up jumped the old woman, all in the dark,
The shanghai crowed fiercely, the dog it did bark—
And then the poor lady began for to cry,
"Marcy sakes! I'm afraid that it really isn't I."[53]

Despite this tongue-in-cheek characterization, neither the act of secession nor the perceptions of England and France altered Lincoln's conception of national identity. Long before his election as president, his positions on the importance of the Union, its priority over slavery, and the inadmissibility of secession were established.[54] These settled views enabled him to act decisively and to reject anything less than the constitutional condition these values defined. One *Harper's Weekly* cartoon caption had Jeff Davis saying to Lincoln, "All I want is to be let alone," but Lincoln had no constitutional choice; his presidential oath of office mandated coercion.[55]

The forbidding threshold of war had been crossed. The long journey from Springfield had transported Lincoln, the commander in chief, to the lone and dreary edges of the battlefield.

The Vagaries of War

By dint of its overwhelming magnitude, the Civil War monopolized the media, became the obsession of illustrators, and turned into the dominant motif in the popular culture. The evolving and dynamic variations on the war theme were legion, running the gamut from its causes to its projected outcome. In time, popular artists from the North, the South, and England presented these themes to their own audiences, in their own terms, for what the artists believed was the benefit, information, or entertainment of their own unique constituencies. Now that the battle lines had been clearly drawn, so were the general parameters of artistic ethnocentrism. Naturally, Northern artists tended to support their own perceived national interests, the Southern illustrators theirs, and comic artists in England invariably sided with the South.

What characterized this war was its uncertainty and unpredictability. From Fort Sumter to the eve of Gettysburg, cyclical vicissitudes of victory and defeat typified the conflict. To the surprise of the North, the South gained the initial edge, but the Northern offensive in the spring of 1862 reversed the trend. However, the South soon regained the initiative with Stonewall Jackson's impressive summer counteroffensive in the Shenandoah campaign and the concomitant defense of Richmond from the Army of the Potomac's ineffective invasion. In September, victory at Antietam temporarily turned the tide, enabling the North to announce its intention to issue the Emancipation Proclamation. This development transformed the war into one of liberation and eventually made it possible for African Americans to strengthen the North's military power. At the close of 1862, at Fredericksburg, the North suffered its most bitter defeat. The national dismay that reverberated from Fredericksburg created a crisis in national confidence and public opinion; lessened the impact of emancipation; generated a quest for sound military leadership; aroused the Copperheads to action against emancipation, conscription, and the tightening vise on civil liberties;

and further divided the Republican Party. Not until the summer of 1863 did the Union show convincing evidence of regaining ascendancy in this tumultuous war. Hence, during the first two years of the Civil War success was hardly more common than defeat. Actually, for North and South alike high hopes and frustrated expectations were common. Such were the vagaries of war, which comic artists amply exposed.

BULL RUN TO THE TRENT AFFAIR

The outbreak of the war at Fort Sumter rallied the country around Lincoln. A nationalistic, patriotic mood prevailed. By summer, the tentative, wait-and-see attitude of *Harper's Weekly* toward the president and his administration was transformed into effusive support: "For our part we are free to confess that thus far Mr. Lincoln seems to us to have been fully equal to the stupendous task which Fate has set before him. We can not thus far detect a single fatal error in his administration of the Government. He appears to be fully conscious of the situation, and to be discharging his duty with a keen perception of his responsibility to God and to the people.... Under these circumstances, we submit that Mr. Lincoln is entitled to the cordial support of every honest man in the country. Nor can we perceive that anything can be gained by carping at the real or supposed errors of the members of the Cabinet."[1] Indeed, some qualms had been expressed about Cameron and Seward's performance, but in general a spirit of harmony and goodwill pervaded the tense atmosphere. Even Horace Greeley's impulsive and impatient clarion call—"Forward to Richmond"—was not initially disruptive. Some deemed Greeley intrusive and presumptuous, but his impatience did not break the spell of Union cohesion.

One week before the battle at Bull Run, popular art reflected this sanguine spirit. A trio of cartoons pictured Jeff Davis and General Beauregard diving for cover from the "Gen. Scott" bombshell, Confederate troops retreating in "double-quick step to Richmond," and "Officer Lincoln" forcing a "compromise" from a submissive Jeff Davis.[2] However, this rash posturing did not pass the test of battlefield reality. At Bull Run, the proud Union forces fled for their lives, and the depth of national loyalty to Lincoln faced its first major test.

The embarrassing defeat at Bull Run nettled the likes of Horace Greeley. He precipitously demanded the resignation of the cabinet and charged the administration with incompetence, but he was unprepared for the firestorm created by his editorial. Newspapers and the illustrated press reprimanded Greeley and the *New York Tribune* for setting a July 20 deadline for the armies to be in Richmond. Greeley's critics thought that the *Tribune's* "Forward to Richmond" editorial placed undue pressure on the administration and army to act prematurely and unwisely. *Harper's Weekly* also mercilessly pounced on the *Tribune's* impetuous editor, "Field-Marshal Greeley, the Mischief-Maker, 'Forward to Richmond' by way of Bull's Run!!!"[3]

DICTATOR GREELEY dismisses the Cabinet, and Warns Lincoln that he will stand no more Nonsense.

"A decimated and indignant people demand the immediate retirement of the present Cabinet from the high places of power, which, for one reason or another, they have shown themselves incompetent to fill. The people insist upon new heads of Executive Departments."—*New York Tribune, July 23.*

"Dictator Greeley,"
Harper's Weekly,
August 10, 1861, 512.
Author's Collection.

Artist John McLenan also made Greeley pay for his impatience. In cartoon, he ridiculed Greeley's irate, impulsive behavior, depicting the editor belligerently jumping up and down on Lincoln's desk while wielding a club and sending official papers flying in every direction. In the background, cabinet members flee from his furor. The caption summarized the cartoon's purpose: "DICTATOR GREELEY dismisses the cabinet, and Warns Lincoln that he will stand no more Nonsense."[4] Paradoxically, Greeley's misguided indignation after Bull Run deflected some adverse reaction from the president to himself.

Although Confederate forces won another significant battle in August at Wilson Creek, Missouri, and still another in October at Ball's Bluff, Virginia, the North did not panic. Most in the North saw these defeats as early aberrations—not disturbing patterns. Moreover, some thought that Bull Run's significance had been grossly over-rated and distorted by an inflammatory press: "The general opinion is that everybody would have considered it a drawn battle, but for that atrocious system the American press has of 'creating sensations' by exaggerating the facts. . . . The next time the American eagle makes a dash at the foe, the Bull Run will be in another direction."[5]

A double-page woodcut in *Frank Leslie's Budget of Fun* reassured the nation that Washington was not in danger and that the Union armies were on their way to Richmond. In fact, the image portrayed an impregnable defense that surrounded the capital city—an ominous portent for Jeff Davis and General Beauregard: "Jeff Davis (to Beauregard)–'But, I say, Bully Beau, are not those fellows running the wrong way?' Beauregard—'That's a fact, our BULL RUN has here come to a pretty sudden stop. Uncle Abe's blockaded the bridges—there's the BANKS of the Potomac above—gunboats below—and there's [General] WOOL gathering near Richmond! We're getting into a pretty tightish fix! Confound that McClellan, why the deuce didn't they keep Patterson? He was the man for us!'"[6] Embedded in such wishful hyperbole were delusive elements of grandeur, but exaggeration temporarily soothed fears and pacified real anxiety.

Unfortunately, the euphoria associated with General McClellan's appointment to command the Army of the Potomac did not last. Within six months of Bull Run some senators were clamoring for McClellan's removal; his obsession with preparation, numbers, and detail had created a debilitating military paralysis. In January 1862, Lincoln impatiently ordered the lethargic McClellan to act. Albert Berghaus's *Harper's Weekly* cartoon echoed the president's sentiments with the sarcastic phrase, "Masterly Activity, or Six Months on the Potomac," but in April, Lincoln was still pleading for action from the passive general.[7] Yet even more newsworthy was the issue of foreign intervention.

Following Bull Run, Lincoln's image in the illustrated press was linked primarily with the question of European neutrality. For example, much ado was made of Prince Joseph Charles Paul Napoleon's official visit to the United States and of Lincoln's firm leadership, which discouraged recognition of the Confederacy.[8] William Newman's cartoon entitled "Recognition, or No" implicitly paid tribute to Lincoln's leadership: "John Bull to Napoleon III.—'Can you recognize that thing they call the C.S.A.?' Nap.—'Well, I think I could, if 'twere not for that Big Fellow who stands in front.'" Even more emphatic was a front-page cartoon in *Vanity Fair* in which John Bull and his associates from France and Spain stood next to a pond that contained fish representations of Jefferson Davis and "Little Aleck [Alexander Stephens]." John Bull pondered whether to cast in his bait, but Lincoln, with a sword in his left hand and his right arm draped over a cannon, warned ("pleasantly, but with some degree of firmness") "Boys, I reckon I wouldn't." *Phunny Phellow*, assuming the European perspective, thought England was enjoying some vicarious satisfaction from the American conflict: "Napoleon III.—'How do you think the fight will terminate, Brother Bull?' Johnny Bull.—'Well, Nap, it's hard to tell; but, slightly altering Shakespeare, I may say: 'Now, whether Jeff kill Abe, or Abe kill Jeff, or each do kill the other, every way makes our gain.'"[9] However, such cartoons represented only the beginning of grave international concerns over the question of neutrality on both sides of the Atlantic. The Trent Affair ignited the explosive elements.

When the news reached England that Capt. Charles D. Wilkes, commander of the USS *San Jacinto,* had captured James M. Mason and John Slidell, two Confederate envoys aboard the British vessel *Trent,* the government, media, and populace were infuriated. How could international law be violated with impunity and so cavalierly? they wondered. Meanwhile, the American media naively celebrated and reveled over the surprising catch, and Captain Wilkes was accorded heroic stature. Soon tensions between Britain and the United States increased, and there was anxiety that the genuine specter of international war hovered perilously over the two nations. As the demands for the release of Mason and Slidell escalated, public revelry over the incident in America subsided and the Lincoln administration apologetically arranged to let the Confederate ministers go.[10] In the end, the United States had to concede that Captain Wilkes had placed his country "Up a Tree." According to the gloating London *Punch,* the "Yankee Coon" in the tree was Lincoln, and Colonel John Bull was holding him hostage. "Coon.—'Air You in Arnest, Colonel?' Colonel Bull.—'I am.' Coon.—'Don't Fire—I'll Come Down.'"[11] In the aftermath of the Trent Affair, neutrality was more tenuous than ever and diplomatic tension more taut.

THE SPRING OFFENSIVE

While Lincoln unhappily continued to spur General McClellan into action, the momentum of the war changed for the better on other fronts.[12] Ironically, England's normally hostile Matt Morgan publicized the spate of Union conquests in *Fun* with a cartoon titled "Sensation Jumble." In it, a bartender mixed "Prof. Lincoln's Great New Yankee Drink," which consisted of "Greatest Naval Victory on Record, Slave Emancipation, Great Victory on the Potomac, Kick Out McClellan, and Great Retreat of the Rebels." Similarly, a humorous woodcut by William Newman captured "The Dream of the Rebel Bill-Poster, Jeff Davis," who sees in vision "The Hand-Writing on the Walls at Richmond," the *Monitor* nullifying the *Merrimac,* riots in Richmond, "Nashville Taken," "Union Sentiment in Tennessee," "Columbus Evacuated," William Tecumseh Sherman in Charleston and Savannah, Nathaniel P. Banks in Manassas and Winchester, the "Execution of Gordon," Burnside in Norfolk, "Mill-Spring," Don Carlos Buell in Memphis, progress "On to Richmond," and "Abraham Lincoln, President" pasted over the "Inauguration of Jefferson Davis."[13] For the most part, these postings were just wistful Union dreams—or irrational Confederate nightmares—but there was tangible evidence of Union progress in the war.

This optimism carried over to other magazines and inspired a wave of creativity. For example, William Newman also envisioned the best of all possible Union worlds in his novel images of "Castle Lincoln—No Surrender" and "Fort Davis—in Ruins."[14] Parenthetically, this cartoon is so cleverly drawn that some readers, unless

"UP A TREE."
Colonel Bull and the Yankee 'Coon.

'Coon. "AIR YOU IN ARNEST, COLONEL?"
Colonel Bull. "I AM."
'Coon. "DON'T FIRE—I'LL **COME DOWN**."

"Up a Tree," *Punch*,
January 11, 1862, 15.
Author's Collection.

they pause for a moment or turn the page on its side for a clearer view of the presidents, may not see the hidden profiles of Lincoln and Davis in the castle and fort scenes.

Idealism about the war also engendered an overly sanguine front-page scene in *Vanity Fair* that depicted "A. Lincoln & Co. Coopers" refabricating the Union barrel. With the vital assistance of his apprentice—a symbol of the valor of Zouave Union soldiers—Lincoln systematically, if piecemeal, commences what seems to be the final task of adding wooden slats for each of the disaffected Southern states to put the finishing touches on the masterpiece of reunion. Congratulating the armed forces with an enthusiastic "Good Boy!" in the caption, Lincoln then places his stamp of approval on cooperation between the North's military and political components, keys to achieving national objectives: "A. L. . . . 'I guess we'll make a Tub of it that'll stand on its own bottom, yet.'"[15]

However, depiction of the pinnacle of hope for peace between North and South appeared in the May 1862 issues of *Frank Leslie's Budget of Fun* and *Phunny Phellow*. Two illustrations, each presented in double-page format, enacted a dramatic "Grand Tableau" of the hostility between the states, confidently predicting a swift end to the war. In meticulous detail typical of the gifted, prolific artist Frank Bellew, *Frank Leslie's Budget of Fun* offered "The Last Act of the Drama." Of course, if this was the "last act," the drama of disunion was almost over. The caption imagined the final scenario before reunion: "The demon of discord descends to perdition—the head of the secession alligator is severed from his body—Old Sesch lies prostrate, with the Zouaves bayonet at his throat—numerous small rebel devils floored—whilst the good genius Lincoln is victorious, and the Union Triumphant for ever!" In the drawing, General McClellan orchestrates the final battle of conquest with his crack Zouave infantry unit, secession is destroyed, Satan ("the demon of discord") and his rebel minions are dispatched to outer darkness, Lincoln honors his oath to defend the "U.S. Constitution," "Liberty" and "Union" ascend to their lofty positions, the flag resumes its rightful place, and cherubs bestow their divine approval on the heroic, grand finale.[16]

"Castle Lincoln—No Surrender; Fort Davis—in Ruins," *Frank Leslie's Illustrated Newspaper,* April 12, 1862, 368. Author's Collection.

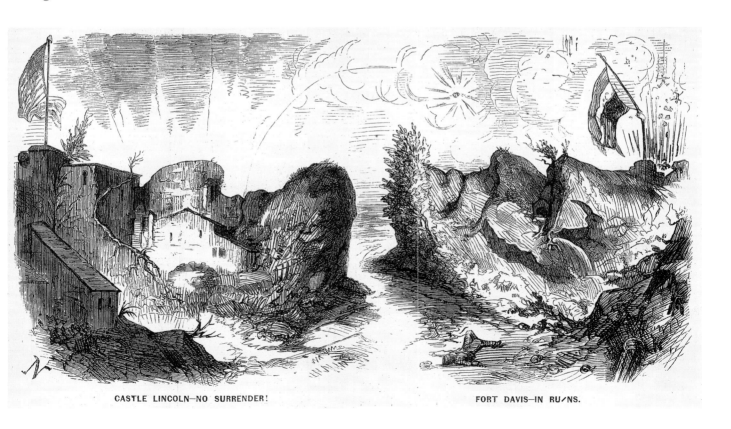

CASTLE LINCOLN—NO SURRENDER!

FORT DAVIS—IN RUINS.

"Cooperation," *Vanity Fair*, April 12, 1862, front page. Author's Collection.

COÖPERATION.

A. L.—"Good Boy! I guess we'll make a Tub of it that'll stand on its own bottom, yet."

The "Grand Tableau" in *Phunny Phellow* was an eighteen-panel serial cartoon that traced the main elements in the war from secession to the projected final victory. The usual tasteless, derisive ethnic language of the period was embedded in the caption:

1. Great Spectacular Drama: Jeff Davis, Stephens, Beauregard, Abe Lincoln, and McClellan. Enter inevitable nigger, author of the piece, showing that the devil is just as black as painted. 2. Two of the Southern chivalry, drunk on gin, attack a defenseless female (Union). Shame on you Jeff and Beauregard. Fort Sumter. 3. Bull Run's lovely virgin still in distress. 4. Sudden appearance of the beauteous fairy (Union). Abe Lincoln granting the maid an efficient protector and metamorphosing her persecutors. 5. Little Mac immediately teacheth those knights a Spanish dance called Mill Spring. 6. Also the true Virginia reel, i.e., Roanoke. 7. Two commiseration friends appear (John Bull and Napoleon). D'ye want help, Jeff? 8. Jeff, Yes. Yes. Yes! Mysterious disappearance of friends Mason and Slidell. 9. He has none to console him but his nigger. 10. Nigger don't seem as friendly as

he ought. 11. Quite the contrary. 12. Jeff's woes drive him insane. He crowns himself king on the 22nd of February 1862. 13. He comforts himself in the possession of a big plum that is called Fort Donelson, but . . . 14. One big plum drops out, but, pa, it's rotten. Floyd. 15. Wicked Jeff loses everything he has, but is obliged to join in [Fort] Donelson, [Fort] Henry. 16. The performance of the real genuine Southern plantation breakdown, and no mistake—nary! 17. Grand Tableau—Retribution. 18. Grand Tableau. Glorious Victory.[17]

In short, optimism reigns supreme.

During this period of unprecedented Union conquest, the only dissonant notes sounded in the illustrated press were due to the Confederate blockade runner *Nashville* and the temporary success of the *Merrimac*. However, due to the timely emergence of the *Monitor*, the *Merrimac*'s effectiveness was not only short-lived but also eventually neutralized. When Union forces took Norfolk, the *Merrimac* had to be scuttled. Although the *Nashville* did very little damage to the Union, the speed of the

"The Last Act of the Drama—Grand Tableau," *Frank Leslie's Budget of Fun*, May 1862, 8–9. Author's Collection.

THE DEMON OF DISCORD DESCENDS TO PERDITION——THE HEAD OF THE SECESSION ALLIGATOR IS SEVERED FROM HIS BODY——OLD SESCH LIES PROSTRATE, WITH THE ZOUAVE'S BAYONET AT HIS THROAT——NUMEROUS SMALL REBEL DEVILS FLOORED——WHILST THE GOOD GENIUS LINCOLN IS VICTORIOUS, AND THE UNION TRIUMPHANT FOR EVER!

sleek vessel enabled it to run the blockade and garner publicity disproportionate to its very modest naval impact. Nevertheless, Lincoln and Gideon Welles were the targets of adverse publicity that resulted. In Frank Bellew's "Sinbad Lincoln and the Old Man of the Sea," the troubled, drenched president emerges from the sea carrying a distraught Gideon Welles to the shore.[18] In the background are the gallant *Merrimac* and the free-spirited *Nashville* unmolested by the federal navy.

Contrary to this image, the Union navy acquitted itself with considerable distinction. Naval support or victories at New Orleans, Roanoke Island, Fort Donelson, Fort Henry, and Norfolk, and the *Monitor*'s confrontation with the *Merrimac* did not go unrecognized. *Punch* begrudgingly portrayed Lincoln with "The New Orleans Plum" in his hand. However, the cartoonist could not resist placing the Confederate victories of Bull Run and Corinth on the map and $250 million of Union war expenditures in the background; still, New Orleans had fallen.

> Big Lincoln Horner,
> Up in a Corner,
> Thinking of Humble Pie;
> Found Under His Thumb,
> A New Orleans Plum,
> And Said, What a Cute Yankee Am I![19]

In *Vanity Fair*, a cartoon by Henry L. Stephens animatedly depicts the "Frisky manner in which the news, 'Norfolk Is Ours,' was received by the President and Secretary of War." In his nightshirt, Stanton leaps from his chair to embrace a startled General Halleck, and Lincoln, bursting his suspenders, enthusiastically grasps Halleck's hand. *Yankee Notions* also feted Com. Andrew Foote and President Lincoln in a cartoon that focuses on the signal role of the navy at Fort Henry.[20]

THE CONFEDERATE COUNTEROFFENSIVE

Suddenly the tide of war began to change. In late May 1862, Stonewall Jackson scored impressive victories at Front Royal and Winchester, Virginia. In June, Robert E. Lee repulsed General McClellan in the Battle of Seven Pines, and in July, Generals Albert Sidney Johnston and Lee defended the gates of Richmond in the Seven Days campaign. Furthermore, Stonewall Jackson concluded his stunning Shenandoah Valley thrust with successes at Cross Keys and Fort Republic.[21] In the fall, the exploits of the CSS *Alabama* and CSS *Florida* took a toll on the shipping lanes.

From the New York press, *Punch* detected this significant shift in momentum and felt that the truth about the war had been adulterated. In a brilliant artistic maneuver, *Punch* borrowed and adapted an idea from Matt Morgan's April 1862 cartoon in *Fun*, which had announced the chain of victories from the Union's spring offensive.

"Sinbad Lincoln and the Old Man of the Sea," *Frank Leslie's Budget of Fun,* June 1862, 4. Author's Collection.

SINBAD LINCOLN AND THE OLD MAN OF THE SEA.

THE NEW ORLEANS PLUM.

BIG LINCOLN HORNER,   FOUND UNDER HIS THUMB,
UP IN A CORNER,   A NEW ORLEANS PLUM,
THINKING OF HUMBLE PIE;   AND SAID, WHAT A 'CUTE YANKEE AM I!

"NORFOLK IS OURS!"

FRISKY MANNER IN WHICH THE NEWS WAS RECEIVED BY THE PRESIDENT AND SECRETARY OF WAR.

"The New Orleans
Plum," *Punch*, May 24,
1862, 207. Author's
Collection.

"Norfolk Is Ours,"
Vanity Fair, May 31,
1862, 263. Author's
Collection.

Morgan had depicted a bartender pouring Professor Lincoln's drink, which consisted of several conquests, from a beaker in his left hand into one in his right. The
cartoonist for *Punch* altered the image only slightly, but the changes entirely reversed
the meaning. Lincoln is now the bartender, but he is obliged to pour the victories out
of his right-hand container into the vessel of defeat in his left hand. According to the
cartoon, the bluster of federal victories was more apparent than real—just "Bunkum," "Bosh," "Bragg," and "Soft-Sawder." The blame for the alleged distortion
was aimed straight at "Old Abe at the Bar of Public Opinion":

> Where dull John Bull would measure out
> Defeat's unmingled bitters,
> In water from truth's well, despite
> Britannia's tears and twitters,
> The caterers for Jonathan
> With bunkum, brag and bluster
> Spice up defeat to victory,
> And call it "raal eye-duster."

There at the bar in Washington
Sits one as honest Abe known,
From his rail-splitting Springfield days
As truthful as a babe known—
But "at the bar 'tis as the bar"—
So honest Abe in fixin'
Despatches up for Jonathan
Has learnt the art of mixin'.

"The Latest from America," *Punch*, July 26, 1862, 35. Author's Collection.

THE LATEST FROM AMERICA;

Or, the New York "Eye-Duster," to be taken Every Day.

From Victory's goblet to Defeat's
This way and that he tosses
Retreats, advances, fronts and rears,
Facts, figures, gains and losses.
Is the draught harsh? A honied lie
Makes questioning palates placid:
Does the draught cloy? Throw in a dash
Of partial loss for acid.

And when he's stirred the stuff about
Till Stanton's taste approves it,
Or Seward's, who bad news can fix
As Jonathan best loves it;
The mixture's handed from the bar,
So cunningly compounded,
Few can pick out the truth with lies
The lies with truth confounded.

"Truth, cold without, Sir," says old Abe,
"With Jonathan is scaarse, Sir:
He's used to take it with a dash
Of hot sensation saarse, Sir.
I guess his stomach 'twouldn't suit,
Perhaps bring on the shakes, Sir,
So palatable at our bar
The naked truth we makes, Sir."[22]

In the history of warfare, this is a nineteenth-century accusation of governmental tampering with battlefield facts.

Corresponding to the changed momentum of the war was an interesting contrast in the pattern of Lincoln's image in English and Union cartoons. In the midst of this shifting context, the British press aggressively censured Lincoln and gloated over the deteriorating Union military situation, whereas the Northern domestic press, emphasizing the positive, tended to protect the president or ignore recent battlefield setbacks.[23] Moreover, added to the scant positive news on the military front was the robust debate on the merits of emancipation, which also helped temporarily modify the content of popular art in the North's graphic media. As always, there were a few exceptions to the rule. For example, O. Morse's front-page cartoon in *Phunny Phellow,* "Grand Milling Match between Abe, the Railsplitter, and Jeff, the Rattlesnake," gave the military edge to the North. "Louis Napoleon.—'Don't you tink, friend Bull, it's time we sall make ze grande interference wiz dis dam fight?' John Bull.—'Well, I carn't say, Mr. Nap. You see, the fact is, Abe has got him in chancery, and it isn't in flesh and blood to stand such punishment long. If Abe should lick him, there's no

GRAND MILLING MATCH BETWEEN ABE, THE RAILSPLITTER, AND JEFF, THE RATTLESNAKE.

LOUIS NAPOLEON,---Don't you tink, friend Bull, it's time we sall make ze grande interference wiz dis dam fight?
JOHN BULL,---Well, I carnt say, Mr. Nap. You see, the fact is, Abe has got him in chancery, and it isn't in flesh and blood to stand such punishment long. If Abe should lick him, there's no knowing but what he might pitch into us while his blood's up if we attempt to meddle with him, and so I think we'd better hold off awhile, ye know.

"Grand Milling Match between Abe, the Railsplitter, and Jeff, the Rattlesnake," *Phunny Phellow*, September 1862, front page. C. Fiske Harris Collection on the American Civil War and Slavery, Providence Public Library.

knowing but what he might pitch into us while his blood's up if we attempt to meddle with him, and so I think we'd better hold off awhile, ye know.'"[24]

Similarly, H. L. Stephens visualized a shivering Jeff Davis, who worried that "That Draft from the North will be the death of me." Jeff Davis's slave "Slidell Alexander" could not stop the draft because "Abe Lincoln's got his back against [the door]." Finally, Thomas Nast pictured Lincoln holding the searing frying pan of Virginia from which Stonewall Jackson was jumping to the hotter coals of Maryland. "Honest Old Abe.—'I s'pose it does burn a little, my dear Stonewall, but you'd better try to bear it. If you jump, you will only be out of the frying pan into the fire!'"[25] These images stubbornly portrayed the federal forces in control, but there was no question that the South and its British advocates were basking in the glory of genuine Southern military achievement.

In England, the images were quite different. Matt Morgan of *Fun* and John Tenniel of *Punch* delivered the most decisive blows to the Union ego, and Lincoln's image sustained major damage. Morgan seemed to relish General McClellan's withdrawal from Richmond and was sure to link Old Abe with the retreat. "After His Last Run," Lincoln had to soak "McClellan's . . . poor feet [in] hot water." In harmony with the visual message from *Fun*, doggerel in *Punch* asserted that, in the

UNHEEDED ADVICE.

HONEST OLD ABE.----I s'pose it does burn a little, my dear Stonewall, but you'd better try to bear it. If you jump, you will only be out of the frying pan into the fire!

"Unheeded Advice," *Phunny Phellow,* November 1862, front page. C. Fiske Harris Collection on the American Civil War and Slavery, Providence Public Library.

North's vocabulary, the words "strategic movement" were just an "American Euphemism" for "rout." If the South had its "Se-ceders," the North was known for its "Re-ceders." *Fun* also had its witty poets; note these "Two Despatches of General McClellan":

No. I.—For Publication
All the rebels have fled,
Stonewall Jackson is dead,
And General Beauregard's banished;
In fact, without bouncing,
They've had such a trouncing,
Secession has totally vanished.

No. II.—Strictly Private and Confidential
Darn them rebels! I guess
We have got in a mess,
For advance you must read retrogression;
My plans are all addled,
The troops have skedaddled,
Once again we are licked by Secession.[26]

For a while, this rhetoric of retreat dogged McClellan and Lincoln in the British press.

At the outset of the war, "Lincoln called for troops to serve only ninety days not because he believed the war would be over quickly but because a 1795 law limited a call-up of militia to not more than thirty days after the assembling of Congress."[27] However, Britain's *Punch* misconstrued the ninety-day enlistment as an indication of the North's irrational optimism that the war would end ninety days after Fort Sumter. Now that the Civil War had lasted a year and a half with no end in sight, John Tenniel gloated that Lincoln's so-called deluded prognostication had not materialized. "Mr. South" hands a troubled president "The Overdue Bill," which states, "I promise to subdue the South in ninety days. [Signed] Abe Lincoln." "Your 'Ninety Days' Promissory Note Isn't Taken Up Yet, Sirree!" chides Mr. South.[28]

In fairness, it must be noted that strident antipathy toward the North in the English comic press was matched by a similar attitude in the Union toward the British; this exchange was not one-sided. As Jonathan, or Uncle Sam, was vilified on one side of the Atlantic, so John Bull was lustily maligned on the other. This exchange was the competitive legacy of the Revolutionary War. However, compared to the blast generated by the comic press in the North, the South's cartoonists barely whispered. Still, the Confederacy stood to gain from these volleys across the Atlantic. Any difficult challenge for Lincoln or the Union armies tended to be magnified or distorted in the English comic press for a laugh, which also provided another way to retaliate against Northern artists.

When Lincoln announced his intention to replenish the federal armies with 300,000 soldiers, England's cartoonists poked fun at the idea. Matt Morgan showed President Lincoln and Secretary of the Treasury Salmon P. Chase baiting their hooks with dollars and postage stamps to lure potential recruits. *Punch* summarized "Lincoln's Two Difficulties" as "No Money" and "No Men."[29] Morgan also featured the flight of "Young Yankeedom to Canada" in caricature and doggerel:

President Abe had a fierce baby,
Who was always a cryin' for slaughter,
But when drafting began he to Canada ran,
So he runs when he didn't oughter.[30]

"The Overdue Bill,"
Punch, September 27,
1862, 131. Author's
Collection.

THE OVERDUE BILL.

Mr. South to Mr. North. "YOUR 'NINETY DAYS' PROMISSORY NOTE ISN'T TAKEN UP YET, SIRREE!"

However, the most compelling comic explanation for the reluctance of young Northerners to become involved in the fighting ascribed the problem to the recent depressing battleground losses and poor military leadership. In England, rampant racism of the time blatantly argued for using African Americans "for these here experiments." Obviously, black Americans were judged to be more expendable.

We're coming, Father Abraam, we're coming all along,
But don't you think you're coming it yourself a little strong?

Three hundred thousand might be called a pretty tidy figure,
We've nearly sent you white enough, why don't you take the nigger?

We've fought, old Father Abraam, and fought uncommon bold,
And gained amazing victories, or so at least we're told;
And having whipped the rebels for a twelve month and a day,
We nearly found 'em liquoring in Washington in May.

Now, really, Father Abraam, this here's the extra ounce,
And we are almost sick, you see, of such almighty bounce;
We ain't afraid of being killed at proper times and seasons,
But it's aggravating to be killed for Mac's strategic reasons.

If you'd be so obliging, Father Abraam, as to write
To any foreign potentate, and put the thing polite,
And make him loan a General as knows the way to lead,
We'd come and list. Jerusalem and snakes! we would indeed.

But as the matter stands, Old Abe, we've this opinion, some,
If you say Come, as citizens of course we're bound to come,
But then we want to win, you see; if Strategy prevents,
We wish you'd use the nigger for these here experiments.

Hereditary bondsman, he should just be made to know
He'd convenience us uncommon if he'd take and strike a blow.
The man as will not fight for freedom isn't worth a cuss,
And it's better using niggers up than citizens like us.

So, Father Abraam, if you please, in this here game of chess,
You'd better take the black men against the white, I guess,
And if you work the niggers off before Rebellion's slain,
Which surely ain't expectable,—apply to us again.[31]

Toward the end of 1862, Matt Morgan caricatured "the real President of the U.S."
as the emissary of death. This cartoon was typical of negative portraits that British
illustrators at that time fashioned of the American president. Since July, Lincoln's
image in the English comic media had not received such a thrashing, and Morgan's
last Lincoln cartoon of the year distilled the essence of this pejorative view. The
president and Columbia, tossed about unmercifully by the angry waves of the ocean,
nervously hold on to their unseaworthy tub. Columbia asks Abe how he is faring.
Lincoln responds, "Quite Well, Thank'ee, Marm. Nothing Could Be Smoother," but
his anxious countenance, taut grip on the sides of the fragile vessel, and sarcasm in
the lead caption, "Abe's Last [Joke]," betray Lincoln's feigned composure.[32] Over

the last few months, except for the North's victory at Antietam, news from the eastern front had not been good for the Union, and the military disaster at Fredericksburg plunged the North into its lowest emotional ebb of the war.

THE CALAMITY AT FREDERICKSBURG

For the most part, Lincoln's image as depicted in cartoons had not fared poorly to this point even in the comic genre of the Northern press, but the watershed of Fredericksburg marked a discernible change in public opinion. Fredericksburg was the last in a series of Union defeats. The grand Army of the Potomac had not proved worthy of its expectations. Cartoonists began asking hard questions: Who is responsible for the loss of life and national disgrace at Fredericksburg? Which leaders are expendable? What changes need to be made to rectify the situation? No longer could Lincoln escape the outrage of illustrators. Even the significance of the official launching of the Emancipation Proclamation was submerged temporarily in the flood of concern.

There was plenty of blame to go around. Lincoln, Secretary of War Stanton, General Halleck, and General Burnside were the principal scapegoats, but the popular art also implicated the secretary of the navy, Gideon Welles. Pointing to the top level, some cartoonists resorted to the stereotype of Lincoln's alleged propensity to trivialize the tragic. A cartoonist for the *New York Illustrated News*, for instance, humorously claimed that Lincoln did not fathom the seriousness of the situation; "This is old mother Lincoln explaining to old mother Stanton how the slaughter of our troops at Fredericksburg reminds him of an anecdote he heard out West." From the cartoonist's standpoint, Lincoln just did not get it. Likewise, for humorous effect *Harper's Weekly* followed the same convenient script of purported indiscriminate, graceless presidential affinity for the light-minded: "Columbia.—'Where are my 15,000 Sons—murdered at Fredericksburg?' Lincoln.—'This reminds me of a little Joke.' Columbia.—'Go tell your Joke at SPRINGFIELD!!'" Still other images argued that "Mr. Nobody" [was] the party really responsible for the Fredericksburg disaster, but even from the rear view, the gangly, top-hatted profile of Mr. Nobody resembled President Lincoln."[33]

Even Thomas Nast did not let Lincoln off the hook, though he distributed the collective fault among Lincoln, Halleck, Stanton, Welles, and Burnside. General Burnside, with a picture of Fredericksburg in the background, asks Columbia whether he should awaken the sleeping Lincoln, Halleck, Stanton, and Welles "for the sake of our wives and children." Lincoln's drowsy head rests on "Bull Run Vols. 1, 2"; "7 Days Battle before Richmond"; and "Lives Wasted Vols. 1-6." His chair is propped against the large volume of "Retreats of 1861 and 1862," and the president's finger points to a document on his lap that says "Emancipation one of these days." Behind Halleck's nodding countenance is the "Plan for Taking Richmond" enshrouded in

THIS IS OLD MOTHER LINCOLN EXPLAINING TO OLD MOTHER STANTON HOW THE SLAUGHTER OF OUR TROOPS AT FREDERICKSBURG REMINDS HIM OF AN ANECDOTE HE HEARD OUT WEST.

"This Is Old Mother Lincoln," *New York Illustrated News*, January 10, 1863, 160. Courtesy of the New York State Library.

"That's What's the Matter, or Who's to Blame—A Tragedy," *Phunny Phellow*, February 1863, 8–9. C. Fiske Harris Collection on the American Civil War and Slavery, Providence Public Library.

cobwebs, and the sarcastic assertion that the "Backbone of the Rebellion" has been "broken 10,000,000,000,000,000,000,000,000 times." Unconsciously, Halleck holds a scroll satirically inscribed, "How I Caught Beauregard at Corinth," and over his head is the inscription "Rotten Vessels of the Bank's Expedition." Next to the snoozing Gideon Welles is a sarcastic sign that indicates Fort Sumter is to be retaken in 1890 and an obscure allusion to "iron-clad vessels." Like his colleagues, the dozing Stanton is proximately associated with "orders which were never carried out [concerning] pontoon bridges, ammunition supplies, ambulances, surgeons, reinforcements, tents, clothing, [and] horses." Next to Stanton's head is the inscription, "Why are the soldiers not paid?" He holds a paper in his hand that asks, "Who stopped the enlistments?"[34] Given this communal affliction of leaders' stupor and lethargy, so argued Nast, Fredericksburg is explicable.

William Newman's double-page explanation of Fredericksburg in *Frank Leslie's Budget of Fun* likened the defeat to a chain of ice-skaters—Uncle Sam, Lincoln, Stanton, Halleck, and Burnside—unwittingly pushing each other toward tragedy but unwilling to assume any individual responsibility. Burnside, first in line, has no one else to push, so he gratuitously condemns Halleck: "Don't be in such a darn'd hurry, Halleck." Halleck replies, "Taint me that's pushing, it's Stanton." Stanton shifts the responsibility to Abe: "It's Abe's fault, and Uncle Sam." Abe doesn't censor anyone.[35]

"An Ice Party, or Letting Things Slide on the Rappahannock," *Frank Leslie's Budget of Fun*, February 1863, 8–9. Courtesy of the American Antiquarian Society.

Several images charitably bypassed Lincoln and accused, at least comically, his subordinates Halleck, Stanton, Welles, and Seward. In successive weeks, Frank Bellew wittily relegated Halleck and Stanton to Lincoln's "guillotine," and Henry L. Stephens passed on the "universal advice" that the president should "drop 'em" from the ship of state. On January 31, Bellew added Gideon Welles to the list of expendable administrators because of his part in the "loss of the *Harriet Lane* and the exploits of the *Alabama*." Later, when Gen. Joseph Hooker replaced General Burnside as head of the Army of the Potomac, "Lincoln's Dream" of the future included the figurative beheading of Seward, Stanton, Welles, and Halleck.[36] Of these figures in the Lincoln administration, only General Halleck, general in chief of the Union armies, would eventually yield his position of leadership.

CRISIS IN MILITARY LEADERSHIP

From the outset of the war, Lincoln had sought, more or less in vain, to staff his army with competent generals. In the Army of the Potomac alone, Commanding Generals McDowell, McClellan, and Burnside had all fallen short of expectations. General Frémont did not last even one year, and Generals Pope, Banks, and Benjamin Butler were all severely criticized. In the midst of the frustration over Fredericksburg, this military game of musical chairs had become a national joke. Cartoonists at home (Confederate and Union) and abroad mined this theme for treasures of humor. There was ample ore to be had by all.

The *Southern Illustrated News* delighted in Lincoln's unresolved plight. A woodcut of "Schoolmaster Lincoln and His Boys" shows the president ready to spank the bandaged and broken McClellan, Banks, John Pope, and Burnside with the ruler of the "Constitution." A protracted caption divulges the grounds for punishment:

Lincoln.—Waal, boys, what's the matter with yer; you haint been hurt, hev yer? *McClellan.*—Them fellers that run away has been beatin' us. *Lincoln.*—What fellers? *McClellan.*— . . . Bob Lee took and bunged me in the eye. *Pope.*—And Stunwall Jackson he kicked me in the rear until he broke my arm. *Banks.*—Yes, and that same feller gouged me and run me until I run my leg off and hev to wear a wooden one. *Burnside.*—All of 'em, Bob Lee, Stunwall and Stuart, jumped on me at Fredericksburg and give me fits; that's the reason my jaw is tied up, to keep my teeth from chatterin', for I've had a fit of the ager ever since. *Lincoln.*—You are a worthless set, all of you. You haint no spunk. I'm agoin' to spank every one of yer. Come up here.[37]

The loss at Fredericksburg resulted in pressure to reform the army. For example, *Frank Leslie's Budget of Fun* portrayed "Uncle Abe trying to straighten things out." With a hot iron, Lincoln attempts to take the ghastly rumples out of the military fabric. To be sure, Lincoln promptly filled Burnside's shoes with General Hooker, and

"Schoolmaster Lincoln
and His Boys,"
*Southern Illustrated
News,* January 31, 1863,
8. Courtesy of the
Western Reserve
Historical Society.

popular illustrators duly noted the change. Meanwhile, the modern metaphor of an incessant revolving door of generals was set by Henry L. Stephens in the nineteenth-century context of the "U.S. Military Shaving Shop." As Burnside gets out of Stanton's barber chair and waits for Lincoln to brush off the clippings, Stanton, "the Head Barber," calls out "Next," and Hooker comes forward. The Confederate version shows Generals Scott, McDowell, Frémont, Banks, Pope, McClellan, and Burnside as puppets on the shelf.[38] The boyish clown is "Master Abraham Lincoln," who "gets a New Toy—Fighting Joe [Hooker]."

On February 13, 1863, when Mary Todd Lincoln held a reception at the White House for the famous diminutive newlywed couple Gen. Tom Thumb and his bride, Livinia Warren, a cartoonist, identified only by the initial "H," exploited the situation. "H" facetiously suggested that Phineas T. Barnum's popular dwarf tandem, Gen. Tom Thumb (Charles Sherwood Stratton) Hand Commodore Nutt, held the solution to the problem of impoverished military leadership. These two "Coming Men" were obvious choices to preside over the army and navy, respectively. Actually, according to the caption, it was the circus entrepreneur Phineas Barnum who was struck with the idea: "The Great Showman.—'Mr. President, since your military and naval heroes don't seem to get on, try mine!' Mr. Lincoln.—'Well, I will do it to oblige you, Friend Phineas, but I think mine are the smallest.'" In the background, Edwin Stanton and Gideon Welles are shaken by the overture.[39]

Other cartoons also belabored the contentiousness that had developed within the highest echelons of the North's armed forces. As war strategy and tactical battlefield

"Master Abraham Lincoln Gets a New Toy," *Southern Illustrated News*, February 28, 1863, 8. Courtesy of the Western Reserve Historical Society.

"The Coming Men," *Frank Leslie's Illustrated Newspaper*, February 28, 1863, 368. Author's Collection.

THE COMING MEN!

THE GREAT SHOWMAN—"*Mr. President, since your naval and military heroes don't seem to get on, try mine!*"
MR. LINCOLN—"*Well, I'll do it to oblige you, Friend Phineas, but I think mine are the smallest.*"

"Uncle Sam's Happy Family of Generals," *Frank Leslie's Budget of Fun*, March 1863, 8–9. Courtesy of the American Antiquarian Society.

execution are foiled, military morale suffers. Consonant with that decline, in *Frank Leslie's Budget of Fun* William Newman satirically displayed "Uncle Sam's Happy Family of Generals" engaged in wholesale fighting, bickering, and faultfinding. On the sidelines, Lincoln mutters, "My Generals Fight Well amongst Themselves, Which Reminds Me of a Little Joke." The same issue of the magazine made a "Tempting Offer for the Unemployed—A Good Smart Napoleon Wanted to Fight Battles, Win Victories, and Make Himself Generally Useful."[40] Such was the state of affairs in the winter of 1863, and spring confrontations of the following year perpetuated dissatisfaction with the management of the war.

In April, "seven monitors and one twin-case-mated experimental craft, the *Keokuk*," tested their mettle against the formidable firepower of the forts in Charleston Harbor. The Confederates won the ensuing battle. The barrage from the land artillery forced the damaged ironclad ship to withdraw to safer waters, and the abandoned *Keokuk* retired humbly to Davy Jones's locker. Offering a foreign editorial commentary on the affair, *Punch* billed the contest in Charleston harbor the "Great American Billiard Match," and John Tenniel's caricature of Lincoln and Davis called it the "Great 'Cannon Game.'" As Jeff Davis calmly strokes the last billiard ball to victory, he exclaims, "Hurrah for Charleston: that's another to me." A disappointed Lincoln wistfully concedes, "Darn'd if he ain't scored ag'in!—Wish I could make a *few winning* hazards for a change." The editorial emphatically gives the edge in the war to Jeff Davis and berates Lincoln for uninspired leadership: "Abe Lincoln may have skill, but he has not yet shown much of it: and certainly he more than once has shown himself out-generalled. His backers say he purposely is playing a slow game, just to draw out his opponent and see what he can do. In ninety days, they say, he is cock-sure of a victory: but this is an old boast, and nobody except themselves now place any faith in it. Abe's famous Bull Run stroke was a bad start to begin with, and his Charleston break has ended in his having to screw back, and thus slip into baulk to save himself from mischief." In *Fun,* Matt Morgan depicted Lincoln as a dog angrily fleeing from the shelling, with cans tied to his tail and the label *Ironside* and *Monitor* attached to him. Honest Abe attributes the blame to his fleet of ironsides, "I'm being licked tarnation well! Only 'cos my rudder won't act."[41]

It is not surprising that the habitually harsh British comic magazines scolded Lincoln for the debacle at Charleston. However, there was also disillusionment at home.

"The Great 'Cannon Game,'" *Punch,* May 9, 1863, 191. Author's Collection.

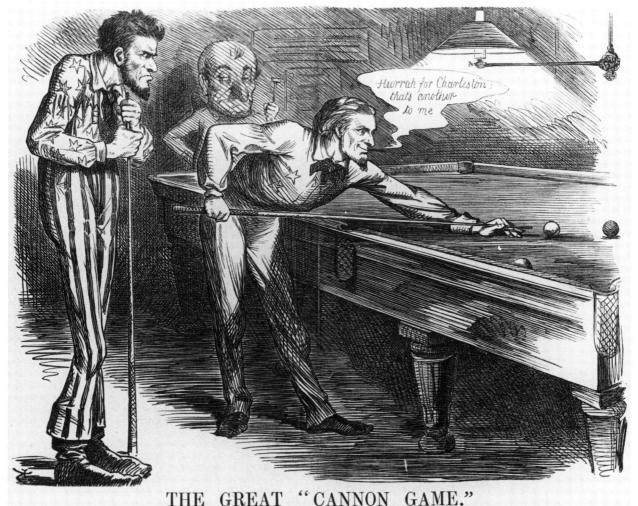

THE GREAT "CANNON GAME."

ABE LINCOLN (ASIDE). "DARN'D IF HE AIN'T SCORED AG'IN!—WISH I COULD MAKE A FEW *WINNING* HAZARDS FOR A CHANGE."

For instance, *Frank Leslie's Budget of Fun* diverted its wrath to the broad shoulders of Gideon Welles. The caption on a cartoon by E. Wyand modified Shakespeare: "All's Well That Ends Welles." The caricature viewed Mother Gideon Welles awkwardly mishandling the valuable "*Monitor* [Tea] Set." Accordingly, Uncle Sam admonishes, "Look here, Mr. Lincoln! That Old Woman is always in mischief—there goes one of my new set! You'd better get rid of her before she smashes everything we have got!"[42] In reality, Adm. Samuel F. Du Pont bore direct responsibility for the failed mission.

The bad news from Charleston hardly faded before Gen. Robert E. Lee beat "Fighting Joe" Hooker at Chancellorsville. The defeat reinforced the Army of the Potomac's tarnished reputation for ineffective generalship. As usual, Matt Morgan aimed his darts at Lincoln. He showed Lincoln and Chase disconsolately looking over their threadbare lists of generals for still another replacement: "Abe.—'Jee-Rusalem! Double or Quits on Hooker, and He's Hooked It.' Chase.—'Lost on All Our Hosses—Freeman, McClellan, Hooker. Oh! Snakes!' Widow.—'I Should Like to Know How They Will Settle with Me.'"[43] In June, Gen. George Meade replaced General Hooker. When would the cycle of defeat end?

"The Monitor Set in Danger; or, All's Well That Ends Welles," *Frank Leslie's Budget of Fun*, July 1863. Courtesy of the American Antiquarian Society.

UNCLE SAM—*"Look here, Mr. Lincoln! That Old Woman is always in mischief–there goes one of my new set! You'd better get rid of her before she smashes everything we have got!"*

THE SETTLING DAY.

Abe :—"JEE-RUSALEM! DOUBLE OR QUITS ON HOOKER, AND HE'S HOOKED IT."
Chase :—"LOST ON ALL OUR HOSSES—FREEMAN, M'CLELLAN, HOOKER. OH! SNAKES!"
Widow :—"I SHOULD LIKE TO KNOW HOW THEY WILL SETTLE WITH ME."

"The Settling Day,"
Fun, May 30, 1863, 105.
Courtesy of the
University of
Minnesota Libraries.

Actually, there was a much brighter and amusing side in contrast to this dismal appraisal. A four-panel caricature in *Frank Leslie's Budget of Fun* predicted that Lincoln would firmly seize the reins of leadership and confidently address the manifold problems of the nation, including the matter of military leadership. Half the panels in the illustration depict him setting out to reform the army and navy. First, as "General Commander in Chief," Lincoln stuffs Stanton into the ample barrel of a cannon to launch him into a new field of endeavor while General Halleck prays for mercy. Second, as "Head of the Naval Forces," Lincoln spares Gideon Welles from total administrative oblivion by waking him up with the scourging lashes of the whip.

AS GENERAL COMMANDER in CHIEF

He disposes of Mess.r Stanton and Halleck in a summary manner

AS HEAD of the NAVAL FORCES

He wakes up Old Mr Welles

AS HIS OWN MINISTER of FOREIGN AFFAIRS
He enforces the Monroe Doctrine

AS PRINCIPAL FINANCIER

With a view to the Early resumption of SPECIE Payments He melts down his Private Plate.

ABE LINCOLN IN HIS NEW CHARACTERS—WHAT HE IS BOUND TO DO.

"Abe Lincoln in His New Characters," *Frank Leslie's Budget of Fun*, May 1863, 9. Author's Collection.

Having addressed the military conundrum, the final two panels deal with Lincoln's roles as "His Own Minister of Foreign Affairs" and as "Principal Financier" of the war. On the diplomatic front, the third panel portrays Lincoln enforcing the "Monroe Doctrine" by kicking Napoleon from the New World to the Old. In the final panel, to the horror of his spouse, the president solves the nation's financial problems when "he melts down his Private Plate [silver] with a view to the early resumption of specie payments."[44]

Meanwhile, as Horace Greeley and other colleagues from the New York press continued to counsel Lincoln about his generals, *Vanity Fair* and *Frank Leslie's Illustrated Newspaper* came to the president's defense. The New York papers used the metaphor of a broom to suggest a clean sweep in Union generals. In a cartoon by John McLenan, when the White House butler announces to Lincoln that the "New York Editor's [are] outside with new brooms [generals] to offer," the president replies, "Hang their new brooms—the old one is good enough, yet!"[45] *Frank Leslie's Illustrated Newspaper* is even more specific. With the discarded brooms of McClellan, Pope, and Hooker on the floor of Lincoln's office, the president contentedly holds in his hand a broom labeled "Grant," and in the caption are the words "Right at Last." Text next to the cartoon further supported the president's judgment: "Greeley be hanged! I want no more new brooms. I begin to think that the worst thing about my *old* ones was in not being *handled* right." On Lincoln's desk is a bust of Horace Greeley, and on the wall is an advertisement: "Greeley, Weed & Company—Wholesale Jobbers in Brooms and other Stocks—McClellan, Pope, Burnside, Hooker."[46]

POTPOURRI OF IMAGES

The malady of war infected many parts of the body politic. The health of the economy, international relations, and domestic tranquility called for special care. Popular art monitored the president's treatment of instability in these areas. As usual, England's comic press, which had already impugned Lincoln's political health and chances for survival, tended toward a more dire prognosis. At home, the illustrated press was not afraid to examine the nation's problems and the state of the president's performance, but verdicts on both counts were more sanguine.

In the realm of finance, *Fun*'s Matt Morgan depicted Lincoln and Chase naively amassing an enormous pile of debt, and the president taking on the aura of a bewildered buffoon.[47] In America, for good reason, the public worried about inflation. From the beginning to the end of the Civil War, both the general price and wholesale farm price indexes in the North grew in a linear pattern.[48] In *Frank Leslie's Budget of Fun*, William Newman's "A Frightful Case of Inflation" highlighted civic

"Right at Last," *Frank Leslie's Illustrated Newspaper*, June 13, 1863, 192. Author's Collection.

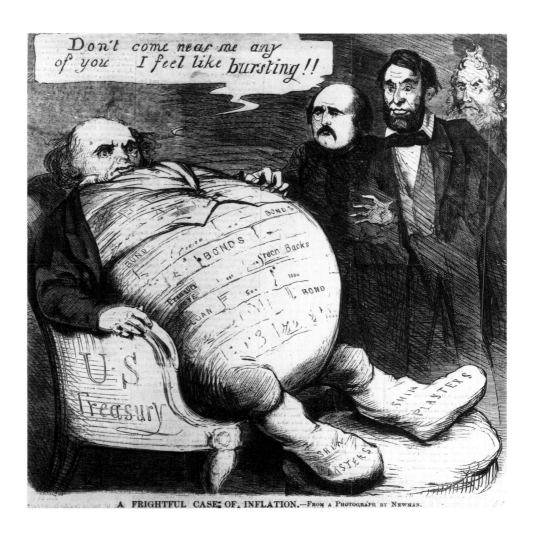

"A Frightful Case of Inflation," *Frank Leslie's Budget of Fun*, April 1863. Courtesy of the American Antiquarian Society.

concern: "Don't come near me any of you. I feel like bursting!! says Chase to Lincoln, Ben Butler, and Gideon Welles. Chases's bloated condition is caused by "greenbacks," "bonds," "treasury notes," and "loans." Nevertheless, in these cartoons the image of Lincoln is not demeaning. Furthermore, reassuring editorials in the news weeklies about the financial status of the nation must have offset some of the nation's economic uncertainty.[49]

In foreign affairs, the American illustrated press carried on a running battle with its media counterpart in England. Typical of imagery in the spring of 1863, three illustrations depict a resolute Lincoln standing firm against the threatened incursions of purported unprincipled interventionists from abroad. One *Harper's Weekly* cartoon by John McLenan depicts Lincoln, backed with a fifteen-inch cannon pointed at John Bull's midsection, summarily dismissing John Bull's attempt to bully the Union on the cotton issue. Another cartoon by E. F. Mullen shows Lincoln confronting John Bull about "England's Neutrality." On the dock are crates of "bombs," "steel-pointed shot," "muskets," "drugs," and "powder" destined for the "C.S.A." Prime Minister Palmerston and John Bull try to rationalize the subterfuge. John Bull claims they are "only boxing up a few harticles for the hemperor of China," but Lincoln is not deceived.[50] Finally, in "Our Administration and No Intervention," Lincoln, Seward, and Columbia hold fast to the anchors of the Constitution and the Monroe Doctrine as they repel the "insidious attempts of European intervention." *New York Illustrated News* artist M. Nevin "furnishes us with the following brief summing up of his allegory":

Secretary Seward, standing upon the Union Rock, and resting upon the Constitution, (under whose volume the Union soldier crawls to die,) repels ... the polite intercession of the wily Machiavel of modern monarchy, whose eager right hand holds the torch of anarchy. The consistent and friendly Emperor of Russia stands behind him—not in an attitude of menace, but of encouragement; with his sceptre elevated, as a warning beacon. The crafty policy of England is shown in the seeming indifference of its nominal chief—the Queen—while her eager guards, with the bearskin shakos and frowning visages, stand expectant of the fray. With a more modified ferocity, Napoleon's "Old Guard," in their panoply of steel armour,

"Our Administration and No Intervention," *New York Illustrated News*, March 14, 1863, 296–97. Courtesy of the Lincoln Museum (Ref. #3693).

await their master's bidding. The Russian Cossacks, on the distant hill, are merely picket observers of the anxious mass below. The most prominent chiefs of the Administration—Lincoln and Chase—stand close in support of Seward, while the Genius of Liberty strangles the Hydra of Rebellion, whose last fold is still around its loyal victim. The retreating Rebels in the background indicate the un-fettered energy of the Goddess in her retributive justice.[51]

One isolated image also deserves mention. The antebellum women's suffrage movement had gained considerable momentum before the outbreak of the Civil War. However, out of deference to the national crisis Susan B. Anthony and Elizabeth Cady Stanton reluctantly decided to defer their drive for suffrage until after the war. This decision stifled and delayed antisuffrage caricature in the illustrated press; how-ever, there were occasional exceptions. One of those rarities, "A Fit for the Ladies League," appeared in *Vanity Fair*. This satirical cartoon by J. H. Howard shows Lin-coln offering a pair of his long pants to the women. "Mr. Lincoln (to Mrs. Mannikens of the business community) 'Well, Ma'am, as the articles you wear don't seem to be large enough for you, I have the honor to present you, by the advice of Mrs. Lincoln, with a pair of mine. They may seem very large, but, at the rate you are progressing, you'll fill them very well by and by!'"[52] Due to the circumstances, Lincoln's level of tolerance was not challenged on this issue.

However, his patience was abundantly tested by the Copperheads. As the North's military goals were frustrated time and again, aversion to war and attraction to a negotiated peace became more appealing to some of Lincoln's opponents. In a car-toon by J. H. Howard, Horace Greeley lauds W. C. Jewett's relatively early overture toward peace: "Nurse Greeley (to Dr. Jewett)—'Well, doctor, I really think, as the patient seems to get worse under Doctors Stanton and Halleck, he can't do better than take your physic!'" However, "Old Abe don't see it." However, compared to the Copperheads, who were largely concentrated in the peace arm of the Democratic Party, Jewett's initiative was only a minor irritation. Ultimately, suspension of the writ of habeas corpus and arrest of the war's foes ignited widespread dissent.[53] The volatile issue of civil liberties came to a head with Clement Vallandigham's arrest.

As early as January 1862, before the Copperhead label came into vogue, *Vanity Fair* had equated "Vallandighamism" with treason:

To aid rebellion day by day
Yet meanly clutch at Union pay;
To stand erect—a living lie
And seem secession to decry,
Still using against Law and Right
The weapons of the hypocrite;
To stand aloof from dangerous strife
And back-stab at the Country's life;

NURSE GREELEY (to Dr. Jewett)—" *Well, doctor, I really think, as the patient seems to get worse under Doctors Stanton and Halleck, he can't do better than take your physic!*"

[Old Abe don't see it.]

"Nurse Greeley (to Dr. Jewett)," *Frank Leslie's Budget of Fun*, May 1863, 12. Author's Collection.

Concord to hate, and worship schism;
This, this is Vallandighamism.[54]

In time, the potent Copperhead sobriquet replaced this pejorative label and tarred more than Vallandigham with the brush of disloyalty. The accusations cut a wide swath: among the accused were prominent people like Fernando and Ben Wood, and Governor Horatio Seymour of New York. Also, newspapers like the *New York Daily*

News, New York World, New York Express, and *New York Herald* were perceived as being among those laced with Copperhead inclinations or sympathy.

In general, the illustrated press formed a broad, united phalanx against the Copperheads. *Phunny Phellow* was incensed that a few extreme Northern voices could utter with impunity the words "Abe Lincoln Ought to Be Hung." *Harper's Weekly* sarcastically featured a "Great Copperhead Orator foaming at the mouth," urging his compatriots to "crush the Lincoln despotism!" For *Vanity Fair,* John McLenan depicted Fernando Wood as "An Extinguished [not distinguished] Visitor to the White House."[55] In "One Kind of Patriotism," another cartoonist pictured Lincoln being mugged by the Democratic Party. The caption explicated the motive: "Resolved, that, as Democrats, we are determined to adopt no affirmative policy, but merely to embarrass the Government by every means in our power, and especially by sympathizing with Traitors, and trying in every way to tie the hands of the President! Resolved, that we base our claim to popular favor on the slowness and inefficiency of the administration in putting down the rebellion." Finally, John McLenan chided the "weak-kneed editors of New York," including Horace Greeley, for being soft on the Copperheads. For such behavior, these editors, plus Fernando Wood, saw the "Handwriting on the Wall"—a stint in the Fort Lafayette prison, courtesy of Abraham Lincoln.[56]

In 1863, the major cause celebre of the so-called Copperheads was the arrest of Clement Vallandigham because of a speech he delivered against the war. After Lincoln banished Vallandigham from the Union to the Confederacy, and Jefferson Davis eventually sent him back north, the presses responded with caricature. *Frank Leslie's Illustrated Newspaper* cast the event as a "Rare Old Game of Shuttlecock." This was a badminton contest at the Mason-Dixon line between "Jeff" and "Abe," with Clement Vallandigham as the shuttlecock: "Jeff.—'No good sending him here. I'll have to send him back.' Abe.—'He's none of mine, anyhow.'"[57] However, the most novel caricature of the incident was the talented William Newman's "A Hard Case—Vallandigham's Reception by His Friend Jeff." While Copperhead snakes nip at "Clem Vallandigham, Passenger to Dixie," Lincoln admonishes, "There now Val—Vanish! Dry Up! You've had so much to say for YOUR FRIEND JEFF. You had better go & live with him." A humbled Vallandigham replies, "I don't want to go; I am a union man NOW." From across the border, Jeff Davis calls out, "No! No! Go back again. We do not want you! 'Twas all very well as long as we could MAKE USE of you ON THE OTHER SIDE."[58] In the long run, Vallandigham survived to run for governor of Ohio in 1864.

One of the strongest anti-Copperhead messages, "A Hint to Father Abraham," came from Thomas Nast. As commander in chief, Lincoln, according to the cartoon, put the Copperheads on the defensive with a full-fledged bayonet assault from the Union army. Fernando Wood, Ben Wood, James Gordon Bennett, the Honorable C. L. Vallandigham, J. Brooks of the *New York Express,* and the editor of the *New York World* are sent on the "Road to Dixie" with a chorus of epithets trailing after them: "Copperheads, Liars, Cowards, Vermin, Blackguards, Scoundrels, Thieves, Traitors but not Democrats, Rebels at Home, and False Men." Nast's advice to "Father

A RARE OLD GAME OF SHUTTLECOCK.
JEFF—"No good sending him here. I'll have to send him back."
ABE—"He's none of mine, anyhow."

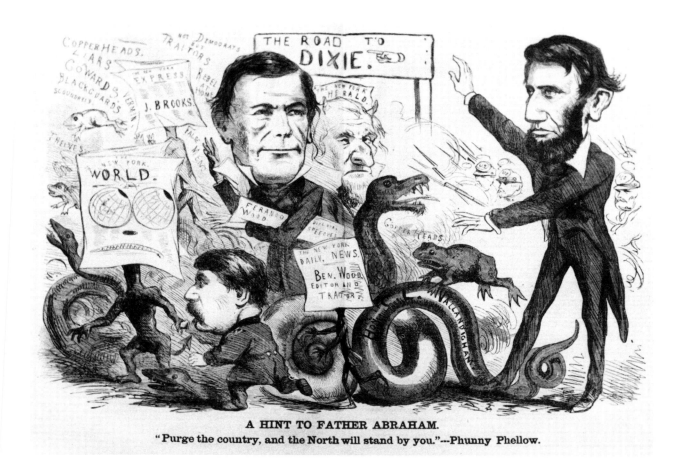

A HINT TO FATHER ABRAHAM.
"Purge the country, and the North will stand by you."---Phunny Phellow.

Abraham" offered even more compelling support against the Copperheads: "Purge the country, and the North will stand by you.—*Phunny Phellow.*[59]

With the exception of McClellan's victory at Antietam in September 1862, a year of almost continuous setbacks on the eastern front (summer 1862 to summer 1863) produced a spate of political caricature, doggerel, and satire that assailed Lincoln. Fredericksburg instigated the political bloodletting, and the failure to find competent military leadership perpetuated it. Actually, although Lincoln was discredited at Fredericksburg, his subordinates—cabinet officers and generals—took the brunt of the criticism. Nevertheless, until the crisis in military leadership passed and Union forces altered the war's momentum, Lincoln's leadership as commander in chief was impugned.

Notwithstanding, the president was surprisingly resilient to whims of public opinion expressed in the Northern illustrated press. On controversial issues such as the suspension of habeas corpus, military arrests, Copperhead sentiment, foreign affairs, financial stability, and the management of the war he received much more favorable treatment in the illustrated magazines than in some newspapers. If not always partisan, both the comic and serious genres were surprisingly fair to Lincoln. They often blunted the criticism of powerful editors like Horace Greeley and James Gordon

Bennett and ignored or repelled the constant thrusts of the British press. While the liberal cannons of caricature preserved the artists' prerogative of self-expression, major illustrators like William Newman, Frank Bellew, Thomas Nast, Henry L. Stephens, John McLenan, J. H. Howard, and E. F. Mullen forged, on balance, a dignified image. Lincoln was not always the recipient of unqualified adulation, but neither was he the butt of indiscriminate carping. *Harper's Weekly* had become his most ardent advocate, but as yet he had no real enemies among the illustrated magazines of the North. From Bull Run to the eve of Gettysburg, despite such vagaries of war as Fredericksburg, the powerful Northern illustrated magazines' visual image of Lincoln was, on balance, respectable.

The victory at Antietam gave the North an unanticipated subtle edge and freed Lincoln to announce the preliminary Emancipation Proclamation. In the long run, this incisive decision changed the balance of power, and hence the complexion and outcome of the war. It also affected another dimension of Lincoln's public stature, and illustrators and writers documented the complex reactions to emancipation in illustrated periodicals from the North, South, and England.

Six

The Evolution of Emancipation

incoln's evolving policy of emancipation was grounded in a solid bedrock of values. The central ideal that drove him toward freedom for black people was articulated in several ways. "We proposed to give all a chance," he declared, "and we expected the weak to grow stronger, the ignorant wiser, and all better, and happier together." In his eulogy of Henry Clay, Lincoln expressed admiration for Clay's "strong sympathy with the oppressed everywhere, and . . . ardent wish for their elevation." This "right to rise," as Gabor Boritt so aptly put it, was the cornerstone of Lincoln's motivation for emancipation, and is the foundation of growth and development for all human beings. Collectively, these concepts were compatible to the historic Declaration of Independence. "I believe," affirmed Lincoln, "the declaration that 'all men are created equal' is the great fundamental principle upon which our free institutions rest, [and] that . . . slavery is violative of that principle."[1] This grand governing constellation of ideals animated his construction of emancipation policy.

Other values tempered the pace and scope of the president's strategy. Lincoln's interpretation of and commitment to the Constitution set limits for change. "By our frame of government," he wrote, "the States which have slavery are to retain it, or surrender it at their own pleasure, and that all others—individuals, free-states and national government—are constitutionally bound to leave them alone about it." The priority that Lincoln accorded to the preservation, and later, the restoration of the Union relative to the cessation of slavery also delineated the propriety of tactical discretion: "Well I, too, go for saving the Union. Much as I hate slavery, I would consent to the extension of it rather than see the Union dissolved, just as I would consent to any great evil, to avoid a greater one." Throughout his political career Lincoln strove to avoid any policy that jeopardized national unity, even if it meant that emancipation would be delayed. However, he would not hesitate to accelerate the timetable if emancipation facilitated union. Furthermore, Lincoln's sensitivity to the interests of both slave and slaveholder suggested a slower tempo for change. As early as 1854 he had argued "that the Southern slaveholders were neither better, nor worse than we of the North, and that we of the North were no better than they. If we were situated as they are, we should act and feel as they do, and if they were situated as we are, they should act and feel as we do; and we never ought to lose sight of this fact in discussing the subject."[2] True to such empathy, the president never abandoned this notion, which was most articulately reflected in the memorable phrase from his second inaugural address, "with malice toward none, and charity for all." Neither slaves nor slaveholders were omitted from his purview. Out of this fertile, expansive seedbed of values came the president's initial moderate policy of containment; his plan for voluntary, gradual, and compensated emancipation; the preliminary emancipation; the Emancipation Proclamation; his backing of the Thirteenth Amendment to the Constitution; and his vision of reconstruction.

Lincoln's position on emancipation was also forged from a complex array of external forces. On the one hand, the president's stance was too moderate for his Radical Republican colleagues, who considered it an agonizing frustration. On the other hand, his philosophy was too radical for the Democratic Party, many in the border states, and more conservative voices among the Republicans. Social pressures from one end of the political spectrum to the other pushed and pulled Lincoln. The lobbying was intense and ran the gamut from personal to public persuasion. Political caricature in the domestic and foreign press was only one of the forms it took. Editorial rhetoric, open letters to the president in newspapers, doggerel, military proclamations from Lincoln's generals, and a host of other messages were used to persuade the besieged president. For a man of principle given to melancholy, this relentless critique was sheer agony.

Of course, the acts of secession and war only intensified the pressure and complicated decision making. Ironically, secession actually expedited the process and broadened the scope of emancipation, and the protracted Civil War provided a constitutional justification. Only when Lincoln saw emancipation as a military necessity within the broad framework of the Constitution was emancipation deemed an instrument to restore the Union and end the war. Only then could the president announce his intention to issue the Emancipation Proclamation. Although the decision was extolled in some quarters, a decline in the stock market, difficulty in attracting army recruits, and the dubious performance of Lincoln's political party in the election of 1862 gave the president little immediate consolation.[3] Just as evidence of progress on the battlefield proceeded lethargically, the fruits of emancipation matured slowly.

Against this dramatic backdrop of events, the images in the illustrated press illuminate dynamic forces at play in the evolution of emancipation. What support did the unauthorized emancipation initiatives of Generals Frémont and Hunter elicit? What were the predominant images in reaction to Lincoln's proposal of compensated emancipation, preliminary emancipation, and the Emancipation Proclamation?

Slightly more than one month after Fort Sumter, the exigencies of war quickly raised the question of what the government should do about slaves who infiltrated federal lines from the Confederacy. Were they contraband, as General Butler considered them? If so, were they free and could they be used in the war? What was the status of the Fugitive Slave Law? Among others, these perplexities nurtured the debate over emancipation.

General Frémont's unilateral military order to free the slaves in his jurisdiction intensified debate. After Lincoln nullified Frémont's premature proclamation, duplicate unsigned cartoons in *Frank Leslie's Illustrated Newspaper* and *Frank Leslie's Budget of Fun* caricatured the president. Tossed overboard from Frémont's ship of proclamation, Lincoln, wearing the life preserver of the Union, survives; yet the president refuses to rescue the symbolic, drowning "Sambo." In fact, while "Fremont's Proclamation" sinks into oblivion, Lincoln pushes "Sambo" under. "I'm sorry to have to drop you, Sambo, but this concern [the Union] won't carry us both."[4]

"I'm Sorry to Have to Drop You, Sambo," *Frank Leslie's Illustrated Newspaper*, October 12, 1861, 352. Author's Collection.

Although few enjoyed humor quite like the president, he would not have appreciated the cartoon's implication that he was abandoning African American interests. Lincoln had explained to Frémont that "there is great danger that the closing paragraph [in Frémont's proclamation] in relation to the confiscation of property, and the liberating slaves of traitorous owners will alarm our Southern Union friends, and turn them against us."[5] Moreover, the president properly concluded that General Frémont had no authority to emancipate slaves. Two weeks after its initial cartoon on the matter, *Frank Leslie's Illustrated Newspaper* ascribed Frémont's action to political ambition. His elbow resting on the Constitution, Lincoln chides Frémont for seeking the 1864 presidential nomination so early. "Well, Master Fremont, that's a rather long reach ain't it? You may fetch it [the presidency], with your sword, perhaps at the proper time, but it isn't ripe yet."[6] *Phunny Phellow* also supported Lincoln's decision. One if its cartoons caricatured "Fremont as a Prestidigitator," magically freeing the slaves in "The Great Chain Trick."[7] Although Frémont's impetuous action was not allowed to stand, the pressure for some form of emancipation escalated.

Exemplifying the clamor from Lincoln's detractors for a more aggressive policy on slavery was a cartoon in the February 1862 issue of *Frank Leslie's Budget of Fun*. Here Frank Bellew suggested that slavery would not go away easily. In the cartoon, Lincoln, apparently diverted from care about slavery, is startled by the loud bleating of a black sheep [labeled slavery] directly in his ear. "Long Abe—'Oh, Thunder! Here's that darned Black Sheep again!'" The text above the cartoon suggests that the sheep represents something more powerful than slavery, however. The text argues that the black sheep in the cartoon is "the famous Greeley ram, Abolition, which our young friend Triangle [Frank Bellew] has sketched." Parenthetically, the docile sheep dog in front of the "Unhappy Shepherd," Lincoln, is General McClellan. McClellan's Radical Republican opponents were unsatisfied with his military leadership, as well as his more casual, conservative philosophical position toward slavery.[8]

In fact, Lincoln had not been diverted from the issue of emancipation. As early as December 1861, the president had confided to Senators Orville H. Browning and Charles Sumner that he was preparing a document based on compensated emancipation.[9] Because the president's plan was voluntary, it was compatible with the earlier Crittenden Resolution, which had passed both the House and Senate and which had declared that the North had no intention of interfering with slavery where it existed. Lincoln hoped that the voluntary, gradual, and compensation incentives would appeal to slaveholders. If so, the essential motivation for slavery, and perhaps even civil war, might be reduced. On March 6, 1862, Lincoln's proposal was sent to Congress.

Although some questioned the feasibility of financing the proposal, *Harper's Weekly* reported that the president's "message has been applauded with equal fervor by the opponents and by the supporters of slavery. It is equally approved by the *Herald* and by the *Tribune*, by the *Evening Post*, and by the *Journal of Commerce*."[10] The House and the Senate seemed to agree and passed appropriate legislation.

Nevertheless, enthusiasm for emancipation varied. For example, William H. Davenport's front-page illustration in the *Comic Monthly* pictured an incensed president

THE PET LAMB AND THE BLACK SHEEP; OR, THE UNHAPPY SHEPHERD.
Long Abe—"OH, THUNDER! HERE'S THAT DARNED BLACK SHEEP AGAIN!"

"The Pet Lamb and the Black Sheep; or, the Unhappy Shepherd," *Frank Leslie's Budget of Fun*, February 1862. McLellan Lincoln Collection, Brown University Library.

holding up an emblem of slavery as the root "Cause and Effect, the Head and Front of the War." Clearly, Lincoln's censorious expression targets Senator Charles Sumner, a proponent of abolition.[11] The president wanted emancipation, but on his own terms and according to his own timetable. Of course, if slavery was the root cause of the war, to remove this blot from the nation was tantamount to ending the war.

Likewise, a cartoon in *Phunny Phellow* expresses relief that the form of emancipation Lincoln initially proposed was conservative. The cartoon heralds Lincoln as the "Guardian" of "the Consititution" against the likes of Horace Greeley and his radical views of emancipation. In another cartoon, this one in *Frank Leslie's Illustrated Newspaper*, Uncle Sam facetiously promotes compensated emancipation: "Bub, there's a quarter for you, and now go and let that poor black bird loose." In the *New York Illustrated News*, Thomas Nast credits "Emancipation" as "Doctor Lincoln's New Elixir of Life—for [slaves in] the Southern States."Lincoln administers the life-giving medication from the cup of "Emancipation" to an afflicted, symbolic denizen of slavery.[12]

Vanity Fair also supported Lincoln's proposal, but unlike the president, it was tainted by harsh racist language. The magazine accused Horace Greeley and Radical

Republicans of "Nigger worship": "We hardly think that the 'Onward to Richmond' men will be delighted at the prospect held out by the President. Gradual Abolition, like cautious Generalship, is distasteful to such hot-headed young fellows as the Editor of the *Tribune,* for instance; and the possibility of there being no chained Nigger for them to worship, by-and-by, may drive these philosophers to their wit's end for a substitute. Meanwhile, all sensible men must congratulate the President upon his project of removing the Black Border from the map of the United States."[13] Though the motives varied, the domestic illustrated press generally gave Lincoln high marks for his gradual, compensated emancipation scheme, if not for colonization. Still, many of the illustrations and much of the rhetoric continued to exhibit considerable contempt and condescension for black Americans—convincing evidence of national ambivalence toward greater freedom for slaves.

Abroad, the press was more critical. In fact, from the Civil War's inception, before emancipation became a central concern, England's comic press had misconstrued Lincoln's views about black Americans. One of *Punch*'s earliest Lincoln images, "The

CAUSE AND EFFECT.
The Head and Front of the War.

"Cause and Effect," *Comic Monthly,* April 1862, front page. C. Fiske Harris Collection on the American Civil War and Slavery, Providence Public Library.

"Doctor Lincoln's New Elixir of Life—for the Southern States," *New York Illustrated News,* April 12, 1862, 368. Courtesy of the New York State Library.

DOCTOR LINCOLN'S NEW ELIXIR OF LIFE—FOR THE SOUTHERN STATES.

American Difficulty," depicted the president lamenting the presence of African Americans in the nation more than their treatment by fellow Americans. "President Abe: 'What a nice White House this would be if it were not for the Blacks!'"[14] More than likely, this was the cartoonist's own racist view projected upon the American president. After all, racism was an international phenomenon.

However, *Punch* also perceived ulterior motives in Lincoln's emancipation program. Popular illustrator John Tenniel had "Oberon" (Lincoln) using a slave (emancipation) as "my henchman." In contrast, "Titania" (Miss Virginia) rejects the overture for compensated emancipation: "Set your heart at rest, the Northern land buys not the [black] child of me." In addition, *Punch* also thought "cash-emancipation" was an impossible financial burden.[15] To the tune of *Yankee Doodle,* the lyricist made the case against compensated emancipation.

> Though not yet clear which stump I'll take,
> That Stump shall be colossal,
> Whether I'm Slavery's advocate,
> Or Liberty's Apostle.
> If I conclude to free the Blacks
> By cash-emancipation,
> Guess I'll run up the biggest bill
> That e'er mocked liquidation
> Yankee Doodle-do is done,

Yankee Doodle dandy;
Here's Mr. Chase in bankrupt case,
And finds your dollars handy![16]

In April, the gathering momentum for emancipation produced more legislation: Lincoln signed a bill, passed by Congress, to abolish slavery in the District of Columbia. Perhaps emboldened by this new wave of liberation, General Hunter, like his predecessor, General Frémont, also abolished slavery within his command. However,

OBERON AND TITANIA.

OBERON (MR. PRESIDENT LINCOLN). "I DO BUT BEG A LITTLE **NIGGER** BOY,
TO BE MY HENCHMAN."

TITANIA (MISS VIRGINIA). "SET YOUR HEART AT REST,
THE **NORTHERN** LAND BUYS NOT THE CHILD OF ME."

"Oberon and Titania," *Punch*, April 5, 1862, 207. Author's Collection.

Lincoln swiftly bridled the general by rescinding Hunter's general order. The comic press also took exception to Hunter's rash initiative. In *Frank Leslie's Budget of Fun*, Frank Bellew caricatured the general as "A Humane but Officious Hunter." The caption contained Lincoln's reproof: "Now then, you boy, that burd [slaves] ain't yours—What do you let her loose for? I'll have you understand that, when I want any burds let loose, I'll let them loose myself." The cartoonist effectively used spelling errors (burd, burds) and slang (ain't) to link Lincoln with the backwoods stereotype, but General Hunter took the brunt of the censure. Parenthetically, again slaves were demeaned by pejorative imagery (the black bird was labeled "Everlastin Nigger").[17]

Vanity Fair also praised Lincoln's resolute action. In addition, it scolded Hunter for his "impudence." The last verse of "Abe and Abolition" chided General Hunter in the racist jargon of the day.

> Upon the whole his Ebony faux pas
> Was scarce more impudent than idiotic,
> "He went for wool to come back shorn" Oh! Bah!
> Was it quick-witted to be thus Quixotic?
> What a reverse! But yesterday supreme,
> Promulging law like Moses from Mount Sinai,
> Today not merely a white joker's theme,
> But food for laughter e'en to Cuff and Dinah.
> Thus do Dave Hunter's prospects to the D—— go,
> Moral—Abe tolerates no alter ego.[18]

Although Lincoln did not countenance the insubordination of General Hunter, he did use the occasion to warn rebellious Southern states that unless they acquiesced to his offer for compensated emancipation they risked more austere measures. *Harper's Weekly*'s analysis of the president's offer left little room for misunderstanding. "He appeals to the people of the slaveholding States to accept the generous offer made to them by Congress while it is yet time. The 'signs of the times' . . . point to the abolition of an institution which is not in harmony with the spirit of the age or reconcilable with the peace of the country. It is for the Slave States to decide whether they will run the risk of having it abolished under the war power, with suddenness and disaster, and without compensation, or whether they will have the sagacity to anticipate necessity, and avail themselves of a Congressional subsidy."[19] Obviously, Lincoln was seriously contemplating the next logical step.

In June 1862, the steady erosion of slavery's foundations continued with legislation that abolished slavery in the territories. Then, in July, the Confiscation Act incorporated major emancipationist features. For example, any slaves within Union lines who were economically sustained by sources that assisted the Rebel cause would be set free. The act also authorized the president to use African Americans as he saw fit to promote Union goals. In *Punch,* "Brother Jonathan's Appeal to Brother Sambo," a condescending oxymoron, satirically envisioned an expanded role for African Americans in the Civil War. The piece was drenched with racial ambivalence. On the

"A Humane but
Officious Hunter,"
*Frank Leslie's Budget of
Fun,* June 1862, 9.
Author's Collection.

one hand, the doggerel gave lip service to freedom, emancipation, brotherhood, and equality in public accommodations. On the other hand, it used vulgar and demeaning racial jargon of the period to put blacks in their place and raise the ubiquitous fears of miscegenation.

Neow, SAMBO, darn it—Brother! There,
I guess that oughter please you:
You know how we in airnest air
From slavery to ease you.

You know we al'ys hev proclaimed
One man's as good as 'nother,
And never hev we felt ashamed
To greet you as a brother.

You know that every slave we've riz,
We hev emancipated;
For ourn the land of Freedom is,
Where all air equal rated

You know between ourselves and you
We've drawn no social line here,
Same car by rail serves for the two,
Same room for both to dine here.

You know we love our gals toe find,
With niggers go a-courtin',
That's nothin' haaf so to our mind—
It's truth that I'm reportin'.

You know in this oncivil war
Your battle 'tis we're fightin',
Your cause we air a-strivin' for,
Your wrongs we air a-rightin'.

Wal, victory our arms has crowned,
Though at some cost in taxes;
And neow we've got on rebel ground
Some help of you we axes.

Up, Niggers! Slash, smash, sack and smite,
Slogdollagise and slay 'em:
Them Southern skunks ain't much toe fight,
So at 'em, darn em! Flay 'em![20]

The visual counterpart to the rhyme was typical of the editorial brevity of the cartoon medium. John Tenniel's "One Good Turn Deserves Another" depicts "Old

Abe" getting right to the point, handing "Sambo" weapons to go to war. "Why I du declare it's my dear old friend Sambo! Course you'll fight for us, Sambo. Lend us a hand, old hoss, du!"[21] Although the president did not immediately use former slaves to bolster the North's military power, this option was readily available at Lincoln's discretion.

"One Good Turn Deserves Another," *Punch*, August 9, 1862, 55. Author's Collection.

ONE GOOD TURN DESERVES ANOTHER.

Old Abe. "WHY I DU DECLARE IT'S MY DEAR OLD FRIEND SAMBO! COURSE YOU'LL FIGHT FOR US, SAMBO. LEND US A HAND, OLD HOSS, DU!"

Independently, the president, disillusioned with the negligible results of compensated emancipation, seized the initiative he had already threatened to implement. He was now ready for the next level, involuntary emancipation. In July, he announced his decision to his cabinet, but he acceded to Secretary of State Seward's recommendation that he postpone the plan until a decisive Union military victory gave more force to this significant change in policy. Unfortunately, that victory did not come until September. Meanwhile, Horace Greeley was growing impatient. Not knowing that a presidential proclamation for preliminary emancipation was imminent, the colorful *Tribune* editor threw down the gauntlet, challenging the president's leadership on this issue. Greeley accused Lincoln of dragging his feet while millions suffered. In turn, Lincoln, concealing his emancipation decision, calmly defended his first priority of union over slavery, asserting that he would resort to involuntary emancipation only if it promoted union and hastened the end of the war.[22]

In general, the illustrated press rushed to the president's defense. *Harper's Weekly* called Greeley's letter "impertinent and very injudicious" and speculated that "Mr. Lincoln will undoubtedly find himself supported by the bulk of the people of the country."[23] *Frank Leslie's Budget of Fun* simply satirized, in verse, the "Correspondence between the President and Horace Greeley," chiding the *Tribune* editor's version of abolition.

> *Horace Greeley, Esq., to his Excellency A. Lincoln*
> Dear Mr. President—It seems to me
> You're very wrong, sir, since we don't agree,
> I want to know if you'll make free and great
> That race which wears short wool upon the pate?
> And also, will you, too put down the knaves
> Now in rebellion, arm our noble slaves?
> That is to say, will you, apart from Crambo,
> Emancipate my dear old friend, our Sambo—
> And prove our great Republic richer, finer,
> By making a great lady out of Dinah?
> And while I've got my pen I here demand
> You make the blacks the white folks of the land.
> You'll never put the scamp, Jeff Davis, down
> Until you elevate the black and brown;
> For I agree with friend Johnny Forney,
> The loveliest of complexions is a tawny;
> And, holding these opinions, 'tis your duty
> To sacrifice the white folks for the sooty.
> I've therefore written this short note to thee,
> That you may know my sentiments.

P.S. If you'll reply to this Horation Caper,
'Twill sell a large edition of my paper.

The President's Reply
The letter you addressed to me, old spoon,
Was duly read by me in the *Tribune*.
If there be any statements in't that I
Know to be false, I won't say now you lie;
And if the inferences drawn aren't true,
I don't intend to argue now with you;
And if it show a dictatorial spirit,
As I believe your heart is right, I'll bear it.
As for the policy I'm pursuing,
I know, sir, very well what I am doing.
I mean to save the union—none should doubt it—
And mean to go the shortest way about it:
The sooner that the Union is restored,
The sooner it will be so, take my word.
Should some refuse to save it, sir, unless
They can save slavery too, they're wrong, I guess;
Should others think it's not worth shucks, without
They can slavery to the right about,
I don't agree with them. Apart from knavery,
I'm for the Union, and don't care for slavery.
If I could save the Union, and not free
A single darkey, that's the way for me.
If I could save it, too, by freeing all,
I'd do it, or I'm not six feet four tall;
And I would do it could I free some blacks,
And leave the others bound as tight as wax.
What I shall do about them, or have done,
Has been in hopes to save the U-ni-on;
And what I haven't done, and shall not do,
Has had the self-same purpose full in view.[24]

Vanity Fair was more emphatic. A cartoon by Henry L. Stephens characterized Horace Greeley as "The Monotonous Minstrel." To Greeley, President Lincoln remonstrates: "Go away, you tiresome vagrant! It's always the same old croaking tune, 'Abolition, Abolition, Marching On!'" In another illustration from the same issue, William Cullen Bryant and Horace Greeley are pictured sculpting a presidential replacement for Lincoln in the 1864 race. In their "unfinished work of art," they have created an "Original Design for President, Major General John C. Fremont."[25] But

The Monotonous Minstrel.

perhaps the cleverest piece, a rhyme entitled "The Late Triangular Duel," was published in *Vanity Fair*, which added a third dimension, the Democratic Party, to the Lincoln-Greeley exchange. The rhyme realistically caught the president between the cross fire of the Democrats and Radical Republicans, but portrayed Lincoln diplomatically holding his own. The verses perceptively depicted the impossibility of pleasing the proponents of both contradictory ideological positions.

First Shot at the President by Greeley and Co.
If you'll free the slave at once,
We'll call you wise, if not a dunce.

Four million heroes wait your nod—
Say they are free, and then thank God!
If you from fear decline to act,
Why not at once announce the fact?
If slavery be not killed by Fall,
Why then the Union's gone: that's all!
                        [Nobody hurt.]

Second Shot at Lincoln, by Democratic Committee
If you forsake your senses now,
And to the *Tribune* idol bow,
The outraged world with fervent hate
Your ill-starred name will execrate.
What! Wisdom shun and justice, too,
To please this Heaven-forsaken crew!
Shall weak philanthropy prevail
On such a monstrous, frightful scale?
If thus the Union you would save,
We'd rather you would dig its grave!
                        [Nobody hurt.]

Third Shot—A Double-Header, by the President
No angry meteor turns my sight
From that pure altar's steady light,
Whereon the flame of duty burns,
And all my heart's best homage earns.
That altar is my Country's Cause—
The cause of Union and her laws:
Whatever helps this cause, I do,
And do not aught with other view.
Slavery, with me, or fails or stands,
Just as the Union Cause demands.
            [The assailing parties put their hands to the spot where the heart
is supposed to be, and turn milky blue.]²⁶

That *Vanity Fair*'s intention all along was to lobby vigorously for the president's gradual, compensated emancipation policy is evident from an earlier, unequivocal editorial. It specifically targeted the abolitionists:

We consider that the so-called "abolition" journals are, for the most part, traitors to their country and abettors of treason, their energies being very generally directed to the purpose of tripping up President Lincoln, by digging trap-holes in the field over which he and his Right-hand Man are steadily advancing to victory.

We insist that nothing sensible was ever suggested on the subject of abolishing slavery, until President Lincoln issued that message to Congress containing his famous Dissolving View, or gradual emancipation policy. Our duty be it to uphold that policy, which we think we can best effect by slashing and cutting around with a two-edged weapon amid the tumultuous throng of soi-disant "abolitionists," who object to the abolition of slavery by gradual process, because that is the only way in which it is ever likely to be abolished. . . . And the affable reader will please take this record of our sentiments as an absolute platform, based upon the great scientific principle of "The Union First."[27]

Meanwhile in Europe, *Punch* misconstrued Lincoln's reply to Greeley as doublethink. The president had opposed slavery; now, they reasoned, he was refuting it.

"What Will He Do with Them?" *Vanity Fair*, October 4, 1862, 163. Author's Collection.

WHAT WILL HE DO WITH THEM?

A. L.—"Darn these here blackbirds!—if nobody won't buy 'em I'll have to open the cages and let 'em fly!"

This is what Lincoln writes to Horace,
Somebody make a glossary for us,
Ignorant owls we are:
For the North has been ranting, raving, blaring,
Scolding, swaggering, cussing, swearing,
Because Britannia was not sharing
In the Anti-Slavery War.[28]

Soon the president removed any doubt about his determined stance on slavery when he announced his policy on preliminary emancipation.

PRELIMINARY EMANCIPATION

If the Greeley-Lincoln exchange of letters on emancipation had lulled the nation into believing that Lincoln would maintain his moderate course, it was gravely mistaken. Lincoln had warned slaveholders that they must take advantage of gradual, compensated emancipation or suffer the consequences. Because there were no volunteers for the president's magnanimous offer, the victory at Antietam gave Lincoln the freedom to proceed. Rebellious states had one hundred days to contemplate the radical alternative of immediate, involuntary emancipation, but they must act.[29]

Vanity Fair's cartoon, "What Will He Do with Them?" correctly ascribed the policy change to the lack of public support for compensated emancipation. Carrying cages of blackbirds, Lincoln exclaims, "Darn these here blackbirds!—if nobody won't buy 'em I'll have to open the cages and let 'em fly!" Although *Vanity Fair* was philosophical about the change in emancipation policy, there was an undercurrent of ambivalence. On a positive note, one cartoonist predicted that the policy portended a boost in army morale. The image contrasted the mood of the military before and after the proclamation. "Before the proclamation" the military mood seemed lethargic and dispirited, but "after the proclamation" an animated and euphoric disposition reigned.[30]

In contrast, there is also indirect evidence that *Vanity Fair* believed Lincoln had acquiesced to Greeley's influence. Because all of this is couched in humor, it is difficult to untangle the comic from the serious. However, when multiple sources allude to persuasion from Greeley, the evidence becomes more tenable. For example, one source sarcastically thanked "Abraham-Lincoln Greeley, Esquire" for "advancing Freedom" and "doomed slave power."[31] Tongue-in-cheek, another asserted that Lincoln, to avoid reading more Greeley editorials, had consented to Greeley's pressure for emancipation.

"What's this?" says Lincoln. "My editorials," says Greeley; "I'm going to read 'em to you. . . . Then, name your terms. Listen, I cannot. Submit, I must. I am ready." Greeley's eyes sparkled. "Will you—will you issue an Emancipation Proclamation, for the Amelioration of the station of the Nigger nation in all creation?"

"Yes, by darnation" cries the worthy but suffering Abraham. . . . "I promise," he murmured faintly, and fell in a swoon. On recovering he found a proclamation, neatly embossed, and wanting only his signature, on the table before him. . . . The President wrote his name with tremulous fingers. . . . Since then the President rides from Soldier's Home to Washington and back escorted by a detachment of cavalry. He is a changed man. . . . But he doesn't think a good deal of the Proclamation. . . . It is the same with others.[32]

Another piece had Lincoln pronouncing another proclamation:

I do hereby declare all persons who shall in any manner be connected with the army of the so-called Confederate States, on the morning of the tenth day of October instant Prisoners of War to the army of the United States. . . . As the President finished signing this paper, he seized my hand . . . and said: "My dear Mr. Emtihed, you have relieved me from great tribulation, and our beloved country from all the horrors of civil war. My proclamation extinguished the cause of the war. . . . I shall have great trouble in satisfying Mr. Greeley with this step; but, inasmuch as I gave way to him and issued the emancipation proclamation, it is his turn to give me my way in this."[33]

Indirectly, this was also a critique of preliminary emancipation. That is, it was asking, can a paper proclamation really make a difference and free slaves who live in the Confederate states?

Doggerel in *Frank Leslie's Budget of Fun* entitled "Upon a Recent Proclamation" also found fault with the new policy. However in this piece, unlike *Vanity Fair*'s conservative critique, *Frank Leslie's Budget of Fun* advocated a more liberal approach. Lincoln's preliminary emancipation had not gone far enough. Was it not paradoxical, questioned the poet, that Lincoln was abolishing slavery in one section of the country and leaving it entirely intact in another?

Old Abe's a wondrous wag, but his last joke
Is, by all odds, the very best e'er spoke.
Since to the slaves he cannot reach nor see,
He nobly says, "Consider yourselves free!
While unto those beneath his very eye—
Slaves you were born," says he, "and slaves you'll die!"
But when he can perform it, says, "I shan't!"
Which shows that Abram has a most invincible
Repugnance to what honest men call principle.
His next attempt, the Budget knows, can't fail—
'Tis to put salt upon Jeff Davis' tail.[34]

Harper's Weekly, loyal to the bone, maintained its support for Lincoln. Although it was temporarily taken aback by the sudden announcement of preliminary emancipation and wondered about the public reaction in both the North and South, the publication's October 4 editorial sensed a gradual change in public opinion toward "abolition views." "How long it will take for these liberal views to permeate society, and stamp themselves on the mind of the working-class, remains to be seen. We do not, for our part apprehend any serious opposition in the North to the president's policy, except in circles whose loyalty to the country may well be questioned."[35]

Just one week later, Frank Bellew's pictorial satire in *Harper's Weekly*, "Lincoln's Last Warning," commended the bold initiative of the preliminary emancipation. In the cartoon, Lincoln corners Jeff Davis in the tree of slavery and warns his Southern counterpart, "Now, if you don't come down, I'll cut the Tree from under you." This image is reminiscent of John Tenniel's clever visual metaphor in *Punch*, "Up a Tree," in conjunction with the Trent Affair. There, Lincoln was impaled on the horns of a dilemma—should he return Mason and Slidell or risk international intervention? Now it is Jefferson Davis's turn—if not voluntary emancipation, then involuntary? Obviously, Lincoln's patience was spent; he would no longer trifle with the South's rejection of incentive-based emancipation. It could mull the proposition over for a hundred days, but if it would not bend, the vise would have to be tightened to the next notch.[36]

In November's *Nick Nax*, Frank Bellew returned to a variation on this theme of intimidation. His "Bogy [Abolition] for a Bad Boy [Secession]" depicts Lincoln threatening the recalcitrant South in a slightly different manner: "Uncle Abe (to naughty little Secesch) 'Now, mind, if you don't drop those things and be a good boy mighty soon, I'll fetch old Bobolition and then what will become of you?'"[37] Unlike *Nick Nax*, the conservative *Vanity Fair* was philosophical but apprehensive about Lincoln's adoption of a more radical strategy. After all, the president had exhausted all

"Bogy for a Bad Boy," *Nick Nax*, November 1862, 208. Courtesy of the Western Reserve Historical Society.

possibilities with a moderate course. Still, Henry L. Stephens admonished Lincoln to "Keep on Track," the constitutional track. "I've got the right fuel now," says engineer Lincoln, "and I guess I can keep her steady."[38] There was still a three-month moratorium, but time was running out for slavery in the rebellious South.

South of the Mason-Dixon line, the confederacy was livid after Lincoln announced preliminary emancipation:

> Ordinary language fails to provide expletives for their wrath: there is no precedent in history fierce enough for the policy they are going to adopt. They call Mr. Lincoln an "ape," a "fiend," a "beast," a "savage," a "highwayman." Their Congress is resolved into a dozen committees, each trying to devise some new form of retaliation to be inflicted upon United States citizens and soldiers, if we dare to carry the proclamation into effect, and tamper—to use the words of the Richmond *Enquirer*—with "four thousand millions' worth of property!" They are going to hoist the black flag. They are going to put to death not only soldiers on the battlefield, but every Northerner found on Southern soil."[39]

The *Southern Illustrated News* pilloried Lincoln in a caricature captioned, "Masks and Faces: King Abraham before and after issuing the EMANCIPATION PROCLAMATION." Removal of King Abraham's mask reveals a beast; the real Lincoln (judging from the cartoon) apparently deserves the gallows in the background. *Phunny Phellow* printed a sketch of "President Lincoln's Proclamation in the 'Rebel Senate.'" Balloon captions above irate Senators capture the emotions: "Horror," "Atrocity," "Shameful," "Barbarous," "From This Day Henceforth All Rules of Civilized Warfare Shall Be Disregarded," "Hoist the Black Flag," "Kill Him," and "All Soldiers or Officers Captured on Our Soil Shall Suffer Death." Facetiously, a cartoon in *Vanity Fair* envisions Jefferson Davis retaliating with his own proclamation, declaring all African Americans "in de Norf States slaves arter de fust ob Janwery Next."[40]

Meanwhile, England's comic press saw emancipation from an entirely different perspective. *Fun* magazine's lead cartoonist, Matt Morgan, minimized the impact of Lincoln's strategy. Morgan pictured a rather mortal "Jupiter Abe" about to launch his emancipation "thunderbolt" from the heavens, and a defiant but unruffled "Southern Ajax" challenging, "Fire away Sir-ree! It amuses you, and won't hurt me." Furthermore, the lead caption disparages Lincoln with the title, "The Penny Jupiter." Morgan also depicted "Abe the Acrobat" awkwardly performing his routine on rings above the boisterous, naive, cheering American rabble. From the balcony, a sophisticated, skeptical, and unimpressed audience of European royalty, including representatives from England, Spain, Italy, Austria, and France, observes the dubious feat with justifiable disdain, for Lincoln is about to plummet from his exalted position. With one foot in the ring of emancipation, he blindly yet surely gropes for the next ring—"utter ruin." "GEE-RUSALEM!" cries Abe, "Guess I'll Smash Myself—and Them [the rabble] too!"[41] For Matt Morgan and London's *Fun*, emancipation was no panacea, nor was Lincoln the agile leader his deceived American partisans thought him to

MASKS AND FACES.

King Abraham before and after issuing the EMANCIPATION PROCLAMATION.

be. From *Fun's* comic standpoint, the American president had been thrust into a role he was ill equipped to perform. Pure and simple, he did not measure up to the requisites of presidential stature.

Punch's interpretation took a different approach. A desperate Lincoln, despairing over a series of Confederate military conquests, seizes the tool of emancipation as a last resort. This theme was repeatedly invoked in doggerel and cartoon.

Although of conquest Yankee North despairs
His brain for some expedient wild he racks,

President Lincoln's Proclamation in the "Rebel Senate."   Sketched by our Artist on the spot.

And thinks that having failed on the white squares,
He can't do worse by moving on the Blacks.[42]

Using a variation on the theme of desperation, a "Serenade to Lincoln" also re-proaches the president for confining emancipation to the Confederacy and for fail-ing to liberate slaves sooner. The epithets in the doggerel underscore the interna-tional scope of racial prejudice.

Stonewall Jackson de ebberlastin' rebel,
And Gineral Lee, dey whip um to de debble.
Says ole Abe Lincoln, "Now mind how you behaves,
If you go on so I shall 'mancipate yer slaves."

Ole Abe Lincoln, he mean to 'mancipate
All de niggers only in ebbery rebel state,
So he don't wipe slick out all slabery dark blot,
But leave someting ob him more dan lilly grease spot.

All loyal States, deir niggers is to keep,
Jes like deir hosses, deir oxes, and deir sheep,

So he reward dem, and punish dem dere udders
Declarin' dat de darkeys is to be deir men and brudders. . . .

You say, ole Abe, now you libbelate de black;
What a pity dat you didn't do it long time back:
Cause all de world would den have stood wid old Abe Lincoln.
Ole Abe Lincoln, dis am berry sad to think on![43]

Likewise, John Tenniel's "Abe Lincoln's Last Card; or, Rouge-et-Noir" shows the
president in dire straits. Lincoln is desperate, his face is etched with anxiety, and he

"A Yankee Olmar,"
Fun, November 15,
1862, 85. Courtesy of
the University of
Minnesota Libraries.

A YANKEE OLMAR.

Abe the Acrobat :—" GEE-RUSALEM! I GUESS I'LL SMASH MYSELF — AND THEM TOO!"

nervously plays his last card: emancipation. In contrast, his Confederate opponent, smiling confidently, holds another card. Is he bluffing, or ready to trump? The card table sits on a keg of gunpowder. The accompanying doggerel concedes military losses "from Bull's Run . . . to Sharpsburg Hill." So, as a last recourse, Lincoln chances emancipation. His hopes are distilled in a few lines of the last verse.

> There! If that 'ere Proclamation
> Does its holy work,
> Rebeldom's annihilation
> It did oughter work.[44]

Ironically, Lincoln had actually used the metaphor of the "last card" in the context of emancipation and the spirit of national urgency. "I am a patient man—always willing to forgive on the Christian terms of repentance; and also to give ample time for repentance. Still I must save this government if possible. What I cannot do, of course I will not do; but it may as well be understood, once for all, that I shall not surrender this game leaving any available card unplayed."[45] To be sure, the president seemed to be using every conceivable option.

However, Lincoln had not entirely abandoned the voluntary, gradual, and compensation components of liberation. On December 1, 1862, the president's Annual Message to Congress proposed a constitutional amendment that would have embraced this principle and extended it to all slaves. Twice he specifically addressed the

"Abe Lincoln's Last Card; or, Rouge-et-Noir," *Punch*, October 18, 1862, 161. Author's Collection.

issue of emancipation. First, "Every State, wherein slavery now exists, which shall abolish the same therein, at any time, or times, before the first day of January, in the year of our Lord one thousand and nine hundred, shall receive compensation from the United States." Second, "All slaves who shall have enjoyed actual freedom by the chances of the war, at any time before the end of the rebellion, shall be forever free, but all owners of such, who shall not have been disloyal, shall be compensated for them." Such views did not rescind the preliminary emancipation, but they rewarded voluntary emancipation for "Maryland, Delaware, Missouri, Kentucky, and such parts of Louisiana, Tennessee, Virginia, and the other rebel States as are now held by the armed forces of the United States." States that accepted the offer would have been granted a generous, flexible, and gradual timetable for emancipation. Moreover, the proposed amendment would have compensated loyal slaveholders whose slaves became free as a result of the war.[46]

Although Lincoln's recommendation broadened the scope of emancipation, his message was misunderstood.[47] The ambiguity in his Annual Message to Congress became a target for cartoonists. One cartoon by John McLenan effectively questions the prolonged projection for the end of slavery. McLenan depicts Horace Greeley and a disappointed group of African Americans reading a sign that announces the delay: "The Great Negro Emancipation Fandango Is Postponed until 1900, Abe Lincoln, Manager." The caption adds, "Sensation among 'Our Colored Brethren' on ascertaining that the Grand Performance to which they had been invited on New Year's Day, was unavoidably postponed to the year 1900!"[48] Although this cartoon does not carry the full weight of an editorial statement, it does reflect some political alienation.

From another angle, a potent, satirical editorial in *Frank Leslie's Budget of Fun* derided the entire annual address. The editorial was a scathing, if comical, indictment of the president. Purporting to constitute the actual text of Lincoln's message, it ridiculed and distorted his ideas. Compensation for emancipation was among the favorite targets of Lincoln's radical detractors.

Again as practice proves more than theory in any case, has there been any irruption [*sic*] of colored people northward, because of the abolishment of slavery in the District of Columbia last Spring? I answer proudly—No! It was quite the contrary, for the slaveowners of the circumjacent counties in Maryland made an exceedingly good thing out of it by bringing all their lame, blind, halt and generally decrepit negroes into the Washington market, and there getting compensated for them at fabulous rates. . . . The idea I have labored to convey is, that if we buy the slaves of the rebels and set them free, paying in U. S. Bonds due January 1, A.D. 2035, that they will immediately lay down their arms, and fall upon our bosoms in a fraternal embrace; for this is all our Southern brethren have been fighting for. It was the hope of "compensated emancipation," even in the dim distance, that nerved them to the enormous expenditures of blood and treasure that they have made in the past two years.[49]

Although the indictment was unfair, the president was nevertheless fair game for such satire. However, because Congress declined to act on the proposed amendment, the brief debate, in comic or serious form, became moot.

THE EMANCIPATION PROCLAMATION

Two factors produced a softer reaction in the media to the Emancipation Proclamation. First, preliminary emancipation had already stolen the thunder, attracting the sharpest criticism from the opposition. Though still a very sore point with some critics, their wounds healed with the passage of time. Second, the December military disaster at Fredericksburg preoccupied the press. Even so, the formal announcement of the Emancipation Proclamation was not overlooked. *Frank Leslie's Budget of Fun* facetiously contrasted a fictitious, Confederate proclamation from Jeff Davis, which announced the hanging of the unpopular scapegoat Gen. Benjamin Butler in retaliation for Lincoln's Emancipation Proclamation. The cartoonist also disparaged Lincoln's proclamation itself. Two subtle elements that pertain to the official document came under fire. First, Lincoln writes the proclamation with "Greeley's Abolition

"Butler Hanged—The Negro Freed on Paper—1863," *Frank Leslie's Budget of Fun,* February 1863, front page. Courtesy of the American Antiquarian Society.

ink," suggesting that it was a product of the editor's ill-conceived influence and the brainchild of Radical Republicanism. Second, the caption, "The Negro Freed—On Paper—1863," sends the additional signal of powerlessness and futility.[50] Obviously, many in the North were struggling with this abrupt change.

A *Yankee Notions* serial cartoon similarly censures the president for yielding to "certain radicals" on emancipation, namely Horace Greeley, and to the Democratic Party on "compromise peace measures." Lincoln, notes the caption, "in trying to please all, pleased nobody." Refusing "further interference," the president comes to his senses and kicks Horace Greeley and the Democrats out of the White House. Only as Lincoln escapes from the bonds of political extremity and firmly grasps the Constitution, argues the cartoonist, does he begin to gain control over the "Rebellion."[51] This was stern chastisement from conservative elements within Lincoln's own party against Radical Republicans and Peace Democrats. As a moderate among radicals and conservatives, Lincoln was buffeted from forces at both ends of the political continuum.

During the Civil War, only rarely, even in the name of emancipation, were African Americans treated with dignity in the comic genre. At best, ambivalence was conveyed. For example, one cartoon ridiculed a generic disciple of New York's Governor Seymour, "Horatio Seymourite," for trying to dissuade Lincoln from emancipation. However, the disdainful image of an African American being worshiped on a pedestal and the language of prejudice in the caption sent another message. "Take their [rebel's] cattle, their houses, their lands, their lives—but, sacrilegious dog! Touch not the sacred nigger!"[52]

This pattern of condescension was common in the cartoons of the illustrated newspapers. In *Harper's Weekly*, although one cartoon celebrates emancipation by depicting a slave giving his master one month's notice of his freedom in January, the dialogue betrays duplicity. "Pompey. 'What day ob de month id dis Massa?' Master. 'Twenty Sixth December, Why?' Pompey. 'Oh! Cause you knows Massa Linkum he gib us our papers on de First January, God bless um; and now I wants to say as hou you allus was a good Massa, and so I'll gib you a Mont's Notice to git anudder Boy. Niggers is powerful Cheap now, Massa!'"[53] African Americans fared slightly better in serious images. For example, Thomas Nast's "The Emancipation of the Negroes" proudly depicts Lincoln's portrait displayed on the wall of a modest African American dwelling. Another cartoon in *Merryman's Monthly* features Dinah dreaming happily "after reading Massa Linkum's proclamation."[54] Such images generally struck a kinder note and tendered a profound compliment to Lincoln.

In England, criticism of emancipation persisted in the comic press. "Old Abe is at his wit's end, not that he has very far to go to get there," joked *Fun*, "for his black proclamation won't go down with Congress any more than wooden nutmegs with a New England pedlar."[55] Doggerel in *Fun* parroted the critique in *Punch*.

Now President Lincoln is beginning to think on
The Union as utterly done for,

Democracy.—IF THEE PERSUADEST HIM WITH THIS HAY, THEE COULD THEN EASILY RIDE THE ANIMAL AS THEE SHOULD.

BUT HE WAS MORE STUBBORN THAN WAS THOUGHT.

NOW BY THE WAYSIDE HE MET CERTAIN RADICALS, WHO SADDLED THE DONKEY WITH THE DARKEY, BUT THE DONKEY SAT DOWN AND LAUGHED, WHICH BROUGHT THE DARKEY TO THE GROUND.

NOW ABRAHAM, IN TRYING TO PLEASE ALL, PLEASED NOBODY. REFUSES FURTHER INTERFERENCE.

WHAT EVERYBODY HOPES THE RESULT WILL BE.

In sheer desperation he frees the black nation,
Swearing niggers the war was begun for.

Yet he has but conceded, the boon so much needed,
To the South in revolt so undaunted,
While he fears to give freedom in loyal Yankeedom
To the slaves with his policy vaunted.[56]

In his cartoon "Scene from the American 'Tempest,'" *Punch's* John Tenniel used the freeing of the slave Caliban in Shakespeare's *Tempest* as an analogue to the Emancipation Proclamation. Caliban is transposed into the stereotypic Sambo, who (speaking of his Confederate master) says to Lincoln, "You beat him 'nough, Massa! Berry little time, I'll *beat him too*."[57] This was perhaps among the most benevolent images on emancipation published in *Punch*, but it was offset by the associated doggerel, "Old Abe in a Fix."

This freedom which we call the great right o' human natur,
I ken give, by word o' mouth, where my word ain't worth a tatur.
But in the States where I could put foot down on liberation,
I must leave the darkies to the chance o' cash-emancipation:

SCENE FROM THE AMERICAN "TEMPEST."

Caliban (Sambo). "*You* beat him 'nough, Massa! Berry little time, I'll *beat him too*."—Shakspeare. (*Nigger Translation.*)

(*Opposite*) "An Old Story in a New Shape," *Yankee Notions*, February 1863, 48. Collection of Richard Samuel West/ Periodyssey.

(*Left*) "Scene from the American 'Tempest,'" *Punch*, January 24, 1863, 35. Author's Collection.

Such freedom as I can give givin' slaves o' rebel masters,
Leavin' slaves ov loyal owners to the mercy o' shin-plasters.[58]

Pessimism about the purported effects of emancipation as characterized by England's comic press was consistently challenged in graphics published in the North. For example, cartoonist William H. Davenport's upbeat rendering in the humorous monthly *Nick Nax* predicted a benign outcome for emancipation. Davenport directly attributed "The Next New Marriage," the union of the North and South, to the dissolution of the chains of slavery.[59] Typically, this optimistic mood reigned in the Union magazines.

THE FINAL PHASE

As the shackles of slavery began to fall from African Americans, hope for the future restoration of the Union increased. However, realization of Lincoln's dream was tied in particular to the performance of black soldiers in the Civil War. The president concurred with "some of the commanders of our armies in the field who . . . believe

"The Next New Marriage," *Nick Nax*, June 1863, 48. Collection of Richard Samuel West/ Periodyssey.

The Next New Marriage.

the emancipation policy, and the use of colored troops, constitute the heaviest blow yet dealt to the rebellion."[60] Not only had they "vindicated their manhood on the battlefield," noted the president, but "they have demonstrated in blood their right to the ballot."[61] Moreover, looking to the future, Lincoln thought "they would probably help, in some trying time to come, to keep the jewel of liberty within the family of freedom."[62] In April 1864, the president declared emancipation an unmitigated success. "More than a year of trial now shows no loss by it in our foreign relations, none in our home popular sentiment, none in our white military force—no loss by it any how or any where."[63] In fact, Lincoln surmised, "Take from us, and give to the enemy the . . . colored persons now serving us as soldiers, seamen, and laborers, and we can not longer maintain the contest."[64] After some suggested that Lincoln "return to slavery the black warriors . . . to conciliate the South," he indignantly replied, "I should be damned in time and in eternity for so doing. . . . [N]o human power can subdue this rebellion without using the Emancipation lever as I have done."[65] Ironically, a cartoonist for *Frank Leslie's Illustrated Newspaper* converted Lincoln's adamant repudiation of this idea into an occasion for wit: "Uncle Abe—'Sambo, you are not handsome, any more than myself, but as to sending you back to your old master, I'm not the man to do it—and what's more, I won't.'"[66] Emancipation to Lincoln was not just a military necessity, but a confirmation of the evils of slavery and the president's corollary principle: "In giving freedom to the slave, we assure freedom to the free."[67]

"Uncle Abe—'Sambo, You Are Not Handsome, Any More Than Myself,'" *Frank Leslie's Illustrated Newspaper,* December 24, 1864, 221. Author's Collection.

In October 1864, Maryland's voluntarily adoption of a new constitution that abolished slavery offered convincing evidence of growing support for broader-based liberation on a national scale. The significance of this signal event was commemorated beyond the state's borders. *Frank Leslie's Illustrated Newspaper* devoted major coverage to a gigantic celebration in Philadelphia, and a large print of the "Abolition of Negro Slavery in Maryland, at Philadelphia, Pennsylvania" embellished its front page.[68] Maryland's sanguine action was a definite precursor of constitutionally sanctioned emancipation on a national scale.

Of course, full emancipation depended upon submission of the South. However, after Sherman's occupation of Atlanta and his powerful drive to the sea, Grant's tenacious pursuit of Lee, and the appearance of increased optimism on all other military fronts, ultimate victory was imminent. John McLenan cleverly linked freedom to the South's surrender. In adjacent full-page cartoons, he compared the motivations of General Lee's defense of slavery with Grant's quest for freedom. According to the chained slave "Cuffee," the grindstone of slavery could no longer sustain the war or a "separate nation." In comparison, for a liberated African American the grindstone of freedom was easy to turn. "Sambo—Golly, Massa Lincum! I've turned dis stun for a good many swords in de las' free years, but dis wun [freedom] is worth um all together. Dat'll do de trick! Yah! Yah!" "I guess he'll take the point of that joke" (a sword), replies Lincoln.[69]

Although the overwhelming majority of Union illustrated periodicals tended to support Lincoln's administration, two magazines, *Funniest of Phun* and the *New York Illustrated News,* broke from ranks during the campaign of 1864 to launch a stinging assault on his presidency. Inspired by Radical Republican disillusionment with the centrist Lincoln, left-wing defectors spearheaded by General Frémont's candidacy on an independent ticket assailed the president for what they perceived as a crisis in leadership. Among their most strident battle cries was the contention that the pace for implementating national emancipation was uninspired and lethargic. They thought Lincoln was too timid on slavery, unprincipled, and vacillating and indecisive, and that he often acted out of moral expediency, and had been in office too long. Lincoln's critics were swept aside, if not buried, by the disarming landslide in the 1864 election, yet the voices of political faultfinding and murmuring were only temporarily muted.

As late as February 1865, there was irrefutable evidence that the bitter residue of resentment among certain elements from the radical flank of his own party still lingered. A virile exhibit of potent antipathy toward emancipation appeared as a cartoon in Lincoln's old enemy, *Funniest of Phun.* Sarcasm targeted at Lincoln oozes from every element of the caption and minute detail of the print. If the cartoon were to be taken seriously, Lincoln, "the gloved hero of Emancipation waiting for the indispensable necessity," was not the hero of emancipation at all. In fact, if one accepted the message, the incompetent president was still holding firmly onto the flag of expediency and military necessity. Too long he had ignored Columbia's incessant importuning for emancipation: "Why not use this weapon?" The query alluded to

the alleged failure of Lincoln to seize the sword of "Justice" and the "Constitution As It Is" to combat the evils of slavery. Instead of quashing slavery with an iron fist, reasoned the cartoon, the president had squandered his political power by donning the symbolic glove of indifference. Had he been as decisive, so the logic went, as his generals in the field, Frémont and Hunter, who had been willing to ban slavery unilaterally, he might have prevailed. The concluding lines in the caption summarize the argument: "'I claim not to have controlled events, but confess plainly that events have controlled me.' Abraham Lincoln—or in other words, 'I have neither exercised my judgment, conscience, or humanity on the moral question of slavery.'"[70]

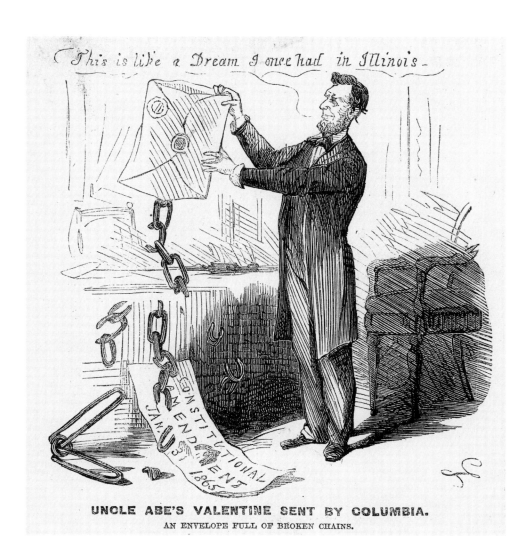

"Uncle Abe's Valentine
Sent by Columbia,"
*Frank Leslie's Illustrated
Newspaper,* February
25, 1865, 368. Author's
Collection.

If Lincoln was not the hero of emancipation, then who was? The cartoonist imputed the honor to General Sherman, who by his adroit military exploits had made emancipation a reality. However, public opinion was not persuaded by this emotional appeal. To the contrary, by 1865 Lincoln's presidential stature was growing significantly.

In time, the Thirteenth Amendment to the Constitution, which abolished slavery, became law. This was Lincoln's crowning achievement. William Newman's artistry featured the accomplishment with different cartoons in two magazines. In *Frank Leslie's Illustrated Newspaper,* the event was celebrated as "Uncle Abe's Valentine Sent By Columbia." The unorthodox valentine is a set of broken chains that symbolize the end of slavery. Upon opening the envelope, Lincoln joyously exclaims, "This is like a Dream I once had in Illinois." The second illustration was done in grand fashion for *Frank Leslie's Budget of Fun.* The double-page cartoon, which focuses on Lincoln's second inauguration, acclaims the president "The Tallest Ruler on the Globe." Carrying the "Amended Constitution" in his hand and passing a replica of the Emancipation Proclamation on the wall of the White House, Lincoln is enthusiastically welcomed back by Columbia for another four years. "The Lesser Luminaries of Europe" are depicted as "deferentially" commending his attainments, and Admiral Faragut, General Sherman, and General Grant publicly parade their recent military feats at Mobile, Charleston, and Richmond, respectively.[71]

To be sure, passage of the Thirteenth Amendment was a high-water mark in American history, worthy of glowing superlatives and national pride, but for African Americans it was only the beginning of the long road toward freedom and respect. A cartoon in *Punch* correctly asserted that black Americans were "More Free Than Welcome."[72] Of three major values—liberty, equality, and fraternity—only a measure of the first had been attained, but this accomplishment was a crucial and essential step in the right direction. To the extent that blacks were liberated, whites could also be transformed. To the degree that prejudice was removed from the national vision, a clearer and brighter light illuminated humanity.

Seven

The Strain
of Conflict

For the first two years of the Civil War, without either side gaining a decisive advantage, the North and South exchanged bitter blows in head-to-head combat. In the western campaign, Union forces had the military edge, but of late, the South had prevailed on the eastern front. Stonewall Jackson and Robert E. Lee's armies had buffeted the Army of the Potomac and accumulated Confederate successes had stiffened General Lee's resolve to invade Pennsylvania. Because the lofty military expectations of the North had not materialized, a subdued and somber mood prevailed. Ironically, to relieve the frustration and tension, this discouraging state of affairs precipitated humor in the comic press. Typical of the wit attributed to Lincoln, though probably apocryphal, was a yarn published in *Nick Nax:* "The latest story they tell of the President is at the expense of a certain individual who, the other day, called at the White House to solicit of the head of the nation a pass for Richmond. Well, said the President, I would be very happy to oblige you, if my passes were respected, but the fact is, sir, I have, within the past two years, given passes to two hundred and fifty thousand men to Richmond, and not one has got there yet."[1] In short, the Union's armies desperately needed to reverse its fortunes.

Britain's humorous magazine *Fun* basked in the North's humiliation. On July 18, 1863, Matt Morgan prominently and proudly trumpeted the South's victories: "Bull Run, Fredericksburg, Port Hudson, and Charleston." His cartoon contrasts the South's substantial "honors" with Abe's ephemeral "tricks" in the North: "South.—'Oh! Don't Give Up, Abe; Try Another Trick. I Don't Mind. I Hold All the Honours.'"[2] By the time Morgan's cartoon was published, he did not know that the fickle momentum of civil war had already abruptly shifted. His premature, smug exultation must have rapidly turned to chagrin, for the South had suffered not one, but three ignominious losses.

TRICKS *v.* HONOURS.

South :—"OH! DON'T GIVE UP, ABE; TRY ANOTHER TRICK. I DON'T MIND.
I HOLD ALL THE HONOURS."

"Tricks *v.* Honours,"
Fun, July 18, 1863, 175.
Courtesy the
University of
Minnesota Libraries.

THE WINDS OF CHANGE

In early July, the North reeled off an impressive series of victories at Gettysburg,
Pennsylvania, Vicksburg, Mississippi, and Port Hudson, Louisiana, that dramatical-
ly affected the course of the war. Beaten severely at Gettysburg, a humbled General
Lee and his army limped south. To be sure, General Meade failed to capitalize on the

rout of Lee's forces by letting Lee elude his grasp and by failing to deliver a crushing blow. Still, despite that disappointment, the Army of the Potomac regained the initiative and fortified its confidence. Moreover, Gen. Ulysses S. Grant simultaneously earned an equally stunning victory at Vicksburg, which combined with General Bank's triumph on July 8 at Port Hudson gave the Union strategic control of the Mississippi River. Truly, the victors at Gettysburg and Vicksburg celebrated Independence Day unlike any since 1776. To date, no Northern Civil War victories had been more gratifying or significant. Although the war was far from over, the Northern juggernaut, commensurate with its advantage in military personnel, equipment, and industrial strength, finally began to assert itself. At last, Lincoln seemed to have discovered a cadre of generals who were equal to the demands of the day. All of this, at least for awhile, quickened the pulse of national optimism.

Merryman's Monthly construed these battlefield successes as "the handwriting on the wall" that signified the ultimate end of the war.[3] In addition, a journalist for *Nick Nax* gloated in whimsical doggerel over the collective conquests of Generals Meade, Grant, and Banks, and, in general, a vastly brighter military prognosis:

Of General Lee, the rebel chief, you all perhaps do know,
How he came North a short time since to spend a month or so;
But soon he found the climate warm, altho' a Southern man,
And quickly hurried up his cakes and toddled home again.

Chorus:
How are you General Lee? It is, why don't you longer stay?
How are your friends in Maryland and Pennsylvania?

Jeff Davis met him coming back; "Why, General Lee," he said,
"What makes you look and stagger so? There's whisky in your head,"
"Not much, I think" says General Lee; "no whisky's there indeed:
What makes me feel so dizzy, I've taken too much Meade."

"But you seem ill yourself, dear Jeff, you look quite sad enough,
I think, while I've been gone, Old Abe has used, you rather rough."
"Well, yes, he has, and that's a fact; it makes me feel downcast,
For they've bothered us at Vickburg, so 'tis Granted them at last."

Chorus:
Then, how are you, Jeff Davis? What is it makes you sigh?
How are your friends in Vicksburg, and in Mississippi?

"Yes, Vicksburg they have got quite sure, and Richmond soon they'll take,
At Port Hudson, too, they have some Banks I fear we cannot break;

While Rosecrans, in Tennessee, swears he'll our army flog,
And prive if Bragg's a terrier good, Holdfast's a better dog."

Says he, "All things are looking queer since them damn Yankees fit
At Gettysburg for Meade-able, where I did have to 'get;"
I feel a kind of choking here, and hemp begins to smell,
I think Secession's "bout played out and kinder goin' to hell."

Chorus:
"How are you, Jeff Davis? Would you not like to be
A long way out of Richmond and the Confederacy?
For with 'Porter' on the river, and 'Meade' on the land,
I guess you'll find that these mixed drinks are more than you can stand."[4]

Artists also boasted of victory. A full-page illustration in *Frank Leslie's Budget of Fun* sharply contested an assertion made by Richmond's *Enquirer:* "Affairs in Maryland are very different now to what they were last August. Maryland now only waits the appearance of General Lee to rise as one man."[5] In effect, based on the experience at Gettysburg, the illustrator argues that General Lee can no longer afford to underestimate the military prowess of the Northern troops. Elsewhere, quoting Lincoln's statement, "What the country requires is military success," *Merryman's Monthly* underscores the field soldier's pivotal role in the "War Pyramid." At the base of the pyramid is the ordinary soldier, on whose shoulders Lincoln sits piggyback; a symbolic African American rides on the "Republican Organ" strapped to Lincoln's body; General Halleck balances delicately above Lincoln, and finally, the secretary of war, Edwin Stanton, constitutes the structure's crest.[6] The artist accurately displays the common soldier bearing the heaviest burdens of war. Few presidents had been more adamant on that score than Lincoln, who often paid tribute to "the men who, by fighting our battles, bear the chief burthen of saving our country." When Lincoln visited the "one-legged brigade" of "convalescent veterans at St. Elizabeth Hospital," the president expressed his deep appreciation for their personal sacrifice. "There was no need of a speech from him," noted the president, "as the men upon their crutches were orators; their very appearance spoke louder than tongues."[7]

However, the cartoon also expressed subtle resentment against black Americans. Implicit in the lackadaisical black image—a self-fulfilling prophecy rooted in slavery—was the spurious notion that African Americans were a burden rather than an asset. The president countered that impression with a number of executive actions. First, when Lincoln attributed the origin of the Emancipation Proclamation to "military necessity," he eloquently and explicitly recognized the indispensable need for African American military participation. Moreover, the proclamation would tend to boost African American morale in the North and South but also undermine Confederate confidence. Second, after the president authorized the organization of black

"What the Country requires is Millitary success"

REPUBLICAN ORGAN

POTOMAC RIVER

THE WAR PYRAMID.

"The War Pyramid,"
Merryman's Monthly,
August 1863, 144.
Collection of the New-
York Historical Society.

military units, which soon distinguished themselves on the battlefield, Lincoln un-
equivocally affirmed their worth to the nation's present welfare and future destiny.[8]
Finally, when Jefferson Davis threatened to single out black Union soldiers for special punishment, Lincoln quickly retaliated to nullify the Confederate leader's move.
On July 31, 1863, Lincoln issued General Orders No. 252:

It is the duty of every government to give protection to its citizens, of whatever class, color, or condition. . . .The law of nations and the usages and customs of war . . . permit no distinction as to color in the treatment of prisoners of war as public enemies. To sell or enslave any captured person, on account of his color, and for no offence against the laws of war, is a relapse into barbarism and a crime against the civilization of the age. . . . The government of the United States will give the same protection to all its soldiers, and if the enemy shall sell or enslave anyone because of his color, the offense shall be punished by retaliation upon the enemy's prisoners in our possession. . . . It is therefore ordered that for every soldier of the United States killed in violation of the laws of war, a rebel soldier shall be executed; and for every one enslaved by the enemy or sold into slavery, a rebel soldier shall be placed at hard labor on the public works and continued at such labor until the other shall be released and receive the treatment due to a prisoner of war.[9]

Harper's Weekly published a cartoon that illustrates the president's "Order of Retaliation." While Jefferson Davis chases a black child with his scourge, Lincoln remonstrates: "Look here, Jeff Davis! If you lay a finger on that boy to hurt him, I'll lick this *Ugly Cub of yours* [a Confederate] within an inch of his life!"[10] For Lincoln, charity mandated the protection of his soldiers without respect to skin color.

Predictably, *Punch* and *Fun* barely acknowledged Union bravery and skill on the battlefield. Ironically, *Punch*'s John Tenniel portrayed Lincoln as "Brutus" and a black American as the "Ghost of Cæsar." In corollary verse, a black minstrel grudgingly concedes that "Brave Massa Meade, him berry strong indeed," but the doggerel's overpowering message is to deride Lincoln as a jokester and exploit his purported betrayal of African Americans.[11]

LINCOLN'S CRITICS AND THE DRAFT

No organ in the illustrated press supported Lincoln more often than *Harper's Weekly*. The editorial page consistently defended him from antagonists, of which there were plenty. "The rebels, and their tools the Copperheads, of course, hate him. The War Democrats doubt some points of his policy. The conservative Republicans think him too much in the hands of the radicals; while the radical Republicans think him too slow, yielding, and half-hearted."[12] For some of Lincoln's detractors, a major point of contention was the draft. The Copperheads organized and orchestrated such opposition. By 1863, Copperhead influence was thriving. In his successful quest to become New York's governor, Horatio Seymour had benefited from opposition to Lincoln in the 1862 election—and the draft was one of Seymour's major concerns. The governor's personal misgivings encouraged public dissent and disillusion with the president's war policies, but he did not anticipate mob disorder in New York in July

THE PRESIDENT'S ORDER No. 252.

Mr. Lincoln. "Look here, Jeff. Davis! if you lay a finger on that boy, to hurt him, I'll
lick this *Ugly Cub of yours* within an inch of his life!"

1863 that fed on such faultfinding, nor did he foresee that black Americans would
become the scapegoats of ethnic violence.

Harper's Weekly interpreted the draft riots as another Copperhead conspiracy.
"The 'revolution in the North' [New York's draft riots] was to counterbalance our
successes on the Mississippi and the retreat of Lee," it surmised.[13] However far-fetched
that rationale, the popular magazine had arrived at the conclusion based on what it
had gleaned from the media in Richmond and London.

Artists in the domestic and foreign illustrated media represented and shaped the diverse national and international sentiment on the draft. On July 4, John McLenan's loyalist cartoon in *Vanity Fair* expressed confidence that the nation would support the draft: "The President.—'Freemen of the North, Arise Again!' The Nation.— 'We come!'"[14] In general, that expectation was valid: the draft riot was something of an anomaly. However, there were pockets of resistance beyond New York's borders, and resentment toward the draft was common.

"Brutus and Cæsar," *Punch*, August 15, 1863, 69. Author's Collection.

BRUTUS AND CÆSAR.
(From the American Edition of Shakspeare.)

The Tent of BRUTUS (LINCOLN). *Night. Enter the Ghost of* CÆSAR.
Brutus. Wall, now! Do tell! Who's you?
Cæsar. I am dy ebil genus, massa LINKING. Dis child am awful Inimpressional.

Nevertheless, the Northern illustrated press rarely sympathized with the Copperhead movement. Although the riots focused the nation's attention on New York, they precipitated adverse publicity and a spirit of censure. *Frank Leslie's Illustrated Newspaper* scolded "The Naughty Boy Gotham, who would not take the draft." The caption contrasts New York's rebellion with Pennsylvania's faithful compliance. "Mammy Lincoln—'There now, you bad boy, acting that way, when your little sister Penn takes hers like a lady!'"[15] *Merryman's Monthly* depicted the president attempting to dissuade a New York draft dodger from fleeing to Canada, but Lincoln's only incentives consist of a rifle, bayonet, sword, and ammunition pouch.[16] The most creative jibe at New York's recalcitrance came from the pen of Frank Bellew, who played on the requirement of potential draftees to accede to the call or else forfeit a three hundred dollar government bounty. On the White House steps, an incredulous Lincoln greets a motly, minuscule group of five disheveled, poor excuses for soldiers

"The Naughty Boy Gotham," *Frank Leslie's Budget of Fun*, November 1863, 13. Author's Collection.

and the disconsolate Provost Marshal James B. Fry, who is burdened by a colossal bag of greenbacks: "Uncle Abe—'Whar in thunder are the rest of the New York army, eh?' Provost-General Fry—'Here they are in this bag—[commutation money for conscripts—] genuine greenbacks!'"[17]

In such cartoons Lincoln appears bewildered, perplexed, and timid, but his actual response to the draft crisis countered that impression. In reality, Lincoln took a firm grip on the situation; he boldly rejected Horatio Seymour's proposal to suspend the draft in New York and wait for a ruling on the draft's constitutionality.[18] As commander in chief, Lincoln could not afford to waste valuable time replenishing the armed forces. The military had seized the initiative, and Lincoln was not about to lose it. Whenever there was a legitimate question about fairness, he was quite willing to negotiate; otherwise, he held his ground.[19] In the context of war, Lincoln was absolutely satisfied that his action was necessary, just, and constitutional. For instance, after certain judges issued writs of habeas corpus to protect specific individuals from the draft, Lincoln used his executive authority to suspend that right throughout the land—an act that pleased his partisans and infuriated his opponents.[20]

Artists in London and Richmond were aroused by Lincoln's suppression of civil liberties. Matt Morgan compared Lincoln to Guy Fawkes, the infamous seventeenth-century British traitor who conspired to destroy the houses of Parliament and King

"The Sinews of War, or How to Bag an Army," *Merryman's Monthly,* October 1863, 208. Collection of the New-York Historical Society.

THE SINEWS OF WAR, OR HOW TO BAG AN ARMY.

UNCLE ABE— *"Whar in thunder are the rest of the New York army, eh?"* | PROVOST-GENERAL FRY— *"Here they are in this bag—genuine greenbacks!"*

James I. In Morgan's print, Lincoln's list of crimes against his country consists of suspension of habeas corpus, emancipation, and the draft. His policies send the "Charter of American Laws," the legacy of George Washington, "States Rights," "Liberty of Subjects," and "Laws" up in flames. In the background, Salmon Chase solicits greenbacks to help "burn the Constitution." Meanwhile, *Southern Punch* used a similar metaphor: the "Abduction of the Yankee Goddess of Liberty." In its cartoon, "the prince of darkness [Lincoln] bears the Goddess of Liberty away to his infernal regions. Goddess.—'Master of perdition, let me go!' Abraham.—'Never! You have been preaching about the Constitution too long already. I was the first to rebel against constituted authority. Hell is murky! You go thither.'"[21]

In contrast, domestic magazine illustrations continued to support the president. In fact, Lincoln's resolute action against the Copperheads won him the plaudits of a full-page illustration by J. H. Howard in *Merryman's Monthly*. The image shows Lincoln taking charge; he personally pulls the rope that propels a cannonball from his powerful "Springfield Gun." His compatriot soldiers are obviously pleased with their distinguished leader's intimate involvement and important contribution to the war. "I guess that will reach 'em," concludes a contented president about the volley sailing toward its Copperhead target. According to the lead caption, this was just the beginning because Mr. Lincoln was "Getting the Range with His Springfield Gun (A Tremendous 'Bore' to the Copperheads) for the 1864 Campaign."[22] Whether the "1864 Campaign" alluded to the following year's military or political campaign did not really matter. The Copperheads stubbornly contested him on both counts—military and political—and they were already geared for the battle.

The British and Confederate comic periodicals had their own ways of caricaturing the draft and the riots. Given the racial and ethnic elements inherent in the draft riots and the antipathy between the English and Irish, it is not surprising that race and ethnicity figured prominent in English cartoons. Irish participants had obviously persecuted black Americans, but the British were overly eager to pin the blame on an inherent flaw in the Irish makeup. However, there were more obvious reasons for the introduction of race and ethnicity. Among these was the almost universal sanction for belittling racial, religious, and ethnic minorities, and efforts to justify slavery on racial grounds compounded the problem. Both African and Irish Americans felt the acute sting of stereotypes in British and Confederate illustrations. Sometimes the misrepresentations were subtle; at other times they were blatant.

Richmond's *Southern Punch* patronizingly created a "Scene in a Yankee Barbershop." An "Intelligent Contraband" propositions his barber: "Maybe I can get yer to go in de army as my substitute? Brudder Linkum say black is no culler an white is no culler, an derfore, ob course, consequently you an me is equals."[23] The suggestion that so-called contraband could be intelligent and that Lincoln's liberal conception of human worth was plausible were incongruous elements on which *Southern Punch* depended for humor in the cartoon.

In London, the initial locus of attention was on the riots. Matt Morgan used the historic tensions between the Irish and English to cast ethnic aspersions. A belliger-

MR. LINCOLN GETTING THE RANGE WITH HIS SPRINGFIELD GUN (A TREMENDOUS "BORE" TO THE COPPERHEADS) FOR THE 1864 CAMPAIGN.

ent Irishman ("King Mob upon His Throne") who uses a black American for his footstool warns: "Now, Abe, How Du You Like Me? Sooner Or Later You Have To Bow, Or You'll Find Me An Ugly Customer." Similarly, Irish and African American images prevailed in "'Rowdy' Notions of Emancipation," but the cartoon's central idea disingenuously attacked Lincoln. In it, John Tenniel portrays a callously indifferent Lincoln ignoring the plaintive pleadings of a black victim being dragged toward the gallows. Contrary to this image, the president effectively used this very setting to teach tolerance: "None are so deeply interested to resist the present rebellion as the working people. Let them beware of prejudice, working division and hostility among themselves. The most notable feature of a disturbance in your city last summer, was the hanging of some working people by other working people. It should never be so. The strongest bond of human sympathy, outside the family relation, should be one uniting all working people, of all nations, and tongues, and kindreds. Nor should this lead to a war upon property, or the owners of property."[24]

Another example from Matt Morgan's portfolio portrays the irony of Irish emigrants fleeing "To the Land of the Free," only to be shackled by Lincoln's war policy, "perpetual draft" tax, and "Union or Death."[25] Ironically, both the genius and defect of caricature involve the use of oversimplification as a tool. In this case, the juxtaposition of the quest of the Irish for freedom with national necessities imposed by war created the indispensable conditions that enabled the cartoon's comic elements.

"Mr. Lincoln Getting the Range with His Springfield Gun," *Merryman's Monthly*, October 1863, 224. Collection of the New-York Historical Society.

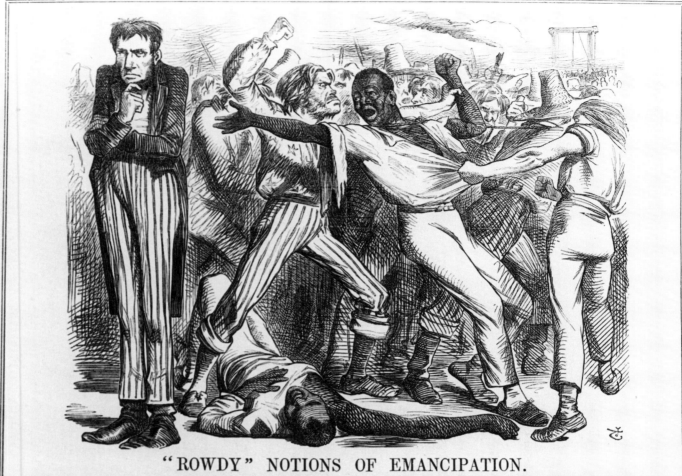

"ROWDY" NOTIONS OF EMANCIPATION.

" THE mob on the corner, below my house, had hung up a negro to the lamp-post. In mockery, a cigar was placed in his mouth. * * * For hours these scared negroes poured up Twenty-seventh Street, passing my house. * * * One old negro, 70 years old, blind as a bat, and such a cripple that he could hardly move, was led along by his equally aged wife with a few rags they had saved, trembling with fright, and not knowing where to go."—MANHATTAN's *Letter in the Standard, July 30th.*

"'Rowdy' Notions of
Emancipation," *Punch*,
August 8, 1863, 57.
Author's Collection.

Lincoln was not a popular figure in British caricature, except as a convenient foil to denounce. Like *Fun*, *Punch* blamed Lincoln's policies for the shortage of willing soldiers and for the future's bleak outlook. The concluding verse of "The American Conscript's Complaint" typifies the standard, pejorative British fare at this time:

Fever, too, and gangrene I regard with infinite aversion,
I had sooner die at once, so let them shoot me for desertion!
Health and home I'd fight to guard, and consequences little think on,
Won't go South to bleed and rot by order of Dictator Lincoln.[26]

In contrast, the domestic illustrated press tended to support Lincoln's stand on the necessity of the draft and its voluntary complement: enlistment. The *New York Illustrated News* printed an upbeat endorsement in a double-page illustration produced by John P. Davis. The caption accentuated the positive: "Urge Enlistments,

Rejoice the Army—We're Coming, Father Abraham." In February 1864, *Yankee Notions* also expressed patriotic loyalty in a front-page illustration entitled "The Last Call." In the caption, "Uncle Abraham calls on Miss Columbia and Uncle Sam for his New Years—300,000 . . . for a victorious prosecution of the war."[27]

NEUTRALITY AND INTERVENTION

One of William Newman's vintage illustrations is an amusing cartoon that depicts the threat of foreign intervention substantially reduced after the Union's victories at Gettysburg and Vicksburg. Newman conveniently arranged for two of the American cartoonists' most popular foreign symbols, John Bull and Napoleon III, to appear with a cargo of weapons at the steps of the Southern White House in Richmond at precisely the right time: "French Visitor.—'Ah, begar! how did you do? Ve have come with our Intervention to recognize your Confederacy!' Colored Servant.—

"The Last Call," *Yankee Notions*, February 1864, front page. Reproduced from the Collections of the Library of Congress.

'Lord sakes! how funny! Why, Massa Confederacy is dead—ya! ya! He died last Fourth July!'"[28] If the danger of intervention had diminished since Gettysburg, it was not evident in the number of illustrations during the fall of 1863.

From the Confederate standpoint, the recent Union military victories were also diplomatic setbacks. Since Fort Sumter, Southern diplomats had hoped and lobbied for the maximum feasible level of British intervention. If possible, recognition as an independent nation; short of that—economic, political, psychological, and military support. It seems reasonable to assume that Confederate diplomatic leverage, for various levels of intervention, decreased in proportion to Union military success. At least temporarily, since the battles at Gettysburg, Vicksburg, and Port Hudson, the Confederate prognosis for winning the war had diminished. Some modest evidence for the sense that some diplomatic momentum might have been lost can even be discerned from England's popular culture. Indeed, a British poet, trying to assume the Confederate diplomatic perspective, articulates the apparent change in political climate in two verses of a poem published in September 1863 in *Punch:*

> Not yet, not yet to interfere does England see occasion,
> But treats our good commissioner with coolness and evasion,
> Such coolness in the premises that really 'tis refrigerant
> To think that two long years ago she called us a belligerent.
>
> But 'tis a speech so plain, my Lord, that all may understand it,
> And so we quickly turn to fight again the Yankee bandit,
> Convinced that we shall fairly win at last our nationality,
> Without the help of Britain's arm, in spite of her Neutrality![29]

London's *Punch* admitted that it was not easy to navigate the precarious waters of neutrality. In one of its cartoons from this period, John Tenniel likens the formidable challenge to the journey of the mythological Ulysses, who tried to get past Scylla (the sea monster) and Charybdis (the whirlpool) without losing any sailors. The modern Ulysses, Lord Russell, is obliged to take his vessel *Neutrality* between the equally hazardous perils of Lincoln and Jefferson Davis.[30] Nevertheless, Russell is not intimidated:

> The Yankee Scylla vainly scowls on you,
> As vainly scowls the Slave Charybdis too.
> I see no terror in those Federal glooms,
> Whence Lincoln's long and rugged visage looms,
> I see no terror in that Southern cloud
> That wraps the face of Davis, keen and proud.
> Let Abraham disport in jocund tales,
> And split his Union as he split his rails;
> Let Jefferson renew his fierce attacks,

And whip his foemen as he whips his blacks;
Neither shall hail Jackides as his friend,
Jackides, sternly neutral to the end.[31]

Neither *Fun* nor *Punch* was reluctant to defend Britain's policy on neutrality. According to these magazines, it was the Confederate and Union governments' importunate and bullying characters that had created the problems. Furthermore, claimed Matt Morgan, "The Neutral Beast" (the British lion) had only breached the boundaries of neutrality when provoked by the "Yankee War Party"—an idea that the *New York Herald* and *New York Times* especially championed.[32]

In the Northern illustrated press, discussions about neutrality revolved around three themes: (1) foreign tests of the Monroe Doctrine's policy of nonintervention; (2) the alliance between Russia and the Union to counter the threat of intervention during the Civil War; and (3) damage inflicted in the past, present, or future by the Confederate ships that Liverpool's Laird shipyards constructed and launched.

THE MONROE DOCTRINE

With respect to the Monroe Doctrine, *Punch* thought it detected double entendre in a proposal by the *New York Herald* that exhorted Lincoln "to enlist the sympathy of all men, North and South, by declaring an intention to drive the English from Canada and the French from Mexico." Surely this was intended as a joke, "a neat way of calling [Lincoln] a fool," claimed *Punch*.[33] *Southern Punch* agreed that Lincoln was a fool, but it based its conclusion on different premises. A cartoon by W. B. Campbell caricatured the president, and the caption portrayed Lincoln as a blundering, ludicrous, and impotent despot:

KING ABRAHAM.—"Look here, Mr. Emperor, I will not submit to having the Monroe Doctrine set aside by your Johnny Darmes (*gens d'Armes*). The United States will put a stop to such jokes. I allow no one to perpetrate a bad joke but myself."
LORD NAPOLEON.—"Ah, Monsieur Lincoln! France no cair for your dis-United States. General Forey will hold Mexico; and bimeby he may make one grand *foray* into your Mexico, east of ze Potomac." KAISER FRANCIS JOSEPH OF AUSTRIA.— "Hapsburgh-Lorraine helps you Napoleon mit 100,000 men." KAISER MAXI-MILLIAN.—"Mine Got! How mad de Yankee man looks. However, mit France und Austria to stand by Mexico, who's afraid?" KING ABRAHAM.—"My Armies and my Iron-clads are teu powerful for all three of you. The Monroe Doctrine shall be maintained." LOUIS NAPOLEON.—"Ah, Monsieur Lincoln! Your Iron-clads have no taken Charleston, nor Semmes, nor Maffitt, nor Maury; your grand Armies can take Richmond. Ze Confederates beat you. Monsieur Davis is all right. He is one grand manager. You zall hold Mexico, Kaiser Max. France does no cair one leetle snap of her finger for de dis-United States. When she does may ze souveniers

"Council between the Crowned Heads of Europe and the United States," *Southern Punch*, October 17, 1863, 8. Reproduced from the Collections of the Library of Congress.

Council between the Crowned Heads of Europe and the United States.

of ze Great Napoleon be forgotten. Your Monroe Doctrine, like ze Grand American Republic, is dead and buried. *Vive la France!*" JOHN BULL.—(aside)"I am neutral. Fight it hout. Old Palm and Johnny Russell have fixed hup haffairs for me. Besides, I am a little hafraid of Canada."[34]

In comparison, William Newman's Northern perspective, "A Peep into the Future—The Monroe Doctrine Triumphant," portrays Lincoln as America's bold, able defender. While the president emphatically kicks Napoleon III and John Bull off the "American Hotel" premises, Uncle Sam (the proprietor) welcomes Canada to the hemisphere's family of nations. Obviously, no feat of social engineering could easily bridge the chasm between these Southern and Northern versions of the Lincoln image. Parenthetically, any apparent American overture to forge a friendlier alliance with Canada, however innocent, made the English uneasy.[35]

THE RUSSIAN-AMERICAN ALLIANCE

Growing friendship between Russia and the North also created nervous tension among foreign observers. In 1863, the second Polish revolt from Russian rule gave Russia and the United States common cause for commiseration, and each sought solace and mutual political advantage from a relationship. Public fear in Britain spawned by such an alliance was expressed in the poetic language of "The President and the Czar:"

> Abe. Bound to this child in bloody sympathies,
> Come to my arms, and let us be allies!
> We'll squelch John Bull, and scuttle Britain's isle;
> But let us go and liquor up meanwhile.[36]

Anxiety among foreign observers increased when an armada of Russian ships was welcomed at New York City's port. *Punch* panned the so-called alliance as the meeting of extremes. However, whereas *Punch*'s John Tenniel depicted the czar and Lincoln warmly shaking hands against the background of their countries' civil wars, *Merryman's Monthly* cleverly countered by highlighting the leaders' affectionate greeting with a radically different twist. Behind Lincoln's office door surreptitiously lurks

"A Peep into the Future—The Monroe Doctrine Triumphant," *Frank Leslie's Budget of Fun*, November 1863, 8–9. Author's Collection.

UNCLE SAM—(to Miss Canada)—"Well, here you are at last! You've often promised to come; now make yourself at home."

the envious, eavesdropping "British lion," which surmises it smells "an enormous rat"—the American-Russian coalition.[37]

The domestic press seemed to relish the leverage such an association might confer. If England and France felt threatened by the Russian-U.S. alliance, they might defer intervention on behalf of the Confederacy. Moreover, a compact between Russia and the United States might also give the Confederates pause to consider the implicit ramifications such an alliance might have on the war. The latter message seems to be the one that John McLenan wanted to convey in his *Harper's Weekly* cartoon for November 28, 1863: "Dr. Lincoln" recommends to his "Smart Boy of the Shop [William Seward] mild applications of Russian Salve for our *friends* over the way [France and England], and heavy doses—and plenty of it—for our Southern patient!!"[38] England's perception of danger in this international liaison is evident in a translated extract from the *Moscow Journal* published in *Punch*. The selection points out the reciprocal advantages for Russia and the United States and the potential existence of ulterior motives.

"Extremes Meet," *Punch*, October 24, 1863, 169. Author's Collection.

EXTREMES MEET.

Abe. Imperial son of NICHOLAS the Great,
We air in the same fix, I calculate,
You with your Poles, with Southern rebels I,
Who spurn my rule and my revenge defy.

Alex. Vengeance is mine, old man; see where it falls,
Behold yon hearths laid waste, and ruined walls,
You gibbets, where the struggling patriot hangs,
Whilst my brave myrmidons enjoy his pangs.

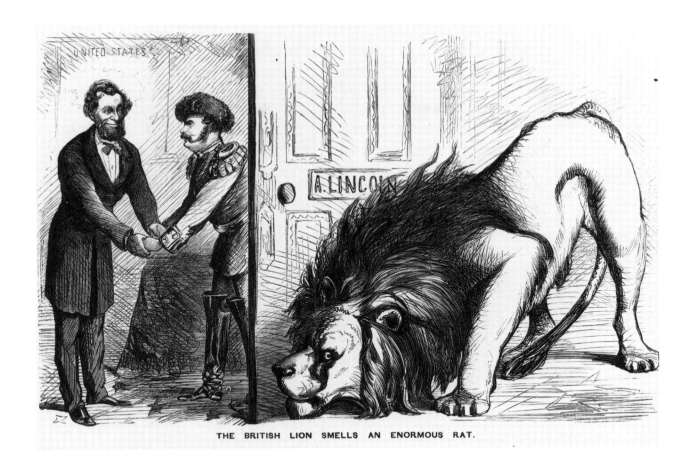

THE BRITISH LION SMELLS AN ENORMOUS RAT.

DRAWING THINGS TO A HEAD.

DR. LINCOLN (to Smart Boy of the Shop). "Mild applications of Russian Salve for our *friends* over the way, and heavy doses—and plenty of it—for our Southern patient!!"

"The British Lion Smells an Enormous Rat," *Merryman's Monthly,* November 1863, 256. Collection of the New-York Historical Society.

"Drawing Things to a Head," *Harper's Weekly,* November 28, 1863, 768. Author's Collection.

Negotiations must be entered into with America, so that, in case of need, she may be able to reckon upon us. The more intimate and solid our alliance with America, the more England will find it to her interest to keep upon good terms with Russia. The commercial world in England shuddered at the news of the Russian squadron having been seen in the Atlantic. Our fleet was useless to us during the Crimean war, but the eight frigates now at sea will render us considerable services in the event of war with the maritime Powers, for they will keep the Commercial Navies of England and France in check. This is the reason why Russia has dispatched them at a favourable time to hold the sea. Our cruisers will find refuge in the neutral ports of America; they will be the terror of the Commercial marine of hostile Powers, and will compel any such to employ half their navies in guarding their merchantmen.[39]

Moscow's inflammatory rhetoric, monitored and reported in England, was not reassuring to John Bull or Napoleon III.

THE LAIRD RAMS

The most acute concern among Union leaders in regard to neutrality involved the Laird shipbuilding firm in Liverpool. This corporation built the *Alabama,* which was delivered to the Confederate navy and played havoc with Union shipping. Reliable intelligence reports asserted that other ships destined for the Confederate navy were in various stages of construction.[40] From the Union perspective, this information did not square with Britain's status as a neutral power. On September 5, 1863, Union pressure resulted in the British government detaining Laird rams. Britain felt pressured from two different sides, as suggested in John Tenniel's cartoon "Neutrality": "Mrs. North" (Lincoln) shakes her finger at John Bull and reprimands: "How about the *Alabama,* you wicked old man?" An equally indignant and adamant Mrs. South counters: "Where's My Rams? Take back your precious consuls—There!!!"[41] The *Southern Illustrated News* cartoon "John Bull—ied" conceded that Union diplomacy was adversely affecting the delivery of more British rams, and it charged the Union with hypocrisy for simultaneously receiving other weaponry from England: "Abraham Lincoln—'. . . You Johnnie, jes' stop them Rebel Rams, or I'll *lamb* you!' Little Johnnie Russell—'Don't be impatient, Mr. Lincoln, I'm just about to paint my broad arrow on them—meanwhile, you see that little Invoice of Arms you ordered is ready for shipment.'"[42] Although English sentiment in favor of the sale of British rams to the Confederacy waxed and waned, even militant, nationalistic *Punch* concluded that it was in the national interest to control the Laird shipyard's involvement in the war:

As I was sailing the Mersey
I saw a wonderful Ram,

NEUTRALITY.

Mrs. North. "HOW ABOUT THE *ALABAMA*, YOU WICKED OLD MAN?"
Mrs. South. "WHERE'S MY RAMS? TAKE BACK YOUR PRECIOUS CONSULS—THERE!!!"

"Neutrality," *Punch*, November 14, 1863, 199. Author's Collection.

"John Bull—ied!" *Southern Illustrated News*, November 14, 1863, 152. Courtesy of the Western Reserve Historical Society.

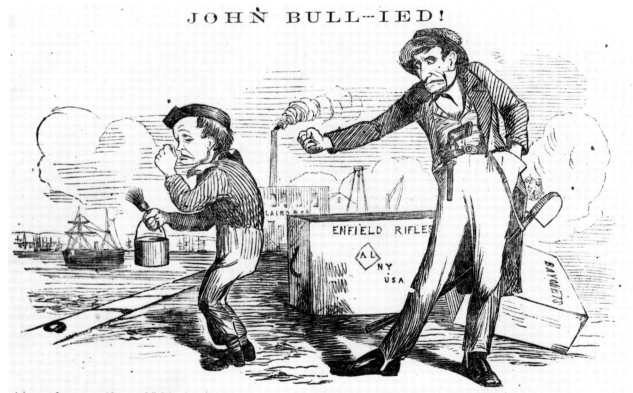

JOHN BULL---IED!

ABRAHAM LINCOLN—(with unparalelled ferocity)—See here—naow—you Johnnie, jes' stop them Rebel Rams, or I'll *lamb* you!
LITTLE JOHNNIE RUSSELL.—Don't be impatient, Mr. Lincoln, I'm just about to paint my broad arrow on them—meanwhile, you see that little Invoice of Arr rdered is ready for shipment.

Which the people there they told me
Had frightened Uncle Sam.

And I think that Policeman Russell,
Who to keep the peace is bound,
Has used a wise discretion
In clapping the Ram in the Pound.[43]

By the early months of 1864, the content and slant of humor in Confederate and British illustrated magazines indicated that the Union had a distinct edge over the Confederacy in gaining favor with France and England. Cartoons in *Southern Punch* in particular lamented the so-called Yankee-British alliance, but the Confederacy had not given up hope.[44] In England, Northern optimism and Southern pessimism over relations with France and England were even more sharply contrasted in "The Two Messages" of Lincoln and Davis, which was printed in *Punch*'s first issue of the new year:

Lincoln
England is behavin' right,
So indeed is France:
Money ain't by no means tight
And our troops advance.
In Arkansas and Tennessee
The Union banner waves,
Maryland and Mis-sou-ree
'S ejecting of their slaves.
Near one hundred thousand blacks,
Free, are in our ranks,
Lots of others making tracks:
For All we offer Thanks.
To such as will submit to us
I promise Pardon free,
Except to Davis (who's a cuss)
And friends of high degree.
But till they own me King and Lord
Nor set me at defiance,
We'll pound away, for in the Sword
Must be our Main Reliance.

Davis
England is behaving ill,
So in fact is France,
Showing towards the North good-will,

Viewing us askance.
Treating the blockade as good,
Though it's no such thing,
Stopping English friends who would
Succour to us bring.
Latterly we licked the foe,
Made the beggar fly,
Now we've had an awful blow,
But we won't say die.
When we first began the fray
O, we little thought
North would fight in such a way,
Which it didn't ought.
Still we'll fight, while we can show
A man to pull a trigger.
All our hope's in pluck, you know,
And Unabating Vigour.[45]

Fun's cartoon version of "The Two Messages" ridiculed both Davis and Lincoln by depicting them with enormous noses. By identifying Lincoln as Aaron and Davis as Moses, it injected a subtle element of anti-Semitism consistent with the period: "Davis and Abe:—'Sez Aaron to Moses, Let's cut off our noses!' 'Sez Moses to Aaron, Oh, no! It's the fashion to wear 'em.'"[46] That Lincoln was Aaron, Moses's subordinate colleague and brother, may have insinuated a slight preference for Davis.

THE WAGES OF WAR TO 1864

Although the collective victories at Gettysburg, Vicksburg, and Port Hudson marked a significant milestone and turning point in the war, they did not defer the steady flow of blood, sweat, and tears. The victories were mingled with defeat, and hope was tinged with despair. War continued to rob the young of their innocence, sound bodies, and whole minds. Pain, sorrow, anguish, and death did not favor one section over another. The glories of war were delusions of grandeur—temporary sedatives that sustained motivation and warded off cynicism.

In mid-August 1863, Gen. Quincy Adams Gillmore's Union forces renewed heavy shelling of Charleston, South Carolina, harbor. *Nick Nax* published a humorous account of a fictitious exchange of letters between the Union and Confederate generals in the area: "To General Beauregard—Dear Sir: I respectfully ask you to allow the United States forces under my command to occupy Charleston forthwith. [signed] General Gillmore. To General Gillmore—Dear Sir: You shan't. [signed] General Beauregard. To General Beauregard—Dear Sir: I shell. [signed] General Gillmore."

Illustrators predicted the outcome of the bombardment. One artist for *Yankee Notions* put Lincoln waist deep in water, holding the American flag in one hand and the uprooted Fort Sumter in the other. Two Union ironclads protect the president, and foreign birds "Louis Napoleon" and "John Bull" encircle the area to satisfy their curiosity. The caption explains the motivation for the assault: "Lincoln.—'Well, Sumpter, as I guess you're about the root of the Rebellion, I'd better pull you up and end the thing where it began.'"[47] Although Fort Sumter did not fall in 1863, Confederate forces yielded ground by evacuating Charleston's Morris Island.

In September, the Confederate army won the Battle of Chickamauga. This Southern setback reminded the Union that every inch of turf would be bitterly contested; nothing could be taken for granted. After the battle, a cartoon in *Frank Leslie's Budget of Fun* reported that John Bull and Napoleon III had dropped by the White House to inquire about Columbia's health: "Dr. Lincoln.— 'She has been much depressed, but I never felt seriously alarmed about her. The fever has now nearly left her, and she will soon be able in person to return your many kind attentions during her illness.'" In London, *Fun*'s Matt Morgan likened the pattern of alternate victories and defeats for the Union to riding on a "See-Saw."[48] Lincoln stands on the ground looking up to his Confederate opponent, waiting for the teeter-totter to hurl him to a more exhilarating and comfortable position. He did not need to wait long, for General Grant soon triumphed in the Chattanooga campaign.

Although cartoons from such foreign and domestic publications as *Frank Leslie's Budget of Fun* and *Fun* had emphasized the incessant challenge of financing the war, 1863 ended optimistically.[49] In Ohio, the political aspirations of Clement Vallandigham—the Democrat's prominent Copperhead candidate for governor—were summarily dashed.[50] For the Union, the prospects for victory were brighter. Both Lincoln's Proclamation of Thanksgiving and his Annual Message to Congress lauded the nation's economic well-being, its robust diplomatic condition, and the country's healthy prognosis for the future. It seemed that the sun was gradually breaking through the clouds of war.

The rosy image in the domestic illustrated press concurred. In *Phunny Phellow*, O. Morse portrayed Lincoln as Santa Claus on Christmas Eve, gladly stuffing the stockings of the United States with victories: "Chattanooga, Morris Island, Vicksburg, Port Hudson, and Gettysburg." Thomas Nast, who consistently backed Lincoln, was just as effusive. His double-page illustration in *Harper's Weekly* depicts a nation at prayer on "Thanksgiving Day." In separate panels, Columbia, Lincoln, Washington, the army, the navy, the town, the country, and emancipated African Americans are all on their knees in appreciation for their blessings.[51] In addition, lighthearted banter playfully complimented the president. Author Charles Halpine created a colorful Irish character, whom he called "Miles O'Reilly." The *Comic Monthly* liked Halpine's wit and featured it in a serial cartoon on its front page: "The Marvelous History of Miles O'Reilly— Poet, Patriot, Politician, and Prisoner." Successive panels developed the story in cartoon and caption: "No. 1.—Miles O'Reilly being

inspired, writes a "pome" on Gen. Gilmore. No. 2.—In consequence of which he is arrested by order of the General. No. 3.—And is punished for being a genius. No. 4.—He however is pardoned by Honest Old Abe, who dearly loves a joke and a Patriot. No. 5.—And is allowed a bit of a holiday to visit his friends in New York,

Santa Claus Visits Uncle Sam!

who receive him with open arms, and tender him numerous offices and drinks. But having quit being a Politician No. 6.—He goes to Washington where he is embraced by his benefactor, who rejoices to meet the rescued prisoner. For full particulars see New York *Herald*."[52]

In the same issue of *Comic Monthly*, Lincoln is shielded from the Copperheads' wrath. An elaborate eighteen-panel, double-page cartoon, "The New Gospel of Peace, According to St. Benjamin," sarcastically sneers at Benjamin and Fernando Wood ("Phernandiwud").[53] The Woods did not like Lincoln's wartime suppression of civil liberties, and they thought he was ignoring the pursuit of peace. Nevertheless, Lincoln emerges unscathed from their lecture at the brothers' expense. In fact, the last panel uses Lincoln's imposing size to stress his ability to "sometimes put down his foot in wrath."

At the end of 1863, the only dissenter from such support for Lincoln in the illustrated press was a familiar and consistent source of criticism: England's *Fun*. After Lincoln called for a national day of Thanksgiving, Matt Morgan accused him of hypocrisy: "Don't you think you'd better wash off your war paint before going to church, friend?" A wary John Bull also warns one of his emissaries to be careful of American shenanigans in diplomacy: "Keep your eye on 'em Johnny—Take care he doesn't drug his grog."[54] However, these images were the usual jaded views of a publication that maintained undeviating opposition to Lincoln and the Union cause. *Fun* was no more a relevant bellwether to the changing Lincoln image than the *Southern Illustrated News* or *Southern Punch*.

DAWNING OF THE NEW YEAR

No year produced more Lincoln imagery than 1864, but most of it focused on his election to a second term. Because election content is reserved for a separate chapter, this segment concentrates on the president's nonpolitical images beforehand. Dur-

"I Wish I Was in Dixie!" *Southern Illustrated News,* February 27, 1864, 64. Courtesy of the Western Reserve Historical Society.

PLAINTIVE AIR—Sung nightly in Washington by that Celebrated Delineator, ABRAHAM LINCOLN.

ing the summer of this year, the level of Northern support for Lincoln reached its lowest point. His Radical Republican colleagues mounted their most serious critique. For the first time in his presidency, two Northern illustrated periodicals defected from the relatively solid phalanx of media support. Even so, except for his traditional critics in the British and Confederate press and the two publications that abandoned him, his image in illustrated magazines did not suffer.

As usual, the New Year began with the annual reception at the White House. The *New York Illustrated News* featured a prominent illustration of the president and the first lady greeting their guests. Except for a few illustrations previously discussed in the sections on the draft and neutrality, cartoons of Lincoln were sparse until March. The most noteworthy of the first two months of the year appeared in the *Southern Illustrated News*. With the "Amnesty Proclamation" in his pocket and a "Map of Richmond" hanging on the wall, Lincoln wistfully strums the guitar and sings the "Plaintive Air—" "I Wish I Was in Dixie!" This Southern image taunted premature Union euphoria, impugned its justification, and touted the view that an imminent end to the war was just a pipe dream. Likewise, *Southern Punch* pictured a downcast "Lincoln and Seward watching over the drooping eagle."[55]

Northern rhetoric that claimed superiority on the battlefield was just as common. In March, William Newman reduced the "Final Issue of the War" to "The Longest Purse Wins." Compared to Lincoln's purse—the "U.S. Treasury"—Jeff Davis's purse

"Final Issue of the War—The Longest Purse Wins," *Frank Leslie's Budget of Fun*, March 1864, 8–9. Author's Collection.

is minuscule. Lincoln can hardly lift his moneybag off the ground, but Davis swings his lightweight purse with ease and alacrity. Unfortunately, Davis's purse also has a hole from which coins and paper money are falling. "Better give in, Jeff," warns Lincoln. "You haven't half a chance! Don't you see, I've the LONGEST PURSE." Next to Lincoln are barrels and boxes labeled "Gold from California" and "Gold Bars." Behind Davis are boxes, too, but they bear the stamp "Uncurrent Money." Furthermore, on the ground is a scroll marked "Repudiation" and a sign entitled "Mississippi Bonds," which does not boost confidence in Southern economic collateral. In the background, John Bull and Napoleon III wager over the war's outcome, but when John Bull realizes what Lincoln has in his financial war chest, he declines to bet against the North. "I sall take you hundred to one in Jeff Davis, Mistaire Boule [John Bull]," remarks France's Napoleon. "No! No! Boney—I back out! I should lose money by it," replies John Bull.[56]

In the spring of 1864, Lincoln promoted Ulysses S. Grant to lieutenant general and commander of the Union army; Lincoln believed this action was an essential prologue to final victory. *Harper's Weekly* acknowledged the honor with a full-page print of Lincoln and Grant. In *Phunny Phellow*, Thomas Nast caricatured General Grant as "Lincoln's New Servant Girl." "I'll have to clean this place out first, Mr. Lincoln, before I can commence to work properly," notes Grant. Looking over Grant's shoulder, his overseers—Lincoln, Edwin Stanton, and Gideon Welles—approving-

"Lincoln's New Servant Girl," *Phunny Phellow*, June 1864, 8–9. Reproduced through permission of the Rare Book and Special Collections Library, University of Illinois at Urbana-Champaign.

Lincoln's New Servant Girl.
MISS GRANT FROM THE WEST.—I'LL HAVE TO CLEAN THIS PLACE OUT FIRST, MR. LINCOLN, BEFORE I CAN COMMENCE TO WORK PROPERLY.

ly observe the new commander getting ready for the spring campaign by sweeping out the debris of obsolete leadership.[57]

On March 14, Lincoln ordered another 200,000 troops from the states for military service. In cartoon, *Frank Leslie's Budget of Fun* saw the draft as one of the "Symptoms of Spring." While Lincoln wields his hoe to cultivate the soil, the rising sun of the secretary of the treasury, Salmon Chase, nourishes the soil with "Greenbacks," "Treasury Notes," "Specie," "5.20 Bonds," and "Coupons." As a result, "Abram's Crop [soldiers] Begins to Shoot" into "Dixie." The image was not far from the truth. In May, General Sherman commenced his historic march toward Atlanta, and Grant began his final offensive in Virginia. *Phunny Phellow*'s Thomas Nast put Grant not only knocking on the door of Lee's "Richmond House" but also claiming possession: "I've rented this house from Abe Lincoln; and if you don't evacuate the premises by 12 o'clock, I'll take possession by main force, for during the last three years you've been most troublesome tenants." In reality, Nast's optimism was not justified. As tenants go, General Lee was most difficult to evict. In the Battle of the Wilderness, at Spotsylvania Court House, and Cold Harbor, Grant's forces suffered enormous

"Symptoms of Spring—Uncle Abram's Crop Begins to Shoot," *Frank Leslie's Budget of Fun*, April 1864, 8–9. Author's Collection.

SYMPTOMS OF SPRING—UNCLE ABRAM'S CROP BEGINS TO SHOOT.

human losses. The death and casualty counts were depressing. The war in Virginia was, at best, a stalemate. Moreover, Sherman's progress also seemed awfully slow. War weariness sapped vital strength from the national will, and disillusionment mounted. Lincoln did not escape the resentment and faultfinding associated with the war's slow cadence. Personally, he agonized over the bitter taste of war; nor did he minimize the horror: "War, at the best, is terrible, and this war of ours, in its magnitude and in its duration, is one of the most terrible. It has deranged business, totally in many localities, and partially in all localities. It has destroyed property, and ruined homes; it has produced a national debt and taxation unprecedented, at least in this country. It has carried mourning to almost every home, until it can almost be said that the 'heavens are hung in black.'" Still the president's will did not weaken. Urged to make a prediction about the war's end, Lincoln ventured that "Grant . . . [would] never be dislodged until Richmond [was] taken."[58] Meanwhile, the visual media in the North kept a stiff upper lip and refused to reflect this darker side, so prevalent in the summer of 1864.

Of course, the Southern and British press contested the reliability of the Northern perceptions. Borrowing an old Union cartoon from *Frank Leslie's Illustrated Newspaper* and appropriating it for its own ends, *Southern Punch* changed the caption to suggest "The Way Lincoln Will Be Lifted Out of Washington City by General Lee"— on the end of several bayonets. In June, *Southern Punch* proclaimed Lincoln's effort to glue the severed Union back together an utter failure.[59] London's *Punch* was also skeptical of any method to mend the Union. As Mrs. Britannia observes Columbia attempting to stitch an ugly tear in the map between America's northern and southern sections, she calmly advises: "Ah, my Dear Columbia, it's all very well; but I'm afraid you'll find it difficult to join that neatly." In the hostile press, Lincoln's image continued to deteriorate. Matt Morgan envisioned the American president as "Columbia's Nightmare."[60] Such opposition was routine and expected, but it was less palatable from Lincoln's own political party.

Although the conservative wing of the Republican Party tended to be less vocal against the centrist Lincoln than either the Democratic Copperheads or Radical Republicans, it, too, expressed discontent. Lincoln's pragmatic adaptation to dynamic conditions brought about change, and that created discomfort. Comparing Lincoln's political philosophies and strategies in 1860 and 1864, one particularly illuminating visual expression of conservatism feared that the president had gone too far. According to this cartoon, the political flavor of the "government porridge" in 1860 and 1864 were radically different. "Mind your seasonings," advises Seward to Lincoln in 1860, "put in plenty of conservatism, and don't forget the Kentucky savory." However by 1864, judging from the cartoon, Lincoln had concocted a radically new recipe: "Bill, scum off that filthy conservatism, it spoils the whole dish, put in more SUMNER savory, and don't be afraid to put in plenty of the radical element."[61] Indeed, Lincoln had not preserved the status quo, but neither had he become the captive or epitome of Radical Republican idealism. He marched to the cadence of his own drum.

This independent, middle-of-the-road strain did not always endear him to either the conservative or radical extremes of his own party.

Intense and frequent criticism from Lincoln's radical colleagues also increased. The *New York Illustrated News* and a new comic magazine, *Funniest of Phun*, supported radical John C. Frémont's negativism. In these political organs, Frank Bellew's cartoons denounced Lincoln for being too conservative on the issue of slavery. In fact, the negative political campaign waged by Frémont against Lincoln for the presidency was ruthless, but material of that kind is reserved for another chapter. However, even cartoons with milder content noted philosophical differences. For example, Bellew disparaged the president's lenient "Amnesty Proclamation" as "Mr. Lincoln's Great National Joke." To lure the rebellious states back into the fold with the paltry incentive of amnesty is preposterous, argued Bellew. He pictured Lincoln naively and futilely "trying to make the rebels acknowledge the corn [Amnesty Proclamation]" he is broadcasting to the scraggly lot of Confederate chicks (states). Meanwhile, the American eagle protects her own plump, healthy brood of states from the envious rooster, Jefferson Davis.[62]

"Bosses of the Government Kitchen," Courtesy of Special Collections Library, Gettysburg College.

1860. SEWARD TO LINCOLN.—Mind your seasonings, old man, put in plenty of conservatism, and don't forget the Kentucky savory.

SEWARD ASIDE.—I've got him just where I want him now.

1864. LINCOLN TO SEWARD.—Bill, scum off that filthy conservatism, spoils the whole dish, put in more SUMNER savery, and don't be afraid to put in plenty of the radical element.

MR. LINCOLN'S GREAT NATIONAL JOKE—TRYING TO MAKE THE REBELS ACKNOWLEDGE THE CORN.

"Mr. Lincoln's Great National Joke," *Funniest of Phun*, July 1864, 15. Courtesy of the American Antiquarian Society.

Actually, when Lincoln enunciated his amnesty and reconstruction policy in his Annual Message to Congress in December 1863, there was reasonably broad support across the political spectrum. However, when implementation of that policy was perceived as facilitating Lincoln's nomination to a second term, the backing rapidly faded. Congress coveted control over the reconstruction process, and the resultant Wade-Davis Bill was designed to give it that power. When Lincoln pocket vetoed that legislation, he triggered a rebellion that seriously threatened the president's political survival.

Radical Republican impatience took other forms, one of which involved the volatile Horace Greeley. In July, Greeley was deceived into believing that authorized Confederate peace negotiators were ready for a serious, confidential rendezvous with legitimate Union representatives at Niagara Falls. Greeley cajoled the skeptical president to agree to the meeting, but to protect himself from any fallout from the event, Lincoln shrewdly assigned the *Tribune* editor as an official U.S. emissary. Furthermore, Lincoln insisted on retaining full control. He firmly specified the parameters for any negotiated peace: "Any proposition which embraces the restoration of peace, the integrity of the whole Union, and the abandonment of slavery, and which comes by and with an authority that can control the armies now at war against the United States will be received and considered by the Executive government of the United States, and will be met by liberal terms on other substantial and collateral points, and the bearer, or bearers thereof shall have safe-conduct both ways."[63]

However, just as Lincoln had suspected, the peace overture was nonexistent. From London, Matt Morgan's artistic sense of humor summarized the result. Greeley, the

"Niagara Doves," *Fun*, August 13, 1864, 219. Courtesy of the University of Minnesota Libraries.

NIAGARA DOVES.

Uncle Abe :—" SAY, GREELEY, WHAT 'AVE YOU BROUGHT BACK?"
Dove Greeley :—" NAREY NOTHINK, NUNKEY!"

dove of peace, perches on Lincoln's finger to give his report: "Uncle Abe.—'Say, Greeley, What 'Ave You Brought Back?' Dove Greeley.—'Narey Nothink, Nunkey!'"[64] Although embarrassment from the failure of this meeting redounded exclusively to Greeley's reputation for overzealous political activism, Lincoln's decision to include the abolition of slavery as a condition of peace further damaged his political stock among some elements of the electorate and galvanized a portion of the opposition, which then sought to scuttle the president's hopes for a second term.

Despite the charade at Niagara Falls, wistful speculation about an imminent peace settlement or the desirability of pursuing it more aggressively was in the air. In fact, another clandestine peace initiative took place in Richmond about the same time. "Rev. Col. James F. Jaques . . . with Mr. J. R. Gilmore, of New York had, with President Lincoln's knowledge, but without his formal permission, paid a visit to the Confederate capital on a peace errand." In a personal interview with Jefferson Davis, the Confederate president disclosed the only terms he would entertain: "Say to Mr. Lincoln, from me, that I shall at any time be pleased to receive proposals for peace on the basis of our independence. It will be useless to approach me with any other."[65] Because some of Lincoln's political enemies continued to perceive him as the sole obstacle to peace, this revelation set the record straight.

The president's able and artistic political ally, Thomas Nast, publicized Davis's response. In a clever cartoon, "The Big Peace Visit to Jeff," Nast quoted Davis's conditions verbatim. The cartoon caption, which got directly to the heart of the issue, emphasized that Davis needed to assume equal responsibility for any failure of efforts in pursuit of peace. All the two sides seemed to have in common was intransigence; Lincoln insisted on Union, and Davis on independence. Fortifying the Union's perspective, Nast jabbed at Davis's credibility on the infamous "history of the Confederacy," which included firing the "first gun at Sumter," "gorilla warfare," "murdering Union men," "Lafayette," "Fort Pillow," "Chambersburg," "hanging Yankees," and "starving Union prisoners."[66] According to Nast's colorful depiction of the Confederate record and Jefferson Davis's clarification of the South's position, a negotiated peace was improbable.

By and large, Lincoln imagery from the domestic illustrated press continued to support him. For example, *Frank Leslie's Illustrated Newspaper* defended him from the Copperheads. In the "Grand Scene from the Last Farce Performed at Albany," it is Horatio Seymour, not the president, whom William Newman chides—because of the governor's criticism of Lincoln's suppression of the press. Nor did bleak reports from the war diminish such support. One illustration in *Frank Leslie's Budget of Fun* surrounds Jefferson Davis with Generals Sherman, Butler, Meade, Hunter, Winfield Scott Hancock, and Grant, while their soldiers shout, "We Are Coming, Father Abraham."[67] In *Comic Monthly*, Frank Beard humorously summarized the war's status. Beard displayed Union generals Grant and Sherman dominating the war arena. To express that accomplishment, Beard portrayed them as dogs and the Confederate generals as rats. On the sidelines, Lincoln urges General Grant to keep digging for Lee at Richmond. General Sherman ruthlessly pummels Gen. Joseph E. Johnston in

Georgia, Stonewall Jackson and General Leonidas Polk die on the battlefield, and the remaining Confederate generals cower in the background. Moreover, Secretary of War Stanton restrains James Gordon Bennett from putting the puppy "Little Mac" back into the arena. General McClellan's puppy image demeans the former general and soon-to-be-named official Democratic rival of Lincoln for the presidency. Finally, John Bull and Napoleon III arrive just in time to witness the one-sided beating.[68]

Although these generally favorable images of Lincoln typified the domestic periodicals' stance on major issues of the day, they do not reflect the intense political opposition waged against Lincoln in conference rooms during the summer of 1864. On the whole, there was a significant disparity between the message of these images and opposition to Lincoln among Radical Republicans, proponents of Frémont's third-party candidacy, and the Peace Democrats. As we shall see, the testament of contemporary illustrated periodicals illuminates how Lincoln survived the challenge for the right to represent the Republican Party in the 1864 presidential election.

"The 'Situation,'" *Comic Monthly,* August 1864. Courtesy of Special Collections Library, Gettysburg College.

The *Comic News,*
Lincoln, and the Civil War

*N*eatly tucked away in the archives of history and hidden from the view of scholars for more than a century are political caricatures, satire, and doggerel of Abraham Lincoln and the Civil War found in the *Comic News,* one of London's humorous illustrated weeklies, and its short-lived successor, the *Bubble.*[1] When the *Comic News* threw its hat into the journalistic ring, English caricature and satire of Lincoln and the Civil War were dominated by the venerable *Punch* and the newcomer *Fun.* In fact, the lengthy shadow cast by *Punch* and *Fun* ultimately doomed the *Comic News* to its early demise in March 1865, approximately nineteen months after its birth on July 18, 1863. Despite the economic realities that destined the rare periodical to obscurity, its robust humor and political posture with respect to Lincoln and the Civil War deserve a better fate in the annals of history.

If for no other reason, this rare comic periodical is valuable for the Lincoln caricatures created by the illustrator Matt Morgan during the last six months of publication. Morgan is well known for his Lincoln cartoons in *Fun.* The Lincoln images in the *Comic News* solve the mystery of why Morgan's seminal Civil War illustrations ceased appearing in *Fun* in October 1864. That same month, Morgan accepted an assignment as the leading illustrator for the *Comic News.* Thus, the *Comic News* illustrations perpetuate an unbroken chain of Civil War art from his years with *Fun* to the beginning of April 1865. Moreover, while the *Comic News* added ten significant "new" Morgan cartoons, it also sponsored Civil War illustration from a few other British illustrators. Hence, Lincoln and Civil War scholarship, as well as art and journalism history, are richer and more complete as a result of the *Comic News.* However, the *Comic News* has much more to offer than Morgan's fine popular art.

The inaugural issue of the *Comic News* was launched under the editorship of Henry Byron. Initially, C. H. Bennett, W. M'Connell, and W. Brunton were its illustrators. At first, Civil War content was sparse. In fact, for the first month, the conflict was completely ignored. In due time, however, the fledgling periodical rivaled *Fun*, if not *Punch*, for its attention to the American conflict.[2] During that first year, Lincoln and Civil War caricatures were rare for the *Comic News*, but significant volleys from the comic editorial and satirical doggerel genres commenced in August 1863.

AMERICAN WANT OF INTELLIGENCE

On August 22, a series of comic editorials under the intriguing and telling title "American Want of Intelligence" was originated by the *Comic News*'s New York–based war correspondent, with the byline "From Our Own Manhattan." From the standpoint of Union sensibilities, consistent with the *Comic News*'s humorous sisters *Punch* and *Fun*, the fairly regular editorial piece was irreverent, satirical, condescending, nationalistic, critical of American leadership, sympathetic to slavery, and by default, slightly more partisan to the Confederate cause. By far, Lincoln was the most frequent target of scorn: "From first to last," noted the initial editorial, "I have maintained the utter incompetence of Abe Lincoln." One week later, the writer predicted, "As long as Lincoln is suffered to remain at the head of affairs, there is no real hope for America." Although "Our Own Manhattan" decried, quite justifiably, the quality of Union generals, including McDowell, Little Mac, Pope, Burnside, and Hooker, he reserved his most potent contempt for the commander in chief.[3]

> Our invincible (except at Bull's Run twice, Fredericksburg, and other battles) troops would long ere this have sprung with a tiger's leap. . . . Why have they been restrained? . . . Simply to suit the purposes of the miserable dotard, the superannuated wood-cutter, Abe Lincoln. . . . Abe has made a bet of half a million dollars with the American representative of the house of Rothschild, that Charleston will not fall before the 22nd September. Of course he means to win. . . . Our peculiar exercise of private judgment in choosing as our ruler not a statesman, not an orator, not even a gentleman, has already cost us half a million lives and a national debt, the largest ever created in so short a time, which we have not the remotest intention of ultimately repaying.[4]

Lincoln continued to absorb the brunt of censure when the October 3 editorial reported, "Rumors are rife as to ministerial changes, both of men and offices." The satirical list of the occupants of new administrative offices included "Dictator—Abe Lincoln; War—Rev. H. W. Beecher (with power to consult Mrs. Stowe); Worship—Brigham Young; Finance—Phineas Taylor Barnum; Army of the Potomac—General Tom Thumb; Public Instruction—James Gordon Bennett; Justice—General Ben Butler, and Indian Relations—Deerfoot." Lincoln did receive some grudging respect from "Manhattan" in conjunction with the naval prowess of the *Monitor,* but it was short-lived.[5] The next editorial resumed the attack, which contained a variety of venom expressly created for its sardonic sting: "The man Lincoln is possibly 'honest,' but a more helpless nincompoop was never raised down in Illinois.... Any citizen of ordinary intellect would have contracted to crush the rebellion in ninety-one days. The plain truth is, that Lincoln and his men do not really desire to put down the South. No, Sir. It pays them too well.... Abe has really been purchasing property down South, that he has bought a plantation in Louisiana; that, as soon as circumstances permit, Mrs. L. will be sent away, and her place supplied by a bevy of African belles; and that the chief overseer, with unlimited powers of using the cowhide, will be our intelligent ... friend, Horace Greeley."[6]

By the last editorial of the series, "Manhattan" was ready to announce his own intention to run for the presidency of the United States. "The time for the fogey and the dotard is gone by. Abraham, stand aside.... Here's the ticket—'Manhattan For President!'"[7]

CIVIL WAR CARICATURE AND DOGGEREL TO JULY 1864

Although Lincoln's image in the British comic press was typically pejorative, there were moments of ambivalence. When Ulysses S. Grant's siege at Vicksburg finally yielded victory and the battle at Gettysburg denied Robert E. Lee's dream for a crushing conquest in the North, Union optimism filtered through the doggerel of the *Comic News*. The title of the piece, "General Bragg's Last Despatch to President Lincoln," refers to a fictitious Union general, "Titus Bragg," who boasts of imminent victory. Three concluding verses sample the substance and flair of the doggerel:

We'll sweep the State with fire and sword,
Secesh! We'll lay a pretty tax on.
Why who is Jeff to set him up,
As if he was old General Jackson?
Why not Calhoun, and Webster too,
Could split our union. No, sirree,
I'd like to see the man who'll dare
To not let every nigger free.

Thunder, if we won't scour the South,
And grind them like their sugar canes.
We'll teach them that we have our wits,
And ain't got pumpkin squash for brains,
Yes, sir, we'll gibbet Davis up
On Charleston steeple, and New Orleans
Shall see old Abe drive tandem there
Over the rebels without reins.

Hurrah! For Congress—Crockett knows
What blessings are in store for us.
Hurrah! For Abe. Secesh is gone.
Then let the rebels cry and cuss;
We've got the pull, now let her nip!
The Union streamers mighty tall;
Let go the hundred-pounder, Sir,
The Stars and Stripes float over all.[8]

Although the first *Comic News* political caricature of Lincoln and the Civil War was actually designed to criticize England's foreign secretary, Lord John Russell, the net effect of the cartoon was to portray Lincoln as a strong leader. This illustration came after another diplomatic confrontation between the United States and Great Britain. When the United States lodged vigorous protests against Great Britain for winking at Confederate contracts for warships with the Laird shipyards in Liverpool, diplomatic relations between the two countries were sorely strained.[9] And when the Confederate vessel *Alabama*, a product of the Laird Brothers' commercial enterprise, began wreaking havoc with the Union naval forces, the cry of foul play reached a new fever pitch. However, supremacy of the seas and in technology or any other category was a matter of pride for the British. The average English citizen did not seem to mind what Lincoln perceived as an unholy alliance between the nation's shipbuilding industry and the Confederacy. In fact, nationalistic fervor resented the perceived retreat by the British government to placate the umbrage taken by the Lincoln administration.

William M'Connell, an adroit political caricaturist, capitalized on this international clash of political will. He contrasted the naturally diminutive Lord Russell to the lanky Abraham Lincoln to underscore the notion that Russell was permitting Lincoln to bully John Bull. Satirizing "British Pluck," M'Connell subtly portrayed Lincoln and Russell as "Licensed Drovers," literally people who drive domestic livestock such as sheep, but in this figurative case, drivers of "Rams"—ships that were characterized by a ramming device. A subdued and deferential Russell is shown kowtowing to Lincoln under a sign that points to "Laird Yards." The caption strengthens the forceful, threatening image of Britain losing face on the diplomatic front: "Lincoln—'Now, drover-boy Jack, if you let out them Rams, I won't answer for the consequences.' Russell (very humbly)— 'No, Sir—please, Sir—I'll do whatever you tells me, Sir—in course, Sir—yes, Sir—please, Sir.'"[10]

That the British followed the fortunes of these ships with interest is especially clear in the case of the *Alabama*. Constructed at the Laird shipyards, the *Alabama* left Liverpool in late July 1862, for the Azores, where it was equipped with armament for service as a Confederate warship. Among its most conspicuous conquests was the sinking of the USS *Hatteras* in January 1863. In the *Comic News*, lyrics that celebrate the *Alabama*'s victories were adapted to a popular air, "The Saucy Arethusa." The last three verses of the song convey the tone of national pride:

"British Pluck," *Comic News*, November 14, 1863, front page. Courtesy of the Western Reserve Historical Society.

BRITISH PLUCK.

LINCOLN.—Now, drover-boy JACK, if you let out them Rams, I won't answer for the consequences.
RUSSELL (VERY HUMBLY).—No, Sir—please, Sir—I'll do whatever you tells me, Sir—in course, Sir—yes, Sir—please, Sir.

The Alabama

This many a year she has been out,
In safety she has sailed about,
And a great deal of damage done, no doubt,
Has the saucy *Alabama*.
The *Vanderbilt* and *Kearsarge*, too,
With other vessels, not a few,
Have been on her track
But have proved so slack
That we cannot help thinking their boasting stuff—
For they've none of them, yet, got near enough
To get hold of the *Alabama*.

The Yankees, they begin to dance,
At finding they've not got a chance
Of putting a check on the bold advance
Of the little *Alabama*:
So now they are turning round on us
And making a very pretty fuss—
"You British," say they,
"Must damages pay!"
"No, not quite, I fancy that can't be,
For she's really got nothing to do with we,
That same saucy *Alabama*."

So let them learn that we will not stand
Their airs and their graces, high and grand—
Instead of Insulting our English land
Let them catch the *Alabama*!
And, when they've driven her ashore,
We shall think of them, p'rhaps, a little more;
But till that's the case
We laugh in the face
Of the nation that talks of its gallant flag,
And its splendid ships—yet, with all its brag,
Can't get hold of the *Alabama*![11]

When the USS *Kearsarge* did finally catch and sink the CSS *Alabama*, a journalist for the *Comic News* wrote three more verses to be sung to the same air. Because of the superior fire power of the USS *Kearsarge*, the final verse triumphantly claims a moral victory:

The fight came off near the Frenchman's land,
Not more than nine miles from the strand,
We fought till not a stick would stand
On board of the *Alabama*.
And then she sank, with flying flag,
The *Kearsarge* got nothing of which to brag.
So now she'll never fight again,
Or spread her sail upon the main,
But still her name
Will leave deathless fame,
For she fought with only a single gun,
'Gainst numbers that were two to one;
On board of the *Alabama*.[12]

Although readers of the *Comic News* were preoccupied for a time with the *Alabama*, Lincoln remained the favorite bull's-eye for derisive humor. Just about any pretext was used to discredit Lincoln while entertaining readers of the *Comic News*. "The ladies, it seems, have wheedled old Abe out of the original draft of the Emancipation Proclamation. They have also persuaded him to give them the shirt that he wore on his way to Washington, when he was nearly murdered in Baltimore."[13]

Even though it had been nearly three years since those charged with Lincoln's safety advised him to slip unobtrusively through Baltimore on his way to his inauguration, that event had neither lost its comic power nor the bite of ridicule. Because England continued to see American manners as unworthy of British societal standards and viewed the rural Lincoln woodcutter as the perfect foil to validate their impressions of this hopeless international gulf in social graces, "The Tale of the President's Shirt" was a natural conclusion to the popular premises of disdain. Furthermore, it was one more arrow in the quiver of the comic genre to send flying at its tall target.

> *The Tale of the President's Shirt*
> At Baltimore Abe had been murdered,
> If he had not been on the alert;
> And so all the Washington ladies
> As a relic have begged for his shirt!
>
> [Chorus]
> Oh, dear me!
> What's become of American manners,
> When they ask for a garment like that
> To cut up into Liberty's banners?
>
> It was marked with A. L. For Abe Lincoln,
> By the President's fingers expert,
> And so all the Washington ladies
> Have an autograph gained in the shirt.
> But whether 'twas linen or long-cloth
> The newspapers do not assert,
> But you'll learn from the Washington ladies,
> The proprietors now of the shirt.
>
> A love for such relics as that is
> The fates long from England avert;
> May no page of our Hist'ry resemble
> The tale of a President's shirt.[14]

Other comic pieces chided Lincoln for the use of paper money, the alleged economic shambles of the Union, the abuse of "Shoddy-Contractors," his supposed unwillingness to entertain diverse opinion, the unsubstantial paper victories, and "the Bunkum he talks about" African Americans.[15]

THE AFRICAN AMERICAN IMAGE

Typical of the media in general and comic journalism in particular, both at home and abroad, the *Comic News* reflected and shaped views about people of color. The Civil War made that issue more salient on both continents. Overwhelmingly, the image was pejorative. Nevertheless, on September 5, 1863, a lengthy piece of doggerel argued that the welfare of African Americans was equally miserable north or south of the Mason-Dixon line. "Whether Hooker win or Lee" predicted the realist poet, the future for slaves was not bright. Included here are six verses of doggerel popularizing that view:

> We blacks, and every shade of brown,
> Creole, Mulatto, and Quadroon
> Do humbly beg to testify,
> With no desire to mystify,
> That we still get drubbed to the old toon.
>
> The bag'nets drill us right and left;
> But North and South give us no quarter;
> They rob us of the dollars, sir,
> They flog our wives and steal our darter.
>
> A plague on both your houses then.
> We are trod on by you friendly Yank,
> And all the while the fierce Secesch
> Drub, beat us, boot us, flog and thresh,
> All down the Mississippi bank.
>
> They talk of 'mancipation time,
> 'Bolition drums go "row-de-dow,"
> That saint, the Reverend Jawboned Debenham
> Says we're "God's own image carved in ebonum."
> But still we cry, Where are we now?
>
> We've got more whales upon our back
> Than wallow in the great Pacific;
> Your nation's stripes we sha'n't forget,
> Your stars are on our noddles set;
> Against the whip we've no specific

They drives us North; they drives us South,
More kicks than half pence come from them.
White broders t'oder side Atlantic
Don't think us niggers cracked or frantic
If we sigh for New Jerusalem.[16]

However, these "White broders t'oder side Atlantic" were not paragons of tolerance or charity either. The *Comic News* justified slavery on the grounds of racial inferiority, rationalized the use of the "lash," maligned the abolitionist movement, and chided Lincoln for his moderate racial views. Illustrations only complemented this negative theme. For example, in one cartoon the famous British illustrator George Cruikshank assembled an Englishman, an African American, and a domesticated gorilla to mock the caption "Are We Not All Brothers?" Later, Yorick, a cartoonist, catered to the fears of ethnic domination. He depicted "The Last (White) Man; or, A Possibility for America in 1874" being auctioned by Senator Jumbo (an African American) as "The only live specimen now existing of the one and indivisible great Republic of the United States."[17]

THE WAR IN AMERICA

Between July and mid-September 1864, a series of comic satires entitled "The War in America" monopolized the Civil War content of the *Comic News*. One had to read between the lines to get any information about the war because, like the earlier series "American Want of Intelligence," this display of raillery was like something the American humorist Artemus Ward might have written. The breezy articles thrived on farce, wordplay, satire, puns, and the absurd. Lincoln, a "tall, gaunt, lean, morose looking figure, with long slender arms, and legs all over the place," continued to attract jocular, demeaning commentary. One version featured a tobacco-chewing president. "Ah, sir, chewing's one of the great in-sti-chew-tions of our country, some of our greatest men has chewed in their time. But the old dominion's almost chawed up! The President here emitted from his mouth an expectoration of the most alarming magni-chew'd, and shot it with a true and steady aim right on the left boot of your amiable and boot-iful correspondent." Later, "our special correspondent in the Federal States" concluded, "So poor America is ruled, and scolded, and schooled, by a buffoon, a monkey, a wretched old donkey, who is more fit for a flunkey than to rule this great country. Old Abe's a muff—or, to pile it strong, 'muffer'; his wisdom's all stuff, and he's a regular duffer."[18]

In the aftermath of Gettysburg, the *Comic News*'s special correspondent derided Lincoln's oratorical ability. "The language of Abraham Lincoln, President of the Minor portion of the Dis-United States of America, is commonly of so vulgar a nature as to be, in the language of the *Comic News* Police Reporter, 'totally unfit for publication.' Mr. Lincoln has made himself almost hymn-mortal by his disgusting song-singing on the flat of Gettysburg, and for further immorality he must get his character improved, or he will never be recognized as a genius by the genial correspondent of the *Comic News*."[19]

For this same period, there were other prey for sneering, too, including Gen. Benjamin Butler. Still, "Beast Butler" was no match for the amount of attention accorded Lincoln. For example, in the summer of 1864, when Lincoln's prospects for reelection were bleak, the *Comic News* predicted that, following the election, Lincoln would be splitting rails again. A cartoon captioned "The Great Donkey Show," the animal rogue's gallery of national leaders, included the "Prussian Mule No. 1," the "German Donkey," and the North's and South's fighting "American Wild Asses." Although Prussia and Germany were not commended by their inclusion in this group, the linguistic regression from "mule" and "donkey" to "wild asses" conclusively designated the Americans as the sole occupants of the bottom rung of the international political ladder. To Napoleon III's suggestion that "those American animals ought to be separated," Britannia replies, "I've spoken to my foreman about it. I'm sorry to say he is not as active as he used to be."[20] The dialogue demonstrates the role

"The Great Donkey Show," *Comic News*, August 13, 1864, 67. Courtesy of the Western Reserve Historical Society.

THE GREAT DONKEY SHOW.

Mons. Nap.—"I THINK THOSE AMERICAN ANIMALS OUGHT TO BE SEPARATED."
Mrs. Britannia.—"I'VE SPOKEN TO MY FOREMAN ABOUT IT. I'M SORRY TO SAY HE IS NOT AS ACTIVE AS HE USED TO BE."

that British public opinion played in keeping pressure on their own leadership to upbraid their cousins' behavior abroad. To be sure, these two "American Wild Asses" might have also easily conjured up the images of the two most salient protagonists, Jefferson Davis and Abraham Lincoln.

THE *COMIC NEWS* ACQUIRES MATT MORGAN

One of the most significant discoveries from the pages of the *Comic News* is nearly a dozen political caricatures of Abraham Lincoln, primarily from the pen of Matt Morgan. Although Morgan, a cartoonist for *Fun*, was one of the principal architects of the Lincoln image in England, he suddenly and inexplicably disappeared from Civil War illustration. His last drawing in *Fun* was published on October 1, 1864. Although one art historian described Morgan's political caricature in *Fun* as "brilliant," compared him to the finest illustrators in *Punch*, and asserted that "his work is amongst the most original of its time," until now his whereabouts during the six months before the close of the Civil War remained a mystery. Lincoln scholars have also neglected to account for Morgan's vanishing act.[21] His transfer of allegiance from *Fun* to the *Comic News* solved the puzzle and extended his known Civil War career in popular art to the end of March 1865. His Civil War illustrations were uninterrupted in the transition from one periodical to another. Exactly one week passed from his last illustration in *Fun* to his first print in the *Comic News* on October 8, 1864.

By the fall of 1864 the survival of the *Comic News,* like the flagging fortunes of the Confederacy, was also questionable. The humor periodical had been steadily losing ground in its head-to-head competition with *Punch* and *Fun*. Extraordinary measures would now have to be taken to resuscitate the dying publication. In the September 17, 1864, issue of the *Comic News,* an announcement alluded to these strong measures: "The next number of the *Comic News* will be conducted under entirely new management." Also noted was the intention of the management to begin offering a "cartoon of great political importance." To accomplish that purpose and bolster sagging sales, Matt Morgan, the leading Civil War cartoonist for *Fun,* was hired.

For nearly three years Morgan had drawn piercing caricatures of Lincoln and some of the central themes of the Civil War. At least ideologically, this was not a difficult transition for Morgan because the two publications shared a common philosophy. *Fun* reveled, too, in criticism of the conduct of the American conflict, specifically in Lincoln's leadership. In fact, Morgan took up his pen with the *Comic News* just where he left off with *Fun*. On September 17, 1864, Morgan's last Lincoln caricature with *Fun* depicted the president as "Columbia's Nightmare." Similarly, his first assault on Lincoln in the *Comic News* portrayed him as the devil. In the vintage Morgan cartoon "Pull Devil—Pull Baker," Lincoln and McClellan, contestants for the presidency of the United States in the 1864 election, are shown tugging for control of a map of the "Northern States," a torn map of the "Southern States" on the ground. Morgan's rendering of Lincoln as Satan casts the cartoon more in the anti-Lincoln camp than in the pro-McClellan category.[22] However, Morgan's felicitous debut in the *Comic News* was not the only significant development of the period.

In the early fall of 1864, written satire and humor were not entirely forgotten. For example, the *Comic News* offered the latest betting odds for the "Richmond Cup" (occupation of the Confederate capital). It wagered "10 to 1 on General Lee's superior science; 50 to 1 against General Grant's inability; . . . 40 to 1 on General Sheridan's advance; . . . and 50 to 1 against Abe Lincoln's lot." The *Comic News*'s special correspondent also occasionally indulged in "showing up, scalping , and tomahawking the Americans, without dreading their vengeance, their bowie-knives, or their six-shooters." Nor could anything, not even American kindness, "deter me from depicting the Americans in their real Character. . . . I could not then . . . have delineated Mrs. Lincoln, nor have given you the character of the immortal rail-splitter! I could not then have accused our American cousins of barbarism! . . . I shall continue, during my stay here, to tear away the mask that hides from view the wretched, hideous, and painful state of things existing in what is called American society."[23] This was typical British satire that was equally at home in the *Comic News*, *Fun*, and *Punch*.

Any political tension between the Lincoln administration and Great Britain created public apprehension in England over the welfare and security of Canada. That anxiety and sense of vulnerability was reflected in the next Morgan cartoon, "Advice

PULL DEVIL—PULL BAKER.

"Pull Devil—Pull Baker," *Comic News*, October 8, 1864, 159. Courtesy of the Western Reserve Historical Society.

ADVICE GRATIS.

Abe:—"NOW, SIR-REE, CUT THAT CONNEXION. I'LL LOAN YOU A SAW!"
Canada:—"YOU'RE BARKING UP THE WRONG TREE, OLD FRIEND; I'M ONLY BINDING UP THE OUTLYING
BRANCHES."

Gratis." The male figure that symbolizes Canada sits on a large branch of a huge tree labeled "Old England." Standing below, "Abe" calls out to "Canada," "Now, sir-ree, cut that connexion. I'll loan you a saw!" Canada retorts, "You're barking up the wrong tree, old friend: I'm only binding up the outlying branches."[24] Canada's precarious position on the branch underscores the destructive consequences that any Canadian break with England would have caused. From England's standpoint, severing the emblematic branch of Canada from the British trunk would have been tantamount to Canada's downfall. The cartoon also conveys the notion that Canada was seeking to strengthen, not weaken, its affiliation with England.

In November, Morgan wistfully ventured a cartoon prediction of the winner of the 1864 presidential election. He missed the mark. Although the winner of the election had not been a foregone conclusion early in the campaign, Lincoln gained popularity as decisive Union victories multiplied. In "Exit Abe," Lincoln is shown falling through a trap door as a result of the verdict of the popular ballot. Columbia appears to be relieved as she casts the deciding vote that sends a disgruntled Abe to political oblivion. However, much to the probable chagrin of Morgan, Lincoln, of course, survived the Democratic challenge. Although *Punch*'s John Tenniel did not go quite so far, he too intimated in cartoon form his desire for Lincoln's defeat.[25]

However, Lincoln's victory did not soften Morgan's cartoon rhetoric toward the president. Rather, it seemed to intensify antipathy, and the tone became more vindictive. For example, Morgan gave a spirited rendition of Lincoln as "The Vampire."

"Exit Abe," *Comic News*, November 12, 1864, 209. Courtesy of the Western Reserve Historical Society.

"The Vampire," *Comic News*, November 26, 1864, 221. Courtesy of the Western Reserve Historical Society.

THE VAMPIRE.

Abe.—"COLUMBIA, THOU ART MINE; WITH THY BLOOD I WILL RENEW MY LEASE OF LIFE—AH! AH!"

This time the president's supposed victim was a helpless Columbia. A menacing Abe threatens, "Columbia, thou art mine; with thy blood I will renew my lease of life—ah! ah!"[26] In effect, Morgan's caption asserted that Lincoln was opportunistically and unscrupulously perpetuating his political power through the immoral tool of civil war.

No British cartoonist was as consistently hostile to Lincoln as Matt Morgan. Neither *Punch* nor *Fun* followed this more critical postelection pattern. As a matter of fact, *Fun* virtually dropped Lincoln caricature when Morgan left and replaced it with a more general, graphic Civil War commentary. And whereas the earlier Morgan exploited the rural simpleton, awkward oaf, incompetent buffoon, and inept president imagery, the later version imputed more malevolent motives. Themes of blood, death, tyranny, intimations of war crimes, and even the propriety of hanging Lincoln exemplify the more hostile content.

Part of this change in image may be due to the bloody character of the later stages of the Civil War. No one could deny the formidable and morbid statistics of casualties and loss of life. Moreover, Lincoln was not the only focus of such criticism. In a brief article titled "American Intelligence," the *Comic News* was uncharacteristically sober as it chided General Grant for his role in the shedding of blood: "The initials of General Grant happen to be U. S. The New York *Herald* and other journals have interpreted these mysterious letters as meaning 'United States Grant,' 'Uncle Sam Grant,' and lastly, in allusion to the fall of Vicksburg, 'Unconditional Surrender Grant,' The names, in their way, are not bad; but Mr. James Gordon Bennett seems to have forgotten another translation of his pet initials, 'Unlimited Slaughter Grant.'"[27] Nonetheless, the gruesome reality of war does not explain away Morgan's singular, aggressive style.

None of this is to say that Lincoln's homespun image disappeared. In fact, the *Comic News* effectively blended the morbid and rural images with the clever use of lower-class dialect in doggerel entitled "The Northern Harmer; or, the Abraham Lincolnshire Farmer."

Where's my man, Seward, tew now? I have drinked to the dregs my cup;
Bring me another gin-sling, mayn't a President tew liquor up?
Doctor, of course, he perhibits; I sit and I listen awhile,
For I guess that the Doctor, leaving, goes out for a private smile!

Do the free electors knaw whet they'd do if they didn't take me?
Whoy they moight be driven back on a feller like Robert Lee!
And if they prefer McClellan, I guess that I pity their taaste;
McClellan? He won a battle; but I laid Virginia waaste!

Dubbut looak at the waaste! There isn't food for a cow!
Nothing but ruin and wrack, that's what I've left there now!
Millions once it were worth, an' now there's lots of dead;
Plenty of comfort once—now, havoc and hell instead!

Feller he says in the play as the times is all out o' jint;
Guess you can't tinker 'em up by your Little Mac from West Pint!
Gentleman born? Git out! He's done no better nor I!
Epaulettes ain't inspiration; and gin I mun lie, I mun lie!

So, Seward, tell ma tha news, I can bear to hear the whole;
"Abraham Lincoln returned, at the very head of the poll!"
Only a four years' tenant; we'll settle thet by-and-bye!
Help, bring cocktails for two, and gin I mun lie, I mun lie![28]

Morgan acknowledged the reelection of Lincoln to a second term in a cartoon that vilified the president as the personification of death. At first glance, Lincoln appears to be a cricket player in the cartoon titled "In for His Second Innings." However, when the president's mask is removed, his true character as the agent of death is exposed. In the background, the dead body of a soldier and crippled war machinery emphasize the point.[29] Morgan tarnished Lincoln with the dual images of duplicity and insensitivity to the brutal consequences of war. In any case, Morgan persistently denounced Lincoln and cast him in the role of villain.

In the same issue, humorous satire imagined what Henry Wadsworth Longfellow, Walt Whitman, and Ralph Waldo Emerson thought of Lincoln and the war. A fictitious Fanny Fern represented the women's view.[30] In poetic style and meter, the satirist imitated and paraphrased Longfellow's classic poem "The Bridge," ascribing these verses about Lincoln's election to the American bard:

I stood on the bridge at midnight,
Whilst the clocks were striking the hour,
A fact which has no connection
With the recent struggle for power;
Except that, whilst watching the wavelets
In moonlight and melody float,
I attempted a slight calculation
As concerns the Electoral Vote!

I found, in the silent midnight,
Under the tranquil skies,
That Lincoln was certain of winning
The costly and coveted prize;
I turned away in the moonbeam,
Orion was bright overhead;
And the night being awfully chlly,
Went quietly home to my bed![31]

Whitman and Emerson were portrayed as partial to Lincoln, but their literary gifts were no more appreciated than the spoof on Longfellow's talent. Fanny Fern, an advocate of women's rights, favored Lincoln over McClellan but concluded, "One man, gals, is very much like another; and a more useless, shiftless, helpless, feckless set of bipeds, . . . a more miserable, incapable gang of human creatures I never saw."[32]

IN FOR HIS SECOND INNINGS.

In the context of the Civil War, the energetic British foreign secretary John Russell was a popular subject for caricature. At the end of 1864, Morgan drew Russell, in
conjunction with France's Napoleon III and America's Lincoln, as "Our Mutual
Friend." However, the implication of friendship was pure sarcasm. Morgan's intent
was to question the foreign policy effectiveness of Russell. Lincoln tries to manipu-
late and coerce Russell; Napoleon III condescendingly waits his turn in the background. Once again, Morgan used the discrepancy in physical size of a short Russell
and taller Lincoln and Napoleon III figures to amplify the notion of influence. The
final print of 1864 shows the Union burning while Lincoln, "The Yankee Nero," gid-
dily plays wooden percussion instruments between his fingers. Like Nero, Lincoln

"Our Mutual Friend,"
Comic News, December
13, 1864, 251. Courtesy
of the Western Reserve
Historical Society.

"OUR MUTUAL FRIEND."

looks upon the burgeoning holocaust with absolute indifference and wears a Roman crown to round out the analogy. This image of Lincoln as a ruthless emperor, king, or dictator who tyrannically usurped power and dominion was more typical of the extreme Confederate view. A milder version, containing elements of this image of the misuse of power, also surfaced among Lincoln's opponents in the Democratic Party.[33] Morgan's linkage of Nero to Lincoln was by no means unique.

Since coming on board as an illustrator for the *Comic News,* Matt Morgan had indeed enlivened the periodical. Quantitatively, in just three months his seven full-page Lincoln caricatures eclipsed any comparable offering in *Fun* or *Punch.* Qualitatively, although pitted against the high standard of John Tenniel's work in *Punch*, Morgan held his own. Like Tenniel, Morgan focused almost exclusively on the anti-Lincoln theme. On the other hand, the artists for *Fun*, perhaps not eager to compete with either Tenniel or Morgan on their specialty—the Lincoln image—wisely opted for more generic Civil War motifs. Unfortunately, Morgan's impressive burst of creative energy was no cure for the ailing condition of the *Comic News*. Within three months it would be history and its successor, the *Bubble*, a two-week flash in the pan.

THE YANKEE NERO.

"The Yankee Nero," *Comic News*, December 27, 1864, 277. Courtesy of the Western Reserve Historical Society.

In January 1865, Morgan's artistry temporarily disappeared from the pages of the *Comic News*. In fact, during that first month of the new year only a single entry of doggerel represented the entire spectrum of Civil War content. That piece chronicled the saga of the css *Florida*. The *Florida* was built in Britain, armed with weaponry in Nassau, and made battle ready by the fall of 1862. Two years later, after a distinguished record at war, the *Florida* anchored temporarily off the coast of Brazil. Lured into a false sense of security by the rules of international warfare, the crew of the *Florida* wrongly assumed that the uss *Wachusett* would abide by the code of international law. Instead, the *Wachusett* captured the *Florida*, towed it to Chesapeake Bay, and unceremoniously sunk its troublesome foe.[34] "The Wreck of the *Florida*" was a parody of Longfellow's "Wreck of the Hesperus." Authorship of the humorous poetry was attributed to "Ab----m L-nc--n, or some other Tall Fellow."

It was the steamer *Florida*,
About to put to sea;
And she was in Brazil's waters
In strict neutralitee.

The skipper he stood by the helm,
A smile was on his mouth,
He was thinking what a glorious craft
She was to serve the South.

Then up and spake an old sailor,
Most weatherwise and vain,
"I pray thee get under yonder fort,
For I smell an American."

"Last night the cook had a silver spoon,
To-day no spoon he'll see."
The skipper he gave a wink with his eye,
"You're a brazen old thief!" said he.

Then there came the ship *Wachusetts*,
Belonging to the foe,
And sent a foe on board to take
The *Florida* in tow.

The skipper's face grew very queer
When he saw it was no go;

And they brought her up in Hampton Roads,
Near the guns of Fort Monroe.

And there a transport steamer ran,
By accident of course,
Full tilt into the *Florida*
With all her engines' force.

The master of that transport seemed
A soft unguarded fool,
But his cruel keelson gored her sides,
Like the horns of an angry bull.

And through the leak, by means unknown,
The sea so swiftly poured;
She settled down on her beam ends;
"Ho, ho!" the Federals roared.

     Moral.
Advice from friends the most obscure,
You never should ignore;
So when J--nny R-ss-ll writes again,
I'll think of the old sailor.[35]

In February, Morgan's first caricature of 1865 was faithful to the usual pattern—another jab at Lincoln. For this cartoon, the level of enmity rose a notch. "A Valentine for Abe" was sent to the White House "from a few admiring friends." The print shows Lincoln looking at the valentine. He is shocked and dismayed as he views a drawing of his own body, his hands tied behind his back, swinging from the gallows. Although rare in England, this kind of Civil War gallows humor was not uncommon in the United States, nor was the theme confined to Abraham Lincoln. Jefferson Davis received comparable treatment from artists in America.[36]

The fear that Lincoln might do something rash with respect to Canada endured in British public opinion until the end of the war. Morgan helped to sustain these apprehensions. He portrayed Lincoln as "The Yankee Eagle," descending on a complacent, sleeping English lion. Lincoln's head is affixed to the eagle. Just before his landing, the eagle warns: "Wake up, old hoss! I'm guin to swoop down on yer biggest jewel."[37] In reality, at this stage of the war, Canada was not even a remote consideration in Lincoln's foreign policy. Nevertheless, international tension and war bred a spirit of suspicion and paranoia.

By March, the demise of the *Comic News* was imminent. Just as irrational measures are sometimes taken by loving associates to prolong the inevitability of a relative's

"A VALENTINE FOR ABE."

death, in desperation the management of the *Comic News* renamed it the *Bubble*, but that bubble was about to pop. Breathing new life into a publication that differed from its predecessor in name only was a futile act. The disease was not going into remission. The reprieve was painfully short. The *Bubble*'s first issue appeared on March 21, 1865, its last, the following week.

As the publication figuratively gasped for breath, Matt Morgan came back for one final encore, a memorable finale for the last issue of the *Bubble*. A despairing, disheveled, Lincoln glances at Columbia, laden with "debt" and "misery." With a broken noose hanging from his neck, a ball and chain around his leg, and a cemetery with

THE YANKEE EAGLE AND THE LION.

YANKEE.—WAKE UP, OLD HOSS! I'M GUIN TO SWOOP DOWN ON YER BIGGEST JEWEL.

"The Yankee Eagle and the Lion," *Comic News,* March 7, 1865, 95. Courtesy of the Western Reserve Historical Society.

crosses and tombstones in the background, Lincoln is condemned by the reproachful Columbia. The verdict seals his destiny to a life of rail-splitting. Indeed, at Lincoln's feet is a bundle of rails and an axe.[38] Thus Morgan's fantasy of poetic justice defined "Abe's Future" as a return to where the cartoonist thought Lincoln belonged—back at his humble beginnings.

Given the imminent defeat of the Confederate forces and the euphoria associated with the triumphal consummation of Lincoln's dreams of Union, Morgan's drawing was ironic. As the final sun set on the destiny of the *Comic News* and the *Bubble,* it rose elsewhere in splendor, marking the dawn of a new era for America. For the wrong reason, Morgan was right about the bleak nature of Lincoln's immediate future. But he was dead wrong about his place in history.

One wonders whether Morgan would have liked one more opportunity, like *Punch*'s John Tenniel or the artistic staff of *Fun,* to make peace with the memory of Abraham Lincoln.[39] Given Matt Morgan's intransigent opposition to Lincoln, the form a conciliatory cartoon of his might have taken tantalizes the imagination. However, in his own way, Morgan was belatedly reconciled to the memory of Abraham Lincoln.

"Abe's Future," *Bubble,*
March 28, 1865, 19.
Courtesy of the
Western Reserve
Historical Society.

ABE'S FUTURE.

With the publication of his volume *The American War*, dominated as it was by his own cartoons, Morgan made a final statement about his lasting image of Lincoln.[40] The images from his repertoire that he selected and omitted for that work, as well as the few images he borrowed from others, are vital to measure Morgan's concluding assessment accurately. What he said about those images in textual commentary is also pivotal. From *Fun*, the evidence is compelling that Morgan's selected mosaic of the Lincoln profile is substantially more benign than the total universe of *Fun* cartoons. Some of the harshest images were simply omitted. Many that were included were softened by the text. Finally, Morgan's inclusion of the sympathetic assassination cartoon published in *Fun*, and his own magnanimous commentary, capped his revision of the Lincoln image. "For once the artist pictures unbiased truth," he wrote. "With his hand on the refreshing Cup of Victory, for which the whole nation with him had been athirst, the ruler whose sterling good sense and unfaltering urbanity under the burden of a vast domain to which the realms of Alexander and Napoleon were but as kitchen gardens had become proverbial, was snatched away. The revulsion of feeling abroad at the news of this tragedy was immense. The veil was torn from all eyes, and the Star of Empire shone in the West with an unflecked radiance which has never since worn a cloud."[41]

None of the caricatures in either the *Comic News* or the *Bubble* were published in Morgan's volume. Why? Only one answer seems plausible. Given the uncharitable tone of virtually all of these cartoons, he must have deliberately chosen to exclude them. That choice obviously had implications for Morgan's evaluation of Lincoln. Morgan may have considered these final caricatures too harsh for the verdict of time. If so, Morgan's "final" appraisal of the deceased president was consistent with the steady, positive transformation of the Lincoln image.

For a year and a half, the *Comic News* entertained its loyal patrons. Subscribers and pay-as-you-go benefactors were treated to a comic perspective from England of the Civil War and Abraham Lincoln much like the publication's more famous peers, *Punch* and *Fun*. To be sure, the *Comic News* liberally borrowed from the tradition established by *Punch* and mimicked by *Fun*. Although true to the pattern, the *Comic News* made a significant contribution to the comic tradition and placed an indelible mark on the archival legacy of Lincoln and Civil War image history in satire, doggerel, and popular art.

Nine

The Drive to Deprive Lincoln of a Second Term

O n February 27, 1864, the *New York Illustrated News* featured "Portraits of the Prominent Aspirants for the Presidency."[1] The roster of nine was dominated by former or current Union generals: Banks, Butler, Grant, Frémont, and McClellan. Actually, it was not clear whether U. S. Grant aspired for the office, but a spontaneous groundswell of support propelled the popular military figure into the public's attention. His heroic image, questions about his availability, and the issue of whether he had any political acumen added intrigue to mystery. Republicans and Democrats coveted Grant's allegiance, and some in each party hoped he might become their standard-bearer. With respect to the other generals, Banks and Butler were the darkest of military dark horses, but they did not entirely escape the purview of the political pundits.

It was flattering to be considered among this august group of potential candidates. After all, the publicity could not hurt, and who knew what might happen in the dazzling glow of American politics? Lincoln had emerged from the shadows in 1860; why could not someone else do the same from the ranks of relative obscurity? The final two generals, John C. Frémont and George McClellan, were the most serious overt military contenders. Both yearned for the right to spoil Lincoln's quest for a second term. Each had been ignominiously relieved of military duty by the president, and resentment and personal ambition only increased their motivation. Already, Frémont had sampled the sweet savor of presidential candidacy in 1856, and he wanted, once and for all, to purge the bitter taste of defeat. In addition, he felt strongly that he was better qualified for the presidency than the incumbent. McClellan, among others, was courted by the Democrats; the odds of winning the party nomination were in his favor. Cartoonists affirmed Little Mac's prominence. For example, a *Phunny Phellow* cartoon portrayed McClellan entranced by a vision of "the ghost of the Presidency (Abraham Lincoln) [who] will never cease to haunt you."[2]

"Well Now, I Never Thought You Would [Fill] That [Congressional] Chair," *Phunny Phellow*, January 1863, 8. C. Fiske Harris Collection on the American Civil War and Slavery, Providence Public Library.

In addition to the incumbent, three distinguished citizen politicians were numbered among the candidates: Fernando Wood, Horatio Seymour, and Salmon Chase. Congressman Wood and Governor Seymour were both from New York. As loyal Democrats, these inveterate opponents of Lincoln would have liked nothing better than to deliver a deadly blow to his political hopes. They had been indelibly labeled as Copperheads, but had effectively rallied Lincoln's foes among the Peace Democrats. In January 1863, Thomas Nast cleverly caricatured Fernando Wood and Lincoln engaged in political banter: "Well now, I never thought you would [fill] That

[Congressional] chair" from New York, noted Lincoln. "Why didn't you?" replied Wood. "Why, I could fill yours!" Although Governor Seymour was also mentioned as a potential Democratic candidate, an editorial in *Harper's Weekly*—a biased Republican source—scoffed at his prospects, asserting that "his obsequiousness to a murderous mob [the New York draft riots] alarmed the most substantial supporters."[3] However, although Fernando Wood and Horatio Seymour were Democratic longshots, the secretary of the treasury, Salmon Chase, was a viable candidate and desired the Republican nomination. For months, Radical Republicans had privately wooed and maneuvered him into a contending position. Chase was convinced that Lincoln was not his intellectual equal, nor did he think the president filled his office with grace and distinction. Lincoln was aware of this condescending, pompous attitude, but he tolerated Chase's vain ambition because of his able service to the nation.

What were Lincoln's chances against these potential contenders? In January 1864, an editorial in Lincoln's single-minded champion, *Harper's Weekly*, claimed that "if the presidential election took place next week, Mr. Lincoln would undoubtedly be returned by a greater majority than any president since Washington." "His election is as sure as the triumph of the nation over the rebellion," continued the editorial. The magazine did concede that certain unlikely contingencies might intervene to prevent the projected landslide. If "he is deserted by his great sagacity, or some huge military disaster befalls the country, or some serious blunder is committed by the Union men in Congress," the bets would be off. To its dismay, *Harper's Weekly* was on the verge of learning a lesson in humility. Before long, political detractors within his own party questioned Lincoln's sagacity; the military strategy failed to yield the expected dividends; Union men in Congress became divided over who to support for the presidency; and some doubted the ultimate triumph of the nation over the rebellion. Alas, this was January, and candidates had not been nominated in either party; U. S. Grant's intentions were still opaque; and rumors about a third party had not been abandoned.[4] Furthermore, two-term presidents were a rare breed; not since Andrew Jackson had a president been reelected. Casual prognostication was inevitable, but at this point not very reliable. Around potbellied stoves, talk was cheap and everyone had an opinion, but no one seemed to have a lock on the presidency. To be sure, the sifting process was shaking down candidates, and Lincoln, McClellan, Grant, Frémont, and Chase were nearest the top.

THE SALMON P. CHASE AFFAIR

The candidates were like boxers in the first round of a fight, trying to feel each other out for early intimations of strengths, vulnerabilities, short-term tactics, and long-term strategies, but not many telling punches were actually thrown. However, there was one sparring casualty, and Salmon Chase was the victim. He was not necessarily damaged beyond repair, but he was pretty banged up.

In the fall of 1863, when rumors of Chase's ambitions for the presidency became public in illustrated periodicals, he found himself on the horns of a dilemma. As a loyal cabinet member in the Lincoln administration, how could he run for the presidency? This was a delicate, if not impossible, undertaking. If he discouraged even spontaneous popular support, he might diminish his chances; but if he was too enthusiastic, his official disinterestedness would be exposed. Even popular artists in London snickered over Chase's plight. In October, Matt Morgan caricatured Lincoln and Seward as sowers who broadcast the seeds of money, debt, and taxes in hopes that the nation would "have a turn of luck soon, and the next president will reap— Eh! Chase?"[5] This was a gentle nudge at Chase's pretensions, but the next month's

THE SOWERS.

№:—"GO IT, SEWARD! SOW ANYTHING! WE SHALL HAVE A TURN OF LUCK SOON, AND THE NEXT PRESIDENT WILL REAP—EH! CHASE?"

"The Sowers," *Fun*, October 17, 1863, 45. Courtesy of the University of Minnesota Libraries.

Frank Leslie's Budget of Fun skewered the secretary of treasury and roasted him slowly over the fire of satire. The vehicle of expression was a parody on Shakespeare's *Julius Caesar,* appropriately entitled "Abraham Caesar." Of course Brutus, the central conspirator, was played by Salmon Chase, alias "Mr. Wildgoose Chase." Among the other characters in the play was a mixture of opponents and allies, including Fernando Wood, Ben Wood, Horatio Seymour, Horace Greeley, J. G. Bennett, H. J. Raymond, John W. Forney, Simon Cameron, Edwin Stanton, William Seward, Charles Sumner, and Gideon Welles. It was Gideon Welles, the soothsayer, who disclosed the conspirator's ulterior motives to Abraham Caesar, the imminent martyr:

> Caesar, these fellows are in caucus sitting,
> You'd better get your hand in for rail splitting.
> They grudge your eminence the nomination,
> Thinking themselves more fit for that high station.

Ultimately, Abraham Caesar's conspirators slay him with the cumulative stab wounds of his own administrative decisions: "the Emancipation Proclamation," "the Confiscation Act," "the Conscription Act," and "the Habeas Corpus Suspension Proclamation."[6] If this were just the usual species of seemingly harmless comic ribbing, it would, nevertheless, not endear Salmon Chase to many undecided voters.

Still, other magazines joined the chorus of misgivings for Chase's impending presidential debut. Concerned that either William Seward or Salmon Chase might be lured to oppose Lincoln's nomination, J. H. Howard's cartoon in *Yankee Notions* warned each against such foolishness. The stern admonition originated in the threatening voice of Uncle Sam: "Bill Seward, you and Sal Chase had better clear out, and tend to yer business till the Apple's Ripe [Presidency 1864]. I've known fellers to get awful sick eatin' fruit afore it was ripe—you can't both of yer have it—p'raps nary one of yer'll get it."[7] The source of *Yankee Notion's* loyalty to the president was twofold. Aside from its respect for his policies and presidential conduct, Lincoln's humor endeared him to the staff of this magazine devoted to wit and whimsy. As a matter of fact, the editors took advantage of every occasion to cite "Abe's last" joke. Making allowance for the usual barbs of political caricature expected by any president, its political content overwhelmingly favored Lincoln.

However, the event that detonated the bomb that blew Salmon Chase out of the presidential race was the Pomeroy Circular. In February, Kansas senator S. C. Pomeroy used his franking privilege to promote Salmon Chase as the sole standard-bearer of the Republican Party. The strategy backfired though, and Chase's integrity and loyalty were immediately impugned. "There can be no doubt," editorialized *Harper's Weekly,* "that the movement to present his name for the Presidency has been fully known to him and not disapproved." *Harper's Weekly* not only underscored the subterfuge, it turned the affair into a testimonial for Lincoln:

If it were true, as the Pomeroy programme sets forth, that the reelection of Mr. Lincoln is impossible; or that his reelection would endanger the country and human liberty; or that he has corruptly used his power of patronage, we should, on any one of those grounds advocate some other candidate. . . . But as Mr. Lincoln's reelection seems to us infinitely more possible and probable than his original election; as his administration can by no impartial spectator be said to have imperiled the country, or to have injured human liberty; and as the imputation of corruption no more cleaves to him than to Washington, we must look for other reasons before sympathizing with any effort to expose the country to the consequences of all the changes that follow a change of the President. It is not that Mr. Lincoln has any other "claim" than his record that we so earnestly wish his reelection. Ability and honesty are the only claims to the Presidency which we recognize.[8]

What irony that the political ploy designed to launch Chase's quest for the nomination effectively removed him from serious contention.

The Chase debacle generated a novel caricature in *Yankee Notions*. À la piggyback, Horace Greeley supports Chase long enough to help him peek into the "government stables" to see what type of race their competitors—the trainer Seward and the jockey Thurlow Weed—are contriving. They did get a glimpse of the two secretly plotting their strategy but they could not fathom the whole picture, because the complete and final plan for the carefully orchestrated race is deliberately withheld from the public until the entry of Lincoln could break from the starting gate. This presumably symbolized the fact that the nomination was still weeks away. The blanket on Seward and Weed's stallion bears the name "Emancipation," revealing a central goal of their race. The dialogue between Seward and Weed discloses their intention to keep their thoroughbred under wraps until the nomination and further signals that the Seward-Weed duo are wholly committed to "the old hoss" Lincoln: "Backer Seward (to jockey Weed).—'Now, then, Thurlow, keep him well blanketed, and don't let him show his ears to the enemy until starting time, you know!' Thurlow.—'All Right, boss, the old hoss for us yet.' Jockey Greeley.—'Oh! Hold quiet, Chase! I'll bet all the greenbacks in your hat that I know that animal by his left ear.'"[9] The "left ear" alluded to Lincoln's reputation for a homely countenance.

Although most imagery about the Salmon Chase affair in the majority of illustrated periodicals militated against his candidacy, a new comic magazine devoted to radical politics—*Funniest of Phun*—tenaciously advanced his cause. *Funniest of Phun* was not about to give up on Salmon Chase, especially when it thought that Lincoln's favorable public image was grossly inflated. On the front page of the magazine's first issue, cartoonist Frank Bellew belittled Lincoln as a clown, who embarrasses himself dancing a jig and playing the banjo to his own unpopular tune—"Amnesty Proclamation." The circus ringmaster just happens to be Salmon Chase, and he engages the "National Joker" in small talk. "Ring-Master.—'Now, Little Joker, what about the next Presidency?' Joker.—'This reminds me of a little story about the Current

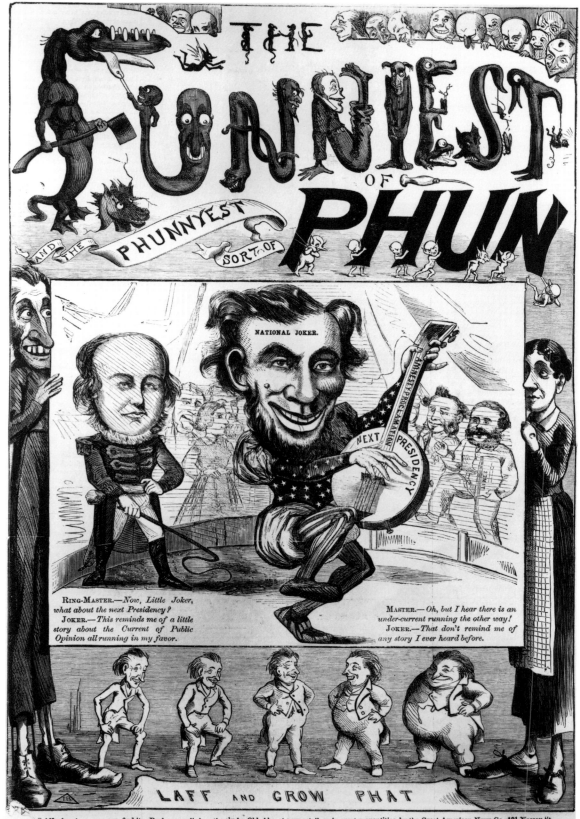

of Public Opinion all running in my favor.' Master.—'Oh, but I hear there is an under-current running the other way!' Joker.—'That don't remind me of any story I ever heard before.'"[10] The suggestion of an "under-current running the other way" was subtle, but there was a kernel of truth to it.

Despite such efforts to vitalize Chase's political aspirations, Salmon Chase withdrew his name for any further consideration for the nomination. A magnanimous editorial in *Harper's Weekly* applied balm to the wound, but it was not powerful enough to heal the strained relationship between Lincoln and Chase. During the summer, any residual "mutual embarrassment" experienced by the president and his secretary of the treasury over this episode ended when Lincoln accepted Chase's resignation from the cabinet. Noting the transition, Frank Bellew showed Lincoln picking at the bones of his filet of Salmon (Chase) and ordering another filet of "Tod." However, David Tod declined the opportunity to replace Salmon Chase. The caption also accounted for that contingency in the waiter's response to Lincoln's aborted request for Tod: "The Tod's out; but can't I fitch something else, Sir?"[11] Eventually, that someone else was William Pitt Fessenden, who became the new secretary of the treasury.

MR. LINCOLN. "MIKE, remove the SALMON and bring me a TOD."
MIKE. "The TOD'S out; but can't I fitch something else, Sir?"

(*Opposite*)
"National Joker," *Funniest of Phun*, June 1864, front page. Courtesy of the American Antiquarian Society.

"Mike, Remove the Salmon," *Harper's Weekly*, July 16, 1864, 464. Author's Collection.

If the Lincoln camp was temporarily relieved that one political rival had fallen by the wayside, this was no time for relaxation. Disgruntled Frémont supporters also intended to block Lincoln's path to the presidency. They could pursue one of three options: Frémont could personally contest Lincoln's nomination at the national convention, throw his political leverage behind a compromise competitor, or "take the field as an independent candidate." In vain, *Harper's Weekly* appealed to Frémont's party loyalty and patriotism to prevent his opposition, but Frémont was not the only threat. In addition, a grassroots movement emerged, urging delay of the Republican nominating convention until September.[12] Among the arguments in favor of doing so was the contention that the efficacy of the Lincoln administration needed to be proven on the battlefield in the summer campaign. This reasoning created conditions for a military resolution to the upcoming election—a political fait accompli. If the armed forces failed to end the war by September 1, Lincoln would be out of the running. Regardless of its merit, this logic favored any opponent of the president, ignored prior battlefield successes in the fall of the year for either side, and restricted the evaluation of presidential candidates to the narrow range of three months. However, the discontent was scattered widely. Unrest in the ranks of Radical Republicanism, even beyond Frémont's loyalists, was growing. Naturally, the Peace Democrats were guaranteed to be implacable rivals and McClellan's stock was increasing. In addition, there was always the outside chance that a military hero like Grant might be willing to become a candidate.

In the midst of this political ferment, what were the visual and verbal messages conveyed in the pages of the illustrated periodicals? A cautious and ambivalent *Merryman's Monthly* was partial to Grant and Lincoln, but there was not much backbone in its verdict to delay its commitment to November: "Presidential Aspirant (to Uncle Sam).—'I have heard Sir, that the White House was to be vacated next Spring by the present tenant, and called to see whether I couldn't get a lease of it for four years, with privilege of four years more.' Uncle Sam.—'Well, I can't exactly say—There's some friends of General Grant's a lookin at the House, and have asked for the refusal of it. The present Tenant likes it purty well—An' I like him tol'ble, though he costs me a heap o' money for repairs. But I'm rather onsartin just yet—ef you could call in towards the end of November, Now I could give you a definite answer.'"[13]

In the *New York Illustrated News,* Frank Bellew's splendid political caricature "Presidential Cobblers and Wire-Pullers Measuring and Estimating Lincoln's Shoes" left ample room for interpretation. On the one hand, the acts of measurement and estimation imply preparation for a replacement, but on the other hand, Lincoln's shoes are huge. Who could fill them? They dwarf the measurers and estimators, including "Bennett, Hudson, Greeley, Raymond, Weed, Seward, [Noah] Brooks, Sumner, Forney, and Miss Anna Dickenson." Was that a satirical commentary on the relative stature of the appraisers, was no political rival big enough to fill the shoes, or was the shoe size just another burlesque on Abe's physique? The last possibility is the only

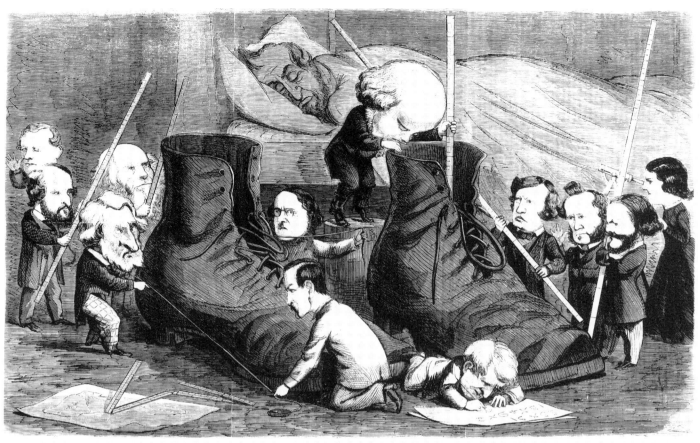

PRESIDENTIAL COBBLERS AND WIRE-PULLERS MEASURING AND ESTIMATING LINCOLN'S SHOES:
INCLUDING BENNETT, HUDSON, GREELEY, RAYMOND, WEED, SEWARD BROOKS, SUMNER, FORNEY, AND MISS ANNA DICKENSON

plausible answer. Given the facts that Frank Bellew eventually edited a magazine that touted John C. Frémont's candidacy and that the *New York Illustrated News* vehemently opposed Lincoln in 1864, it is obvious that the caricature was not designed to discourage the emergence of radical political antagonists.[14] What is also transparent, by even any cursory inspection of the print, is that, by any measure, this is classic popular art from conception through execution.

In "The Rival Bill Posters," the *Comic Monthly* emphasized the variety of candidates and their proponents. The *Tribune*'s Horace Greeley posts placards for "Chase or Welles." The *New York Herald*'s James Gordon Bennett carries signs for U. S. Grant. Henry Raymond, editor of the *New York Times,* vouches for Lincoln. Senator Sumner paints letters on behalf of the Thirteenth Amendment to the Constitution. The Copperhead reputation of Fernando Wood is reinforced with his poster—"Vote for Jefferson Davis." Prominent signs are also displayed for Frémont, McClellan, and lesser luminaries like Haney and Thurlow Weed.[15] However, if quantity of publicity placards means anything, Grant and Lincoln take the honors.

At this time, the field seemed wide open. For example, a cartoon in *Merryman's Monthly* maintained that Ben Butler ought to occupy the "Presidential Chair."[16] In

"Presidential Cobblers and Wire-Pullers Measuring and Estimating Lincoln's Shoes," *New York Illustrated News,* March 5, 1864, 297. Courtesy of the New York State Library.

Nick Nax, Lincoln's humor was discussed in consecutive issues. In April, Old Abe, at the expense of Irish immigrants, supposedly ventures a witty prophecy about the next president:

> My opinion as to who will be the next President, said Mr. Lincoln, not many days ago, is very much the opinion that Pat had about the handsome funeral. You see Pat was standing opposite the State House in Springfield, with a short black pipe in his mouth and his hands in his empty breeches pockets. "Pat, whose funeral is that passing?" inquired old Jake Miller, who seemed impressed with a belief that an Irishman must know everything. "Plaize yer honor," replied Pat, removing his pipe for a moment, "it isn't meself can say for sartin, but to the best o' my belief, the funeral belongs to the gintleman or lady that's in the coffin!" Now it's very much the same, continued Mr. Lincoln, about the next presidency. I can't say for certain who will be the people's choice; but to the best of my belief, it will be the successful candidate![17]

In May, it was more of the same drollery:

> Uncle Abe, in elucidating his estimate of Presidential honors, tells a clever story, as he always does when he sets about it. It seems that Windy Bill, who is a politician of no ordinary pretensions, was a candidate for the Consulship of Bayonne, and urged his appointment with the eloquence of a Clay or a Seward. He boasted vociferously of his activity in promoting the success of the Republican ticket, and averred with his impassioned earnestness that he and he alone had made Old Abe President. "Ah!" exclaimed the sage of Springfield, "and it was you who made me President, was it?" a twinkle in his eye all the time. "Yes," said Billy, rubbing his hands and throwing out his chest, as a baggage master would a small valise, "Yes, I think I may say I am the man who made you President." "Well, Billy, my boy, if that's the case, it's a d——d of a muss you got me into, that's all."[18]

Drawing for *Phunny Phellow*, Thomas Nast displayed his talent for caricature in "May the Best Man Win!" On his hobby horse, Uncle Sam reviews "the Army of Candidates for the Presidential Chair." Nast, a master of his craft, exploited the word *army*. Not only are many of the political hopefuls generals in the army, but the list of candidates is so long that it resembles an army. Nast's sketch includes close-ups of the major candidates, but an apparently infinite line of other political aspirants extends into the distance. The major figures from left to right appear to be Fernando Wood (background), General McClellan, John C. Frémont (background), Abraham Lincoln, Salmon Chase, General Butler, General Banks, General Pendleton, and William Seward.[19]

If Lincoln's preeminent defender, *Harper's Weekly*, was not engaged in protecting his flank from intraparty bickering, it was trying to deflect criticism from the Copperheads. The Copperheads controlled the inside track to the Democratic Party

(*Opposite*)
"The Rival Bill Posters," *Comic Monthly*, April 1864, 26–27. C. Fiske Harris Collection on the American Civil War and Slavery, Providence Public Library.

MAY THE BEST MAN WIN!--UNCLE SAM REVIEWING THE ARMY OF CANDIDATES FOR THE PRESIDENTIAL CHAIR.

UNCLE SAM REVIEWING THE ARMY OF CANDIDATES FOR THE PRESIDENTIAL CHAIR.

"May the Best Man Win!" *Phunny Phellow*, April 1864, 8–9. Reproduced through permission of the Rare Book and Special Collections Library, University of Illinois at Urbana-Champaign.

nomination and desired a candidate whose pacifist political ideology was diametrically opposed to the president's and offensive to Radical Republicans. No political faction was more abrasive to Lincoln and his policies; even Frémont's personal rancor did not match Copperhead antipathy. When the Copperheads maligned Lincoln, the president's advocates retaliated. For example, *Harper's Weekly* specifically accused Fernando Wood and the *Metropolitan Record* of subversion. This was harsh language, but it was not uncommon for *Harper's Weekly* editorials to label "Copperheads and Peace men at the North" as "accessories of the rebels" and those who "pander to . . . the South."[20] However, when Lincoln suspended the right of habeas corpus to protect the nation from political subversion, he also incurred the wrath of representatives from a broader political spectrum, including some in his own party. This cross section of opponents feared that suspension also jeopardized the preservation of civil liberties.

Suspension involved a fragile distinction. Quelling subversion and conserving liberty was like navigating treacherous rapids. On the one hand, inherent in the decision was the risk that someone might get hurt. On the other hand, the venture was deemed worth the peril. Discouraging political subversion entailed dangers, but the risk of overzealous application was also problematic. Inevitably, the arrest of foes on grounds of subversion awakened resistance. One publication that joined the ranks of those who had serious reservations was *Frank Leslie's Budget of Fun*. Would the suppression of civil liberties affect freedom of the ballot? queried the magazine. The meter of the popular poetry critical of suspension was set to the tune of "Coming through the Rye," and the doggerel contained the usual insensitive ethnic denunciation:

If you meet, no matter who,
Coming up to vote
Without a nigger on his ticket,
Take him by the throat.
If he will not vote for Abe,
Pray what right has he
Where the bayonet rules the ballot
And the polls are free (to all that vote for Abraham)?

If he offers to resist you,
From your pocket draw
The test oath; should he dare refuse it,
Swear he's broke the law—
And quickly brand him as a traitor,
For what right has he
Where the bayonet rules the ballot
And the polls are free (to all that vote for Abraham)?

If this from the poll should drive him,
Mark him on your card;
But should he still persist in voting,
Call the provost guard,
And let him take him off to prison,
For what right has he
Where the bayonet rules the ballot
And the polls are free (to all that vote for Abraham)?

When election day is over
You may let him slide,
And swear it was a fair election
On the winning side.
Shoddy papers will sustain you,
For the sake of fee,
Where the bayonet rules the ballot
And the polls are free (to all that vote for Abraham)?[21]

For the most part, this strain of criticism focused on specific issues; it did not necessarily supplant the typically respectful view of Lincoln. However, the Frank Leslie series of publications did seem to adopt a more negative tone through the summer of 1864.

U. S. GRANT AND JAMES GORDON BENNETT

After Ulysses S. Grant assumed responsibility for Union military forces, hope for his presidential candidacy began to fade. In two cartoons in *Yankee Notions*, illustrators criticized James Gordon Bennett's persistent advocacy of Grant. In each case, Lincoln was the felicitous beneficiary. The first illustration was accorded front, full-page status. Cartoonist J. H. Howard reasoned that it was time for Bennett to stop throw-

"Humiliating, But What He Must Come to at Last," *Yankee Notions*, May 1864, front page. Reproduced from the Collections of the Library of Congress.

HUMILIATING, BUT WHAT HE MUST COME TO AT LAST.

J. G. B.—"PLEASE, SIR, LET ME TAKE ALL THAT MUD BACK AGAIN—WILL YOU, SIR?"

The Next Presidency—A Marvelous Prophecy.

BETWEEN THE TWO TREES PLANTED ON THE POLITICAL GRAVE OF OLD ABE. AND NAMED RESPECTIVELY GRANT AND McCLELLAN, MAY BE SEEN THE UNSUSPECTED FORM OF THE "RAIL SPLITTER," AS LARGE AS LIFE AND TWICE AS NATURAL.

"The Next Presidency—A Marvelous Prophecy," *Yankee Notions*, May 1864, 145. Reproduced from the Collections of the Library of Congress.

ing political mud at Lincoln, repent, and return to the fold. Howard moralized that, though "humiliating," such action was "what he [Bennett] must come to at last." Showing the president splattered with Bennett's soiled aspersions, the subdued New York editor brings "soft soap," a pan of water, and a towel to begin removing the dirt. Deferentially, Bennett supposedly makes amends: "Please, sir, let me take all that mud back again—will you, sir?"[22]

In the second illustration, a cartoonist with the initials "M. D." employs the classic figure-ground illusion for novel artistic effect. In this illusion, what we normally perceive as the figure (a black image on white paper) becomes the ground; the white, in turn, becomes the figure. Again, Bennett is the butt of the humor, and the element of prognostication is repeated in "The Next Presidency—A Marvelous Prophecy." The eagle Seward—loyal exponent of Lincoln's candidacy for a second term—perches on "Old Abe's" premature political tombstone, which was erected "by his loving J. G. B," and watches as the ghost of Bennett returns to the site of Lincoln's burial place expecting either Ulysses S. Grant or George McClellan to emerge as Lincoln's successor. Instead, Bennett sees a shocking apparition of Lincoln distinctly outlined "between the two trees [labeled Grant and McClellan] planted on the political grave of Old Abe." Bennett's surprise confrontation with the "unsuspected form of the 'Rail Splitter,' as large as life and twice as natural" is an eerie harbinger of Lincoln's ultimate triumph over Bennett's stable of candidates. Ironically, the tall trees, "Mc-Clellan" and "Grant," form the ground for the stately figure (in white) of Lincoln, the next president. The twisted, dying trees of "Butler" and "Fremont" are tokens of their projected political fate.[23] However, although the *Yankee Notions*'s cartoon was intended to foil Bennett's campaign for Grant (or McClellan), other images still gave him an outside chance.

In *Frank Leslie's Budget of Fun*, a cartoon by William Newman contends that unless Grant ends the war soon he must forego the 1864 election. Uncle Sam and Jefferson Davis anxiously watch Robert E. Lee and U. S. Grant don fisticuffs and go toe-to-toe. Although the cartoon gives Grant a distinct advantage, time conspires against any chance that he has for the presidency. Under his arm, Uncle Sam holds the prize (a cake marked "White House"), but the major caption concedes that "The Cake [Is] in Danger."[24] Indeed it was—at least for 1864—and Bennett would need to find a new presidential protege.

That is exactly what Frank Bellew attempted (that is, solve the puzzle of what candidate Bennett would then champion) in a fine cartoon of his that appeared in the *New York Illustrierte Zeitung* and *Funniest of Phun*. The caption describes James Gordon Bennett as "the journalistic Barnum with his great blowing elephant—'Satanic,' performing his bombastic feats of political strategy for ministerial honors in Paris." The elephant's function is to trumpet the qualities of Bennett's latest political infatuation, but there is obviously some uncertainty in the most recent tune from Satanic: "I've given a terrible blast this morning, and am most blowed out [for U. S. Grant]. I wonder who my master will want me to blow for next?" As Grant falls from Bennett's grace, the *New York Herald* editor boosts McClellan into prominence, while Frémont enviously waits for his chance. Bennett disdainfully ignores Lincoln, who, lying on the ground in front of Satanic, is still hurting from the indignity of rejection.[25]

Bellew's imagery was as much a critique of James Gordon Bennett's alleged desire to gain a ministerial appointment or ambassadorship as it was a commentary on his fickle political appetite and a tool to promote or embarrass any particular candidate. Given the dubious reputation of Bennett, Lincoln did not necessarily lose stature. To be sure, Grant's heroic military prowess and political credibility were touted, but his loyalty to Lincoln defused any gain that might have accrued to Lincoln's rivals. Exemplifying the flawed public image of James Gordon Bennett was doggerel articulated by his circus elephant that lightheartedly impugned the moral foundation of Bennett's political intentions and behavior:

> I'm most blow'd out,
> But again will try,
> Tho' I've got no wool for a good deal of cry
> But master's resolved on having a shy,
> By aiding Mack who is all my eye,
> Or the great Pathfinder good and high,

Or by any means, I own with a sigh,
From telling the truth to forging a lie,
Turning his coat, or any tom fooleries
For the ministerial post at the Tooleries.

I'm nearly blowed out—alas! And alack,
And I want a new coat to cover my back;
Also one for my boss, who to Paris would go,
But that (boo!) Depends upon whether or no
We can name the first horse in the President Race,
I tried hard down people's throats brave Grant to cram,
But I only succeeded his chances to d_ _n.
So far, it's "all cry and no wool," as all know,
But I'll try it again—now, who makes the best show,
To bestow an Ambassador's place?
(It's not easy to know how the folks will be "goosed,"
But Fremont I guess I shall give the next boost.)

"The Journalistic
Barnum with His Great
Blowing Elephant,"
Funniest of Phun, June
1864, 8–9. Courtesy the
Lincoln Museum (Ref.
#2613).

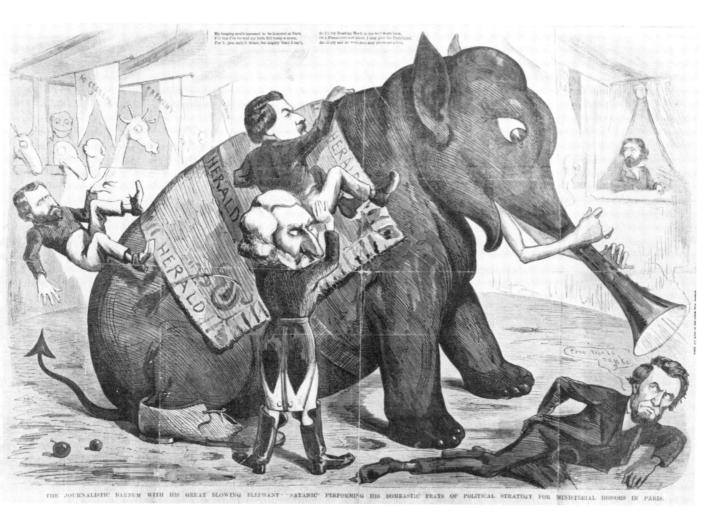

THE JOURNALISTIC BARNUM WITH HIS GREAT BLOWING ELEPHANT—"SATANIC" PERFORMING HIS BOMBASTIC FEATS OF POLITICAL STRATEGY FOR MINISTERIAL HONORS IN PARIS.

My longing soul's harassed to be honored at Paris.
For this I've blowed my horn full many a morn,
For U. (You and) S. Grant, but might fraid I can't,
So I'll try boosting Mack on the well-worn hack,
Or a Fremont sort kinder I may give the Pathfinder,
As all cry and no wool soon may prove me a fool.[26]

LINCOLN'S NOMINATION

For several reasons, forces within the Republican Party that gathered to derail Lincoln's ambition for a second term settled on a policy of postponement. If the party's nominating convention could be delayed from June until September, the probability of his political success would decline. As noted above, Grant's supporters hoped that a decisive battlefield victory might end the war in time for him to become the front-runner. However, *Harper's Weekly* saw U. S. Grant firmly committed to Lincoln, and it systematically divided the opposition into "three classes of persons engaged in manufacturing opinion hostile to the Union Convention called at Baltimore."[27] The motives and agenda for each class varied, but the overall objective to forestall the convention was the same:

> First, the enemies of the American Government and human liberty known as Copperheads. Second, the declared opponents of Mr. Lincoln's nomination in any case whatever. This class calls the Baltimore call "insolent!" and criticizes the administration with all the acridity of the fiercest rebel journals. Third, the class which is wholly devoted to the country and to liberty, but is dissatisfied with the influences that surround the President, and are persuaded that Mr. Seward and Mr. Blair are almost as dangerous to the good cause as Jefferson Davis or Lee. This class wishes the Convention to be postponed until after General Grant has fought, and, in any case, asks that the terms of the call may be so changed as to include War Democrats and all other loyal Union men.[28]

The intentions of the first two classes were deemed most irrational and reprehensible; the third was just ill advised. If there is opposition to specific cabinet members, reasoned the editorial, let the evidence be openly and fairly presented, but do not let that investigation delay the convention. Furthermore, *Harper's Weekly* defended what it considered sensible principles upon which the rhetoric of the call for a convention was founded: "It is addressed to 'all qualified voters who desire the unconditional maintenance of the Union, the supremacy of the Constitution, and the complete suppression of the existing rebellion, with the cause thereof by vigorous war and all apt and efficient means.'" Of course, the bottom line for *Harper's* Weekly's "determination that Mr. Lincoln shall be nominated is only a very profound conviction that it is best for the country that he should be."[29]

In preparation for the Baltimore convention, illustrators were glad to gratify the appetites of their own constituents for graphics. William Newman's splendid "House-Clearing at Washington" shows Lincoln and Seward attempting to control the infestation of rival political rats. Salmon Chase is already confined to a cage, but Banks, Butler, Seymour, Wood, Frémont, and McClellan are still loose. Lincoln brandishes a broom to push Frémont into a political appointment and lunges with his foot to step on McClellan. Seward swings his shovel at Ben Butler, while Fernando Wood waits for his comeuppance. "Raymond's Rat-Bane" delivers its toxin to Governor Seymour's system, and General Banks looks for some route for escape. "Greeley's Poison" is held in reserve on a table for some unwitting victim. (Ironically, Greeley hoped to administer a lethal dose to Lincoln.) The slogan "Vote for Old Abe" is written in bold letters on an overturned table, and the caption catches Abe expressing his own political motives: "Be spry, Billy, or some of these will eat us out of house and home! It's too bad of these chaps to want us out, we ain't half fat enough yet." In another cartoon, William Seward is depicted as sympathetic to Lincoln's political demise. In *Phunny Phellow*, Seward avers that the president's shoes are not all that difficult to fill, and to that jolting assessment Lincoln has no humorous retort.[30]

"House-Clearing at Washington," *Frank Leslie's Budget of Fun*, June 1864, 8–9. Author's Collection.

BE SPRY, BILLY, OR SOME OF THESE WILL EAT US OUT OF HOUSE AND HOME! IT'S TOO BAD OF THESE CHAPS TO WANT US OUT, WE AIN'T HALF FAT ENOUGH YET.

S——D, THE BOOTBLACK, GIVES AN OPINION:

S——d —Thunder! Abe! What a shoe! I don't see why it should be so difficult to find somebody to stand in your shoes!

L——n, Well, Bill, I can't say that your remark reminds me of any anecdote!

On June 8, 1864, Lincoln was nominated to head the ticket of the National Union Party, a hybrid organization intended to woo War Democrats to the Republican banner. Among the National Union Party's campaign planks was support for a constitutional amendment to abolish slavery. A second-term nomination for the president was not a good omen for Jefferson Davis. The Confederate government had hoped that Lincoln might not survive the political winnowing; they desired a less intractable and more conciliatory leader. Popular artists avidly grasped this theme, noting that "Jeff Davis's breakfast [was] spoilt by a shot from Baltimore—the hardest shell yet."[31] Still Lincoln had not won reelection, and the Richmond White House banked on a new president.

When the Baltimore convention adjourned, *Harper's Weekly* defended the nominee against "the charges made against him of the exercise of arbitrary power by the Copperheads, and of indifference to the slavery question by Mr. Wendell Phillips."[32] With an imposing circulation, this powerful magazine also celebrated the nomination with "The Latest Portrait of the President."[33] While Lincoln was shown with his secretaries, John George Nicolay and John Hay, the political association in the text, for whatever political mileage that connection might deliver, deliberately linked the president with the popular General Grant. Furthermore, the cartoon asked readers to examine the obvious evidence in Lincoln's countenance of his qualifications—a subtle reliance on the contemporary "science" of physiognomy. The editorial helped readers complete the association and draw the intended conclusion:

> Look thoughtfully at this rugged face. In its candor, its sagacity, its calmness, its steadiness and strength, there is especially conspicuous the distinctive American. The hardy, simple traits of the best American character are there. Turn then to the portrait of General Grant in our paper of three weeks ago, and there you see another purely American face. There are the same homely honesty, capacity, and tenacity, the same utter freedom from every kind of cant and affectation in each. It is to such men, one in the council, the other in the field, in every fibre, in every heart-beat, in every hope and thought and word, in every instinct and quality, American, that the salvation of American institutions has been providentially intrusted. Children of the people, both of them sprung from the poorest and plainest ancestry, as unpretending and unselfish in their high places to-day as in the time when they were both unknown, these two men illustrate at once the character of American civilization and of the American people. There is but one power in the great multitude of American hearts today, God bless President Lincoln and General Grant![34]

In essence, Lincoln and Grant embodied the quintessential homespun, frontier contrived American. For Lincoln, this portrait resembled the classic rail-splitter image refurbished for the 1864 election. What red-blooded, patriotic citizen could defy such political logic? Among such opponents was Gen. John C. Frémont.

FRÉMONT'S NOMINATION

As early as General Frémont's military proclamation in 1861 to free the slaves, he was suspected of coveting the 1864 presidential election. In a confidential letter to Orville H. Browning, Lincoln surmised that the proclamation was "purely political." In contrast, cartoonists were less reticent to expose the transparency of Frémont's motivation. *Frank Leslie's Illustrated Newspaper* bluntly portrayed him prematurely trying to pluck the fruit of the 1864 nomination from the political tree: "Well, Master Frémont, that's a rather long reach ain't it? You may fetch it with your sword, perhaps at the proper time, but it isn't ripe yet."[35] In 1864, however, the fruit was ripe and Frémont was reaching for it.

One week before Lincoln's nomination at the Baltimore convention, Gen. John C. Frémont was nominated at another convention in Cleveland and thus officially contested Lincoln's right to a second term. This development created a significant schism within the Republican Party. Frémont's radical platform consisted of five major components: (1) a call for a constitutional amendment to abolish slavery; (2) a plank that supported the preservation of free speech; (3) another plank in support of habeas corpus; (4) advocacy of the confiscation of rebel land; and (5) support for a single-term limitation for the office of president. This combination was politically astute. Like the Copperheads, it protested the executive action to suspend certain civil liberties, but, unlike the Copperheads, it called for a more spirited quest to abolish slavery.

In one of its editorials, *Harper's Weekly* described the defectors as "extreme abolitionists," a "few who are morbidly angry with the administration," and "the friends of the rebels, who hope to divide the Union vote and thereby secure the success of the Copperhead candidate." As for Frémont, the editorial deplored his judgment and patriotism for rending a united political front, but the publication's response in a cartoon was "so what"? Frémont was no match for Lincoln. The illustrator portrayed a confident Lincoln sloughing off the political challenge with equanimity and indifference: "Frémont. —'Well, Sir! I am nominated, you see!' [John F.] Cochrane.—'Yes Sir; WE are nominated.' Lincoln.—'Well, Gentlemen; and what then?' Frémont and Cochrane.—'Oh! Nothing, Sir; nothing—that's all!'"[36]

However, the amount of space devoted to Frémont's candidacy in *Harper's Weekly* belied any sense of indifference. Although Frémont might not generate enough votes to triumph in the upcoming election, he could dilute the plurality and spoil Lincoln's chances. If the Peace Democrats happened to choose a worthy competitor, the probability increased. In that event, surmised the editors of *Harper's Weekly*, "the practical question, then, for every sincere Union man, will be whether he wishes to sit at a feast of which these gentlemen [Peace Democrats] are the hosts."[37]

In July, a cartoon by Frank Bellew identified personal spite and political revenge as Frémont's motivation to run against Lincoln. When Miss Columbia takes little John C. Frémont to Doctor Jonathan to find out what ails him, the physician notes the name "Lincoln" written on John C.'s scalp: "Mrs. Columbia.—'Tell me, Doctor, what is the matter with him? Do you think his Brain is affected?' Doctor Jonathan.—'Oh! no, my dear Madam; it's only a rather aggravated case of Sore Head!'"[38] Regardless of the accuracy of this diagnosis, the Lincoln campaign was in for a long, hot summer.

THE SUMMER OF 1864

More than any other time in Lincoln's presidency, the summer of 1864 witnessed the apogee of opposition to him. During that period, the wear and tear of war wrenched the nation's soul. The enormous sacrifice of life, the toll of casualties, the emotional drain on families, the seeming futility of fighting, and the economic burden seemed to go on and on. War weariness affected Lincoln's public approval. In addition, the exigencies of war wrung from the president a series of arduous, unpopular decisions that also damaged his reputation. The Peace Democrats disliked the draft, the suppression of civil liberties, the trend toward the abolition of slavery, and Lincoln's purported unwillingness to negotiate a peace settlement. The radical wing of the Republican Party eschewed his lenient policy of amnesty and reconstruction and lamented the sluggish rate of full implementation for emancipation. Meanwhile, the conservative segment disdained the president's radicalism.[39] These swirling eddies of opposition engulfed Lincoln in a struggle for political survival.

When such combustible elements of discontent are linked with political rivalry, the outcome is volatile. Ironically, Lincoln's most intense opposition originated within his own Republican Party. Among those who instigated the movement were Horace Greeley, Senators Benjamin F. Wade, Henry Winter Davis, Zachariah Chandler, Sumner, and General Frémont. By August, the discomfort became so intense that Lincoln, his advisors, and closest friends believed that only extraordinary intervention on the order of the miraculous could preserve his political existence. However, before we examine that phase, the difficult summer of 1864 begs consideration.

Frémont's Campaign

In the illustrated press, it was John C. Frémont's third-party movement that generated the most hostile opposition to Lincoln. Shortly after Frémont's nomination, two illustrated magazines enlisted in his cause. Spearheading the break in ranks from the relative solidarity of the illustrated press in support of Lincoln was the *New York Illustrated News*. Joining the opposition from the comic flank was a new publication called the *Funniest of Phun,* which was edited by talented artist Frank Bellew. Just before Frémont's nomination, these magazines contained generic anti-Lincoln content, but more invidious comparisons that favored Frémont over Lincoln followed the Cleveland convention.[40] The relatively large volume of anti-Lincoln material in these Frémont political organs was greatly disproportionate to the modest anti-Frémont content generated by the Lincoln magazines. There was also a similar qualitative distinction: the Frémont periodicals published significantly more harsh anti-Lincoln imagery than the comparable stereotypes of Frémont produced in magazines friendly to Lincoln.

The *New York Illustrated News* struck the first blow for Frémont. It celebrated his nomination in the June 18 issue and on June 25 depicted the ticket of Frémont and John F. Cochrane leaving Lincoln and Andrew Johnson far behind. The artist, probably Frank Bellew, used Lincoln's spontaneous remarks on swapping horses in midstream for his theme: "I have not permitted myself, gentlemen, to conclude that I am the best man in the country; but I am reminded, in this convention, of a story of an Old Dutch farmer, who remarked to a companion once that it was not best to swap horses when crossing streams."[41] The cartoonist portrayed Lincoln fording what looks more like a huge river than a stream. Riding the mule "Expediency," the president is up to his neck in water and sinking fast, and Andrew Johnson, his running mate, is on the verge of drowning. Frémont and Cochrane, on the other hand, are not experiencing any difficulty. Frémont confidently rides the horse "Principle" and holds the sword of "Justice." As he passes Lincoln, Frémont sarcastically remarks, "Wouldn't you rather like to swap horses, after all? Eh, Abe?"[42]

An article in the *New York Illustrated News* informs us what provoked the accusation of expediency. General Frémont's partisans were set on edge by a sentence in an earlier editorial in *Harper's Weekly*: "The Presidential question, like every other question in politics, is one of expediency, not of abstract, absolute right." This expression generated a potent new derisive theme. Thus, "expediency" became a convenient, popular, and malevolent political shibboleth in the Frémont camp. Cartoonists and journalists (so inclined) enthusiastically embraced it: "The critical condition of the Union today, the question of its perpetuity undecided, the scales of battle hanging almost even, springs from this same flagitious principle of expedience, a principle which seems to govern the Administration in all it does or fails to do." As evidence of presidential culpability, the editorial cited Lincoln's famous reply to Horace Greeley: "My paramount object is to save the Union, and not either to save or destroy slavery." "Could anything be plainer, could anything be meaner, could any thing be more diabolically selfish?" continued the *New York Illustrated News*. "Not a word of right, not a word of justice, but only 'is it expedient, will it benefit the Saxon race?' We arraign that entire passage as one of the foulest insults to humanity on record," fumed the periodical. This was bitter partisan politics in action. Ironically, Lincoln

"Old Abe's Last Joke," *New York Illustrated News*, June 25, 1864, 560. C. Fiske Harris Collection on the American Civil War and Slavery, Providence Public Library.

OLD ABE'S LAST JOKE.

"I am reminded in this connection of a story of an old Dutch farmer who remarked to a companion once that it was not best to swap horses when crossing streams."

continued to reiterate, almost simultaneous with this attack, his hope and expectation "that a constitutional amendment, abolishing slavery throughout the nation, may be adopted."[43]

Trying to gather political dirt from the dust of controversy, the *New York Illustrated News* thought it had the elements of a scandal in the Arguelles case. In one of its issues, a cartoonist assumed the Lincoln administration had "a severe task" explaining why it had turned José A. Arguelles over to Spanish authorities without consulting the Senate. "Boss Seward.—'There, Mr. Raymond [editor of the *New York Times* and Lincoln's campaign manager], I wish you to make a good case out of this for Mr. Lincoln.' Journeyman Raymond.—'Tell you what, Boss, that's a mighty tough job—However, give us hold, I'll do my best any how.'" In fact, insofar as the Lincoln administration was concerned, this was much ado about nothing. José A. Arguelles, a Spanish officer in Cuba, had seized a ship full of slaves and been awarded with $15,000 in prize money and a leave to visit New York City for discovering the illicit traffic in slavery. However, he falsely reported the death of over one hundred slaves, whom he had actually sold for personal profit. When the crime was discovered, Spanish authorities wanted Arguelles extradited for trial. However, because there was no treaty of extradition between the United States and Spain, "nor any act of Congress directing how fugitives from justice in Spanish dominions shall be delivered up," Seward had pragmatically resorted to "the law of nations and the Constitution of the United States."[44] Any potential for political liability dissolved quickly after Seward explained his rationale for extraditing Arguelles.

However, in July a far more serious accusation was leveled at the Lincoln administration. The *New York Illustrated News* printed a ruthless anti-Lincoln sketch, charging him with protecting slavery. The captions and cartoon imagery denounce Lincoln, "alias J. Shackles, Slave Dealer," for running a "Slave Pen" under the guise of a "Constitutional Institution." "Our Republican Form of Government" is a travesty and in shambles. Satan endorses the operation with his salutation "Hail Columbia." The flag that flies on the corner of the institution publicizes the hypocrisy and incongruity of freedom and slavery: "The Flag of the Free, and the Home of the Slave." Henry Ward Beecher, standing on his soapbox at Exeter Hall in England, defends slavery as "a Constitutional Institution." In effect, he has decorated the administration's institution with his own brand of "Beecher Paint—Prejudice." To the left of the institution, almost under the nose of Lincoln, "slaves, horses, and other cattle" are auctioned to the highest bidder. On the side of the building, slaves are kept in place with "Constitutional Guarantees." At the right corner, Seward, Hopkins, Ben Wood, John Breckinridge, Clement Vallandigham, and Henry J. Raymond whitewash the edifice with a litany of "states rights," "domestic incentives," and the so-called Bible and missionary defense of slavery. In front, Lincoln declines to use his keys to open the slave pen. Instead, he bows to the demands of border states who assert, "I want my [slave] property," while an oppressed slave asks, "Massa is we gowin to be free?"[45] This is heady, negative campaign rhetoric and an intoxicating message from Lincoln's radical rivals.

THE POPULAR PREJUDICE AND JUDICIAL BLINDNESS OF THE PEOPLE ON THE U.S. CONSTITUTION,—OR THE CONSTITUTION AS PEOPLE HAVE BEEN ACCUSTOMED TO SEE IT.

"The Popular Prejudice and Judicial Blindness of the People on the U.S. Constitution," *New York Illustrated News,* July 2, 1864, 569. C. Fiske Harris Collection on the American Civil War and Slavery, Providence Public Library.

To counter the effect of such blatant assaults on Lincoln's slavery policy, *Harper's Weekly* cited a litany of tangible administration accomplishments on the issue: "Slavery has been prohibited in the national Territories. It has been abolished in the District of Columbia. A more strenuous treaty with England for the suppression of the Slave trade has been negotiated. The Fugitive Slave law has been repealed. Colored men have been allowed to carry the mails, and their right to give testimony in courts of law has been established. Slaves have been enrolled as free soldiers of the United States, receiving equal wages with all others. The President has emancipated by proclamation the slaves in all the rebel section. The Convention of loyal Union men have declared with the utmost enthusiasm for an amendment of the Constitution making slavery impossible."[46] Although *Harper's Weekly* was on the defense, this checklist of inroads against slavery was impressive. Lincoln was surely not the villain that the attacking cartoon made him out to be, but partisan political imagery was not known for sensitivity to fair play and goodwill.

To disparage Lincoln, Frémont image makers doubtless employed the theme of expediency most frequently. On July 9, in the upper right-hand corner of a double-page illustration in the *New York Illustrated News*, Frémont, on the strength of "Principle," rides comfortably on the back of the American eagle toward the White House. Because of Lincoln's expediency, the eagle also carries the president just long enough to dump him ingloriously into "Salt River." Also in the illustration, McClellan is precariously close to the edge of that same symbolic river of defeat.[47]

The *New York Illustrated News* continued its unrelenting attack on the president into August. Once again, expediency is the principal motif of one significant cartoon. In it, Lincoln and Seward dine on "Humble or Slavery Pie" seasoned with the sauce of "expediency": "Old Abe.—'Capital Sauce this, Mr. Seward!' Mr. S.—'Splendid, it gives a fine flavor to the pie. How impatient our dogs are to get their share.'" The collars identify the dogs as the *Evening Post*, *Times*, and *Tribune*. The *Illustrated News* reproves these newspapers for acquiescing too eagerly to Lincoln's so-called expediency. On the shelf above Lincoln and Seward, the most exquisite dessert, the cake of "Principle," is reserved "For President Fremont."[48] Such was the gist of pro-Frémont and anti-Lincoln imagery in the *New York Illustrated News*, but the criticism from its sister publication *Funniest of Phun* was just as severe.

When *Funniest of Phun*'s maiden issue was published in June, an editorial in the magazine warned that it was not "the organ of the President, between whom and ourselves not the slightest resemblance exists."[49] In July, the periodical cast its lot with John C. Frémont's radical independent party politics and commenced its attack upon Lincoln. As in the *New York Illustrated News*, the anti-Lincoln illustrations tended to focus on slavery, free speech, habeas corpus, and expediency. The first three of these items were pillars of the Frémont platform.

"Humble or Slavery Pie," *New York Illustrated News*, August 6, 1864, 652. Courtesy of the Department of Special Collections, the University of Chicago Library.

OLD ABE.—Capital sauce this, Mr. Seward!
MR. S.—Splendid, it gives a fine flavor to the pie. How impatient our dogs are to get their share.

Assuming that George McClellan would eventually end up as the nominee on the Democratic side, *Funniest of Phun* gratuitously compared candidates Frémont, Lincoln, and McClellan. The self-serving contrast left Lincoln and McClellan beyond the pale of legitimate leadership. "Leading, Following, and Rebelling" are the labels applied to Frémont, Lincoln, and McClellan, respectively. In the lead, Frémont rides a high-stepping steed that crushes the Copperhead serpents, "Jeff Davis, Vallandigham, Wood, Long, Saulsbury, and the New York *Herald*." Frémont holds the reins of "Constitutional Law" and "Vox Populi." He grips the sword of "Justice," and uses "Principle" to pull the "car of freedom." "War" is the only bonafide instrument of "Peace," and the pillars that support the canopy of freedom include "Universal Freedom and Justice," "The Sanctity of the Marriage Relation," and "Education." The banners of "Common Law, Equity, Liberty, and Justice" billow in the breeze. Frémont's pledge to obliterate the last vestiges of slavery (simultaneous with his inauguration on March 4, 1865) is formulated in one of the balloon captions: "Impelled by the claims of humanity, justice and the constitution, I proclaim that all persons heretofore held as slaves in the United States, in violation of the plainest principles of Equity and the Sacred Guarantees of Personal Liberty embodied in the Constitution, are hereby declared now and forever free, and that every such person, will be protected in all their just rights under the Constitution, any Law or Statute of any State to the contrary, notwithstanding. Will be signed, J. C. Fremont." Suspended in

"Leading, Following, Rebelling," *Funniest of Phun*, July 1864, 8–9. Courtesy of the American Antiquarian Society.

the air just above Frémont, an angel announces the "Nation's Verdict" for Frémont's contemplated executive action: "Well done, good and faithful servant."

Lincoln, on the other hand, is invidiously "weighed in the balance" and found wanting. He is maligned as a monkey who, unable to keep pace with the exuberant strides of Frémont, assumes the undignified stance of a jockey riding the ineffective hobby horse of "Expediency." On the legs of the wooden horse are inscribed Lincoln's alleged weak, vacillating, morally bankrupt policies: catering to the "Border States," the "Amnesty Proclamation," "Conservatism," and "Colonization." The epithet "National Choker" is extracted from Lincoln's reputation for joking and his supposed leadership flaws. To support the indictment of the president's leadership style, which the cartoon describes as "follower," the caption cites the evidence of Lincoln's own words: "When, early in the war, General Frémont attempted military Emancipation, I forbade it, because I did not then think it an indispensable necessity. . . . I was driven to the alternative of laying a strong hand on the Colored Element. . . . I claim not to have controlled events, but confess plainly that events have controlled me."

That McClellan brings up the rear in this parade of political contenders is no accident. From Frémont's perspective, McClellan's conservative political philosophy on slavery is even more offensive than Lincoln's moderate stance. McClellan rides a stubborn mule that has to be forcefully pulled behind Frémont's drive for freedom. Whereas Frémont is applauded by an angel, McClellan receives commendation from a satanic demon. Furthermore, McClellan's earlier statements, as in the case of Lincoln, are also used against him: "Understand one thing, not only will we abstain from any interference with your slaves, but will on the contrary with an iron hand crush any attempt at insurrection on their part."[50] Obviously, restraints on negative electioneering in the Victorian period were minimal.

In August, *Funniest of Phun* continued the bitter invective against Lincoln. Physically, the anti-Lincoln periodical pictured him as an arbitrary, autocratic beast. Prominently displayed is a royal crown, which connotes blatant and irresponsible usurpation of kingly authority. The title, "Abraham the Last," suggests his reluctance to relinquish dictatorial power. The infelicitous slogans—"My Will Is Law" and "Necessity–My Only Law"—signify intransigent, tyrannical behavior. Finally, the cartoonist accused Lincoln of two unconscionable policies: (1) the inconsistent application of emancipation; and (2) the breach of civil liberties. On emancipation, the president simultaneously tantalizes and frustrates the slaves's aspirations for freedom. Lincoln offers it, only to pull it back when just within reach. According to the caricature, this is Lincoln's "emancipation joke"; there is no substance to his emancipation pretensions. However, the beast's central attack on liberty shows him trampling on the constitutional guarantees of "Habeas Corpus" and "Freedom of the Press." Lincoln's obedient lieutenant William Seward (an appendage of the Lincoln beast) unscrupulously orchestrates a system of political persecution. To be sure, "Seward . . . had once been in charge of arrests of disloyal persons in the North." In fact, "rumor had

"Abraham the Last," *Funniest of Phun*, August 1864, front page. Courtesy of the American Antiquarian Society.

it that Seward had once boasted to the English ambassador that he could ring a little bell and cause the arrest of anyone in the United States." This apocryphal story wove its way into this political caricature: From "Seward's Liberty Pole," the secretary of state has only to ring "that little bell ... [to] imprison any man in the United States."[51]

In September, the image of the president as a dictator persisted in a front-page print of *Funniest of Phun:* "The Herod of the Nineteenth Century." Unfaithful to Miss Liberty, the libertine Lincoln abandons her and succumbs to the wiles of the siren "Union with Slavery." "Ask what you will," entreats Herod, "and I will give you even to half of my Kingdom." "Give me the Head of Liberty," replies Miss "Union with Slavery." While liberty languishes in captivity, Lincoln seals this unholy pact with a toast from the jug of expediency. The narrative further embellishes the scene:

> The most estimable gentleman in the foreground, Mr. Abraham Lincoln Esq. D.F. &c &c with the taste which ever distinguishes him, is enchanted by the beauties of the fair and blooming hag, slavery, and in those mellifluous tones which no female could resist, declares his passion for "the dear charmer."
>
> That neglected lady whom it is the fashion nowadays to snub in her own house, we refer to Mrs Hail Columbia Liberty, beholding the man who has sworn to love, cherish, and obey her, seduced from his allegiance and ready to comply with the request of her enemy for her head, cries "who will protect me?"[52]

However, the poet waxed even more eloquent on this "modern Herod":

Our modern Herod drunk with power and popularity,
Is blind to every claim of justice and humanity,
Sees double, like all drunken men, and thinks the wanton croaker,
A sweet enchantress, come to charm the high and mighty joker.

He offers any sacrifice that his charmer may demand,
What e're can be secured by war, or half the nation's land.
Vice slavery takes him at his word, and makes an urgent plea
She wants within her blood-stained hands the head of Liberty.

O our Herod knows her wish requires a fearful crime,
And yet he whispers in her ear, "Sweet Syren, give me time."
Declares he will protect her claims through all the border States,
While sad and weak humanity still suffers on and waits.

To serve and save your system a monstrous oath I've taken,
My pledge 'twas most sincere, and must not be forsaken,
With your "local institutions" I will never interfere;
Though I sacrifice poor Liberty, for my oath and friends are dear.

"The Herod of the Nineteenth Century," *Funniest of Phun*, September 1864, front page. Author's Collection.

Thus Liberty is sacrificed by her pretended friends,
When e'er they use their power to serve their selfish ends.
But, Phoenix like, she yet will rise above the scorching flame
And reign a LIVING PRESENCE, not a mocking and a name!

But where's Lank Herod's seven league boots, and where the cap and cloak,
He traveled to the White House in? To us a sorry joke,
The people soon will vote him out the Presidential chair!
Where's friends and reputation then? faint echo answers where?[53]

Two other images in the same issue also disparage Lincoln. One portrays "The National Joker" dressed in an outlandish jester costume. While he blithely and obliviously performs his light-minded clown routine in the circus ring, the temple of lib-

"The National Joker,"
Funniest of Phun,
September 1864, 16.
Author's Collection.

THE NATIONAL JOKER — SALARY 25,000 DOLLARS PER ANNUM — Conditions need not apply to the Situation

A PRESIDENTIAL CONDIDATE SIMMERING DOWN.

OLD ABE.—"Well, it's awful hard to keep the pot bilin, so it is; I guess somebody has bin and throwed cold water on my fire-wood."

"A Presidential Candidate Simmering Down," *Funniest of Phun*, September 1864, 16. Author's Collection.

erty perishes in flames and soldiers fight and die in vain. If Nero fiddled, Lincoln jokes, asserts the cartoon; the incendiary result is no different. The other image depicts the president coaxing a smoldering fire to ignite his "presidential election." The kindling consists of volatile, flammable material: "reconstruction, colonization, Blair family, Amnesty Proclamation, habeas corpus, expediency, and Arguelles." The naive president surmises, "Well, it's awful hard to keep the pot bilin, so it is; I guess somebody has bin and threw cold water on my fire-wood."[54] Ironically, the dawning of September sparked a blaze in Lincoln's camp that transformed a simmering, sputtering election campaign into a boiling cauldron.

Although Frémont's campaign had generated a volume of robust anti-Lincoln imagery in three months, the caricature must be put in perspective. Only two magazines from the illustrated genre championed Frémont's cause; one was a newcomer, and the other, for want of circulation, was in the throes of transition and death. These were not ideal vessels to transmit Frémont's message, which furthermore lacked imagination. Given Lincoln's overall track record on slavery, the radical argument had limited appeal, and expediency was not a convincing rallying point. Some faulted the president's leadership, sophistication, and political sagacity, but few questioned his fundamental integrity. There was some disenchantment with Lincoln's executive decisions in regard to civil liberties, but the Copperheads, who protested the loudest, were among the least popular political interest groups. Finally, Frémont's charisma left much to be desired; he did not emerge from the 1856 presidential election as the unequivocal leader of the Republican Party. Nor did his experience during the Civil War anoint him as a gallant military figure after the pattern of U. S. Grant. Hence, neither the medium, the message, nor the man—nor any mixture of these elements—created conditions necessary to drive sufficient numbers of the electorate into Frémont's camp.

The Threat from Party Regulars

Simultaneous with Frémont's audacious campaign, a more substantial threat to the Lincoln presidency surfaced. The preponderance of disenchanted Radical Republicans had not defected into Frémont's independent political party. Although they may have sympathized with his political convictions, they were either persuaded that Frémont could not prevail or believed that he was not the right person to lead the country. Among these Republicans was the influential abolitionist Wendell Phillips, who did "not expect the [Frémont] movement as such to succeed, but [was] willing to unite with anybody who will be more radical than Mr. Lincoln."[55] Phillips obviously hoped for a compromise that would yet create the conditions for the emergence of a consensus Radical Republican who could defeat all comers. This hope assumed that a deal could be cut so that Frémont would step down out of deference to the ideals of radical politics. When Lincoln pocket vetoed the Wade-Davis reconstruction bill in early July, the probability of this eventuality dramatically increased. Radical Republican party regulars were livid, Lincoln's political stock plummeted, and he and his advisors despaired. Even if this radical movement could not ultimately prevail, the president thought that it might unwittingly harm the Republicans and that the Democrats would triumph as a result.

In early August, when the Wade-Davis Manifesto publically rebuked the president for scuttling the bill, Lincoln's prospects for a second term became more dismal. The manifesto, printed in Horace Greeley's *Tribune*, blasted Lincoln for executive arrogance, castigated him for his lack of leadership, and gave him a vote of no confidence. It did not take Lincoln long to realize that a significant portion of his own party leadership declined to support him and that the resolve of some of his closest advisors was badly shaken. Indeed, Lincoln feared the worst political scenario. *Frank*

Leslie's Budget of Fun reflected the gravity of Lincoln's political condition in doggerel that suggested Columbia's hand was "forced to swap horses when crossing a stream." The turtle-like pace of the war; the national debt; "three years of [Lincoln's] follies"; obsequious deference to Britain, France, Russia, and Spain; and the premature firing of Frémont and McClellan were blamed for the national malaise in doggerel entitled "Abraham and Columbia":

Lank Abraham lolled in his library chair,
Consulting "Joe Miller" and "Vanity Fair,"
When in swept Columbia, careworn and pale,
But dauntless and haughty 'mid Fortune's assail—
"Come, steward," she said, "now explain if you can!
Why shan't I discharge you and try a new man?"

Then Abraam the wily replied with a grin,
"A Dutchman once said, in the county Quinn,
(The story is old, but in point, as I deem)
'Taint safe to swap horses when crossing a stream."

"Cease, sirrah, your jesting! remember," she said,
"My fields with the blood of my yeomanry red!
The wail of the widow, the orphan's sad eye
Rebuke the rude trifling of lowly or high.
My children are warring along my green slopes—
I come for your counsels, your plans and your hopes."

Quoth Abraam, "Don't swap; for as sure as a gun,
This thing, it is certain, must never be done.
Your biler will bust if you bother the steam—
'Taint safe to swap horses when crossing a stream."

"But, steward," she answered, "my debts are untold
Account for my treasures of silver and gold!
Hard taxes are wrested from labor's brown hand.
Yet pledged is my income, and mortgaged my land.
Your squanderings waste what the plunderers miss;
Three years of your follies have brought me to this!"

And Abraam replied, as he straddled his chair,
"You know, my dear madam, I'm honest and square;
To shelve a tried President, don't ever dream—
'Taint safe to swap horses when crossing a stream."

"You crouch to John Bull, for French despots hurrah,
You cringe to the Spaniards and toady the Czar;
My shield cannot shelter a poor refugee;
My commerce is hunted all over the sea.
How fallen am I—the young Queen of the West,
Who walked among nations more proud than the best."

"Tis true," said the steward, "I notice your fix,
But let the pot bile, and jest tote up the sticks.
Don't muddle the milk, if you hope to get cream:
'Taint safe to swap horses when crossing a stream."

"Sir, since you persist in your quips and your cranks,
Where is Rosecrans, Cameron, Scott, and Nat Banks,
Pray, why do you 'swap,' if removal won't cure,
When Frémont was fast and McClellan was sure?"
And quelling her tears, she demanded reply
With clouds on her brow and flame in her eye.

"That 'minds me," said Abraam of old Deacon Bruce—
"What's sass for the gander ain't sass for the goose—
Things aint at all times," sez he, "quite what they seem—
'Taint safe to swap horses when crossing a stream."

"Enough!" cried Columbia, "my future I see—
Ruin, havoc and death in the homes of the free;
Fair Liberty stabbed by the lords of misrule,
While, thoughtfulness, she laughs at the freaks of their fool;
Thieves, clowns and usurpers in council preside,
And fraud, force and folly my destinies guide."
"I have it!" quoth Abraam, "as slick as a mice!
Squash Hamlin! and Government's rid of its vice;
But don't turn tail at a copperhead scream—
'Taint safe to swap horses when crossing a stream."

Columbia disgusted, would listen no more,
But cried in a rage, as she stormed through the door—
"I have kept an old donkey for nearly four years,
Who brings me but scorn and disaster and tears!
I vow I will drive a respectable team,
Though forced to swap horses when crossing a stream."[56]

Although other images in the same issue were more favorable and offset this conclusion, the ambivalence toward Lincoln was not a good omen for his political future. Even *Harper's Weekly* winced when its editors "read with pain the manifesto of Messrs. Wade and Winter Davis; not because of its envenomed hostility to the president, but because of its ill-tempered spirit, which proves conclusively the unfitness of either of the gentlemen for grave counselors in a time of national peril." "The President may be wrong," conceded the editorial, "but no such distempered critics of his course can be right." Nevertheless, *Harper's Weekly* was engaged in serious damage control, and it attempted to soften the impact of the manifesto in the remainder of the editorial: "Nor is the censure of the manifest of Messrs. Wade and Davis a party matter. There is no party consideration in the case. The Union men of the country have nominated Mr. Lincoln upon the strength of the general course of his administration and of his personal patriotism. They do not profess to approve every act, or to agree with every measure of that administration; but under all the circumstances of the time and country, and his unswerving fidelity to the cardinal principles which the rebellion attacks, they think it best for the country that he should be re-elected. Whatever, therefore, tends to defeat him helps to throw the country into the hands of the enemies."[57] No doubt, Lincoln was in trouble.

If the Radicals could select a viable candidate, persuade Frémont to step aside, convince Lincoln that the odds against him were insurmountable, and rally the state governors to new leadership, the political miracle they envisioned might well become reality. On August 30, they met to plot and execute strategy, but two unforeseen events soon intervened. First, Sherman's capture of Atlanta utterly transformed the prospects of war and the political landscape. Second, when the Democratic Party nominated General McClellan, he disavowed important elements of its controversial peace platform, which divided the Democratic Party. Both of these developments substantially weakened the opposition and infused new life into Lincoln's campaign. In the midst of this sudden political upheaval, Republican governors repudiated the radical plan and closed ranks behind the president. In the interest of party unity, Lincoln reluctantly deposed Postmaster General Montgomery Blair—a relatively small concession to heal political wounds and vastly improve the president's prognosis. Finally, more out of opposition to McClellan than deference to Lincoln, Frémont withdrew from the race. This act removed residual political debris from the Republican pathway to the White House. Afterward, only George McClellan and the Democratic Party stood in Lincoln's way.[58]

Ten

The Olive Branch
or the Sword?

ew presidential elections in American history have been infused with new life more quickly and dramatically than Lincoln's second quest for the White House. Within days of the president's own dire prediction that "it seems exceedingly probable that this Administration will not be re-elected," he was catapulted back into the role of the "favorite."[1] Among the reasons for this sudden change were the stunning capture of Atlanta and the collapse of the Radical Republican effort to replace Lincoln on the ballot. These events ultimately doomed Frémont's third-party opposition. The removal of these political distractions enabled Lincoln to focus exclusively on defeating the Democratic Party's candidate, George McClellan.

Yet even the Democrats oiled the track on which Lincoln glided to an electoral and popular landslide. Duplicating the political division of 1860, the Democrats suffered an identity crisis. To broaden constituent appeal and placate the War Democrats, the Chicago convention delegates nominated a military leader, but the platform, conceived by Copperhead mentality, catered to the olive branch more than the sword. By succumbing to the ideology of compromise and peace without victory, the Democrats gambled their political fortune. Then when General McClellan's letter of acceptance for the nomination shrugged off the peace platform, the Democrats had a problem. To make matters worse, the vice presidential candidate, George Pendleton, endorsed the Chicago platform. Not only was McClellan at odds with his party's official philosophy, but he and his running mate also did not see eye to eye with each other. Furthermore, pacification was rendered less appealing with Sherman's conquest of Atlanta. Hence, the timing of the Chicago platform, its philosophy, and the emergence of tension between national figures at the head of the Democratic Party all seemed out of step with conditions in the embattled nation. These political conditions created a Democratic campaign manager's nightmare and an answer to prayer for zealous Republicans.

By the end of September 1864, the illustrated domestic press overwhelmingly supported Lincoln; the Democrats could not claim a single magazine from the genre. When Frémont dropped out of the race, opposition to Lincoln evaporated among illustrators. After *Funniest of Phun* realized it had been abandoned by Frémont, it redirected its criticism toward McClellan and gradually softened its attitude toward Lincoln.[2] At the end of the summer, Lincoln's other opponent in the illustrated press, the *New York Illustrated News,* also gracefully yielded, on economic grounds, its stake in this medium to competitors *Harper's Weekly* and *Frank Leslie's Illustrated Newspaper.* Hence, insofar as the illustrated periodical was concerned, Lincoln enjoyed smooth political sailing almost from the time of McClellan's nomination to the election. The Democrats had limited exposure in separately published prints and in the usual campaign propaganda, but they did not enjoy visual support in illustrated magazines anywhere near that of Stephen A. Douglas in the 1860 election. This state of affairs did not bode well for the Democrats.

Harper's Weekly maintained its allegiance to Lincoln and *Frank Leslie's Illustrated Newspaper,* though more tepid and ambivalent in its support, also championed his cause. The comic genre, which included *Phunny Phellow, Comic Monthly, Yankee Notions, Frank Leslie's Budget of Fun,* and *Merryman's Monthly,* also united behind

"Don't You Wish You May Get It?" *Phunny Phellow,* May 1864, 8–9. Reproduced through permission of the Rare Book and Special Collections Library, University of Illinois at Urbana-Champaign.

"Don't You Wish You May Get It?"

Lincoln. Thus, principal members of the magazine cartoonist's guild—Thomas Nast, Frank Bellew, Frank Beard, William Newman, J. H. Howard, and the like—were devoted to Lincoln's reelection.[3] This formidable collection of talent, especially the tandem of Nast and Bellew for *Harper's Weekly*, arguably made a major difference in Lincoln's quest for reelection. In fact, Nast and Bellew were two major elements in a three-pronged attack against McClellan. The third component was the editorial page.

Nast's specialty was the grand double- and single-page work of political art designed to elevate Lincoln and embarrass McClellan.[4] Nast had a unique knack for stimulating the emotions of the electorate and provoking political thought. Frank Bellew's gift involved the comic touch. To achieve the same end sought by Nast, Bellew adroitly entertained his readers on the cartoon page, though he was equally at home with caricature. Ironically, this was the same illustrator who had so powerfully vilified Lincoln in the pages of *Funniest of Phun* and the *New York Illustrated News*. Apparently, Bellew identified with Radical Republican politics, but he sided with Lincoln just long enough to defeat the Democratic candidate, whose conservative views he found more offensive than Lincoln's moderation. Whatever energy Bellew had expended earlier for Frémont he zealously diverted to Lincoln's campaign. Meanwhile, the editorial staff at *Harper's Weekly* carefully selected its themes and systematically argued its case. The result was a finely honed political editorial policy. Thus, *Harper's Weekly* became an effective instrument of propaganda. Week after week, the combination of popular art and essay drove its message home: McClellan was not worthy to replace Lincoln. To McClellan's dismay, the Democratic Party had no comparable system of communication. Given the pivotal historical role of political caricature, pro-Lincoln material in the press was a formidable political power to overcome.

THE CAMPAIGN

Well before McClellan's nomination, cartoonists correctly surmised that the final choice for presidential contenders might come down to Lincoln and McClellan. In May, Thomas Nast depicted a playful Lincoln, shown as a monkey, toying with "Little Mac," a dog. In his right hand Lincoln dangles a tempting rat dinner—"The White House, 1865"—before McClellan's nose, but with his left hand the president restrains Little Mac by the tail. "Don't you wish you may get it?" teases the president. Judging from the cartoon, Little Mac was under Lincoln's spell; virtually at will or at the president's whim, Lincoln could present or withdraw the White House prize and facilitate or curb McClellan's political destiny.[5] At this point in the race, such imagery represented political wishful thinking.

Early imagery from the campaign also intimated that the Democrats might again be their own worst enemies; the insistence on a peace plank could hopelessly divide the party. In one cartoon, "Fernandy Wood" threatens "Say peace! Or, by thunder,

I'll split it up the middle."[6] To be sure, this parody of the Democratic Party came from the Republican press, but Democrats eventually fulfilled the prophecy as if the Republicans had orchestrated it. Copperhead influence that committed the Democrats to the policy of appeasement would have generated a profound political peril, especially if the Union armies had significantly changed the war's prognosis, which they did.

As the news of a peace platform filtered out of the Chicago convention, *Harper's Weekly* defined the most compelling election issue as "shameful surrender," versus patriotism: "On one side in this election, all who stand for the unconditional maintenance of the Union and the Government, and for waging the war for that purpose until the rebels yield and ask to be heard, will vote for Lincoln and Johnson. On the other side . . . all who wish peace upon any terms or 'conciliatory' war, which is merely shameful surrender, will vote for the Chicago candidate. He will be the candidate of the enemies of the war, and whoever he may be, knowing who his supporters are, he will justly regard his election as a sign that the first wish of the people is to stop the war, not to maintain the Union."[7] When news of Sherman's victory at Atlanta followed just days after the Chicago convention, the Democrats knew they had an acute political problem.

Thomas Nast's memorable full-page cartoon "dedicated to the Chicago Convention" and entitled "Compromise with the South" hit the electorate with emotional force. As a consequence of the Democratic convention, Nast portrayed a broken-hearted Columbia kneeling and weeping over the grave of the Union. A smug Jefferson Davis stands irreverently with one boot on the grave over the shattered sword of "Northern Power." Leaning on a crutch, a mortified, one-legged Union veteran loathes the humbling obligation to clasp hands with the triumphant Jefferson Davis. On the tombstone is the inscription "In memory of our Union heroes who fell in a useless war." The Union flag ignominiously flies upside down, upon it a list of Civil War victories, and the words "Emancipation of the Slaves" billow in the wind. In contrast, the Confederate flag celebrates war atrocities—"guerilla warfare barbarities, Fort Pillow, Lawrence, starving Yankee prisoners, no quarter, burning Chambersburg, Pennsylvania, Yankee killers, murderers, bayoneting the wounded, [and] scalping."[8] This powerful Nast illustration attempted to persuade readers that the Democratic program was irresponsibly disloyal and detrimental to the Union.

Soon the Republicans had more political ammunition. "It matters little who is nominated there," claimed *Harper's Weekly*, "because the Convention represents opposition to the war, and its candidate can not escape the fate of his position." However, George McClellan's letter of acceptance as the Democratic nominee did, indeed, attempt to "escape the fate of his position." To the dismay of the Copperhead faction, he disavowed the peace elements of his party's platform. McClellan's action complicated the Democratic Party's election strategy. Exploiting this new development, *Phunny Phellow*'s Thomas Nast caricatured the Democratic Party as only he could. He pitted McClellan against two Copperhead newspapers, the *Metropolitan Record* and Ben Wood's *New York Daily News*, and outspoken Copperhead personalities Clement L. Vallandigham, Horatio Seymour, and Fernando Wood. As McClellan whitewashes the Chicago platform—"We demand immediate efforts for a cessation of hostilities with a view to peace at the earliest practicable moment; We wish to shake hands with the South; Slavery is right; Angels of peace meet here; [and] Treason"—his antagonists stand symbolically on it, rail furiously at Little Mac, and watch in horror as their candidate defaces their ideological masterpiece. With Copperhead snakes nesting in his hair, Vallandigham animatedly protests: "Let the platform alone. If you don't like it, don't meddle with it." The Copperhead newspapers bellow "We will no longer support Little Mac." Attired as Satan, Fernando Wood grimly utters: "The Peace party will not consent to have their principles betrayed, and then do homage to the betrayer. We are all going to the d———." Horatio Seymour and vice presidential candidate Pendleton stare in disbelief.[9] Although the cartoon tended to exaggerate the gravity of the situation, its depiction of internal friction, debate, and schism laid bare the Democratic Party's political vulnerabilities. Nast's cartoon raised questions about the propriety of the peace policy, the cohesion and direction of the Democratic Party, and the wisdom of Copperhead influence.

Harper's Weekly also pilloried the controversial Copperhead personalities.[10] Such guilt by association added to the unsavory reputation of the Chicago convention proceedings, reinforced the view that the Democrats were out of step with their times, and muted the voice of the War Democrats. In fact, the Republicans went out of their way to publicize the ascendancy of the Peace Democrats over the War Democrats.

The Republicans offered many reasons to vote for Lincoln: the Democratic Party's ineffectual peace strategy, the party's lack of harmony, Copperhead influence among Democrats, alleged Democratic complicity with the enemy, McClellan's tarnished war record, the potential threat that Pendleton might succeed McClellan, the likelihood of imminent final victory for Union forces, spontaneous Lincoln support among the soldiers, the futility of changing horses midstream, and Lincoln's leadership prowess. For two months leading up to the election, Lincoln's campaign reiterated these themes.

The ratio of pro-Lincoln to anti-McClellan imagery in Republican magazines was heavily weighted against McClellan. Negative campaigning was prevalent not only with Lincoln's campaign, but also with virtually all other political parties during the Civil War. Although the rhetoric of the Democrats maligned Lincoln more than it praised McClellan, it could not match the Republicans illustration for illustration and editorial for editorial.

As for the Democratic side, McClellan was favored in Britain's comic press (*Punch, Fun,* and *Comic News*) and in the *Illustrated London News*, but he was most often slighted in domestic magazines. London's *Fun* asserted that the "Voice of America," the "Voice of Abe," and the "Voice of Fun" all conspired against Lincoln's reelection. A sample of verses from "The Three Voices," September 24, 1864, demonstrates the anti-Lincoln message:

The Voice of America
Ugly Abe, he sat in his lair,
Worked his nails in his shaggy hair,
And struck his desk a blow;
Abe was vicious and Abe was glum,
He scratched his nose with his tawny thumb,
And he got him up to go.

Away with the humbug! Cast off his yoke,
Who while thousands are bleeding is brewing a joke,
And fiddles while towns are ablaze;
Who hounds at our throats war's ravenous dogs—
He who sewed up the eyes of a cargo of hogs,
In his raffish younger days.

The Voice of Abe
Foul is the treason of little Mac,
He has stolen my wind, my sails are slack,
My hold on the helm is gone;
That slip of a chap preferred to me?
Able-bodied and six feet three—
The modern Washington?

The Voice of Fun
Surely 'tis a monstrous bore,
Skilled in pettifogging lore,
He should get the rout;
Very rude of Syracuse,
Poor old Abe to abuse,
As well as kick him out.[11]

On the same date, a cartoon by John Tenniel depicted Lincoln in deep political trouble. Mrs. North, losing her patience with Lincoln's leadership, says, "You see, Mr. Lincoln, we have failed utterly in our course of action; I want peace, and so, if you cannot effect an amicable arrangement, I must put the case into other hands." The "other hands" were obviously those of George McClellan. The *Illustrated London News* concurred that "the voice of the people is for Little Mac." Still, an article in *Fun* conceded that "McClellan's chances of election for president seem to be of the smallest just now—thanks to the manifesto of principles he has thought fit to issue."[12]

Indeed, McClellan had little hope of stealing the election from Lincoln. After months of being on the defense, *Harper's Weekly* relished the shift to the offense, and it relentlessly hammered away at McClellan's candidacy. One of the periodical's major contentions was that the Peace Democrats threatened to disgrace the nation. Any time the rebel press encouraged Lincoln's opponents, *Harper's Weekly* accused the Democrats of befriending the enemy. For example, in September 1864 *Harper's* reprinted a recent passage from the *Atlanta Register,* which asserted that "If they [the Democrats] will use the ballot-box against Mr. Lincoln while we use the cartridge-box, each side will be a helper to the other." Such quotations gave the appearance of complicity, even if there actually was none. Democratic Party ideology was also accused of being subversive: "The platform of the Chicago Convention will satisfy every foreign and domestic enemy of American Union and Liberty," claimed *Harper's Weekly*.[13] Of course, the Copperhead movement within the Democratic Party was repeatedly indicted for befriending the enemy.

Cartoonists belittled General McClellan, both physically and psychologically. In caricature, Frank Bellew contrasted the lanky Lincoln at his White House desk with a puny, toylike McClellan, who barely fits in the palm of Lincoln's hand. The words that emanate from Lincoln's mouth in the balloon caption also diminish McClellan's importance: "This reminds me of a little joke."[14] This is generic denunciation, but before the election was over McClellan's character, military performance, and polit-

"This Reminds Me of a Little Joke," *Harper's Weekly*, September 17, 1864, 608. Author's Collection.

ical sagacity were also specifically impugned. To a lesser extent, especially in the domestic illustrated press, Lincoln faced similar demeaning comic scrutiny.

Aware that Lincoln had taken a beating in the partisan Frémont press and at the hands of the radical wing of his own political party, *Frank Leslie's Budget of Fun* depicted the president as a resilient survivor: "Mr. Lincoln said recently that he was like Blondin on the tightrope, with all that was valuable in America, the Union, in a barrow. Some of the spectators cried, 'A little faster, Mr. Lincoln.' Another said, 'A little slower, Mr. Lincoln.' A third said, 'Straighten your back a little more.' Others shouted, 'Stoop a little lower.' Others cried, 'A little more to the South.' Some, 'A

"The Political Blondin," *Frank Leslie's Budget of Fun*, September 17, 1864, 8–9. Reproduced through permission of the Rare Book and Special Collections Library, University of Illinois at Urbana-Champaign.

THE POLITICAL BLONDIN.

Mr. Lincoln said recently that he was like Blondin on the tightrope, with all that was valuable in America, the Union, in a barrow. Some of the spectators cried, "A little faster, Mr. Lincoln." Another said, "A little slower, Mr. Lincoln." A third said, "Straighten your back a little more." Others shouted, "Stoop a little lower." Others cried, "A little more to the South." Some, "A little more North." What would be thought, if, when Blondin was in the performance of his dangerous task, the spectators bothered him with advice, and even went so far as to shake the rope? So with me—keep quiet, and I'll wheel my barrow across.—NEW YORK PAPER little more to the North.' What would be thought, if, when Blondin was in the performance of his dangerous task, the spectators bothered him with advice, and even went so far as to shake the rope? So with me—keep quiet, and I'll wheel my barrow across."[15] One balloon caption expresses Lincoln's sentiments: "If my friends will only leave me alone, I'm all right." On each side of the wheelbarrow, which holds the hopes of the Union, two wounded veterans encourage and support Lincoln's tightrope performance. Prominent generals in the audience appear to urge Lincoln forward. On Lincoln's shoulders ride Edwin Stanton and Gideon Welles. Meanwhile, Salmon Chase has fallen from his exalted position. Frémont and Cochrane conclude, "If he reaches the other side, we must bolt." Parenthetically, Frémont and Cochrane did withdraw from the race just five days later. In another segment, perennial sceptics John Bull and Napoleon III lament Lincoln's astounding feat; "Blarst it, I always told you he would," remarks John Bull, and Napoleon III responds, "By gar, Mistare Bull, dat Ole Lincoln will do it."[16] This image, perhaps like no other, reflected the spectacular mood swing in Lincoln's camp from the despair of August to renewed faith during September that he would regain the White House.

Whereas the official Democratic philosophy touted peace negotiations, the Republicans pushed for unconditional surrender. "Union for Victory and Victory for Union," blared the headline of one editorial.[17] Another calculated the extent of the political benefits from Sherman's defeat of Confederate forces at Atlanta: "There is not a man who did not feel that McClellan's chances were diminished by the glad tidings from Atlanta. . . . When people solemnly resolve, as the party which had nominated General McClellan did at Chicago, that the experiment of war to maintain the Government and restore the Union is a failure, how can they be glad to hear of a great and vital victory which belies their theory? . . . Sherman has done more in his capture of Atlanta, for a cessation of hostilities than Vallandigham and his Convention could do in twelve months of abuse of the administration and of the war."[18]

In a double-page spread, Thomas Nast's art recorded "The Blessings of Victory" and eloquently argued, "Victory will bring us Peace." Wisely, he depicted the liberation of prisoners of war, soldiers coming home to their families, the emancipation of slaves, the incarceration of traitors, and the honoring of war heroes.[19] These images heralded an honorable end to the war and the accomplishment of a lasting peace. This was the peace the nation had hoped for and sought since the first volley at Fort Sumter, and judging from Nast's message, such hope undercut the spurious prospects offered by the Peace Democrats.

The theme of peace through war went through several variations. In *Frank Leslie's Budget of Fun*, an illustration by William Newman features "General Bombshells, the True Peace Candidate," who espouses the "War Path [as] the True One." Newman fashioned the robotic "True Peace Candidate" out of familiar patriotic icons such as cannon barrels and balls, a sword inscribed "Right makes Might," and a cape that resembles the American flag. General Bombshells crushes the "Chicago Platform"; dumps "McClellan's Report" on the ground; knocks over Jewett, who was carrying peace papers from the aborted Niagara Falls peace conference; and sends

G. F. Saunders, Fernando Wood, Judah Benjamin, Jefferson Davis, James Gordon Bennett and his *New York Herald*, the *Metropolitan Record*, and the *New York World* scurrying for cover. The belligerent general confidently introduces Generals Grant and Sherman and Adm. David G. Farragut to the "Rebs" as "Uncle Sam's only authorized negotiators—They know how to make peace!" Behind these illustrious military figures march the invading Union military forces singing "We are coming Father Abraham." On the front page of another periodical, *Phunny Phellow*, Thomas Nast rendered his own comic version of peace through victory. Nast's stable of "Lincoln's Peace Commissioners to Jeff" includes the bellicose "Farragut, Unconditional Surrender Grant, Sherman, Hancock, [and] Old Butler."[20]

Among Thomas Nast's most effective tactics was one that countered the Democratic Party's proposal for an "immediate cessation of hostilities" with a patriotic appeal to "final victory." Nast's memorable "Rally, Round the Flag, Boys" was brilliantly conceived and executed.[21] So that readers could not miss Nast's artistic tour de force, the double-page print was highlighted and described in the lead article on the front page:

> The constitutional standard-bearer [Lincoln], who through good ... and evil report has held the flag of the country aloft and triumphant, is represented surrounded by his gallant fellow-citizens of the army and navy, who on land and sea have maintained the honor and integrity of the nation. Neither he nor they ask for an immediate cessation of hostilities—neither he nor they are ignorant of the great price of constant sacrifice of every kind that must be paid for the final victory of the people over their enemies; of loyal men over traitors; of the great mass of men who live by their own labor over a privileged class that call workmen "mud-sills" and the triumph of the true Democracy over the only aristocracy in the land.
>
> Soldiers, said the President a few days since to a returning regiment, I thank you in behalf of the country for the services you have rendered.... The war is for the perpetuation of the principle of equal rights to all. In this government the sober and industrious have an equal chance. I occupy the White House now; but there is an equal chance that your father's son may be as fortunate as my father's son.
>
> These are the words of a true Democrat and honest man, sprung from the people, and conscious that he is upholding their cause against traitorous enemies everywhere. This is your war, he says. Boys, rally round your Flag![22]

Nast depicted a host of army and navy men rallying around Lincoln and the flag, and poetry augmented the power of the message, as noted in this single, representative verse:

> Rally, round the flag, boys!
> Rally once again;
> There are traitors in the camp, boys,
> And pirates on the main:

There are rebels in the front, boys,
And foes across the sea,
Who hate the proud Republican,
And scoff at you an me.[23]

(*Opposite*)
"Rally, Round the Flag,
Boys," *Harper's Weekly*,
October 1, 1864, 632–33.
Author's Collection.

Apparently, Nast's earlier illustration, "Compromise with the South, published in the weekly of September 3, . . . had already attracted universal attention." At least *Harper's Weekly* thought so: "It is the most complete commentary upon the principles which the Chicago candidates represent, and which, we believe, the people will repel with as overwhelming and just an indignation as they did the rebel shot at Sumter." Reinforced by the reaction to Nast's September print, the *Harper's Weekly* staff anticipated that "Rally, Round the Flag, Boys" contained similar compelling rationale "which no man [could] escape." The staff urged "any Union Club" to hang the illustration on its walls and political committees to circulate the "inspired document."[24]

Numerous letters to the editor apparently continued to provide evidence that Nast's campaign pictures made a positive difference. "From among the letters from all parts of the country approving them [Nast's work]," reported *Harper's Weekly*, "we select this hearty one from a Captain in the Michigan Cavalry":

Mr. Editor—Allow me to suggest that those two excellent designs of Mr. Nast—Compromise with the South, and Blessings of Victory—published in your Weekly, be offered to the public on durable paper, that they may be framed and hung up in every hotel, railroad depot, and other places of general resort throughout the North, as being the most truthful and powerful explanations of the issues to be settled by our armies and by the November election.

I am here recovering from a wound received before Atlanta, and when I return to my regiment I shall carry with me those pictures to show to my boys, though your truly loyal and superior paper circulates so generally in the army that they may see them before my return; but I shall make sure of it.[25]

Several factors eloquently argue for the probable impact of Nast's art: that the origin of such letters was widely dispersed, that individual copies of Nast's prints were solicited, that public exposition was advocated "in places of general resort," that the illustrations enjoyed some credibility as being both "truthful" and "powerful," that private individuals of potential influence were motivated to distribute them among those for whom they were responsible, and that such periodicals "circulate[d] so generally in the army" among the soldiers. Even a contemporary magazine targeted at the Union's youths, the *Little Joker*, contained serial political cartoons that touted Lincoln over McClellan. In satire, Frank Bellew professed that the only justification for electing McClellan was to lower the price of liquor. In the "Comic Picture Gallery" were claims that "the great Copperhead card, the Ace of Spades [McClellan], . . . will be trumped on the 9th of November."[26] Basing its claims on a "recent canvass in the First New York Dragoons," the magazine also projected "how the soldiers [will] vote: 'McClellan, 1; Grant, 5; Lincoln, 750.'" Two other political polls predicted similar results, and the commentary concluded, "We receive the above votes from gentlemen direct from the localities named, and there is no mistake about them. The assertion the army is for McClellan is all gammon. The soldiers know what they are about as well as we do, and they know the Rebellion a great deal better."[27]

On September 24, Frank Bellew's cartoon "Politics Makes Strange Bedfellows" chastened the *London Times* for supporting the Democratic Party. The *Harper's Weekly* cartoon pictured John Bull in bed with the stereotypic Democratic Irishman, "Pat," under the covers of the "Chicago Platform." John Bull's loaded valise of "British Gold," to finance the Democratic cause, sits conspicuously at the foot of the bed. A week later, in *Harper's Weekly*'s sequel to "Politics Makes Strange Bedfellows," the bed collapses under the collective weight of the infelicitous and incongruous Irish-British alliance.[28]

Obviously, Frank Bellew's work was in demand. *Frank Leslie's Illustrated Newspaper* also commissioned him to draw its principal cartoon. Bellew sketched the broken-down nag, "Peace," pulling the coach of the "Chicago Platform": "Little Mac.— 'Yes. Mr. Vallandigham, I certainly took the situation of coachman, but I didn't know I was expected to drive such a wretched concern as that!'"[29] Unwittingly, the Chicago platform had become a significant political ally to Lincoln during his reelection campaign.

"The patriotism of the American people rejected with such instant scorn and indignation the craven platform of the McClellan and Pendleton party," reasoned *Harper's Weekly*, "that the managers are now painfully struggling to separate the candidates from the Convention and platform."[30] The Republicans suspected that changing national conditions might persuade the Democrats to try to refocus the attention of voters away from their platform toward their candidates, but the Republicans would not allow that to happen. The Chicago platform remained an integral part of the election strategy, and a salient, vulnerable target for editorial and political caricature.

In fact, *Comic Monthly* matched the "Baltimore Platform" and the "Chicago Platform" in a race of trotters. To portray the division in the Democratic Party, astute cartoonist Frank Beard symbolically harnessed two horses, "Peace Democracy" and "War Democracy," to McClellan's ineffective carriage, the Chicago platform. Try as he might, McClellan, the troubled jockey, cannot coordinate the balky pair or keep up with Lincoln's fine single trotter, "Emancipation." In contrast, Lincoln's horse responds with alacrity and fluidity to its jockey's finesse at the reins; it pulls the streamlined Baltimore platform with ease. As Lincoln joyously pulls away going down the stretch, a despondent Frémont, standing next to his broken-down carriage, "Cleveland Platform," hollers from the sidelines, "O ye darned long legged Old Ape! What made you run against me?" Parenthetically, with Frémont officially out of the race, *Harper's Weekly* editorialized on the notion that the Republicans were finally unified

and that the Democrats were increasingly in political disarray. Although the race was not over, it appeared that neither the jockey, the carriage, nor McClellan's tandem horses were equal to their formidable rival. Furthermore, when the individual parts are considered as a whole, Lincoln's splendid race team is even greater than the sum of its parts, whereas McClellan's unit does not synchronize with any measure of precision.[31]

Frank Bellew represented this unevenness with various visual metaphors, but his principal image emerged from the Chicago platform. In *Frank Leslie's Illustrated Newspaper*, McClellan unsuccessfully attempts to walk on war and peace stilts of grossly unequal lengths. To offset this disparity, McClellan tries to balance his equilibrium with an olive branch on the peace side and a sword on the other. Pendleton's task is even more difficult; he is virtually immobilized by having to walk on just one stilt—peace. Another metaphor is a "Marvelous Equestrian Performance on Two Animals by McClellan and Pendleton. Smoking a peace pipe and wearing a bonnet, McClellan, flaunting a sword, incongruously rides a war horse. Pendleton, on the other hand, mounts "his wonderful Disunion Steed, Peaceatanyprice." Dressed as Satan, Pendleton carries the dove of peace. Of symbolic significance is the fact that Pendleton's

"The Presidential Race," *Comic Monthly*, October 1864, 8–9. Courtesy of the Department of Special Collections, the University of Chicago Library.

peace animal is a slow mule. The caption notes that the "beautiful creature Peaceat-anyprice, recently imported from Europe, was sired by John Bull, and dam'd by America."[32]

However, the most powerful assault on the Chicago platform came from Thomas Nast's double-page satire of the same title. According to Nast, the document preserved slavery, slave auctions, and corporal punishment of slaves. It made a mockery of the Constitution, perpetuated the probability of racial conflict, "demand[ed] that immediate efforts be made for a cessation of hostilities with a view to an ultimate convention of all the states," and chastised Lincoln for "arbitrary military arrest [and] imprisonment," "the suppression of Freedom of Speech and of the Press, the denial of the right of asylum, [and] the open and avowed disregard of state rights."[33] The editorial page of *Harper's Weekly* spelled out the purpose of the illustration and encouraged its use in the campaign:

> We publish today, in Mr. Nast's illustration of the Chicago Platform, one of the most overwhelming and convincing speeches that can be made for the Union and its standard-bearers Lincoln and Johnson. It represents the exact meaning of the Chicago resolutions, of which General McClellan and Mr. Pendleton are the official representatives. It reveals the secret and express tendency of the whole policy of the party of surrender to rebellion, and compromise with treason.
>
> Union committees and clubs . . . can circulate no documents more effective than the series of political pictures and caricatures which have appeared in the late numbers of this paper. They can either procure quantities of the paper itself, or they can be furnished with electrotypes of the pictures to be printed and issued as they choose.[34]

For all intents and purposes, these illustrations were used like separately published prints: they could be displayed in public locations or circulated as handbills to advance the Republican agenda.

By mid-October, Lincoln's reelection seemed certain. In early elections, Pennsylvania, Indiana, and Ohio all spurned the Democratic Party, and the generous Republican vote signaled a probable Lincoln landslide. Yet the artists continued to produce political cartoons as if the race would go down to the wire. Neither Bellew nor Nast missed a magazine deadline, and they were aided by the comparable skills of other illustrators like William Newman. In *Frank Leslie's Illustrated Newspaper*, Newman answered the common query of why General McClellan had not resigned his major generalship: "A bird in the hand is worth two in a bush." Newman could see McClellan's bid for the presidency slipping away, so he drew Little Mac as a duck hunter who had bagged just one bird—his major general commission. McClellan holds the bird in his hand, but the duck labeled "Presidency" eludes him as it flies over Salt River—a body of water that politicians dread.[35]

Meanwhile, Frank Bellew was poking holes in "The Copperhead Plan for Subjugating the South." Because Copperheads believed the war could never restore the

Union, Bellew chuckled at their peace strategy. The Copperheads, surmised Bellew, intended to accede to every wish and placate every desire of the rebellious South: "Our picture represents the successful operation of this exceedingly humane and ingenious device. We will do everything you want. We are very humble, please come back." By so doing, boredom would ensue, and the South would gladly return to the Union to relieve the frustration.[36] At the expense of the opposition, Bellew was having fun practicing his craft, and his devoted readers must have enjoyed the results.

However, *Harper's Weekly* saved one of its most compelling images for the waning days of the campaign. It is a fine sketch by illustrator Theodore Jones. From Jones's perspective, lightning bolts from Lincoln, Grant, Sherman, Farragut, and Sheridan strike mortal blows to the beleagured sinking ship of secession. Ironically, McClellan, Confederate vice president Alexander Stephens, and the Copperheads mount a last-ditch, though futile, effort to rescue secession from its stormy predicament.[37] A brief article on the editorial page explicates the meaning of the print:

Upon page 697 of this paper is a vivid picture of the wreck of the great pirate ship Secession. She is dashed upon the rocks, and is rapidly going to pieces in the terrible storm of Patriotism which beats upon her. Smitten by the fatal thunderbolts of Lincoln, Grant, Sherman, Farragut, and Sheridan she lies a helpless hulk amidst the waves. One ray of hope—Stephen's Hail, holy light!—strives to cheer her from the Chicago Lighthouse, on whose summit blows the national flag, union down [the Union flag symbolically flies upside down]. But the foundation of the Lighthouse itself is fast crumbling away, dashed to pieces by the irresistible waves of popular indignation.

Meanwhile the copper-bound boat, *Peace-at-any-Price*, is launched by the famous Chicago wreckers, SEYMOUR, [August] BELMONT, VALLANDIGHAM, WOOD, COX, AND VOORHEES, while PENDLETON strains at the stern to shove her off, and a gentleman in a Major-General uniform, upon a prancing war-horse—that seems to recoil in disgust—cheers them and warns them on. Among the crowd the most conspicuous wrecker carries under his arm a huge plank—Immediate Cessation of Hostilities—over which they hope the pirate crew may safely escape, to ship for another voyage. But the storm is overwhelming. Escape is impossible; and the ship Secession, "built in the eclipse, and rigged with curses dark," is going down forever.[38]

As the electioneering drew to a close, illustrators increasingly engaged in political forecasting. Both Frank Bellew and Frank Beard used railroad metaphors. Bellew contended that McClellan was "On the Wrong Track." In the cartoon's caption, Bellew's pun on platforms explicates his intent: "A Certain Distinguished General.—'Say! When does this train start for Washington?' Conductor.—'Law! If you want to go to Washington, you ought to have taken the Baltimore Train, which starts from the other platform. Didn't you know the Chicago train don't run to Washington?'" Curiously, Frank Beard's mind-set independently led him to frame a cartoon of his in *Merryman's Monthly* in rather similar railroad jargon. August Belmont, McClellan's campaign manager, and McClellan find themselves on "Salt River R.R"— the wrong train. Although too late, Belmont warns his political protege (riding in the caboose), "Don't stand on the [Chicago] Platform; I tell you it's Dangerous!" However, McClellan's hat, letter of acceptance, and report are swept away in the wind, while the Democratic presidential contender is jarred and rattled up and down on the Chicago platform.[39]

Frank Beard's featured front-page illustration in *Merryman's Monthly* did not prolong the suspense about McClellan's political fate. Bearing an olive branch in his hand, the "Chicago Platform" poking out of his back pocket, McClellan answers Miss Columbia's advertisement for a potential vacancy at the White House: "Mac.— 'I have seen an advertisement stating that you wanted a new servant, one more peaceably inclined and all that sort of thing, than the old one was, so I thought I'd drop in, you know.' Columbia.—'I'm sorry you gave yourself the trouble, as I have concluded to retain the services of the man I have now. Abraham, wait on this gentleman to

"Abraham, Wait on this Gentleman to the Door," *Merryman's Monthly*, November 1864, front page. Courtesy of the General Research Division, New York Public Library Astor, Lenox, and Tilden Foundations.

MAC.—*"I have seen an advertisement stating that you wanted a new servant, one more peaceably inclined and all that sort of thing, than the old was, so I thought I'd drop in, you know."*
COLUMBIA.—*" I'm sorry you gave yourself the trouble, as I have concluded to retain the services of the man I have now. Abraham, wait on this gentleman to the door."*

the door.'" Lincoln, Columbia's obedient servant, holds the staff of power in one hand and the American eagle in the other and happily acquiesces to Columbia's bidding. James Gordon Bennett and an accomplice sadly peek around the corner just in time to observe Columbia's abrupt rebuff.[40]

Because the British comic press and selected news media, including the *London Times* and the *Illustrated London News*, promoted hopes that McClellan would stage a colossal election upset, the American magazines, confident Lincoln would conquer his foe, needled the president's antagonists across the sea. *Harper's Weekly* pictured John Bull failing to get his American counterpart, Jonathan, to adopt a "British bantling," the Chicago platform: "John Bull.— 'Now, then my friend Jonathan there is a child [Chicago platform] I want you to adopt.' Jonathan.—'Looks a kinder sickly— got peace on the Brain, ain't he? Guess ye better take keer of yer own children. I don't wish ye to interdooce any of yer rickety stock uner my family!'"[41] *Frank Leslie's Illustrated Newspaper* also chided the English illustrated media. After the discouraging preliminary election results from Ohio, Indiana, and Pennsylvania, John Bull inquires how the Democratic Party is faring in the political fight. A limping and battered Democratic chief replies: "Oh, splendidly! Glorious victory—only broke my arm and leg and lost one of my eyes, and it took three quarters of an hour to whip me." "If that's your hidea of a victory, you needn't come to me to borrer any more money," rejoins John Bull. For his part, Frank Bellew returned to the popular theme of swapping horses midstream. Jonathan summarily rejects John Bull's offer to dismount his trustworthy steed, "Old Abe," for the uncertain fortunes of the Chicago nag of "Compromise" and "Peace."[42]

Meanwhile, in England, the *Comic News* and *Punch* retaliated, especially against Lincoln. For the *Comic News*, Matt Morgan confidently predicted Lincoln's ignominious upset. In comparison, *Punch*'s John Tenniel settled for a scathing critique of the fratricidal war between the "American Brothers." Although Tenniel portrayed both Lincoln and Jefferson Davis entangled in debt, it is Davis who clearly has the upper hand. As a matter of fact, Davis is almost free from indebtedness, whereas Lincoln is forced by circumstances to acknowledge his dire straits.[43] Thus did political ideology continue to shape images of Lincoln at home and abroad, sometimes in defiance of reality. Soon, however, these English comic periodicals would be compelled to admit that they had been out of touch with the jarring events of politics and war in the United States.

In a few instances, the comic press's appreciation for humor in any form led it to overlook political partisanship. For example, *Frank Leslie's Budget of Fun* had apparently saved a satirical piece entitled "Our Campaign Biographies," which focuses on Lincoln, McClellan, and Frémont, for publication just before the election. In this piece, no candidate escapes the strokes of burlesque and travesty. Even Frémont's withdrawal from the race did not save him. This work was "written expressly for the *Budget*, and compiled from original and reliable statistics, invented for the occasion, for the exclusive use of Frank Leslie."[44] For Frémont, Lincoln, and McClellan, respectively, the "reliable statistics" included,

DON'T SWAP HORSES.

JOHN BULL. "Why don't you ride the other Horse a bit? He's the best Animal."
BROTHER JONATHAN. "Well, that may be; but the fact is, OLD ABE is just where I can put my finger on him: and as for the other—
~~~ they say he's some when out in the scrub yonder—I never know where to find him."

"Don't Swap Horses,"
Harper's Weekly,
November 12, 1864, 736.
Author's Collection.

Fremont

1863—Having made the most masterly arrangements for the capture of his entire foreign legion by the Rebels, he is maliciously relieved of his command by President Lincoln, who envies him, his military genius, his brass band of foreigners, his fine head of hair parted in the middle, and the golden locks of his Mary Poser, who knocks Mrs. Lincoln into a Cock-ed Hat.

1864—Is despatched by David Field, George Opdyke, Gov. [William] Sprague, Horace Greeley and little Gay on a Wild-goose Salmon Chase after his own remains, which started on a similar expedition in 1856.

Lincoln

1808—Came into the world with a joke which nearly split his poor mother's sides. Heartless indifference of the young monster, who takes an edition of Joe Miller out of his pocket and begins to read. Four feet high when born.

1814—His mother having no wood to boil her kettle, he falls on his knees, kisses her, begs her blessing, and then silently goes into the forest. Returns home in ten minutes with enough wood on his back to cook her goose and taters for three centuries.

1814—His mother having sent him for coals, he embezzles the thirteen cents, steals some wood and then comes home, saying he has lost his money. Jokes his mother about the black (republicanism) of coals. N.B.—Our hero grows three feet this year.

1860—Through Greeley's jealousy of Seward he receives the nomination, and is smuggled into Washington as a short Scotchman carved in wood for a snuff establishment. N.B.—Grows five feet six inches.

Private Note by Frank Leslie—If the biography of Mr. Samuel Some Body, Esq., is to be believed, Abraham Lincoln, Esq., is the greatest man in the world; for if he was four feet high when born, grew four feet in 1810, three feet in 1814, two and a half feet in 1816, four feet in 1817, and for the next twenty years grew four inches a year—saying nothing of the five feet six inches when he received the Chicago nomination in 1860—our dear Abraham is now over thirty-nine feet high. . . . We have sent a special tailor to Washington to measure him. Exact dimensions in next number. Buy a copy.

McClellan

While the Battle of Malvern Hill was in progress he was thirty-nine miles off, seated in a gunboat at the edge of a canebrake, drinking tanglefoot juice and playing pennypoke with a one-armed fragment of the Southern Confederacy. . . . He is in favor of peace on earth and good will to Jeff Davis. . . . He did not capture Atlanta. He is at present negotiating with Maximillian and Max Maretzek for a division of this country, using Jeff Davis as a go-between. Treason lurks within our borders. Beware of Mac. May he dig forever.[45]

Harper's Weekly's election issue was distributed well before its official November 12 publication date to have maximum influence on the decisions of voters.[46] It was packed with voter information and political illustrations. The editorial page emphasized the pivotal nature of the election: It would decide whether the "national Government . . . has the right to defend its existence by force against foreign enemies and domestic rebels; or it is about to declare that John C. Calhoun and Jefferson Davis and George H. Pendleton are right, and George Washington, Alexander Hamilton, Henry Clay, Andrew Jackson, Daniel Webster, and Stephen A. Douglas were wrong in their theory of government."[47] An editorial also paid tribute to the yeoman service of Thomas Nast and Frank Bellew, and then described Nast's illustration of "Election Day":

Mr. Nast and Mr. Bellew have done admirable pictorial service in this paper for the Union cause. The grave and poetic designs of Mr. Nast, and the clear, comic pungency of Mr. Bellew's caricature have brought home the issues of this canvass to many a mind more forcibly than any argument or speech.

This week Mr. Nast shows us the significance of the scene at the ballot-box. Surrounded by illustrations of the various persons and classes who decide at the polls the fate of the country and of free popular institutions, the figures of Peace, with drooping head and clipped wings, as if prostituted to a hateful purpose, with her hands manacled behind her, stands before the sacred urn, while the twin Satans of secession and sympathy with it push their ballots into her hand. But opposite to her—calm, erect, and majestic, the consciousness of victory in her heart and its fire beaming in her eye—the ripe and noble figure of the Country, American Union and Liberty, drops her ballot into the box. You can read upon it the name of ABRAHAM LINCOLN, whom the heart of that country desires to see the next President of the United States.[48]

Nast not only sketched his impressive double-page election day scene, he also revealed "How the Copperheads Obtain Their Votes." Falling prey to the dubious though effective practice of negative campaigning, Nast claimed that the Copperheads fraudulently scavenged voter names from the tombstones of Union soldiers killed in action. While the Copperhead sleuths supposedly invaded cemeteries by night, surreptitiously recording names by the light of a lantern, the spirits of deceased veterans rose in indignation: "A Curse upon You for Making Me Appear Disloyal to My Country for Which I Have Fought and Died."[49]

There was also the usual last minute political skulduggery that consisted of outlandish charges. These were often lighthearted. For example, *Frank Leslie's Budget of Fun* offered a sinister conspiracy theory. Robert E. Lee secretly plots with Jefferson Davis to take the life of George B. McClellan so the Peace Democrat, Pendleton, can ascend to the role of president: "Jeff.—'Well, this War-Democrat President Won't Suit Us a Bit!' Gen. Bob.—' No; But Hem! Accidents Will Happen, You Know. Trains May Be Upset—Torpedoes Might Explode—and Then, You Know, We Have a Peace Man Who Will Succeed to the Chair.' Jeff.—'That's So!'"[50] The contextual cues of the cartoon medium implicitly neutralized much of the image's power; nevertheless, the suggestion was planted and, in some cases, probably noted. However, these eleventh-hour machinations constituted political overkill. In this election, the Democratic Party would get nowhere. As forecast, a devastating Lincoln landslide buried the McClellan-Pendleton ticket.

Typical of Lincoln, even before the official results were known, he initiated the healing process. If he were to win, he wanted to do so with grace and dignity, just as if he were to lose. "I do not impugn the motives of any one opposed to me," he noted. "It is no pleasure to me to triumph over any one." Instead, he thanked the "Almighty for this evidence of the people's resolution to stand by free government and the rights of humanity." Lincoln was gratified that "the election . . . demonstrated that a people's government can sustain a national election in the midst of a great civil war," but "now that the election is over, may not all, having a common interest, re-unite in a common effort to save our country. . . . While I am deeply sensible to the high compliment of a re-election," Lincoln continued, "it adds nothing to my satisfaction that any other man may be disappointed or pained by the result."[51] This compassionate, sensitive rhetoric of reconciliation did not necessarily typify the postelection demeanor of the illustrated press, however. Even Lincoln did not elude the critics, but McClellan and the Democratic Party, of course, faced the bulk of disdain.

POSTELECTION ANALYSIS

On November 19, *Harper's Weekly* editorialized on the lessons of the election. The "grandest lesson . . . is its vindication of the American system of free popular government," wrote the editors. Three other lessons were also enumerated: (1) the international community needed to know that there was nothing for it to gain from the nation's division; (2) the rebels needed to understand that they must acquiesce to the constitutionally sanctioned Union; and (3) everyone needed to comprehend that the people of the North "expect the utmost vigor in the prosecution of the war by every legitimate method."[52] This was a clarion call, a caveat that warned everybody about the determination of the North to maintain the Union, however costly the price.

One editorial in *Frank Leslie's Illustrated Newspaper* called the recent election the "most imposing . . . momentous, and . . . critical ordeal . . . in the history of the United States." The editorial saw the election as a mandate to bring the rebellious states "to the point of submission to the supreme authority of the Union." It chided the Democratic Party for its untenable antiwar positions and for "blindly casting away a golden opportunity for a great success."[53] Implicit in the last phrase was the magazine's conviction that the Lincoln administration would have been vulnerable to defeat had the Democratic Party adopted a more astute and defensible political position.

The two major illustrated weekly news magazines also articulated their views of Lincoln's presidential stature. *Harper's Weekly* paid tribute to Lincoln's "unwearied patience, perfect fidelity, and remarkable sagacity . . . the representative of the feeling and purpose of the American people." However, to *Frank Leslie's Illustrated Newspaper*, Lincoln won only by default. Its argument followed the Radical Republican line: Although the nation wisely elected him, given the program of the opposition, it really had no other choice. This rather ordinary, though likable, man was really unworthy of the honors and responsibilities of high office. Although the country sorely needed different leadership, no one else of authentic political stature emerged to take the reins. Neither Lincoln's character, competence, intellect, nor leadership qualified him for the task. Even Lincoln's official prose was reviewed caustically.[54] His election was a fait accompli. However, the editorial did allow that Lincoln's heart was in the right place:

> Under ordinary circumstances Mr. Lincoln would neither have been nominated or elected. It was not belief in his abilities that induced his nomination, nor was he elected from faith in his capacities or consistency. It was because the rebellion had made him the impersonation of the National cause by its vilification of his character, its slanders on his life and habits, and its thorough identification of him with the war and its objects. . . . Whereas he was and is almost womanly in his

sympathies, more than womanly weak in his concessions to treason and in his forgiveness of crime, and, in the plenitude of his kindly nature, mingled with a Spartan devotion to justice, more likely to sacrifice a friend than punish an enemy. It is better that the nation's heart should be represented in the executive chair than its head—the latter often errs, the former seldom. Mr. Lincoln is far from representing the National intellect; but his pulses keep tune with the National heart. He does not lead, but rather follows public convictions. His greatest errors have been an obstinacy which he has mistaken for consistency, more especially in all matters relating to individuals. His pigheadedness in retaining McClellan after events had demonstrated his incapacity, and when he of all men knew best the necessity of a change, and his present folly of retaining men in his cabinet whose worthlessness none know so well as himself, in defiance of the strongly expressed contempt of Congress and the country, are all proofs that he does not clearly appreciate his own position, nor always reflect the popular will. Per se, there is no man of less consequence in the United States than Abraham Lincoln of Illinois. A schoolboy would deserve flogging for sending out documents of such prodigious moment as come from his pen in phrases so mean and unbecoming. The dignity of this war has been sadly marred by the so-called State papers which it has called out on both sides—and by none more than by Mr. Lincoln's.

What we are driving at is this, that Mr. Lincoln owes his reelection, an event over which all good and true men devoutly rejoice, to no personal ability, or character, or distinction of his own. Nine-tenths of the men who voted for him—outside of Illinois, where every male of puberty is an office-holder—did so from no high appreciation of him as a man or a statesman, but because, by so doing, they conceived they were best promoting the welfare of the country. To use one of the President's favorite similes, "we could not swap horses while swimming the river."[55]

It was obviously too early to debate Lincoln's place in history objectively. Moreover, he was a war president, and the war was not yet over. From any angle, the emotions and biases of partisan politics distorted the vision. Only the revolution of time would expose his work to more qualified judges of the period. The uncritical enthusiasm of his proponents in *Harper's Weekly*, the faint praise of disgruntled Radical Republicans, the critique of Peace and War Democrats, the judgment from abroad, and the appraisal of his ardent foes in rebellion would all have to be filtered through the lens of time and the give-and-take of scholarly debate—a dynamic, open-ended, and perpetual discussion. However, now that we are the beneficiaries of a seasoned perspective and of that durable, ongoing debate, the message of the editorial in *Frank Leslie's Illustrated Newspaper* strikes us as ludicrous. By the same token, the preponderance of over a century of scholarship vindicates Lincoln as one of the nation's finest presidents.

"Long Abraham
Lincoln a Little
Longer," *Harper's
Weekly*, November 26,
1864, 768. Author's
Collection.

Long ABRAHAM LINCOLN a Little Longer.

What did the postelection illustrations say about Lincoln? As the victor, Lincoln's visibility obviously increased. This was a quantitative change in pattern. Two factors diminished the output of Lincoln illustrations between McClellan's September nomination and the November election. First, the propensity of political campaigns for negative electioneering guaranteed that the Lincoln camp would highlight McClellan's blemishes more than Lincoln's virtues. Second, the failure of the Democratic Party to mount a comparable illustrated media blitz of Lincoln left McClellan dangling as the principal target of popular artists.

Because illustrated periodicals declined to support the Democratic Party in the 1864 election, the qualitative assessment of the candidates naturally reflected a bias in favor of Lincoln. Frank Bellew's memorable caricature "Long Abraham Lincoln a Little Longer" was typical.[56] Indeed, the gist of the cumulative message from contemporary prints affirmed that Lincoln was standing taller than ever.

Political caricature in magazines sponsored by Frank Leslie also offered a far more sanguine portrait of the president than the critical editorial from *Frank Leslie's Illustrated Newspaper*. For example, *Frank Leslie's Budget of Fun* saturated its December issue with benign Lincoln caricature. The front page depicted Lincoln and McClellan at odds over which plank to cross over the "Abyss of War." Each tries to persuade Columbia—the custodian of the "Rights of Man," the "Constitution," and "Laws"—to choose the best platform to bridge the chasm. Napoleon III and John Bull encourage Columbia to adopt McClellan's "worm-eaten," pieced-together plank of "Peace Democracy" and "War Democracy." "Go vid dis leetle man, Ma'am, Ve recommend him," urges Napoleon III. "I hope she'll take Little Mac's road. I should like to see her COME TO GRIEF," adds John Bull. Lincoln, on the other hand, asserts that the "Only Path to UNION CITY Is through WAR. . . . Don't trust that rickety concern, Madam, it's Unsound, and will come in two before you are half way over." Grasping Lincoln's arm, Columbia takes Lincoln's advice and repudiates the unstable McClellan platform.[57]

In "A Parcel for the White House," another illustration portrays Columbia testing which candidate was prepared to carry the heavy responsibilities implied in the "Presidential Vote 1865." To bear off the major national issues of the day—"Emigration, the Monroe Doctrine, Emancipation, and the Pacific Railroad"—McClellan pushes an inadequate, rickety, and minuscule cart, the "Chicago Platform." "Trust Me & MY TRUCK, It's as safe as a GUNBOAT," boasts McClellan. Parenthetically, the pejorative gunboat image stereotyped General McClellan as an inept and timid military figure commanding his forces at the Battle of Malvern Hill from the relative safety of a remote vessel. Compared to McClellan's toy cart, "A. Lincoln's Union Express" easily accommodates the imposing issues in a gigantic wagon; "Guess I'm the man to carry it, I CARRIED IT BEFORE," observes Lincoln.[58]

To portray Lincoln's victory, Frank Bellew designed multiple comic prints for *Frank Leslie's Budget of Fun*. One depicted the "Giant Majority Carrying Abe Lincoln Safely through Troubled Waters to the White House." Significantly, the important role of the military in Lincoln's election is acknowledged by the club labeled

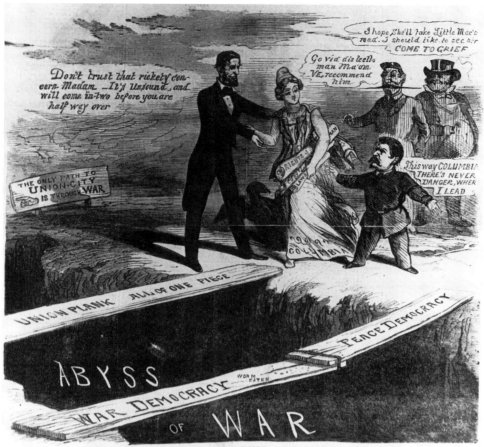

THE TWO PLATFORMS—COLUMBIA MAKES HER CHOICE.

A PARCEL FOR THE WHITE HOUSE; OR, THE PRESIDENTIAL VOTE.

"army" in the giant's left hand and the emblem of the navy anchor hanging from his pocket. Whereas a dry Lincoln is carried away triumphantly by the giant majority, a thoroughly drenched McClellan—a victim of shipwreck—staggers out of the water, literally shouldering the blame for defeat at the polls, which is signified by an imp designated as "minority." While debris from the "Chicago Platform" floats between the legs of the giant, the donkey of peace still flounders in deep water.[59]

The shipwreck image took on a different appearance in *Yankee Notions*. In that periodical, J. H. Howard's comic portrayal "Poor McRobinson Crusoe!" depicts McClellan exiled to a remote island. Humbled by the disaster, McClellan helplessly watches his sinking ship, "Democracy," disappear into the depths of the sea under the brilliant rainbow ("Abraham Lincoln") from the storm. The caption spells out McClellan's plight: "McCrusoe.—'Stranded, by Jove! with nothing left but my sword, camp chest, and my commission—and precious little good they'll do me in this situation, I'm thinking.'"[60]

Frank Bellew also drew a piece entitled "The Good Uncle and the Naughty Boy," a reference to Uncle Sam and McClellan, respectively. Holding the torn map of the

United States, Uncle Sam interrogates Lincoln and McClellan, wanting to know who offered McClellan the stewardship of the divided nation. A submissive and shackled symbol of the Confederate States of America listens in on the conversation:

> Uncle Sam.—"I Hear That Somebody Has Been Offering to Sell this [map of the United States] to That Boy [McClellan] There, and I'm Bound to Find Out Who Did It. Abraham Lincoln, Where Were You During the Election?"
> Abe Lincoln.—"I Was at the Top of the Poll, Sir."
> Uncle Sam.—"George McClellan, Where Were You, Sir?"
> George McClellan.—"If You Please, Sir, I Wasn't Anywhere."
> Uncle Sam.—"Hum! Weren't Anywhere! That Looks Suspicious—Very Suspicious!"[61]

Several postelection images focused on the avalanche of votes cast for Lincoln. William Newman built upon that theme. In the "Winter of Their Discontent," he used the metaphor of a "Snowstorm of Ballots" to characterize the mood of Jeff Davis and Robert E. Lee—for they were the ultimate election losers. Newman

THE WINTER OF THEIR DISCONTENT—JEFF AND HIS LIEUTENANT OVERTAKEN IN A SNOWSTORM—OF BALLOTS.

Lee—"'PON MY SOUL, JEFF, I CAN'T PROTECT YOU MUCH LONGER! I SHALL HAVE TO DROP THIS UMBRELLA—I'M PRETTY NEAR WORN-OUT!"

portrayed Davis and Lee inundated by a storm while on a duck hunting expedition. While Lee and Davis are unmercifully pelted by the onslaught of ballots, Lee attempts to shield Davis with his umbrella. Finally, Lee concedes: "Lee.—'Pon My Soul, Jeff. I Can't Protect You Much Longer! I Shall Have to Drop This Umbrella— I'm Pretty Near Worn-Out!'" Yet the storm is not the only indignity: the hunters had failed to bag any birds. Jeff Davis had wasted his "Last Shot" in hopes of securing the bird of "Independence," and the duck of foreign "Recognition" was already in free flight, having eluded Davis once and for all. All Davis and Lee can do is wait out the storm. As the ballots—"Abe & Andy, Old Abe, Uncle Abrahm, Split-Rails Forever, Rail-Splitter, Union, War"—fall, it is as if no power can salvage the Confederates' hunting expedition or assuage the disconsolate gloom that hovers over them.[62]

Like the storm metaphor, "Jeff Davis's November Nightmare" also focuses on the depressing election news from the North. The disquieting apparition of Old Abe leads to this dialogue: "Is that you, still there, LONG ABE?" asks Davis. "Yes! And I'm

"Jeff Davis's November Nightmare," *Frank Leslie's Illustrated Newspaper*, December 3, 1864, 176. Author's Collection.

JEFF DAVIS'S NOVEMBER NIGHTMARE.

going to be FOUR YEARS LONGER," responds Lincoln.[63] Psychologically, the president's landslide was a devastating blow to the South.

Inexplicably, Thomas Nast did not sign his clever caricatures in *Phunny Phellow*, but they unmistakably bore Nast's indelible signature of talent. To the end, Nast exploited the peace-war ambivalence of the Democratic Party. Nast heralded McClellan's defeat as "The Peace-War Eagle Brought to Grief." Protected under McClellan's peace wing are McClellan's supporters Fernando Wood, Clement Vallandigham, Horatio Seymour, and George Pendleton. Signficantly, no supporters stand under the war wing. From a distance, Union generals disparage McClellan: "You can't get this chicken under that [war] wing"; "Old Abe is the boy for us, he will let us finish the war"; "No compromise, down with the Rebs"; "You are played out"; and "How are you Gunboat?"[64]

In a double-page spread Nast called "Election Day," McClellan and Pendleton are the Humpty Dumpties of the Democratic Party: "Mac and Pen went up the hill, to fetch a pail of water; Mac fell down and broke his crown, and Pen came tumbling after." In the distance, Lincoln can be seen in front of the White House with one of his generals; together they watch the American eagle deliver Jeff Davis to the door. Union soldiers and prominent generals jubilantly celebrate the spectacle. With a tear in his eye and an olive branch in his hand, General McClellan laments the outcome.[65]

In the midst of this overwhelming and impressive support, a single dissenter from the Northern comic media emerged. It was Lincoln's old nemesis from the Radical Republican tradition, the *Funniest of Phun*. The political stance of this periodical forced it to choose Lincoln over the Democratic candidate, McClellan, but it nevertheless did so with reluctance and great ambivalence. It was *Funniest of Phun* that had embraced General Frémont's candidacy before he left the race. *Funniest of Phun* had spared neither animosity nor vituperation when it had attacked Lincoln before the election. Afterward, it returned to harsh slogans of antipathy—failure to pursue justice, elevation of expediency over principal, demonstration of spineless leadership, and reticence to translate a constitutional mandate on the slavery question into an act of authentic presidential decisiveness. It mocked Lincoln as "the gloved hero of Emancipation." The glove symbolized his purported refusal to crush slavery with a bare-fisted blow. It was not Lincoln, but General Sherman, the real emancipator, who slew the dragon of "slavery," "prejudice," and "avarice." Lincoln was only holding the flag of the "Emancipation Proclamation" because of "expedience" and "military necessity." In fact, the caricature had Lincoln confessing: "I have neither exercised my judgement, conscience, or humanity on the moral question of slavery."[66] Ironically, this unsigned print was most likely drawn by Frank Bellew, who, along with Thomas Nast, so eloquently championed Lincoln's cause in *Harper's Weekly*. Was this Bellew's own private pledge of allegiance to Radical Republican politics? This question still remains a matter of speculation, but Radical Republicanism seems to be a plausible hypothesis.

Begrudgingly, *Punch*, the *Comic News*, and *Fun* all acknowledged Lincoln's triumph. Bitterly, the *Comic News* vilified Lincoln as the merchant of death, "In for His

The gloved hero of Emancipation waiting for the indispensable necessity.

"The Gloved Hero of Emancipation Waiting for the Indispensable Necessity," *Funniest of Phun*, February 1865, 8–9. Collection of Richard Samuel West/ Periodyssey.

"TO SECURE JUSTICE AND LIBERTY,"————"SHALL GUARANTEE TO EACH STATE A REPUBLICAN FORM OF GOVERNMENT"————"NO PERSON SHALL BE DEPRIVED OF THEIR LIBERTY WITHOUT OUR PROCESS OF LAW—U.S. CONSTITUTION AS IT IS."

"I am unprepared to declare a constitutional competency to Congress to abolish slavery in the States"—A. Lincoln;—or in other words, "The incompetency of Congress to do what they were expressly elected and delegated to do, to enact law to protect and enforce the object, letter and spirit of the Constitution."

"I claim not to have controlled events, but confess plainly that events have controlled me." Abraham Lincoln—or in other words, "I have neither exercised my judgment, conscience, or humanity on the moral question of slavery."

Second Innings." From *Punch* John Tenniel's Lincoln miraculously emerged as the "Federal Phœnix" from the cinders of "Habeas Corpus, Free Press, State Rights, Credit, Commerce, and United States Constitution."[67] By the same title, doggerel elaborates the meaning of the clever print:

As the bird of Arabia wrought resurrection
By a flame all whose virtues grew out of what fed it,

So the Federal Phœnix has earned re-election
By a holocaust huge of rights, commerce, and credit.[68]

London's *Fun* published a requiem for the solemn occasion, but let it be known that it still sympathized with the South. Four of the seven verses follow:

The rowdy strolls into the bar,
And quaffs the cheering cup;
'Tis "Cousin, take a change o' breath;"

"The Federal Phœnix,"
Punch, December 3,
1864, 229. Author's
Collection.

THE FEDERAL PHŒNIX.

Or, "Stranger, liquor up."
The North is bound to win the day,
As she hath done before;
Our President hath ruled so well,
We'll give him four years more.

Now shall brave Gilmore's fierce Greek fire
With tenfold splendour blaze;
Now will we, level with the ground,
The Southern cities raze;
Now shall their smoke ascend to heaven,
And when the deed is done,
A grand Te Deum shall proclaim
A glorious victory won.

What saith the South? Oh, God of heaven!
She lifts her arm on high,
And points with her ensanguined brand
To the wrath-crimsoned sky:
"Help me, oh warriors' God," she prays,
"Long as thou givest me breath,
To fight for home and liberty—
If needful, to the death.

"Then let the North Te Deums sing
O'er slaughtered wives and maids;
Let Northerns in our daughters' hearts
Plunge deep their vengeful blades;
And be the praise of 'Honest Abe'
In every Northern mouth.
This, this our heartfelt prayer shall be,
'Oh, God! Avenge the South!'"[69]

However, these sour grapes from abroad could not reverse Lincoln's electoral victory or detract from the tangible progress of achieving national goals since the 1860 election. Then the fear of Black Republicanism was Lincoln's political nemesis, and the specter of slavery, secession, and war his formidable presidential obstacles; in 1864 anxiety over Black Republicanism was no longer the central theme, and emancipation, union, and peace for all Americans were plausible realities.

If there was ambiguity in 1860 about whether the illustrated periodicals had materially influenced the outcome of the presidential election, that uncertainty was swept away in the election of 1864. The visual and verbal creations of illustrated periodicals were integral parts of Lincoln's political machine. Nowhere is the evidence more compelling than in the pages of *Harper's Weekly*, but no single magazine could hoard the praise. Lincoln's election was a collective effort, an informal and loose partnership that involved *Frank Leslie's Illustrated Newspaper* and almost the entire comic medium. For his contribution, Thomas Nast deserved much credit and was personally thanked by the president, but Frank Bellew, William Newman, Frank Beard, J. H. Howard, John McLenan, and others, conspicuous and inconspicuous, had also earned plaudits, as did the signal contribution of photographers. Likewise, creators of the written word of all kinds (satire, editorials, doggerel, and news) made their mark, never to be obliterated by the passage of time. And, of course, the unsung artisans and laborers who performed the less glamorous tasks of engraving, printing, marketing, and circulation also helped make it all possible. If 1860 marked the humble beginning of a media political revolution, the 1864 election celebrated its coming of age.

Now that Lincoln's last political race was history, he finally held in his hands what amounted to a firm mandate from the people. They had given him a sword and reserved the olive branch for that unlikely contingency of a negotiated peace on the terms Lincoln had already clearly specified to the Confederate administration. The end of the national ordeal was in sight.

Enduring to
the End

In 1864, an immense electoral mandate that endorsed the continuation of war and the Union's military strategy temporarily muted Lincoln's staunchest critics; consolidated Northern unity; empowered anew the administration for decisive, prudent action; and transfused a surge of confidence into the body politic. Not since the earliest days of the war had there been such optimism. All the crucial indicators pointed in the right direction: Maryland's initiative to abolish slavery was enacted, the political groundwork for the Thirteenth Amendment to the Constitution was established, national consensus over the direction of the country was forged, and the North's military juggernaut surged inexorably toward victory. In December, impressive battlefield victories at Nashville and Savannah reinforced the upbeat mood.

MEDIA EUPHORIA

This effervescent spirit was also discernible in the press. The message of national optimism fairly saturated the illustrated magazines. In a double-page spread that retrospectively celebrated the Thanksgiving holiday, Thomas Nast "thank[ed] God for Maryland freeing her slaves" and "for our Union victories"; touted Lincoln's "re-election in the United States"; reveled that John Bull, Napoleon III, and "rebeldom" are all confounded by northern success; invoked a benediction—"Blessed are the Peacemakers"—on the army, navy, and their leaders; and summed it all up in the phrase "United We Stand."[1]

Around Christmas, the seasonal theme of Santa Claus and gift giving (especially to Jefferson Davis) preoccupied the comic media. To be sure, a few of the gifts were dubious. For example, *Merryman's Monthly* equipped Santa Claus with a sack full of bombs for "Jefferson Davis and his friends."[2] Other gifts are contingent on Davis's

ultimate submission to Union authority. In each case, the gifts are mutually exclusive—Davis must select one or the other. In the *Comic Monthly*, Frank Beard dressed
Lincoln in a Santa Claus outfit for a surreptitious nocturnal visit to the Richmond
White House. Santa Claus Lincoln's gifts are customized for the occasion: he offers
either an "olive wreath" or a "sword." Although Lincoln's personal preference is to
bestow the olive wreath, if absolutely necessary he will deliver the sword: "Hm! Let
me see, what shall I give little Jeffy—this nice olive wreath or the pretty little sword?
Well, I'll put the wreath in his stocking and if he gets restive in bed, he shall [have]
the sword."[3] Either way, the rebellion is doomed.

Similarly, in *Phunny Phellow* Thomas Nast drew two Christmas boxes for Lincoln
to give to his nemesis, Jeff Davis. Unlike most presents, the contents of these boxes
are not mysterious; a sign on each identifies the contents and specifies the consequences for choosing one over the other. Again, the peace/war dilemma confronts
Davis. Will it be box one—"Four Years More War," or box two—"Peace and Union"?
Lincoln warns the Confederate president, "You pays your debts and you takes your
choice." If Davis selects more war, he is guaranteed "Extermination, Confiscation,
U.S. Soldiers to have your lands, Death to all traitors, No Armistice, [and] Slavery

"United We Stand,"
Harper's Weekly,
December 3, 1864, 776–
77. Author's Collection.

and Rebellion [to] fill the same grave." If Davis chooses peace, he opts for "No Slavery, . . . Surrender, . . . and [obedience to] the laws of the United States." In this classic double-bind decision-making context, Lincoln controls the contingencies; and from the South's perspective, Davis can only select the lesser of two "evils."[4]

Of course, these images of Santa Claus and gifts passed with the season, but the underlying message remained: victory is inescapable. Any Union setbacks would be temporary and reversible. Illustrators practiced their craft as if the war were about over and reunion imminent. Typifying confidence in the Union among artists was a cartoon in *Frank Leslie's Illustrated Newspaper*. Holding Jeff Davis's head in a hammerlock by his left arm, Lincoln uses his right fist to pummel his adversary unmercifully. Davis staggers from the beating. The caption reflects the disparity of power: "Now, Jeffy, when you think you have had enough of this, say so, and I'll leave off (Vice President's Message)."[5]

Toward the close of December, Thomas Nast anticipated "The Union Christmas Dinner." In this drawing, Nast contemplates not only "Peace on earth and good will toward men," but also a host of other desirable conditions: "The return of the Prodigal Son; Lay Down Your Arms and You Will Be Welcome; Unconditional Surrender; Victory Holding out the Olive Branch to Submission; The Home Toast—God

"Santa Claus Lincoln," *Comic Monthly*, December 1864. Courtesy of the Lincoln Museum (Ref. # 432).

Lincoln's Christmas Box to Jeff Davis.

OLD ABE--"You pays your debts and you takes your choice."

Bless Our Soldiers and Sailors; One Country, thy sins be forgiven thee; No Slavery, Freedom to All; All Men are Free and Equal; Love thy neighbor as thyself; United We Stand; Union, North and South; The U.S. Government must be maintained, but if we do not forgive, neither will your Father which is in heaven forgive your trespasses; And if a house be divided against itself, that house cannot stand."[6]

In the meantime, elements of England's comic media perceived the North's military domination as ruthless and vengeful, and they laid the blame directly at Lincoln's feet. A cartoon by Matt Morgan laments, "You have swollen the earth with the blood of my children." To be sure, the carnage was vast, but the evidence is devoid of any indication that Lincoln operated with vengeance or malice. "I wish you to do nothing for revenge, but that what you may do, shall be solely done with reference to the security of the future," counseled Lincoln to General Rosecrans.[7]

HAMPTON ROADS PEACE CONFERENCE

In December, *Harper's Weekly*'s lead editorial reported that "the air is full of rumors of peace."[8] Ironically, the combination of military success and resounding support

"North and South,"
Frank Leslie's Illustrated Newspaper, December 24, 1864, 221. Author's Collection.

NORTH AND SOUTH.

" *Now, Jeffy, when you think you have had enough of this, say so, and I'll leave off.*"—(*Vide* President's Message.)

for war in the recent election spawned these rumors. *Harper's Weekly*'s editorial staff attempted to articulate the logical base for this phenomenon. The periodical also ventured to explain just why this was a propitious time for the Union to test the political climate for a just peace: "Having ascertained how unanimous the country is for war, if necessary, it is a good time to ascertain whether it be necessary. It is a good time, because there can be no possible misunderstanding. An invitation to the rebels to lay down their arms could not be misinterpreted now, as it might have been at any other period of the war, as a sign of doubt upon the part of the Government. It would be the indication of conscious power and conscious right. It would be the summons to a doomed fortress to surrender after the irresistible strength of the besiegers had been displayed to the garrison in full view."[9] In short, the transformation of the military and political environments substantially changed the balance of power between the North and South. This enhanced position of strength for the Union made ultimate victory more certain and a negotiated peace more plausible. Hence, rumors of peace followed naturally.

To convert rumor into reality, though, required a catalyst. With more zeal than wisdom, Francis Preston Blair stepped forward. With a grandiose scheme in his pocket,

Blair pestered Lincoln for a pass to Richmond. Although Lincoln was put off by Blair's outlandish plan and disavowed any official connection, he finally yielded to constant importuning and granted the pass. After all, what harm could Blair do? Surely he could do no more harm than Horace Greeley had done at Niagara Falls.

In January, Blair managed to meet with Jefferson Davis. A cartoon in *Frank Leslie's Illustrated Newspaper* ridicules the peace adventurer's gall. It caricatures Blair as a "Self-Appointed Envoy" and whimsically disguises him as an old lady carrying "sugar plums" and "barley water" to Richmond to sweeten his chances for a negotiated peace. The image and caption confirm the public skepticism that surrounded this latest odyssey in the checkered history of private Civil War diplomacy: "Old Lady.—'Please . . . will you let me take these notions to Richmond. I kind of think they'll convert 'em.' Gen. Grant.—'Guess not! This other [a pile of cannonballs] is the sort of sugarplum just now.'"[10]

In *Comic Monthly,* a cartoon by Frank Beard also poked fun at Blair; and it threw in Horace Greeley, Lincoln, and General Sherman for good measure. Beard spoofs Blair, who is ineffectually striving to catch the dove of peace in his net of "conciliation." However, his net, like his strategy, is full of holes and the elusive dove easily escapes. Meanwhile, Horace Greeley pleads with Lincoln for just one more chance at

"The Union Christmas Dinner," *Harper's Weekly,* December 31, 1864, 840–41. Author's Collection.

the peace enterprise: "Darn up that old net of Blair's, Abe, and let me try." Lincoln's humorous reply smacks of the earlier debate about emancipation between Greeley and himself: "No matter, 'taint indispensable necessity yet." Behind Blair, General Sherman calmly holds the docile, captive "Georgia" dove in his right hand and the net of "Subjugation" in his left. "This is the only net [subjugation] to catch that bird [the dove of peace] with," asserts Sherman.[11]

In December, *Harper's Weekly* argued that conditions for peace had never been better, but after Frank Blair launched his diplomatic foray it did an abrupt about-face. The success rate for such diplomatic ventures was abysmal during the Civil War. Why should Blair's experience be any different? was the question that vexed *Harper's Weekly.* Who could blame its editorial staff for being nervous about this latest experiment? This reversal was not so much a philosophical change for the magazine as it represented a crisis of confidence over Frank Blair's diplomatic credentials.

With the press in the dark about the "whirring" and "cooing of doves and the rustle of olive boughs," *Harper's Weekly* cynically compared Blair's mysterious excursion to Richmond with Greeley's vain rendezvous at Niagara Falls: "It is to be seen whether the cooing of the one is more effective than that of the other." Aside from skepticism about the outcome, the venture seemed misguided and flawed: "An infinite mischief is done by this well-intentioned private cooing." Finally, the editorial settled into the comfortable conclusion that though the "doves are very obliging,

"This Is the Only Net to Catch That Bird With," *Comic Monthly,* February 1865. McLellan Lincoln Collection, Brown University Library.

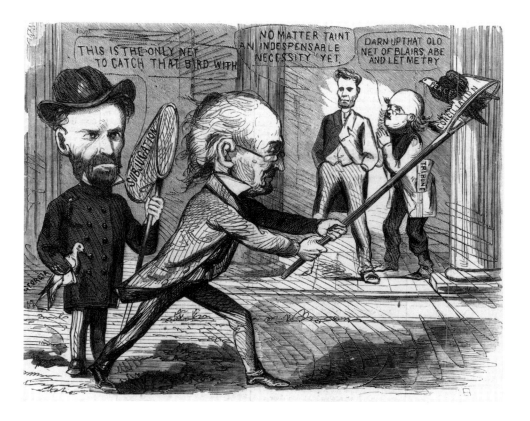

... the eagle is quite competent to conclude and confirm peace."[12] In other words, if Blair was the emissary, it was safer and wiser to abandon the peace dove for the war eagle—or it could also be taken to mean that there was nothing to lose; if Blair fails, they could always resort to the sword.

Harper's Weekly was also troubled by the *New York Tribune*'s speculative assessment about the eventual results of Blair's private diplomacy. Although the *New York Tribune* did not expect Blair to "effect a pacification," noted *Harper's Weekly*, it did think that "he will yet have done his country a signal service by assuring the South that our Government is not vindictive, and does not insist on an unconditional surrender." However, *Harper's Weekly* did not share that sanguine view. Such disagreement was typical of the great divide between these two venerable publications. Not until Blair was removed from the diplomatic scene and official representatives from the Confederate and federal governments were formally authorized to broach the question of peace did *Harper's Weekly* express relief.[13] Even so, credit should be given to Blair for engaging the two sides in a brief interlude of serious dialogue.

On January 28, Jefferson Davis appointed three peace commissioners—Alexander Stephens, R. M. T. Hunter, and John A. Campbell—to meet with federal authorities. Meanwhile, Lincoln gave Seward instructions that clearly specify the parameters essential for any negotiated settlement: "You will proceed to Fortress-Monroe, Virginia, there to meet, and informally confer with Messrs. Stephens, Hunter, and Campbell, on the basis of my letter to F. P. Blair, Esq. of January 18, 1865, a copy of which you have. You will make known to them that three things are indispensable, to wit: 1. The restoration of the National authority through all the States. 2. No receding by the Executive of the United States on the slavery question from the position assumed thereon in the late Annual Message to Congress, and on preceding documents. 3. No cessation of hostilities short of an end of the war, and the disbanding of all forces hostile to the government."[14]

That Lincoln took this opportunity for peace seriously is attested to by his personal appearance at the Hampton Roads Peace Conference. For hours he and Seward negotiated in good faith with the Confederate team. One cartoonist wistfully envisioned the Confederate "Peace Commission" submissively "Flying to ABRAHAM's Bosom," but it was not to be. Afterward, war was the only recourse. The next day, Lincoln ordered Grant to spare no effort to bring the war to a speedy conclusion. *Harper's Weekly* could offer only one consolation: "It can certainly no longer be charged against the Administration that it has neglected an opportunity to obtain peace on the basis of Union."[15]

Lincoln's detractors soon assailed the proposal. Most of the criticism came from the usual sources like Greeley's *New York Tribune*. Although its faultfinding varied in kind and intensity, *Frank Leslie's Illustrated Newspaper* chose to criticize Lincoln on a relatively minor point—the linguistic style of his report on the peace conference— and it did so with fervor and self-righteous indignation: "We have not the space necessary for the reproduction of the reports of the various parties to the late Peace

THE PEACE COMMISSION.

Flying to ABRAHAM's Bosom.

Conference at Fortress Monroe. That of the Rebel Commissioners is clear, straightforward, precise and compact. That of the President muddled, voluminous, technical, and full of that astounding (not to say characteristic) style of composition which has made most of the State papers that have come from the same source a disgrace even to the imperfect common school education of the country."[16] As ever, though, the loyal *Harper's Weekly* jumped to Lincoln's defense.[17]

COURTSHIP AND COERCION

Early in 1865, a clever drawing by William Newman invited the rebellious states to the "Great Union Ball." In the cartoon, the loyal states dance to the harmonies of an "orchestra of old men who voted for Washington." Lincoln is the band's distinguished musical conductor. In the foyer, General Benjamin Butler invites the reluctant debutantes from North Carolina, South Carolina, Virginia, Mississippi, Louisiana, Alabama, Georgia, Arkansas, and Florida to the grand social affair; and he presents elegant evening gowns, all labeled "freedom," to the attractive Southern belles. The invitation on the wall notes that these gowns are considered "wedding garments": "Now, Wayward Sisters, if you wish to come in, and be happy with the rest, put on these WEDDING GARMENTS and be Welcome."[18]

(*Opposite*)
"The Peace Commission," *Harper's Weekly*, February 18, 1865, 112. Author's Collection.

"Great Union Ball—An Invitation," *Frank Leslie's Budget of Fun*, January 1865, 8–9. Courtesy of the American Antiquarian Society.

Given Ben Butler's reputation of insensitivity toward Southern women and the noteworthy antipathy of the Confederacy toward Butler, one wonders what William Newman was thinking when he drew Butler as the diplomatic intermediary between North and South. It is ironic that Butler was removed from his command just days after this print was published in *Frank Leslie's Budget of Fun*. Lincoln was anxious to press for every military advantage and was disappointed with Butler's performance, especially his failure to open the port at Wilmington. This minor episode was also the subject of comic commentary: "Old Abe.—'I don't deny it, Ben, you've been a good servant; but what's the use of a Butler that can't open my port?'" When Butler openly criticized the president for his removal, *Harper's Weekly* tried to make the best of the situation by lauding Butler's administrative ability but censoring his battlefield leadership.[19]

Meanwhile, Confederate rebels had launched guerrilla attacks across the Canadian border into the United States.[20] These irritated military and political officials were charged with defending the boundary. Gen. John A. Dix had threatened to cross the

"What's the Use of a Butler That Can't Open My Port?" *Frank Leslie's Budget of Fun*, March 1865, 3. Collection of Richard Samuel West/ Periodyssey.

OLD ABE—" *I don't deny it, Ben, you've been a good servant; but what's the use of a Butler that can't open my port?*"

border in pursuit of the insurgents and had ordered military personnel to shoot any participants, regardless of nationality. Though Lincoln rescinded Dix's order, the press magnified bluster over the affair. The English comic media detected too much American swagger. Careless threats of war were no more than sensational journalism, but they piqued the staff egos of London's *Punch*. They retaliated with their most brutal weaponry—comic satire:

> War with England, indeed, you long-faced, wizened, ugly, ignorant Occidentals. Do you know what you are talking about? Defy the flag that has braved a thousand years the battle and the breeze. Laugh at the Lion and give umbrage to the Unicorn. Bah! . . . Do you know what we should do in the flash of a lucifer match? We should recognize the Confederacy, proclaim Davis King of the South, and steam into all the Confederate ports at once with three hundred thousand guards, all six foot and most six and three-quarters, sinking all your blockading ships to Davy Jones, except such as we should seize for our own use in bombarding New York. . . . We should then walk over you all, and straight into Canada, where we should instantly hang every Yankee who had dared to set his hoof on the sacred soil, and then we should annex the North to the colony, making Quebec the empire city.[21]

After the Senate overreacted by considering legislation to abrogate Canadian treaties, *Punch* credited Lincoln with exercising rare statesmanship. This was one of those uncommon occasions when Lincoln was commended in English caricature; John Tenniel actually portrayed Lincoln sensibly discussing the matter with Uncle Sam: "Attorney Lincoln.—'Now, Uncle Sam, you're in a darned hurry to serve this here notice [Abrogation of Canadian Treaties, by Order of the Senate] on John Bull. Now, it's my duty, as your attorney, to tell you that you *may* drive him to go over to that cuss, Davis'—(Uncle Sam Considers)." Although the *Comic News* also expressed some concern over the security of Britain's North American colony, the issue gradually faded away.[22]

Days before Lincoln's second inauguration, *Frank Leslie's Budget of Fun, Phunny Phellow, Comic Monthly,* and *Yankee Notions* published a number of images that focused on Lincoln. William Newman drew Columbia and Lincoln attempting to rescue a drowning Jefferson Davis by pulling him back into the Union boat, which is outfitted with that safest of all devices for troubled swimmers—the Constitution. Unhappily, "Old Mr. Secesh [Jefferson Davis] prefers annihilation to salvation in the Union boat. In his rapid descent [to Davy Jones's Locker] he sees some agreeable visions." Those "agreeable" visions include "Libby Prison," "Vote for Secession," "Fort Sumter, 1861," "Millen Pen," and a set of ghosts that haunt him—presumably victims of the Civil War.[23]

In *Phunny Phellow,* Thomas Nast depicted Lincoln conducting "The Grand Peace Overture to 'Our Wayward Sisters.'" The lyrics of which include "We have missed you. We are coming Father Abraham, [and] United We Stand, Divided We Fall."

THE THREATENING NOTICE.

ATTORNEY LINCOLN. "NOW, UNCLE SAM, YOU'RE IN A DARNED HURRY TO SERVE THIS HERE NOTICE ON JOHN BULL. NOW, IT'S MY DUTY, AS YOUR ATTORNEY, TO TELL YOU THAT YOU *MAY* DRIVE HIM TO GO-OVER TO THAT CUSS, DAVIS——" *(Uncle Sam Considers.)*

Among the noted instrumentalists who play under Maestro Lincoln's baton are Frank Blair (concert master), Horace Greeley, James Gordon Bennett, Henry Raymond, Edwin Stanton, William Seward, and Gideon Welles. New York newspapers that contribute to this symphony of peace include the *World*, *News*, *Express*, and *Post*. Believe it or not, this diverse group is finally creating harmony. Similar to *Phunny Phellow*, *Yankee Notions* featured the "National Philharmonic Society" rehearsing pieces such as "Union Forever," "Mobile," "Savannah," "Nashville," and "Lowell." In the background, Jefferson Davis hangs "On the One Stringed Instrument"—the gallows.[24]

Finally, a cartoon by Frank Beard in *Comic Monthly* anticipated "Jeff Davies" and "Alex Stevens" having to walk the path of "Union and Submission to Government" to get from the desolate land of "Secession" to the land of promise—"The Union." "The Narrow Path" across the "Last Ditch" is not easy to cross. Although Seward

"Old Mr. Secesh Prefers Annihilation to Salvation in the Union Boat," *Frank Leslie's Budget of Fun*, March 1865, 9. Collection of Richard Samuel West/ Periodyssey.

steadies the plank on one end, Sherman and Grant prod Davis and Stephens with their swords. Meanwhile, Lincoln tempts them with his "Amnesty Proclamation" and beckons them to take the final steps. Davis is having second thoughts: "No! No! Stevens that plank is too narrow." The caption records the exchange among Davis, Stephens, and Lincoln: "Alex Stevens.—'Come, Jeff, let's go over, I don't like this side of the ditch.' Jeff. Davies.—'don't like it any better than you do, but I don't like to say so, and if they'd only make the gangway a little wider, I think I'd go. Why don't they put down that State Rights' plank.' Father Abraham.—'Narrow as the path is, it is the only way in which you can come over; and you will have to come soon, for I perceive there are two fellows behind you that will leave you nothing but the inside of the ditch [their graves], where so many of your friends agreed to meet, if you don't hurry up.'"[25] This rare depiction of the mixture between courtship and coercion characterized tensions between the incentives of reconstruction and war.

SECOND INAUGURATION

For *Harper's Weekly*, it did not take the trauma of presidential assassination to awaken appreciation for the merits of Abraham Lincoln or to accelerate the pace of political idolization. In the eyes and hearts of its editorial staff, he had earned the admiration and respect of a nation, never to be relinquished. The staff's vision was well ahead of its time, though some dismissed its admiration as a serious case of overzealous partisanship. In anticipation of the nation's quintessential political and social event of the year—Lincoln's second inauguration—*Harper's Weekly* produced an eloquent and effusive tribute:

> On this day President Lincoln enters upon his second term amidst the benedictions of the loyal citizens of the United States. No man in any office at any period of our history has been so tried as he, and no man has ever shown himself more faithful to a great duty. His temperament, his singular sagacity, his inflexible honesty, his patient persistence, his clear comprehension of the scope of the war and of the character and purpose of the American people, have not only enabled him to guide the country safely in its most perilous hour; but have endeared him

"The Narrow Path," *Comic Monthly*, March 1865, 8–9. Courtesy of the American Antiquarian Society.

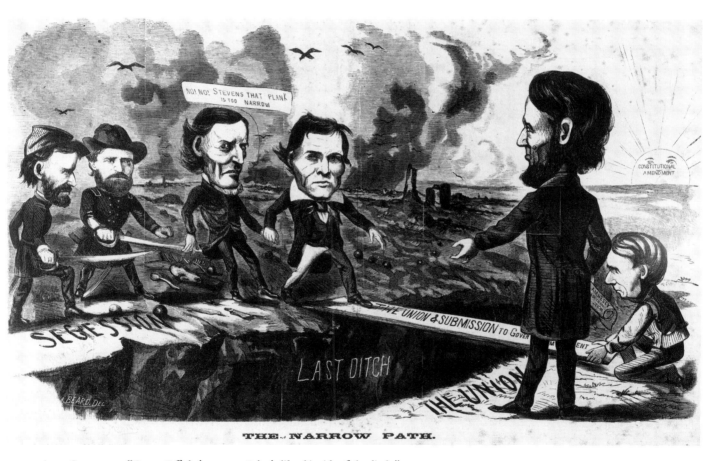

THE NARROW PATH.

ALEX STEVENS—*"Come, Jeff, let's go over, I don't like this side of the ditch."*

JEFF. DAVIES—*"Don't like it any better than you do, but I don't like to say so, and if they'd only make the gangway a little wider, I think I'd go. Why don't they put down that State Rights' plank, and the . . . ."*

FATHER ABRAHAM—*"Narrow as the path is, it is the only way in which you can come over; and you will have to come soon, for I perceive there are two fellows behind you that will leave you nothing but the inside of the ditch, where so many of your friends agreed to meet, if you don't hurry up."*

forever to the popular heart. . . . Party hate has dashed itself to pieces against his spotless patriotism. Friendly impatience has long since hushed its hot criticism. Foreign skepticism and affected contempt at length recognize in him a purely characteristic representative of that America which conquers by good sense and moral fidelity. . . . And that he is to-day inaugurated amidst universal applause, that the nation has not been deluded by the vehement party assaults which every civil war makes so practicable and specious, but has known and approved a man so just and faithful, is the noblest proof of the truly conservative character of that popular Government with which the name of Abraham Lincoln will henceforth be associated.[26]

On March 18, the date *Frank Leslie's Illustrated Newspaper* and *Harper's Weekly* circulated their inauguration issues, a profound irony was captured by one of Alexander Gardner's fine photographs of the ceremony. Salmon Chase—chief justice of the U.S. Supreme Court, former cabinet colleague, and political nemesis of Abraham Lincoln—administered the oath of office. On December 6, 1864, Lincoln had appointed Chase to the highest judicial position in the land. Despite the fact that Chase had treated the president with condescension, coveted his political office, and left the cabinet because of "mutual embarrassment," Lincoln overlooked past differences and awarded Chase for his keen legal mind. It was a sterling example of the major theme of Lincoln's second inaugural address: "With malice toward none, with charity for all, with firmness in the right, as God gives us to see the right."[27]

The two illustrated weeklies embellished their pages with grand prints of the inauguration scene; these issues would become future collectors' items.[28] Yet the comic genre also exhibited its talent. In a "Diplomatic Reunion at Washington," presumably at the inaugural ball, *Nick Nax* caricatured the angular Lincoln in animated conversation with two representatives from the European foreign service. However, the finest visual tribute to Lincoln may have come from William Newman's fine work in *Frank Leslie's Budget of Fun*. In Newman's own ingenius way, he heralded Lincoln at his inauguration as "The Tallest Ruler on the Globe." Crowned with the laurel of peace, bearing the mantle of the flag of his country, and carrying an "Amended Constitution" purged of slavery, Lincoln is welcomed to the White House by appropriate icons of patriotism: Columbia (who holds in her hand the Missouri Compromise), the American eagle, flags, decorative wreaths, and a copy of Lincoln's own masterpiece, the Emancipation Proclamation. Physically, Lincoln dwarfs royalty from other lands, which symbolizes singular international stature. Napoleon III and Britannia follow closely behind Lincoln to keep his flag-like mantle off the ground, and each pays a glowing, but short tribute. Napoleon III fairly worships him: "Shades of MON UNCLES—How he has GROWN!" To this observation Britannia is in full accord, and she adds with admiration: "Goodness me! Yes! And he keeps on growing!" One monarch even invokes the blessings of Allah: "May his shadow never be less." Bearing gifts of victory embellished with olive branches, Admiral Farragut, General Sherman, and General Grant offer, respectively, Mobile, Charleston, and Richmond to

PRESIDENT LINCOLN TAKING THE OATH AT HIS SECOND INAUGURATION, MARCH 4, 1865.—PHOTOGRAPHED BY GARDNER, WASHINGTON.—[SEE PAGE 164.]

"President Lincoln Taking the Oath at His Second Inauguration," *Harper's Weekly,* March 18, 1865, 161 (front page). Author's Collection.

this "Tallest Ruler." Even *Punch* doffs his hat from the humbling perspective of the "dirt," and the Democratic Irishman concedes, "Bad luck to me, but this is gay."[29] Artist William Newman was in fine form.

TRIUMPH AND TRAGEDY

On every front, the Union's spring offensive mauled the retreating or defensively entrenched and besieged Confederate forces. Physically and psychologically beaten, though gallantly holding on to a taut and slender thread of hope, weary soldiers of the Confederacy wondered how long it would take before someone raised the white flag of surrender. To the last breath of war, the Copperhead minority abused Lincoln

"A Diplomatic Reunion at Washington," *Nick Nax*, April 1865, 190. Courtesy of the Western Reserve Historical Society.

A Diplomatic Reunion at Washington.

with complaints. As late as April 8, *Harper's Weekly* shielded Lincoln from unwelcome faultfinding by those who impatiently petitioned the president to offer the rebels "fresh terms of peace":

> That the malignant Copperhead opposition should seek to embarrass the situation by representing [Lincoln] as averse to peace is natural; but that loyal papers should persistently poison the public mind with the impression that the President is reluctant or obtuse in the matter is most unfortunate. To destroy public confidence in the chief executive by incessant complaint that he does not act wisely; to insinuate that peace is at every moment possible, if only the President chose; to declare that the rebels are merely waiting for a kind word from him before laying down their arms, is to be guilty of the greatest injustice to him and the gravest injury to the country.[30]

The following day the criticism was moot; Gen. Robert E. Lee surrendered his army at Appomattox. A few days earlier, Lincoln had been given a tumultuous welcome at

Richmond, especially by grateful representatives of the black population.[31] Parenthetically, this poignant scene was memorialized by popular artists, including Thomas Nast. On April 12, Mobile, Alabama, fell. Now the dominos lay in shambles; the rebellion was all but over.

Since Fort Sumter, Lincoln had longed for this day, perhaps as no other citizen. His last public address, given "not in sorrow but in gladness of heart," followed the evacuation of Petersburg and Richmond and the surrender of General Lee at Appomattox. Some loose ends still existed before peace could come, so Lincoln's joy was not full. Still, he anticipated "a righteous and speedy peace whose joyous expression can not be restrained."[32] Unfortunately, the hand of an assassin robbed Lincoln and the nation of that "joyous expression." The black shrouds of national mourning displaced the festive mood of triumphant victory celebration, and the nation wept. Ironically, Lincoln's last experience in mortality validated his fabled doctrine of necessity; events had, indeed, exercised considerable control over his mortal fate.

There were two other coincidental but ironic twists to the assassination. The first involved the raising of the U.S. flag at Fort Sumter. On April 14, 1861, the flag over the battered fort had been lowered and removed. On April 14, 1865—four years later to the day, and on the very day Lincoln was assassinated—it was triumphantly elevated again to the top of the pole.

"The Tallest Ruler on the Globe," *Frank Leslie's Budget of Fun*, April 1865, Courtesy of the McLellan Lincoln Collection, Brown University Library.

THE TALLEST RULER ON THE GLOBE IS INAUGURATED AT WASHINGTON—THE LESSER LUMINARIES OF EUROPE ASSISTING DEFERENTIALLY.

"President Lincoln
Entering Richmond,
April 4, 1865," *Harper's
Weekly*, February 24,
1866, 120–21. Author's
Collection.

The second irony was associated with the incongruous timing of a Lincoln cartoon in *Harper's Weekly*. When fresh copies of *Harper's Weekly* were distributed for
sale on the regularly scheduled date of April 15, Lincoln had already passed from
mortality into the eternities early in the morning. On the last page of that historic
issue was a relatively obscure, mundane cartoon. Curiously, it portrayed Lincoln as a

"Special War Correspondent" sending in his last report: "'All seems well with us.'—A. Lincoln."[33] This was a fitting epitaph for Lincoln and a succinct summation of the imminent unified state of the nation.

Because of the time necessary to print such magazines, *Harper's Weekly* and *Frank Leslie's Illustrated Newspaper* could not get their assassination reports out until they released their April 29 issues. That delay makes especially poignant a brief essay on Lincoln written long before the assassination and published in Belfast, Ireland. It was printed, though, in *Harper's Weekly* on April 22: "When the heat of party passion and international jealously have abated, when distraction has spent its malice, and the scandalous gossip of the day goes the way of allies, the place of Abraham Lincoln, in the grateful affection of his countrymen and in the respect of the world, will be second only, if it be second, to that of Washington himself."[34] The acid test of that prophetic proposition came sooner than its author had surmised.

In crisis, the magazines scrambled to cover the singular, shocking news of Lincoln's death. The sensationalist *National Police Gazette* scooped both *Frank Leslie's Illustrated Newspaper* and *Harper's Weekly* by one week in the race to publish the earliest graphics on the assassination. An artist by the name of Risdon sketched the "Scene at the Death-Bed of the President" and the "Assassination of President

"From Our Special War Correspondent," *Harper's Weekly*, April 15, 1865, 240. Author's Collection.

FROM OUR SPECIAL WAR CORRESPONDENT.

"City Point, Va., *April* —, 8.30 A.M.
"All seems well with us."—A. Lincoln.

Lincoln." However, from April 29 well into June both *Frank Leslie's Illustrated Newspaper* and *Harper's Weekly* provided more, and higher quality, images of Lincoln's assassination, death, funeral, and the disposition of the assassins.[35]

The assassination presented a special problem for magazines that had been critical of Lincoln. It seared a benign image into the hearts of the nation through the overwhelming national grief; the nefarious nature of the brutal deed; the conjunction of assassination and victory; Lincoln's popularity with the masses; and eulogies that spared no hyperbole. Furthermore, death is not only a great leveler of human beings, but also a forgiving editor of real or imagined frailty. Martyrdom effaces blemishes and highlights the nobility of the victim at an accelerated rate. This was not an atmosphere congenial to political critique. Editors and artists more or less quickly made peace with this transformation.

From abroad, *Punch* and *Fun* sincerely lamented Lincoln's assassination. *Fun*'s F. Wilfred Lawson depicted Lincoln as Caesar reaching for the cup of victory just as his life is taken by Brutus. However, *Punch* went one step further; its able artist John Tenniel, who had created so many derisive political caricatures of Lincoln, humbly drew a penitent image, "Britannia Sympathizes with Columbia."[36] In an unprecedented move, *Punch* publicly and self-consciously apologized to readers for its misrepresentations of the fallen American president. Tom Taylor's pen wrote the combined poetic confession and eulogy:

> You lay a wreath on Lincoln's bier,
> Yes, who with mocking pencil wont to trace,
> Broad for the self-complacent British sneer,
> His length of shambling limb, his furrowed face,
>
> His gaunt, gnarled hands, his unkempt, bristling hair,
> His garb uncouth, his bearing ill at ease,
> His lack of all we prize as debonair,
> Of power or will to shine, of art to please.
>
> Yes, whose smart pen backed up the pencil's laugh,
> Judging each step, as though the way were plain:
> Reckless, so it could point its paragraph,
> Of chief's perplexity, or people's pain.
>
> Beside this corpse, that bears for winding-sheet
> The Stars and Stripes he lived to rear anew,
> Between the mourners at his head and feet.
> Say, scurril-jester, is there room for you?

Yes, he had lived to shame me from my sneer,
To lame my pencil, and confute my pen—
To make me own this hind of princes peer,
This rail-splitter a true-born king of men.

My shallow judgment I had learnt to rue,
Noting how to occasion's height he rose,
How his quaint wit made home-truth seem more true,
How, iron-like, his temper grew by blows.[37]

What makes this admission so fascinating is that the magazine gives us a glimpse of salient characteristics used to create Lincoln's caricature ("length of shambling limb, . . . furrowed face, . . . gaunt, gnarled hands, . . . unkempt, bristling hair, his garb uncouth, his bearing ill at ease, his lack of all we prize as debonair"). Taylor then proceeded to negate that contrived image out of deference for the substance of Lincoln's genuine character:

How humble yet how hopeful he could be:
How in good fortune and in ill the same:
Nor bitter in success nor boastful he,
Thirsty for gold, nor feverish for fame.

He went about his work—such work as few
Ever had laid on head and heart and hand—
As one who knows, where there's a task to do,
Man's honest will must Heaven's good grace command;

So he went forth to battle on the side
That he felt clear was Liberty's and Right's,
As in his peasant boyhood he had plied
His warfare with rude Nature's thwarting mights—

So he grew up, a destined work to do,
And lived to do it: four long-suffering years'
Ill-fate, ill-feeling, ill-report, lived through,
And then he heard the hisses change to cheers.

The taunts to tribute, the abuse to praise,
And took both with the same unwavering mood:
Till, as he came on light, from darkling days,
And seemed to touch the goal from where he stood.[38]

Even *Frank Leslie's Illustrated Newspaper*, whose image of Lincoln was sometimes ambivalent, elevated its evaluation of the martyred president to highest praise. Compared to its February editorial, which severely faulted Lincoln's leadership and stingingly critiqued the linguistic style of his report from the Hampton Roads Peace Conference, there was not a trace of ambivalence in the April eulogy of *Frank Leslie's Illustrated Newspaper*. Its rhetoric was the kind to which *Harper's Weekly* readers were accustomed. No, it was even better: "All that was mortal of Abraham Lincoln, the man of the people; the tried but always faithful President, will soon be consigned to the grave; but that grave will be the Mecca of a great nation, and will divide the reverential tribute of mankind with that which has made Mount Vernon holy, and a shrine before which all good men bow, as before the symbol of our faith and the emblem of our salvation."[39] In view of Lincoln's humor and apparent apprehension of earlier pieces of criticism, such a testament in *Frank Leslie's Illustrated Newspaper* would surely have drawn at least a chuckle if Lincoln could have returned long enough to read it.

Lincoln imagery did not entirely disappear from the comic magazines after the assassination. For example, *Phunny Phellow* and *Yankee Notions* published serious tributes to Lincoln.[40] However, the assassination and sudden end of the war wreaked havoc with the May issue of *Frank Leslie's Budget of Fun*. Artistic and printing deadlines probably precluded any other course for the magazine; the editors simply had to go to press with what they had. Not that a major gaffe was perpetrated, but the timing of two images in particular was not ideal for this period of sorrow and mourning. One, a double-page illustration, gently poked fun at "Abe's Jokes" and "Seward's Foreign Policy," and Lincoln was conspicuously omitted from an honor role of contributors to the war's anticipated end, though Seward was included.[41]

The other cartoon did not disparage Lincoln, but was slightly anachronistic because the war was over. In fact, it meshed better with the Hampton Roads Peace Conference imagery in March. Its inspiration came from the *London Times*, which may account for the time lag. This second cartoon proposed that the "'First Step of Peace' . . . at Fortress Monroe" might have been for Lincoln and Jeff Davis to unite in an attack against the meddling John Bull and Napoleon III. In fact, it showed the "North and South polishing off the 'Innocent Neutrals.'" "Bully for you Jeff," says Lincoln; "Give the fat one another jab in his bread-basket." "Go in again, Abram," replies Davis: "put their darned heads into Chancery."[42] The humor was well meant, but the timing of the cartoon was incompatible with national sorrow. Yet these were minor blips on the screen of history against the vast panoramic parade of mourning.

In a plethora of editorial commentary, one strain of reason and compassion stood above the rest. An editorial writer for *Harper's Weekly* was impressed and stirred by the specter of "national mourning," "cities . . . solemnly tapestried with the signs of sorrow," the movement of the "funeral train . . . across the land amidst tolling bells . . . and slow pealing dirges," and "orators impassioned eloquence." However, this inspired journalist was more deeply touched by "one class of mourners little seen . . . yet whose grief for Abraham Lincoln is profounder and more universal than all." The writer, who was anonymous, called this unobtrusive group "The Truest Mourners":

To the unhappy race upon whose equal natural rights with ourselves this nation had so long trampled—upon our dusky brothers for whom God has so long asked of us in vain while we haughtily responded that we were not our brothers' keepers, the death that bereaves us all falls with an overwhelming and appealing force. The name of Abraham Lincoln meant to them freedom, justice, home, family, happiness. In his life they knew that they lived. In his perfect benignity and just purpose, inflexible as the laws of seed-time and harvest, they trusted with all their souls, whoever doubted. Their deliverer, their emancipator, their friend, their father, he was known to them as the impersonation of that liberty for which they had wept and watched, hoping against hope, praying in the very extremity of despair, and waiting with patience so sublime.[43]

"The Proposed 'First Step to Peace,'" *Frank Leslie's Budget of Fun*, May 1865, 16. Author's Collection.

THE PROPOSED "FIRST STEP TO PEACE;" OR, EXTRINSIC POLICY ENTERTAINED AT FORTRESS MONROE.
NORTH AND SOUTH POLISHING OFF THE "INNOCENT NEUTRALS."—[See London *Times*, just received.]

At Gettysburg, Lincoln had seen the Civil War as a test whether this nation, "conceived in Liberty, and dedicated to the proposition that all men are created equal . . . could long endure." He also resolved to honor those who had given "the last full measure of devotion" in the war with "a new birth of freedom."[44] Lincoln lived just long enough to see the nation pass the test of national endurance and to witness the fulfillment of his resolve for "a new birth of freedom." Yet no honor, in life or death, from his country would have been more satisfying or meaningful than that spontaneous tribute conferred by the humble, grateful gatherings of "The Truest Mourners."

Notes

CHAPTER ONE

1. On published prints, see Harold Holzer, Gabor S. Boritt, and Mark E. Neely Jr., *The Lincoln Image* (New York: Charles Scribner's Sons, 1984); on song sheet covers, "In the Lincoln Memorial University Collection: Lincoln Sheet Music," *Lincoln Herald* 79.3 (Fall 1977): 123–27; on campaign papers, William Miles, comp., *The People's Voice, An Annotated Bibliography of American Presidential Campaign Newspapers, 1828–1984* (New York: Greenwood Press, 1987), and "The Rail Splitter," *Lincoln Lore* (July 1958): 1–4; on patriotic envelopes, George N. Malpass, "'Anti-Lincoln' Patriotic Envelope Designs," *Lincoln Herald* 57.3 (Fall 1955): 25–30, and "Lincoln Patriotics," *Lincoln Lore* (Oct. 1967): 1–4; on pamphlets, *Abraham Africanus I.* (New York: J. F. Feeks, 1864); on newspapers, Robert S. Harper, *Lincoln and the Press* (New York: McGraw-Hill, 1951), and Herbert Mitgang, ed., *Abraham Lincoln: A Press Portrait* (Athens: Univ. of Georgia Press, 1989).

2. Frank L. Mott, *A History of American Magazines*, 5 vols. (Cambridge, Mass.: Harvard Univ. Press, 1957), 2:192.

3. John Ebert and Katherine Ebert, *Old American Prints for Collectors* (New York: Charles Scribner's Sons, 1974).

4. Sarah McNair Vosmeier, "Photographing Lincoln: The Transformation of American Photography, 1846–1860," *Lincoln Lore* (July 1989): 1–4; (Aug. 1989): 1–4; (Sept. 1989); 1–4; (Oct. 1989): 1–4.

5. Charles Hamilton and Lloyd Ostendorf, *Lincoln in Photographs: An Album of Every Known Pose* (Norman: Univ. of Oklahoma Press, 1963); and Stefan Lorant, *Lincoln: A Picture Story of His Life*, rev. ed. (New York: W. W. Norton, 1969).

6. Comparing the number of James Buchanan or Frémont prints (pro and con) in the 1856 election with the comparable Lincoln prints in 1860 reveals a significantly larger number of political caricatures for Lincoln than for either Buchanan or Frémont. (That same comparison holds up when comparing Lincoln caricatures in the 1864 election with those of President-elect Ulysses S. Grant in the 1868 election.) As illustrated periodicals became entrenched in the 1860s, separately published prints, including political caricature, began to decline. See Frank Weitenkampf, *Political Caricature in the United States in Separately Published Cartoons* (New York: New York Public Library, 1953). For a generic history of graphic humor, see William Murrell, *A History of American Graphic Humor, 1747–1865*, 2 vols. (New York: Cooper Square Publishers, 1967).

7. Mott, *A History of American Magazines*, 2:455, 475–76.

8. Albert Shaw, *Abraham Lincoln: A Cartoon History*, 2 vols. (New York: Cooper Square Publishers, 1967), 2:53.

9. Holzer, Borritt, and Neely, *The Lincoln Image*, xx.

10. Rufus Rockwell Wilson, *Lincoln in Caricature* (New York: Horizon Press, 1953).

11. Holzer, Borritt, and Neely, *The Lincoln Image*, xxi.

12. Actually, this battle was not confined to the magazines; newspaper content on both sides of the Atlantic also figured in stimulating graphic and visual commentary.

13. Although this study traces the evolution of Lincoln's image from the entire illustrated periodical genre, this is not the first work to examine Lincoln from the perspective of contemporary magazines. See, William S. Walsh, *Abraham Lincoln and the London* Punch (New York: Moffat, Yard, 1909).

CHAPTER TWO

1. Norman Cousins, *Human Options* (New York: Berkley Books, 1981), 192.

2. Frederick Douglass, "Frederick Douglass Cuts through the Lincoln Myth to Consider the Man," in *Lend Me Your Ears: Great Speeches in History*, ed. William Safire (New York: W. W. Norton, 1997), 184.

3. "Speech at Hartford, Connecticut," *The Collected Works of Abraham Lincoln*, ed. Roy P. Basler (New Brunswick, N.J.: Rutgers University Press, 1953–55), 4: 5 (hereafter cited as *Collected Works*).

4. "Temperance Address," *Collected Works*, 1:273.

5. Douglass, "Frederick Douglass," 183.

6. "Happily for the country, happily for you and for me, the judgment of James Buchanan, the patrician, was not the judgment of Abraham Lincoln, the plebeian." So wrote Frederick Douglass in gratitude for Lincoln's commonplace background. Ibid., 184.

7. David Herbert Donald, *Lincoln* (New York: Simon and Schuster, 1995), 236.

8. Holzer, Boritt, and Neely, *The Lincoln Image*, 132; "By the People, For the People: Lincoln in Graphic Art, 1860–1865," *Lincoln Lore* (Aug. 1980): 3.

9. "First Debate with Stephen A. Douglas at Ottawa, Illinois," *Collected Works*, 3:12–30. The pattern of joviality was sustained throughout the debates.

10. "As one of the neighborhood's stalwarts, Coleman Smoot, expressed it, 'Not only did his wit, kindliness, and knowledge attract people, but his strange clothes and uncouth awkwardness advertised him. . . . Soon the name "Abe Lincoln" was a household word.'" Douglas L. Wilson, *Lincoln before Washington* (Urbana: Univ. of Illinois Press, 1997), 32. "He told Herndon a great many things about the Lincoln of these years. . . . Not surprisingly, the first thing he stressed was Lincoln's humor, that 'the People would flock to hear him—loving jokes—humor &c -.' 'When he first came among us his wit & humor boiled over.'" Douglas L. Wilson, *Honor's Voice* (New York: Alfred A. Knopf, 1998), 186.

11. Donald, *Lincoln*, 274.

12. Actually, the most notorious negative allusion to Lincoln's humor did not come from the magazine genre, but from a separately published print: "The Commander-in-Chief Conciliating the Soldiers' Vote on the Battle Field." The Democratic Party used this alleged incident of Lincoln joking in the midst of human carnage at Antietam to smear his reputation in the 1864 presidential election. For Lincoln's attempt to refute this allegation see, "Memorandum Concerning Ward H. Lamon and the Antietam Episode," *Collected Works*, 7:548–50.

13. "The Marvelous History of Miles O'Reilly, Poet, Patriot, Politician, and Prisoner," *Comic Monthly*, Nov. 1863, front page; "Old Abe's Jokes," *Harper's Weekly*, Apr. 2, 1864, 223; "Uncle Sam Spreading Himself and His Greenbacks at the Great Sanitary Fair," *Frank Leslie's Budget of Fun*, May 1864, 8–9; "This Reminds Me of a Little Joke," *Harper's Weekly*, Sept. 17, 1864, 608.

14. "Old Abe's Last," *Yankee Notions*, July 1864, 221. For other examples in *Yankee Notions* of drollery either attributed to Lincoln or written about him, see "Uncle Abe's Last," Jan. 1862, 11; "Honest Abe's Hilarity," Mar. 1863, 67; "Old Abe Not a Temperance Man," Mar. 1863, 77; "Another of Lincoln's Jokes," Sept. 1863, 258; "Miles O'Reilly," Feb. 1864, 35; "An Elucidation of Mr. Lincoln's Estimate of Presidential Honors," June 1864, 182; "Abe Lincoln's Latest and Best Joke," Oct. 1864, 300; "Mr. Welles," Apr. 1865, 126.

15. "The Fight in Congress—One of 'Abe Lincoln's Illustrations,'" *Yankee Notions*, June 1858, 165; "Preface," ibid., Apr. 1861, 2; "Jonathan to His Readers of Volume 11," ibid., Dec. 1862, 382.

16. "Field Marshall Jonathan to the Grand Army of Funny Fellows," *Yankee Notions*, Jan. 1863, 2.

17. "Jonathan to All Creation," ibid., Dec. 1863, 381.

18. "Proclamation," ibid., Dec. 1864, 383.

19. Donald, *Lincoln*, 259.

20. Søren Kierkegaard, *Either/Or*, part 1, ed. Howard Hong and Edna Hong (Princeton, N.J.: Princeton Univ. Press, 1987), 20.

21. "The Yankee Nero," *Comic News*, Dec. 27, 1864, 277; "The Herod of the Nineteenth Century," *Funniest of Phun*, Sept. 1864, 4, front page.

22. Neutral scores were ascribed to descriptive scenes like Lincoln and his cabinet, or in those relatively rare instances when an image seemed to contain counterbalancing positive and negative components.

23. The *Illustrated London News* and *Punch* each produced just one relatively nonpartisan Lincoln illustration to note the presidential election.

24. Although these percentages reflect the quantity of Lincoln images in the magazines, they do not necessarily indicate the importance of the magazines or their illustrations for Lincoln's image. In 1861, *Vanity Fair* and Henry L. Stephens were probably more influential than *Phunny Phellow* and its artists in the development of the public Lincoln.

25. Although the anti-Lincoln imagery in the British comic press tended to become more hostile as the Civil War went on, there was far more kinship to the Confederate cause than that of the Union.

26. Mark E. Neely Jr., *The Abraham Lincoln Encyclopedia*, paperback ed. (New York: Da Capo Press, 1984), 66.

CHAPTER THREE

1. Although L. Edward Carter alluded to a revolution in journalism—which includes illustration—coincident with the Civil War, he did not treat the proliferation of the illustrated periodical as a revolutionary development. L. Edward Carter, "The Revolution in Journalism during the Civil War," *Lincoln Herald* 73.4 (Winter 1971): 229–41.

2. "To Lyman Trumbull," *Collected Works*, 4:45.

3. For examples of such Lincoln and Douglas images, see "Scene from the Impending Crisis," *Frank Leslie's Budget of Fun*, Mar. 1860, 4; and "Grand Match for the Presidential Collar," *Phunny Phellow*, Apr. 1860, 1.

4. "The Impending Crisis at Charleston," *Frank Leslie's Budget of Fun*, Apr. 1860, 11. This reference was also linked to Hinton R. Helper's inflammatory book *The Impending Crisis of the South*: *How to Meet It*.

5. "Reply to Oliver P. Morton at Indianapolis, Indiana," *Collected Works*, 4:193–94.

6. "Prominent Candidates for the Republican Presidential Nomination at Chicago," *Harper's Weekly*, May 12, 1860, 296–97.

7. "A Link on (A. Lincoln) the Light-House at Chicago," *Momus*, May 23, 1860, 3. *Momus*'s journalistic coup d'état was an artifact of its status as a daily periodical from its inception on April 28, 1860, to its transformation to a weekly on May 24, 1860, until its premature death in July of the same year. With the exception of the weekly *Vanity Fair*, *Momus*'s competitors were publishedbimonthly or monthly. The same illustration appeared in *Momus*'s new weekly edition on May 26, 1860, 49.

8. The accompanying editorial is "Presidential Qualifications," *Momus*, May 22, 1860, 1.

9. "The Republican Fizzle," *Vanity Fair*, May 26, 1860, 349.

10. One source attributes the "two-shilling candidate" aspersion to the editor of "the home organ of James Buchanan," *The Lancaster (Pa.) Intelligencer*. "Can't Tell the Truth," *Chicago Rail Splitter*, July 1860, 2. For the *Vanity Fair* cartoon, see "Another Two Shilling Candidate," *Vanity Fair*, June 2, 1860, 357. For a while, the disdainful "two-shilling candidate" metaphor continued in the pages of *Vanity Fair*. See three cartoons in the June 9, 1860, edition: "Side-Splitting Humors of the Rail-Splitters," 371; "Personal Intelligence," 376; and "The Rails Good for Something After All," 380.

11. "The Last Rail Split by 'Honest Old Abe,'" *Momus*, June 2, 1860, 61; "To Henry Asbury," *Collected Works*, 3:339; "To Anson S. Miller" 3:340; "To M. M. Inman," 3:341.

12. "The Democratic Split," *Momus*, May 3, 1860, 1.

13. "There Was a Convention at Charleston," ibid., May 15, 1860, 1.

14. "Burst, Charleston May 3, 1860," ibid., May 7, 1860, 3. Later, a Frank Bellew caricature rightly ascribed the conflict to slavery. "The Rock upon which the Democratic Party Split," ibid., June 30, 1860, 108–9; "A Peep into Futurity or the Funeral," *Frank Leslie's Budget of Fun*, Aug. 15, 1860, 8–9.

15. "The Tribune Offering the Chief Magistracy to the Western Cincinnatus," *Momus*, June 9, 1860, 73; "A Piece De Circonstance," ibid., June 2, 1860, 64. A ballad also scolded Greeley for the political demise of Seward: "Who Killed Bill Seward?" ibid., June 9, 1860, 75.

16. The textual elaboration of the cartoon appears under the title "The New Brutus," *Vanity Fair*, June 2, 1860, 360. The cartoon "Et Tu, Greeley?" follows on page 361. For other illustrations of similar spirit on the Greeley and Seward convention episode, see "The Slaughter of Seward," *Campaign Plain Dealer and Popular Sovereignty Advocate*, July 7, 1860, 3; "Billy Seward, TheCelebrated Black Republican Minstrel, Retiring from the Stage," *Frank Leslie's Budget of Fun*, July 15, 1860, 1; "Back from Chicago," ibid., July 15, 1860, 15.

17. "Brutus Greeley to Caesar Seward," *Vanity Fair*, June 23, 1860, 412; "P. S. 1860, Brutus Greeley," ibid., June 23, 1860, 412–13. For additional examples of such doggerel, see "The Burial of Sir William Seward," *Momus*, June 2, 1860, 56; and "Who Killed Bill Seward?" ibid., June 9, 1860, 75.

18. "The Story of Five Little Pigs," *Vanity Fair*, June 16, 1860, 392.

19. "Shaky," ibid., June 9, 1860, 377. A similar image appeared in *Harper's Weekly:* "The Coming Man's Presidential Career," *Harper's Weekly*, Aug. 25, 1860, 544. Moreover, one of Stephen A. Douglas's campaign papers also depicted the "rotten rail," Lincoln, Greeley, and African Americans, as a political liability. "'Old Abe' finds the Negro too heavy a load—the rail is rotten—and a breakdown is inevitable. Horace Greeley also finds that his end of the load is more than he bargained for," *Washington Democratic Expositor and National Crisis*, Sept. 1, 1860, 112.

20. *Democratic Expositor and National Crisis*, July 4, 1860, 7; "Speech at Cincinnati, Ohio," *Collected Works*, 3:440.

21. "Abe, the Giant Killer," *Momus*, July 21, 1860, 120.

22. "Serene above Them All," *Vanity Fair*, July 7, 1860, 19.

23. "The Humors of the Presidential Canvass," *Comic Monthly*, Aug. 1860, 8–9. The stick figure centerpiece illustration from the larger serial cartoon was also published separately. See Wilson, *Lincoln in Caricature*, 15. Standing alone, the image describes Lincoln "as nothing more substantial than a scarecrow, literally strung together from his familiar log rails." Holzer, Boritt, and Neely, *The Lincoln Image*, 38. However, when the image is placed within the framework of "The Humors of the Presidential Canvass," serially embedded within a matrix of almost twenty oth-

er images, the quality and meaning of the collective image is materially enhanced by its contextual cues, including the contrast between Bellew's other Lincoln images and those of Lincoln's political rivals—Douglas, Bell, and Breckinridge. Obviously, the serial version is much richer than the solitary stick figure.

24. "Black Draught," *Frank Leslie's Budget of Fun*, Aug. 1, 1860, 9.

25. "Columbia and Her Suitors, *Frank Leslie's Budget of Fun*, Aug. 1, 1860, 9.

26. "Which Horn of the Dilemma?" *Phunny Phellow*, Aug. 1860, front page; "A Settler," Aug. 1860, 13. As for nativism, Lincoln tried to dispel any uncertainty about his position. "I have some little notoriety for commiserating the oppressed condition of the Negro; and I should be strangely inconsistent if I could favor any project for curtailing the existing rights of white men, even though born in different lands, and speaking different languages from myself." "To Theodore Canisius," *Collected Works*, 3:380.

27. "That Horrid Darkey Who Won't Let Folks Sleep," *Frank Leslie's Budget of Fun*, Sept. 1, 1860, front page.

28. "Three to One You Don't Get It," *Vanity Fair*, Sept. 1, 1860, 117. Other pictorial periodicals picked up the three-to-one theme. "Three to one ain't fair exactly, but come on boys" was the caption for two other cartoons. See "The Political Sensation," *Comic Monthly*, Nov. 1860, 8–9; and "The Battle in New York," *Wide Awake Pictorial*, Nov. 1860, 7. A political deal between Bell and the Democratic Party was broached the very next week in another Henry L. Stephens cartoon, "Keeping Queer Company," *Vanity Fair*, Sept. 8, 1860, 129. Lincoln was convinced that fusion was the only strategy that could defeat him. "No one this side of the mountains pretends that any ticket can be elected by the People, unless it be ours. Hence great efforts to combine against us, are being made, which, however, as yet, have not had much success." "To Anson G. Henry," *Collected Works*, 4:118.

29. "A Galvanized Split Rail," *Phunny Phellow*, Sept. 1860, 9; "Great Swimming Match to Come Off on the Fourth of November," *Frank Leslie's Budget of Fun*, Sept. 15, 1860, front page (brackets in original).

30. "Aminadab Sleek at Jones' Wood," *Vanity Fair*, Sept. 22, 1860, 153 (brackets in original).

The character "Aminadab Sleek" was often used in nineteenth-century caricature to portray hypocrisy. For example, see "Mr. John Bull in some of his favorite characters," *Frank Leslie's Budget of Fun*, Aug. 1863. Humors of War, folder 2, William A. Smith Collection, American Antiquarian Society (hereafter cited as AAS).

31. "Honest Old Abe and the Little Boy in Search of His Mother—A Sensation Story," *Phunny Phellow*, Nov. 1860, front page. Among the prints that Currier and Ives published separately on the topic of Douglas visiting his mother were "'Taking the Stump, or Stephen in Search of his Mother" and "Stephen finding 'his mother.'" Weitenkampf, *Political Caricature*, 121.

32. "Scan. Mag. at Washington," *Vanity Fair*, Sept. 29, 1860, 165.

33. All three of the principal news weeklies gave substantial coverage—in full, double-page illustrations to the New York Wide Awake parade of October 3. "Torchlight Procession of the Wide Awake Club," *Frank Leslie's Illustrated Newspaper*, Oct. 13, 1860, 326–27; "The Political Demonstration," *New York Illustrated News*, Oct. 13, 1860, 360–61; and "Grand Procession of Wide Awakes at New York on the Evening of October 3, 1860," *Harper's Weekly*, Oct. 13, 1860, 648–49. For coverage of the Prince of Wales, see "The Prince of Wales and the Wide Awakes," *Comic Monthly*, Oct. 1860, 8–9.

34. "Seward's Grand Starring Tour," *Vanity Fair*, Oct. 13, 1860, 189. Satirical articles about the Wide Awakes also appeared in *Vanity Fair*: "The Wide Awakes," Sept. 29, 1860, 168; "On the Great Wide Awake Procession," Oct. 13, 1860, 192; and in a Wide Awake advertisement, Nov. 3, 1860. As for the coat, see "What Will He Do With It?" ibid., Oct. 20, 1860, 201. In 1856, James Gordon Bennett's *New York Herald* supported Frémont's election, but it supported Douglas in 1860.

35. "Old Buck's Shaving Saloon," *Phunny Phellow*, Oct. 1860, 4.

36. Reinhard E. Luthin, *The First Lincoln Campaign* (Cambridge, Mass., Harvard Univ. Press, 1944), 185–86.

37. "The Presidential Pot-Pie," *Frank Leslie's Budget of Fun*, Oct. 1, 1860. Given the penciled date on the cartoon, October 1860, and what we know about the content of the other issues of theperiodical in the fall of that year, October 1, 1860, is the most plausible estimated date. The cartoon is located in Humors of War, folder 2, AAS.

38. "The Perilous Voyage to the White House," *Frank Leslie's Budget of Fun*, Oct. 15, 1860, 8–9. This cartoon is located in Humors of War, folder 2, AAS. The penciled notation on the illustration is October 1860. The source and specific date of October 15, 1860, are confirmed by an advertisement for *Budget of Fun* in its sister publication, *Frank Leslie's Illustrated Newspaper*, Oct. 13, 1860, 332.

39. "Sich a Gittin Up Stairs," *Vanity Fair*, Oct. 27, 1860, 213. Also in October, a full-page engraving of a Mathew Brady photograph of Lincoln was published to the benefit of the future president. "Abraham Lincoln of Illinois," *Frank Leslie's Illustrated Newspaper*, Oct. 20, 1860, 347. Additional exposure in cartoons also helped Lincoln. For example, see "*Harper's Weekly*," Oct. 27, 1860, 688.

40. "The Political Sensation," *Comic Monthly*, Nov. 1860, 8–9.

41. "Wonderful Surgical Operation," *Vanity Fair*, Nov. 3, 1860, 225.

42. "Honest Old Abe Marching Forth to the White House," *Wide Awake Pictorial*, Nov. 1860, front page. Virtually all other illustrations in the *Wide Awake Pictorial* were borrowed from comic papers like *Momus* and *Comic Monthly*, but this illustration was original. The *Wide Awake Pictorial* was a single-issue campaign paper rather than an illustrated periodical.

43. "Deplorable Result of Lincoln's Election," *Vanity Fair*, Nov. 10, 1860, 236.

44. "The Next Sensation," *Frank Leslie's Budget of Fun*, Nov. 15, 1860, 12; "The Result of the Election," *Phunny Phellow*, Jan. 1861, 3. In virtually all ethnic illustrations, there were condescending elements that represent deeply ingrained racism.

45. "Monkey Uncommon Up, Massa!" *Punch*, Dec. 1, 1860, 220.

46. "Good Gracious, Abraham Lincoln! How Did You Manage to Get the Situation of Overseer of My Farm?" *Frank Leslie's Budget of Fun*, Jan. 1861, 16.

47. "The Smothering of the Democratic Princes," ibid., Nov. 15, 1860, front page. Although the cartoonist did not sign the illustration, it appears to be the work of Henry L. Stephens.

48. The word "Curtin" was not a misspelling of the stage curtain, but a play on words. Andrew Curtin was the governor of Pennsylvania.

49. "Richard the Third," *Frank Leslie's Budget of Fun*, Nov. 15, 1860, 4 (brackets in original).

50. "The Great Original Wide-Awake," ibid., Dec. 15, 1860, page unknown.

51. "Old Abe and His Electors," ibid., Apr. 15, 1861, 8.

52. "The Successful and Unsuccessful Candidates at Breakfast the Morning After," ibid., Dec. 15, 1860, page unknown. The date is estimated but probable, based on a *Frank Leslie's Illustrated Newspaper* advertisement (Dec. 15, 1860, 62) that mentions an "Abe and Douglas cut" in the December 15 issue of the *Budget of Fun*.

53. "A Phenomenon of Portraiture," *Frank Leslie's Budget of Fun*, Dec. 15, 1860, page unknown. Although the cartoon is signed with a "W" over an "N," the identification is still somewhat problematic because the two most likely candidates, William North and William Newman, both drew for this publication. Typically, Newman signed his works with a single capital "N." North signed his illustrations with a "W" on top of an "N," but also usually included a drawing of a pair of spectacles. In this example, there are no spectacles. However, a comparison of the style of Lincoln's hair, especially in the first portrait, with other drawings of the two artists favors William North as the artist. For a similar humorous study of the facial expres-sions of emotion in Jefferson Davis, see "The Passions Illustrated by Jeff Davis," *Phunny Phellow*, July 1862, 12.

54. *New York Herald*, Dec. 20, 1860, in *Lincoln Day by Day: A Chronology, 1809–1865*, rev. ed., ed. Earl Schenck Miers and C. Percy Powell (Washington, D.C.: N.p., 1960; reprint, Dayton: Ohio, Morningside, 1991) 301; Benjamin P. Thomas, *Abraham Lincoln* (New York: Alfred A. Knopf, 1952), 267. Thomas depicts Greeley as indulging in the same sport: "Greeley noted after an interview with Lincoln that 'his face was haggard with care and seamed with thought and trouble. It looked care-ploughed, tempest-tossed and weather-beaten.'" Ibid., 506.

55. For a good example of Douglas's preconvention image in the comic press, see "The Little Giant as the Modern Gulliver," *Comic Monthly*, June 1860, 7.

CHAPTER FOUR

1. For human interest drawings from this time, see *Frank Leslie's Illustrated Newspaper*, Nov. 17, 1860, 414; Nov. 24, 1860, 4; Dec. 15, 1860, front page; *Harper's Weekly*, Nov. 10, 1860, front page; *New York Illustrated News*, Nov. 17, 1860, front page; Nov. 24, 1860, 41; and *Illustrated London News*, Dec. 8, 1860, 543. On Buchanan passing the torch, see "Dogberry's Last Charge," *Vanity Fair*, Dec. 15, 1860, 297. Anxieties from this period are reflected in "Divorce A Vinculo," *Punch*, Jan. 19, 1861, 27; "What on Airth Are You Doing to That Bird of Mine?" *Budget of Fun*, Feb. 1861, 13.

2. "Coming Round," *Vanity Fair*, Nov. 17, 1860, 249.

3. "Badgering Him," *Vanity Fair*, Dec. 29, 1860, 321.

4. "To Nathaniel P. Paschall," *Collected Works*, 4:139–40; Speech at Buffalo, New York, ibid., 221; Speech at the Astor House, New York City, ibid., 230–31.

5. "Mr. Lincoln Has Spoken," *Vanity Fair*, Jan. 12, 1861, 16.

6 "The Ingratitude of the Republic-ans," *Frank Leslie's Budget of Fun*, Dec. 15, 1860. Humors of War, folder 2, AAS. The date and source of this illustration are confirmed by an advertisement of the contents of *Budget of Fun* in *Frank Leslie's Illustrated Newspaper*, Dec. 15, 1860, 62.

7. "The Inside Track," *Vanity Fair*, Mar. 2, 1861, 103.

8. "To David Davis," *Collected Works*, 10:54. The historical record affirms that these were not the only criteria for Lincoln. "He could not afford to dispense with the best talent, or to outrage the popular will in any locality."

9. "Grand Distribution of Government Pap," *Frank Leslie's Budget of Fun*, Apr. 1, 1861, Humors of War, folder 2, AAS. The source and date are confirmed by an advertisement of *Budget of Fun* in *Frank Leslie's Illustrated Newspaper*, Mar. 30, 1861, 303. In 1864, *Southern Punch* appropriated the same cartoon for its

own partisan purposes. Only the caption was changed. "Hungry Government School in Lincolniana," "Seward.–'Don't give Horace a single spoonful of United States Pap, Aunt Aby. He favored you only because he hated me.' Aunt Aby–'Hush Billy.I must pin him to my Baltimore apron. If I don't stop his mouth, he will go to the fleshpots of Cleveland or Chicago. These boys must be well fed or they will turn out their school marm.'" *Southern Punch*, July 19, 1864, 8.

10. "The 'Ins' and the 'Outs,'" *Frank Leslie's Budget of Fun*, Apr. 15, 1861. The source and date of this illustration are confirmed in an advertisement of *Budget of Fun* in *Frank Leslie's Illustrated Newspaper*, Apr. 13, 1861, 335. The cartoon is not signed, but it appears to be the work of William North.

11. "Remarks to a Pennsylvania Delegation," *Collected Works*, 4:180.

12. "Cameron at Springfield," *Vanity Fair*, Feb. 2, 1861, 55. Cameron arrived in Springfield on Dec. 30, 1860. The next day, Lincoln wrote a letter that expressed his desire to have Cameron serve as secretary of war or secretary of the treasury. Miers and Powell, *Lincoln Day by Day*, 304. For the allegations of fraud against the Winnebago Indians, see Donald, *Lincoln*, 266.

13. "A New Song to an Old Tune," *Vanity Fair*, Sept. 21, 1861, 144.

14. "Artemus Ward on His Visit to Old Abe Lincoln," *Vanity Fair*, Dec. 8, 1860, 279. On the same page, to embellish the humor, Henry L. Stephens also illustrated Lincoln shaking hands with Ward.

15. "Gulliver Abe, in the White House, Attacked by the Lilliputian Office-Seekers," *Frank Leslie's Budget of Fun*, Mar. 15, 1861, front page.

16. "Artemus Ward on His Visit to Old Abe Lincoln," 279–80.

17. "Old Abe and His Electors," *Frank Leslie's Budget of Fun*, Apr. 15, 1861, 8. Although the offices held by Uncle Sam were to Prussia and Sardinia, Carl Schurz actually received an appointment to Spain. See also, "The Ingenious Manner in which President Lincoln Receives Those Who Apply for an Office," ibid., June 1861, 16. In 1863, the same cartoon appeared in another humorous magazine with the caption, "Uncle Abe.—'Here, New York, don't go to Canada, but take these [weapons]. They'll just fit you.'" *Merryman's Monthly*, Oct. 1863, 200.

18. "Old Abe Invokes the Spirit of St. Patrick to Rid Him of the Reptiles that Destroy His Peace," *Phunny Phellow*, May 1861, 16.

19. "To the Victors Belong the Spoils," *Frank Leslie's Budget of Fun*, Apr. 15, 1861 (brackets in original). An advertisement of the contents of *Budget of Fun* in *Frank Leslie's Illustrated Newspaper*, Apr. 13, 1861, 335, confirms the source and date of this illustration.

20. With the exception of the subcaption, this was the same drawing as the one described above. "To the Victors Belong the Spoils," *Merryman's Monthly*, Dec. 1863, 284.

21. "Abrahm, Spare This Head," *Nick Nax*, Dec. 1860, 592. These verses were also published under the title "An Office-Holder's Appeal," in *Phunny Phellow*, Aug. 1861, 6.

22. "Mr. Whippletrot's Plum Pudding," *Comic Monthly*, Jan. 1861, foldout.

23. "Mr. Longlank in Pursuit of an Office under Difficulties," *Phunny Phellow*, May 1861, 8–9.

24. "A Political Wire Puller Visits Old Abe," *Yankee Notions*, Feb. 1861, 56–57.

25. "A Model Minister," *Frank Leslie's Budget of Fun*, May 1861.

26. See, *Frank Leslie's Illustrated Newspaper*, Mar. 2, 1861, front page, 232–33, 236; *Harper's Weekly*, Mar. 2, 1861, front page; Mar. 9, 1861, front page; and the *New York Illustrated News*, Mar. 2, 1861, 264, 265; Mar. 9, 1861, 280, 281.

27. "Progress of 'Honest Old Abe' on His Way to the White House," *Phunny Phellow*, Apr. 1861, 8–9. Except for the anomaly of the Baltimore fiasco, it is unlikely that this parody would have appeared. The late date of the illustration (April), the reference to Baltimore, and Lincoln's Scotch attire disclose the source of the motivation.

28. "How Abe Lincoln Escaped the Fire-Eaters of the South and the Flames of Secession," *Frank Leslie's Budget of Fun*, Mar. 1, 1861, front page. In the caption, Lincoln's allusion to "Indian Bonds" refers to a Buchanan administration scandal.

29. "The Flight of Abraham," *Harper's Weekly*, Mar. 9, 1861, 160.

30. "Arrival of Mr. Lincoln at the Camden Station, Baltimore, at 4 o'clock on the Morning of February 23," *New York Illustrated News*, Mar. 9, 1861, 280; "Awful Consternation of the Old Party at the White House, and Sudden Appearance of Lincoln," ibid., Mar. 9, 1861, 288. In Wilson, *Lincoln in Caricature* (91), this cartoon is erroneously credited to *Frank Leslie's Illustrated Newspaper*, Mar. 9, 1861. "Mr. Lincoln's Arrival at the Camden Station, Baltimore, on the Morning of the 22nd Inst. Hour, 4 O'Clock," *New York Illustrated News*, Mar. 9, 1861, 113.

31. "Mr. Lincoln's Flight," *Vanity Fair*, Mar. 2, 1861, 102; "The MacLincoln Harrisburg," ibid., Mar. 9, 1861, 113; "The New President of the U.S.," ibid., Mar. 9, 1861, 114.

32. "Incidents in the Career of President Lincoln," *Comic Monthly*, Apr. 1861, 8–9.

33. "Here is Old Abe," *Yankee Notions*, Jan. 1862, 17.

34. "The Tale of the President's Shirt," *Comic News*, Dec. 19, 1863, 182.

35. "Our Presidential Merryman," *Harper's Weekly*, Mar. 2, 1861, 144.

36. "No Communion with Slaveholders," ibid., Mar. 2, 1861, 144; "The War," ibid., May 4, 1861, 274.

37. "Our Great Iceberg Melting Away," *Vanity Fair*, Mar. 9, 1861, 115.

38. *Frank Leslie's Illustrated Newspaper*, Mar. 16, 1861, 264–65; *Harper's Weekly*, Mar. 16, 1861, 168–69; *New York Illustrated News*, Mar. 16, 1861, 299–302. The British press also acknowledge the inauguration. *Illustrated London News*, Mar. 30, 1861. The Nast caricature is entitled "The President's Inaugural" and appears in the *New York Illustrated News*, Mar. 23, 1861, 320.

39. "Old Abe's First Night in the White House," *Frank Leslie's Budget of Fun*, Apr. 1, 1861, 9.

40. "His New Facial," *New York Illustrated News*, Mar. 2, 1861, front page. Judging from advertisements, entrepreneurs jumped at the chance to make money on Lincoln's bearded countenance. See "Bellingham's Stimulating Onguent for the Hair and Whiskers," *Vanity Fair*, Mar. 2, 1861, 272. The quotation comes from "Agency for the Lincoln Whiskeropherous," ibid., Mar. 16, 1861, 126.

41. In regard to handshaking, see "A Fancy Portrait," *New York Illustrated News*, Mar. 30, 1861, 336. Handshaking was a trial of sorts. "But there are sufficient people out here to keep me shaking hands for six hours. I will shake as long as I can shake, and then will content myself with a look that will answer the same purpose. That's the way I have done in other places, where large crowds of people have called upon me, and so I must do here." "Remarks in Philadelphia, Pennsylvania," *Collected Works, First Supplement*, 10:61. For the other cartoons, see "A Manager's Apology," *Phunny Phellow*, Apr. 1861, 12; "A Black Republican Damsel," ibid., Apr. 1861, front page; "Consulting the Oracle," *Harper's Weekly*, Apr. 13, 1861, 240; and "Homeopathic Treatment," *Yankee Notions*, Apr. 1861, 109.

42. Memorandum, July 3, 1861, John G. Nicolay Papers, Library of Congress, quoted in Miers and Powell, *Lincoln Day by Day*, Mar. 4, 1861, 26; "To Duff Green," *Collected Works*, 4:163; "Speech at Cincinnati, Ohio," ibid., 199.

43. "A Job for the New Cabinet-Maker," *Frank Leslie's Illustrated Newspaper*, Feb. 2, 1861, 176. Three years later, *Southern Punch* borrowed the same cartoon for its own purposes. For it, the caption read "Lincoln vainly endeavoring to cement the old union." *Southern Punch*, June 11, 1864, 4. "Winding Off the Tangled Skein," *Harper's Weekly*, Mar. 30, 1861, 208; and "The Theory of Coercion," *Frank Leslie's Budget of Fun*, Mar. 15, 1861, 13 (two cartoons). The last cartoon discussed in this paragraph also appeared in *Frank Leslie's Illustrated Newspaper*, Mar. 2, 1861, 240.

44. "Hurt You, Uncle Bill?" *Frank Leslie's Budget of Fun*, Mar. 1, 1861, 8; "Fragment: Last Speech of the Campaign at Springfield, Illinois," *Collected Works*, 3:334.

45. "President Lincoln and His Cabinet in Council at the White House," *Frank Leslie's Illustrated Newspaper*, Mar. 30, 1861, 297. On the same date, another news weekly also pictured Lincoln and his cabinet meeting with Gen. Winfield Scott, *New York Illustrated News*, Mar. 30, 1861, 328. See also, "Prof. Lincoln in His Great Feat of Balancing," *Vanity Fair*, Mar. 23, 1861, 139.

46. "Great and Astonishing Trick of Old Abe, the Western Juggler," *Frank Leslie's Budget of Fun*, Apr. 15, 1861.

47. "The Generous Rivals, " ibid., Apr. 15, 1861.

48. "An Anxious Mama and a Fractious Child," *Phunny Phellow*, Apr. 1861, 16.

49. "Taking the Pill," ibid., May 1, 1861. Although Frank Bellew did not sign the illustration, the striking likeness of the visage of Lincoln in another signed Bellew cartoon strongly suggests him as the probable artist. See the lower right corner face of Lincoln in "Humors of the Presidential Canvass," *Comic Monthly*, Aug. 1860, 8–9.

50. "The Last Advice," *Vanity Fair*, Apr. 20, 1861, 187; "Old Abe, Ain't There a Nice Crop?" ibid., May 4, 1861, 211.

51. "Great Fight for the Championship," broadside advertisement for *Phunny Phellow*, May 1861, McLellan Lincoln Collection, Brown University Library, Providence, R.I.

52. Harlan Hoyt Horner, *Lincoln and Greeley* (Urbana: Univ. of Illinois Press, 1953) 220, 221. *New York Tribune* editorials dealt with the crisis on Apr. 13, 17, and 22; and May 2 and 13.

53. "The Old Woman in Trouble," *Frank Leslie's Budget of Fun*, May 1, 1861.

54. "That 'union is strength' is a truth that has been known, illustrated and declared, in various ways and forms in all ages of the world. That great fabulist and philosopher, Aesop, illustrated it by his fable of the bundle of sticks, and he whose wisdom surpasses that of all philosophers, has declared that 'a house divided against itself cannot stand.'" "Campaign Circular from Whig Committee," *Collected Works*, 1:315. "Well I too, go for saving the Union. Much as I hate slavery, I would consent to the extension of it rather than see the Union dissolved, just as I would consent to any Great evil, to avoid a Greater one." "Speech at Peoria, Illinois," ibid., 2:270.

55. "But the Union, in any event, won't be dissolved. We don't want to dissolve it, and if you attempt it, we won't let you." "Speech at Galena, Illinois," ibid., 2:354. "Robbery of the National Apple Orchard," *Harper's Weekly*, May 18, 1861, 307.

CHAPTER FIVE

1. "The Leaders of the Nation," *Harper's Weekly*, July 13, 1861, 434.

2. The three cartoons were entitled "The Bombshell (Gen.

Scott) and the Rat-Holes," "Double-Quick Step to Richmond," and "The Situation," ibid., July 13, 1861, 448.

3. For the newspaper reaction against Greeley's clamor for censure of the administration and the cabinet, see Horner, *Lincoln and Greeley*, 229–30. "Field-Marshall Greeley," *Harper's Weekly*, Aug. 3, 1861, 496.

4. "Dictator Greeley," *Harper's Weekly*, Aug. 10, 1861, 512.

5. "Frank Leslie to the Budgetonians," *Frank Leslie's Budget of Fun*, Sept. 1861, 1.

6. "How It Was That Jeff Davis Didn't Take Washington," ibid., Sept. 1861, 8–9. Other cartoons in the same issue and other magazines also minimized the importance of Bull Run. For example, see ibid., "There's a Good Time Coming," 16; and "The First Great Battle—Bull Run. First Blood for Jeff. Uncle Sam.—'Yer think yer've whipped me, d'yer? Wait a while, my little man!'" *Phunny Phellow*, Oct. 1861, 13. Immediately following Bull Run, George McClellan was assigned to replace Gen. Irvin McDowell.

7. "Masterly Activity, or Six Months on the Potomac," *Harper's Weekly*, Feb. 1, 1862, 176. The idea for this caption may have been culled from the pages of a Confederate newspaper. In September 1861, the *Charleston Mercury* reproved the "'masterly Inactivity' of the Confederate army in Virginia, which it said had been stationary for six weeks with the capital at Washington nearly in sight." The paper called for an offensive to force the United States "to defend themselves." E. B. Long, ed., *The Civil War Day by Day: An Almanac, 1861–1865* (Garden City, N.Y.: Doubleday, 1971; reprint, New York: Da Capo Press, 1985), 115.

8. See "Prince Napoleon Visiting President Lincoln at the White House," *Frank Leslie's Illustrated Newspaper*, Aug. 17, 1861, 213; "Horrid Nightmare of John Bull on Hearing of Prince Napoleon's Visit to Washington," *Harper's Weekly*, Aug. 17, 1861, 528; "Old Moses Davis," *New York Illustrated News*, Aug. 19, 1861, 256; "Presentation of Prince Napoleon by Secretary Seward to the President," *Harper's Weekly*, Aug. 24, 1861, front page; and "John Bull and the American Loan," *New York Illustrated News*, Aug. 26, 1861.

9. "Recognition, or No," *Harper's Weekly*, Sept. 14, 1861, 592; "Mr. Lincoln to England, France, and Spain," *Vanity Fair*, Nov. 16, 1861, front page; "The Fight across the Line from a European Point of View," *Phunny Phellow*, Oct. 1861, 16.

10. For media examples of national pride over the capture of Mason and Slidell, see "Overhauled," *Vanity Fair*, Nov. 30, 1861, 243; "Jonathan on Slidell and Mason," ibid., 248; and "The Mason Who Built His Own Cell," Dec. 14, 1861, 263. Naturally, the tone of official U.S. diplomacy inresponse to the British demand for reparations was measured more carefully than the corresponding response in the media. For example, see "If England must have reparation for the Trent business, we might be induced to open a Port [cannon] for her—so," *Vanity Fair*, Dec. 28, 1861, 279 (front page); "Mr. Secretary Seward is about as much alarmed at John Bull's mail-clad Man-of-War as Trabb's Boy was at Pips," ibid., 283; "The Knife-Thrower Who Nailed John Bull to the Plank," ibid., Jan. 11, 1862, 23; "Jonathan on the Late Surrender of Mason and Slidell," ibid., 25; "Complimentary to Messrs. Mason and Slidell," ibid., Feb. 1, 1862, 53 (front page). The British media also assumed a militant stance with "her weapons ready": "Waiting for an Answer," *Punch*, Dec. 14, 1861, 238, 239; "The American Dilemma," ibid., Dec. 21, 1861; "A Likely Story," 249. However, there were also examples of a more conciliatory mood: "A Safe Delivery and a Wise Deliverance from War," ibid., 253; and "Columbia's Fix," ibid., Dec. 28, 1861, 259. According to these comic images, England essentially left the ball in the American court.

11. "Up a Tree," *Punch*, Jan. 11, 1862, 15. Lincoln was rarely caricatured during the Trent Affair. In any case, the resolution was gingerly handled in the Northern press to save face: "John Bull.—'Mr. Lincoln, I demand Messers Mason and Slidell!' Abe Lincoln.—'I see there is a clause wherein you can have them," *Phunny Phellow*, Feb.1862, 13.

12. Lincoln to McClellan: "I beg to assure you that I have never written you, or spoken to you, in greater kindness of feeling than now, nor with a fuller purpose to sustain you, so far as in my most anxious judgment, I consistently can. But you must act." "To George B. McClellan," *Collected Works*, 5:185.

13. "Sensation Jumble," *Fun*, Apr. 4, 1862, 25; "The Hand-Writing on the Walls," *Harper's Weekly*, Mar. 22, 1862, 192.

14. "Castle Lincoln—No Surrender; Fort Davis in Ruins," *Frank Leslie's Illustrated Newspaper*, Apr. 12, 1862, 368. This is just one case of artistic novelty. In a later chapter, we will encounter an artist's creative use of the figure-ground illusion, which conceals Lincoln's image (figure)between two trees. "The Next Presidency—A Marvelous Prophecy," *Yankee Notions*, May 1864, 145.

15. "Cooperation," *Vanity Fair*, Apr. 12, 1862, front page.

16. "The Last Act of the Drama—Grand Tableau," *Frank Leslie's Budget of Fun*, May 1862, 8–9.

17. "The Great Im-Moral Negro Extravaganza—Dis-Union Foreber," *Phunny Phellow*, May 1862, 8–9. Two months later, another double-page serial cartoon trumpeted the triumphs of the Union. "Old Abe as He Will Shortly Appear in His Great Character of the Father of His Country. Me Che-ild! Me Long Lost Ch-ild! Dost Not Know Me? Embrace Thy Dad." "The Political Theater," ibid., July 1862, 8–9.

18. "Sinbad Lincoln and the Old Man of the Sea," *Frank Leslies's Illustrated Newspaper*, May 3, 1862, 32. For the same print, see *Frank Leslie's Budget of Fun*, June 1862, 4. For a full account of the blockade runner *Nashville*, see Richard S. West

Jr., *Mr. Lincoln's Navy* (New York: Longmans, Green and Co., 1957), 275.

19. "The New Orleans Plum," *Punch*, May 24, 1862, 207.

20. "Norfolk Is Ours," *Vanity Fair*, May 31, 1862, 263; *Yankee Notions*, July 1862, 197.

21. During this period, the federal armies were not without success. For example, Confederate forces evacuated Corinth, Mississippi, and Fort Pillow, Tennessee. In the Battle of Memphis, the Union armies also prevailed. In September, McClellan defeated Lee at Antietam. Nevertheless, the momentum largely remained with the Confederate armies until they experienced major setbacks in July 1863 at Gettysburg, Vicksburg, and Port Hudson.

22. "The Latest from America," *Punch*, July 26, 1862, 35; "Old Abe at the Bar of Public Opinion, ibid., July 26, 1862, 33. *Punch* also created "Bunkum, General-Commanding" to exploit the idea of managed news from America. "Latest American Despatch," ibid., 40.

23. Illustrators did report on Lincoln's review of the troops in the Army of the Potomac, but the graphics they published were descriptive in nature. "The President's Visit to the Army of thePotomac," *Harper's Weekly*, Oct. 25, 1862, 684; "President Lincoln and General McClellan," *New York Illustrated News*, Oct. 25, 1862, 397.

24. "Grand Milling Match between Abe, the Railsplitter, and Jeff, the Rattlesnake," *Phunny Phellow*, Sept. 1862, front page. In this cartoon, there was substantial disparity between the Abe in the caption and the illustration. Apparently, Morse did not write the caption because the illustrated Abe did not have a beard or resemble the real Lincoln. The figure of "Abe" is actually Uncle Sam.

25. "That Draft," *Harper's Weekly*, Oct. 4, 1862, 640; and "Unheeded Advice," *Phunny Phellow*, Nov. 1862, front page.

26. "After His Last Run," *Fun*, Aug. 2, 1862, 195; "An American Euphemism," *Punch*, Aug. 2, 1862, 50. *Fun* also panned McClellan's retreat in verse: "Yankee Notions," *Fun*, Aug. 2, 1862, 193. In addition, see "Proper Names," *Punch*, Aug. 9, 1862, 53; and "Two Despatches of General McClellan," *Fun*, Sept. 6, 1862, 250.

27. Donald, *Lincoln*, 296.

28. "The Overdue Bill," *Fun*, Sept. 27, 1862, 131.

29. "Recruiting A La Mode," ibid., Aug. 23, 1862, 225; "Lincoln's Two Difficulties," *Punch*, Aug. 23, 1862, 77.

30. "Young Yankeedom to Canada," *Fun*, Aug. 30, 1862, 235.

31. "To Abraham Lincoln," *Punch*, Aug. 16, 1862, 72.

32. "Go It Ye Cripples," *Fun*, Oct. 11, 1862, 35; "Abe's Last," ibid., Dec. 27, 1862, 145.

33. "This Is Old Mother Lincoln," *New York Illustrated News*, Jan. 10, 1863, 160; "Columbia: 'Where are my 15,000 Sons—Mur-

dered at Fredericksburg?'" *Harper's Weekly*, Jan. 3, 1863, 16; "Mr. Nobody," ibid., Jan. 3, 1863, 3. One source blamed the mud at Fredericksburg for Lincoln's failure to drive Jeff Davis from his comfortable nest. "The Bad Bird and the Mudsill," *Frank Leslie's Illustrated Newspaper*, Feb. 21, 1863, 352.

34. "That's What's the Matter, or Who's to Blame—A Tragedy," *Phunny Phellow*, Feb. 1863, 8–9.

35. "An Ice Party, or Letting Things Slide on the Rappahannock," *Frank Leslie's Budget of Fun*, Feb. 1863, 8–9. Humors of War, folder 2, AAS. A copy of the full issue in the Richard Samuel West/Periodyssey Collection confirms the date and page numbers.

36. "Those Guillotines—A Little Incident at the White House," *Harper's Weekly*, Jan. 3, 1863, 16; "Universal Advice to Abraham: Drop 'Em!" ibid., Jan. 10, 1863, 32; "Manager Lincoln," ibid., Jan. 31, 1863, 80; "Lincoln's Dream; Or There's a Good Time Coming," *Frank Leslie's Illustrated Newspaper*, Feb. 14, 1863, 336.

37. "Schoolmaster Lincoln and His Boys," *Southern Illustrated News*, Jan. 31, 1863, 8.

38. "Uncle Abe Trying to Straighten Things Out," *Frank Leslie's Budget of Fun*, Jan. 1863. Humors of War, folder 2, AAS. "U.S. Military Shaving Shop," *Harper's Weekly*, Feb. 21, 1863, 128; "Master Abraham Lincoln Gets a New Toy," *Southern Illustrated News*, Feb. 28, 1863, 8.

39. "The Coming Men," *Frank Leslie's Illustrated Newspaper*, Feb. 28, 1863, 368.

40. "Uncle Sam's Happy Family of Generals," *Frank Leslie's Budget of Fun*, Mar. 1863, 8–9. The date and source are very plausible but unconfirmed. The date was handwritten on the cartoon, and the illustration was among a collection of caricatures largely, but not exclusively, gleaned from *Frank Leslie's Budget of Fun*. The inclusion of the capture of the "Harriet Lane" in the illustration on January 1, 1863, adds credence to the probability of the estimated date. Humors of War, folder 2, AAS. "Tempting Offer for the Unemployed—A Good Smart Napoleon Wanted to Fight Battles, Win Victories, and Make Himself Generally Useful," ibid. A penciled date of March 1863 is also inscribed on this print.

41. West, *Mr. Lincoln's Navy*, 232; "The Great 'Cannon Game,'" *Punch*, May 9, 1863, 191; "Great American Billiard Match," ibid., May 9, 1863, 190; "Honest Old Abe's Rudder," *Fun*, May 9, 1863, 75. A few months later, this idea was plagiarized, a common nineteenth-century media practice in America. The only change was the wording on the rudder from *"Monitor"* and *"Ironsides"* to "Halleck," "McClellan," and "Stanton." "Honest Old Abe's Rudder," *Phunny Phellow*, Aug. 1863, 16.

42. "The Monitor Set in Danger; or, All's Well That Ends Welles," *Frank Leslie's Budget of Fun*, July 1863. Although un-

confirmed, the source and date are plausible because there is an advertisement for *Frank Leslie's Ladies Magazine* on the back side page of the caricature and the apparent date is written on it, the source and date are plausible but unconfirmed. American Caricatures, folder 3, Samuel B. Woodward Collection, AAS.

43. "The Settling Day," *Fun*, May 30, 1863, 105.

44. "Abe Lincoln in His New Characters," *Frank Leslie's Budget of Fun*, May 1863, 9.

45. "Brooms! Brooms!" *Vanity Fair*, May 23, 1863, 75.

46. "Right at Last," *Frank Leslie's Illustrated Newspaper*, June 13, 1863, 192. After Union victories at Gettysburg, Vicksburg, and Port Hudson, this cartoon surfaced again as if to say, "Indeed we have the right generals!" *Frank Leslie's Budget of Fun*, Aug. 1863, 13.

47. "Yankee Pancakes," *Fun*, Feb. 21, 1863, 225.

48. For rates of inflation, see J. G. Randall and David Donald, *The Civil War and Reconstruction*, 2d ed. (Lexington, Mass.: D. C. Heath, 1969), 482. Actually, an editorial in *Harper's Weekly* put a positive twist on inflation: "The Practical feature of the Administration policy will be, must be, continued inflation. Great wars can not be waged on a specie basis. Issues of Irredeemable paper are as essential to their prosecution as issues of shot and shell from government arsenals." "Our Financial Policy," *Harper's Weekly*, Feb. 28, 1863, 130.

49. "A Frightful Case of Inflation," *Frank Leslie's Budget of Fun*, Apr. 1863. Both the source and date of this illustration are estimated. As with other prints, this illustration was found among many *Frank Leslie's Budget of Fun* illustrations. Thus the source seems plausible, but it is unconfirmed. Establishment of the date is more problematic because it is based on a process of elimination that involves what the author knows about the illustrations in the surrounding issues of the magazine, the date (Jan. 20, 1863) on a set of satirical letters on the back page of the illustration that places this illustration sometime afterward, and the secretary of the treasury's work on banking legislation. The illustration is from American Caricatures, folder 3, AAS.

50. "The Financial Situation and the Prospect," *Harper's Weekly*, May 9, 1863, 290; "Mr. Bull: 'Hi Want My Cotton . . . ,'" ibid., May 16, 1863, 320; "England's Neutrality," *Vanity Fair*, May 9, 1863, 56.

51. "Our Administration and No Intervention," *New York Illustrated News*, Mar. 14, 1863, 291, 296–97.

52. "A Fit for the Ladies League," *Vanity Fair*, June 13, 1863, 86.

53. "Nurse Greeley," *Frank Leslie's Budget of Fun*, May 1863, 12; Mark E. Neely Jr., *The Fate of Liberty* (New York: Oxford Univ. Press, 1991).

54. "Vallandighamism," *Vanity Fair*, Jan. 18, 1862, 37.

55. "Abe Lincoln Ought to Be Hung," *Phunny Phellow*, Nov. 1862, 12. Also, see "Last Tableau in the Play of Treason at Home," ibid., May 1863, front page; "How the Bowery Boys Amuse Themselves," *Harper's Weekly*, Mar. 28, 1863, 208; "An Extinguished Visitor to the White House," *Vanity Fair*, June 27, 1863, 135.

56. "One Kind of Patriotism," *Harper's Weekly*, June 27, 1863, 416; "The Handwriting on the Wall," *Vanity Fair*, June 27, 1863, 140.

57. "A Rare Old Game of Shuttlecock," *Frank Leslie's Illustrated Newspaper*, June 20, 1863, 208, which also appeared in *Frank Leslie's Budget of Fun*, Aug. 1863, 13.

58. "A Hard Case—Vallandigham's Reception by His Friend Jeff," *Frank Leslie's Budget of Fun*, July 1863. The date of this cartoon is unconfirmed, but very probable. Lincoln ordered Vallandigham sent behind Confederate lines on May 19, 1863. The date, July 1863, is also written in hand on the cartoon. Humors of War, folder 2, AAS.

59. "A Hint to Father Abraham," *Phunny Phellow*, July 1863, 8–9.

CHAPTER SIX

1. "Fragment on Slavery," *Collected Works*, 2:222; "Eulogy on Henry Clay," ibid., 2:126; Gabor Boritt, *Lincoln and the Economics of the American Dream* (Memphis, Tenn.: Memphis State Univ. Press, 1978), 281; "To James N. Brown," *Collected Works*, 3:327.

2. "To James N. Brown," 327; "Speech at Peoria, Illinois," *Collected Works*, 2:270; "Speech at Bloomington, Illinois," ibid., 2:230.

3. "It is six days old, and while commendation in newspapers and by distinguished individuals is all that a vain man could wish, the stocks have declined, and troops come forward more slowly than ever." "To Hannibal Hamilton," ibid., 5:444.

4. "I'm Sorry to Have to Drop You, Sambo," *Frank Leslie's Illustrated Newspaper*, Oct. 12, 1861, 352. The same cartoon appeared in *Frank Leslie's Budget of Fun*, Nov. 1861, 5. Frémont's proclamation was issued on August 13, but it took time for the illustrated media to respond.

5. "To John C. Frémont," *Collected Works*, 4:506. In fact, Lincoln soon cited evidence to support his contention. "Gen. Anderson telegraphed me that on the news of Gen. Fremont having actually issued deeds of manumission, a whole company of our volunteers threw down their arms and disbanded. I was so assured, as to think it probable, that the very arms we had furnished Kentucky would be turned against us. I think to lose Kentucky is nearly the same as to lose the whole game." "To Orville H. Browning," ibid., 4:532.

6. "Well, Master Fremont, That's a Rather Long Reach Aint It?" *Frank Leslie's Illustrated Newspaper*, Oct. 26, 1861, 368. Lincoln did construe Frémont's proclamation as "purely political." "To Orville H. Browning," *Collected Works*, 4:531.

7. "The Great Chain Trick," *Phunny Phellow*, Dec. 1861, 16.

8. "The Pet Lamb and the Black Sheep; or, the Unhappy Shepherd," *Frank Leslie's Budget of Fun*, Feb. 1862. A front-page cartoon in *Vanity Fair* illustrates the opposition to McClellan's stance on slavery. "General McClellan, don't go strong 'nuff for Bobolition—Dat's what's de matter!" "Brudder Greeley on the Crisis," *Vanity Fair*, Mar. 29, 1862, front page.

9. Miers and Powell, *Lincoln Day by Day*, 80, 85.

10. "Abolition in High Places," *Harper's Weekly*, Mar. 22, 1862, 178.

11. "Cause and Effect, the Head and Front of the War," *Comic Monthly*, Apr. 1862, front page.

12. "The Constitution and Her Guardian," *Phunny Phellow*, Apr. 1862, 13; "There, Bub, There's a Quarter for You," *Frank Leslie's Illustrated Newspaper*, Apr. 5, 1862, 336; "Doctor Lincoln's New Elixir of Life—For the Southern States," *New York Illustrated News*, Apr. 12, 1862, 368.

13. "Some Sense About the Nigger at Last," *Vanity Fair*, Mar. 14, 1862, 130. With regard to colonization, Lincoln was right in believing that the cessation of slavery would not end intolerance and inequality, but he was wrong in thinking that African American "comfort would be advanced by it." "Address on Colonization, to a Deputation of Negroes," *Collected Works*, 5:372. Although *Harper's Weekly* generally supported Lincoln, the magazine wisely opposed the president's advocacy of colonization. "Shall We Cut Off Our Noses," *Harper's Weekly*, June 28, 1862, 402. For a more general treatment of Lincoln's "Presidential Leadership" on the race issue, see LaWanda Cox, *Lincoln and Black Freedom* (Columbia: Univ. of South Carolina Press, 1981).

14. "The American Difficulty," *Punch*, May 11, 1861, 193.

15. "Oberon and Titania," ibid., Apr. 5, 1862, 137. Uncharacteristically, *Punch*'s competitor, *Fun*, listed "Slave Emancipation" among the recent military victories of the North. "Sensation Jumble," *Fun*, Apr. 4, 1862, 25.

16. "Tall Doin's," *Punch* Apr. 5, 1862, 139.

17. "A Humane but Officious Hunter," *Frank Leslie's Budget of Fun*, June 1862, 9.

18. "Abe and Abolition," *Vanity Fair*, July 7, 1862, 274.

19. "The President's Proclamation," *Harper's Weekly*, May 31, 1862, 338.

20. "Brother Jonathan's Appeal to Brother Sambo," *Punch*, Aug. 9, 1862, 54.

21. "One Good Turn Deserves Another," ibid., Aug. 9, 1862, 55. Six months later, the *Southern Illustrated News* virtually cop-

ied the *Punch* cartoon. Only slight artistic nuances and a Scottish cap differentiated the English and American illustrations. "One Good Turn Deserves Another," *Southern Illustrated News*, Mar. 14, 1863, 8.

22. For the text on Lincoln's reply to Greeley, see "To Horace Greeley," *Collected Works*, 5:388–89.

23. "The President and Slavery," *Harper's Weekly*, Sept. 6, 1862, 562. The following week, *Harper's Weekly* summarized the president's "perfectly distinct statement." "He says that he is the Chief Magistrate of the Union; that he is sworn to maintain it; and that he means to maintain it at any price. But what exact price must be paid he says that he must determine. He will take every step, including emancipation, just as fast as it shall seem to him necessary." "The President's Policy," *Harper's Weekly*, Sept. 13, 1862, 578.

24. "Correspondence between the President and Horace Greeley," *Frank Leslie's Budget of Fun*, Sept. 1, 1862. For Lincoln's clearest statement on the relationship of Union and slavery, see "Speech at Peoria, Illinois," 270.

25. "The Monotonous Minstrel," *Vanity Fair*, Sept. 6, 1862, 115; "An Unfinshed Work of Art," ibid., Sept. 6, 1862, 120.

26. "The Late Triangular Duel," ibid., 119 (brackets in original). This piece also appeared in *Nick Nax*, Nov. 1862, 204.

27. "Preface," *Vanity Fair*, July 5, 1862, 3.

28. "Jump Out of the Bag, Puss!" *Punch*, Sept. 13, 1862, 105.

29. "Preliminary Emancipation Proclamation," *Collected Works*, 5:434. The clearest public warning from the president was contained in the proclamation of his that revoked General Hunter's unauthorized general orders of emancipation. "Proclamation revoking General Hunter's Order of Military Emancipation of May 9, 1862," *Collected Works*, 5:222–23. However, the *Harper's Weekly* interpretation of the order, quoted earlier in this chapter, was even more direct. Elsewhere, Lincoln had noted, "I have not decided against a proclamation of liberty to the slaves, but hold the matter under advisement. And I can assure you that the subject is on my mind, by day and night, more than any other. Whatever shall appear to be God's will I will do." "Reply to Emancipation Memorial Presented by Chicago Christians of All Denominations," *Collected Works*, 5:425. This was about as close as the president could come on the issue without tipping his hand that the decision had already been made.

30. "What Will He Do with Them" *Vanity Fair*, Oct. 4, 1862, 163; "President Lincoln's Political Governor," ibid., Oct. 4, 1862, 168.

31. "Sole Stirring Words," ibid., Oct. 4, 1862, 167.

32. "Our War Correspondence," ibid., Oct. 11, 1862, 172.

33. "Another Blow for the Union," ibid., Nov. 1, 1862, 210. Later, *Vanity Fair* satirically attributed the removal of General McClellan from his post as commander of the Army of the Potomac

to "the fault of his advisors." "Our War Correspondence," *Vanity Fair*, Nov. 22, 1862, 245.

34. "Upon a Recent Proclamation," *Frank Leslie's Budget of Fun*. American Caricatures, folder 3, AAS.

35. "Slavery Practically Abolished," *Harper's Weekly*, Oct. 4, 1862, 626.

36. "Lincoln's Last Warning," ibid., Oct. 11, 1862, 656; "Up a Tree," *Punch*, Jan. 11, 1862, 15.

37. "Bogy for a Bad Boy," *Nick Nax*, Nov. 1862, 208.

38. "Keep on Track," *Vanity Fair*, Nov. 22, 1862, 247. Democratic gains in the recent election had sobered the president. Thus, in this cartoon William Seward fuels the engine with wood labeled "Democratic Majority."

39. "The President's Proclamation in Secessia," *Vanity Fair*, Oct. 18, 1862, 658. See also, "The Emancipation Proclamation in Secessia," ibid., Oct. 18, 1862, 659; and "The Proclamation in Richmond," *Frank Leslie's Illustrated* Newspaper, Oct. 18, 1862, 50.

40. "Masks and Faces," *Southern Illustrated News*, Nov. 8, 1862, 8; "President Lincoln's Proclamation in the 'Rebel Senate,'" *Phunny Phellow*, Dec. 1862, 8–9; "Latest from Ethiopia," *Vanity Fair*, Oct. 25, 1862, 204.

41. "The Penny Jupiter," *Fun*, Oct. 18, 1862, 45; "A Yankee Olmar," ibid., Nov. 15, 1862, 85.

42. "The American Chess Players," *Punch*, Oct. 18, 1862, 157.

43. "Serenade to Lincoln," ibid., Oct. 18, 1862, 158. Only verses three through five, and seven are quoted.

44. "Abe's Lincoln's Last Card; or, Rouge-Et-Noir," ibid., Oct. 18, 1862, 160, 161.

45. "Proclamation of the Act to Suppress Insurrection," *Collected Works*, 5:341.

46. "Annual Message to Congress," *Collected Works*, 5:530; "The Message," *Harper's Weekly*, Dec. 13, 1862, 786.

47. "But both the friends and enemies of freedom misunderstood Lincoln's admittedly ambiguous message. Some failed to notice his promise that all slaves freed 'by the chances of war'—including his Proclamation—would remain forever free. The Proclamation was a war measure applicable only against states in rebellion. Lincoln's gradual emancipation proposal was a peace measure to abolish the institution everywhere by constitutional means." James M. McPherson, *Battle Cry of Freedom* (New York: Ballantine Books, 1988), 562–63.

48. "The Great Negro Emancipation Fandango Is Postponed until 1900," *Harper's Weekly*, Dec. 20, 1862, 816.

49. *Frank Leslie's Budget of Fun*, Feb. 1863, front page. Humors of War, folder 2, AAS. Lincoln's eloquent, and now famous "We cannot escape history" portion of the address was also mocked. "In conclusion, fellow-citizens, I beg to state that we cannot hope to escape History, who will be after us with a very

sharp stick. No personal significance or insignificance can spare one or another of us. My own hopes of being spared on the latter count are consequently dashed, in which I share a disappointment common to nearly all of you."

50. "Butler Hanged—The Negro Freed—On Paper—1863," *Frank Leslie's Budget of Fun*, Feb. 1863, front page.

51. "An Old Story in a New Shape," *Yankee Notions*, Feb. 1863, 48.

52. "A Solemn Warning," *Frank Leslie's Budget of Fun*, Dec. 1862, 16. This print is located in the Richard Samuel West/Periodyssey Private Collection of Political Caricature, and in American Caricatures, folder 3, AAS.

53. *Harper's Weekly*, Jan. 10, 1863, 32.

54. "The Emancipation of the Negroes," *Harper's Weekly*, Jan. 24, 1863, 56–57; "Dinah's Dream," *Merryman's Monthly*, Apr. 1863, 29.

55. "North and South," *Fun*, Jan. 3, 1863, 159.

56. "President Lincoln's Slave Policy," ibid., Jan. 24, 1863, 219.

57. "Scene from the American 'Tempest,'" *Punch*, Jan. 24, 1863, 35.

58. "Old Abe in a Fix," ibid., Jan. 24, 1863, 34.

59. "The Next New Marriage," *Nick Nax*, June 1863, 48.

60. "To James C. Conkling," *Collected Works*, 6:408–9.

61. "To James S. Wadsworth," ibid., 7:101.

62. "To Michael L. Hahn," ibid., 7:243.

63. "To Albert G. Hodges," ibid., 7:282.

64. "To Charles D. Robinson," ibid., 7:500.

65. "Interview with Alexander W. Randall and Joseph T. Mills," ibid., 7:507.

66. "Sambo, You Are Not Handsome, Any More Than Myself," *Frank Leslie's Illustrated Newspaper*, Dec. 24, 1864, 221.

67. "I have always thought that all men should be free, but if any should be slaves it should be first those who desire it for themselves and secondly those who desire it for others. Whenever [I] hear anyone, arguing for slavery I feel a strong impulse to see it tried on him personally." "Speech to One Hundred Fortieth Indiana Regiment." *Collected Works*, 8:361. "Annual Message to Congress," ibid., 5:537.

68. "Celebration of the Abolition of Negro Slavery in Maryland," *Frank Leslie's Illustrated Newspaper*, Nov. 19, 1864, front page.

69. These prints are attributed to the periodical *Fun, Fact, and Fancy*, 24–25. However, they may have appeared in the *Comic Monthly* or *Phunny Phellow*. In any case, the prints are located in the rare book room of the Regenstein Library at the University of Chicago.

70. "The Gloved Hero of Emancipation Waiting for the Indispensable Necessity," *Funniest of Phun*, Feb. 1865, 8–9. This

print appears in chapter 10, below, "The Olive Branch or the Sword?"(see page 320).

71. "Uncle Abe's Valentine Sent By Columbia," *Frank Leslie's Illustrated Newspaper*, Feb. 25, 1865, 368; "The Tallest Ruler on the Globe," *Frank Leslie's Budget of Fun*, Apr. 1865. The latter print appears in chapter 11, below (see page 343).

72. "More Free Than Welcome," *Punch*, Oct. 18, 1862, 160.

CHAPTER SEVEN

1. "Old Abe's Last," *Nick Nax*, July 1863, 86.

2. "Tricks *vs.* Honours," *Fun*, July 18, 1863, 175. It is appropriate to note that the Southern victories at Port Hudson and Charleston were temporary defensive achievements not comparable to the South's earlier successes at Bull Run and Fredericksburg.

3. "The Handwriting on the Wall," *Merryman's Monthly*, Sept. 1863, 165.

4. "How Are You General Lee?" *Nick Nax*, Nov. 1863, 203.

5. "Jeff Davis Reckoning without His Host," *Frank Leslie's Budget of Fun*, Aug. 1863, 5.

6. "The War Pyramid," *Merryman's Monthly*, Aug. 1863, 144; "To Montgomery Blair," *Collected Works*, 6:346. The ebullient aura of victory was also trumpeted in a front-page cartoon of *Merryman's Monthly* August issue. The caption conveys the essence of Union euphoria: "A pretty man you are for a president sending off Lee to capture Washington and leaving us poor helpless women at Richmond unprotected!! Ugh! A Richmond Curtain Lecture. Mr. and Mrs. Jeff Davis as Mr. and Mrs. Caudle. Time, Night of 4th July 1863."

7. "Remarks to the 'One-Legged Brigade,'" ibid., 6:226.

8. "To James C. Conkling," ibid., 6:408–9.

9. "Order of Retaliation," ibid., 6:357.

10. "The President's Order No. 252," *Harper's Weekly*, Aug. 15, 1863, 528.

11. "Brutus and Cæsar," *Punch*, Aug. 15, 1863, 69, 71.

12. "The President," *Harper's Weekly*, Aug. 29, 1863, 546.

13. "The Draft," ibid., Aug. 29, 1863, 546.

14. "Once More," *Vanity Fair*, July 4, 1863, 147. Unfortunately, *Vanity Fair* discontinued publication in 1863.

15. "The Naughty Boy Gotham," *Frank Leslie's Illustrated Newspaper*, Aug. 29, 1863, 372. This cartoon was reprinted in *Frank Leslie's Budget of Fun*, Nov. 1863, 13.

16. "Uncle Abe, 'Here, New York, Don't go to Canada,'" *Merryman's Monthly*, Oct. 1863, 200. Actually, this illustration was used in the aftermath of Lincoln's first election. Only the caption was changed to fit the 1863 setting. For the original cartoon source, see *Frank Leslie's Budget of Fun*, June 1861, 16.

17. "The Sinews of War, or How to Bag an Army," *Merryman's Monthly*, Oct. 1863, 208.

18. "To Horatio Seymour," *Collected Works*, 6:369–70; "Proclamation Suspending Writ of Habeas Corpus," ibid., 451–52.

19. For the record of Lincoln's resolute correspondence with Governor Seymour, and for other documents on this issue, see "To Horatio Seymour," *Collected Works*, 6:381–82, 389–91, 391–92, 416–17; "Draft of Proclamation, ibid., 6:388; "Opinion on the Draft," ibid., 6:444–49.

20. "Proclamation Suspending Writ of Habeas Corpus," 451–52. Lincoln's suspension of habeas corpus also commanded military officers to resist any judicial action based on writs, including resistance of warrants for their own arrest. "Draft of Order Concerning Writ of Haebeas Corpus," ibid., 6:460.

21. "The Yankee Guy Fawkes," *Fun*, Nov. 7, 1863, front page; "Abduction of the Yankee Goddess of Liberty," *Southern Punch*, Nov. 14, 1863, 4.

22. "Mr. Lincoln Getting the Range with His Springfield Gun," *Merryman's Monthly*, Oct. 1863, 224.

23. "Scene in a Yankee Barbershop," *Southern Punch*, Oct. 10, 1863, 4.

24. "King Mob upon His Throne," *Fun*, Aug. 8, 1863, 205; "'Rowdy' Notions of Emancipation," *Punch*, Aug. 8, 1863, 57; "Reply to New York Workingmen's Democratic Republican Association," *Collected Works*, 7:259–60.

25. "To the Land of the Free," *Fun*, Sept. 26, 1863, 15.

26. "The American Conscript's Complaint," *Punch*, Sept. 26, 1863, 128.

27. "Urge Enlistments, Rejoice the Army," *New York Illustrated News*, Jan. 2, 1864, 152–53; "The Last Call," *Yankee Notions*, Feb. 1864, front page.

28. "Too Late," *Merryman's Monthly*, Aug. 1863, 145.

29. "England's Neutrality," *Punch*, Sept. 5, 1863, 97.

30. "Scylla and Charybdis, or the Modern Ulysses," ibid., Oct. 10, 1863, 149.

31. "Ulysses," ibid., Oct. 10, 1863, 148. Also, see "Scylla and Charybdis," ibid., 154.

32. "Mr. Bull to His American Bullies," ibid., Oct. 3, 1863, 138; "John Bull's Neutrality," ibid., 139; "The Neutral Beast," *Fun*, Sept. 12, 1863, 255.

33. "A Poke at President Lincoln," *Punch*, Aug. 22, 1863, 81. In doggerel, *Punch* also distanced the British from the French violation of the Monroe Doctrine. "Mexico and Monroe," ibid., Aug. 29, 1863, 85.

34. "Council between the Crowned Heads of Europe and the United States," *Southern Punch*, Oct. 17, 1863, 8.

35. "A Peep into the Future—The Monroe Doctrine Triumphant," *Frank Leslie's Budget of Fun*, Nov. 1863, 8–9. For an excellent example of this anxiety over Canada, see "A Slip-Shod

Serenade—Canny Seward to Canada," *Punch*, Sept. 26, 1863, 125.

36. "The President and the Czar," *Punch*, Oct. 24, 1863, 168. Later, this cordial climate between the two nations was the basis of the sale of Alaska to the United States.

37. "Extremes Meet," ibid., Oct. 24, 1863, 169; "The British Lion Smells an Enormous Rat," *Merryman's Monthly*, Nov. 1863, 256.

38. "Drawing Things to a Head," *Harper's Weekly*, Nov. 28, 1863, 768.

39. "Yankees and Russians," *Punch*, Nov. 7, 1863, 194. For additional evidence of British anxiety on this issue, see "Federal Proclivities," ibid., Nov. 14, 1863, 196.

40. "The Anglo-Rebel Ironclads," *Harper's Weekly*, Sept. 5, 1863, 562.

41. "Neutrality," *Punch*, Nov. 14, 1863, 199; Encouragement from the *Comic News* in England was also present to resist the pressure from the Union. "British Pluck," *Comic News*, Nov. 14, 1863, front page. This illustration appears in chapter 8, below: "The *Comic News*, Lincoln, and the Civil War" (see page 228).

42. "John Bull—ied!" *Southern Illustrated News*, Nov. 14, 1863, 152.

43. "The Ram of Liverpool," *Punch*, Nov. 14, 1863, 203.

44. "Yankee-British Alliance against France," *Southern Punch*, Feb. 27, 1864, 8; "Lincoln Is Rather Indisposed–The Effects of an Overdose of British Neutrality," ibid., Mar. 12, 1864, 8.

45. "The Two Messages," *Punch*, Jan. 2, 1864, 9. The origin and substance of Lincoln's message was likely abstracted from his "Annual Message to Congress" on December 8, 1863, and then embellished. *Collected Works*, 7:36–53. A comparable report from President Jefferson Davis must have constituted the basis for the poet's assessment of "The Two Messages."

46. "The Two Messages," *Fun*, Jan. 2, 1864, 153.

47. "Laconic Generals," *Nick Nax*, Nov. 1863, 200; "Getting at the Root of It," *Yankee Notions*, Oct. 1863, front page.

48. "How Kind of Them," *Frank Leslie's Budget of Fun*, Oct. 1863. Humors of War, folder 2, AAS; "See-Saw," *Fun*, Nov. 14, 1863, 85.

49. "The Bill Presented," *Frank Leslie's Budget of Fun*, Nov. 1863, 16; "The Sowers," *Fun*, Oct. 17, 1863, 45.

50. A cartoon by William Newman rejoiced in Vallandigham's loss. "Vallandigham Ball(ot)ed Out," *Frank Leslie's Budget of Fun*, Dec. 1863 (probable date). Humors of War, folder 2, AAS.

51. "Santa Claus Visits Uncle Sam," *Phunny Phellow*, Dec. 1863. Humors of War, folder 2, AAS. "Thanksgiving Day," *Harper's Weekly*, Dec. 5, 1863, 778–79.

52. "The Marvelous History of Miles O'Reilly, Poet, Patri-ot, Politician, and Prisoner," *Comic Monthly*, Nov. 1863, front page.

53. "The New Gospel of Peace, According to St. Benjamin," ibid., Nov. 1863, 8–9.

54. "Thanksgiving," *Fun*, Dec. 5, 1863, 115; "A Hint," ibid., Dec. 5, 1863, 111.

55. "Receiving New Years Calls at the White House," *New York Illustrated News*, Jan. 23, 1864, 196; "I Wish I Was in Dixie!" *Southern Illustrated News*, Feb. 27, 1864, 64; "Lincoln and Seward watching over the drooping eagle," *Southern Punch*, Jan. 2, 1864, 5. For another cartoon that poked fun at the Yankee drive to end the war, see "The Little Joker," *Southern Illustrated News*, Feb. 13, 1864, 48.

56. "Final Issue of the War—The Longest Purse Wins," *Frank Leslie's Budget of Fun*, Mar. 1864, 8–9.

57. "General Grant Receiving His Commission," *Harper's Weekly*, Mar. 26, 1864, 197; "Lincoln's New Servant Girl," *Phunny Phellow*, June 1864, 8–9.

58. "Symptoms of Spring—Uncle Abram's Crop Begins to Shoot," *Frank Leslie's Budget of Fun*, Apr. 1864, 8–9; "I've Rented This House from Abe Lincoln," *Phunny Phellow*, June 1864, front page; 78. "Speech at Great Central Sanitary Fair, Philadelphia, Pennsylvania," *Collected Works*, 7:394, 395–96.

59. "The Way Lincoln Will Be Lifted Out of Washington City by General Lee," *Southern Punch*, May 7, 1864, 8. Although the caption was altered, the cartoon image was copied from *Frank Leslie's Illustrated Newspaper*, Mar. 2, 1861, 240. "Lincoln Vainly," *Southern Punch*, June 11, 1864, 4. The cartoon of Lincoln trying to repair the Union was also borrowed from *Frank Leslie's Illustrated Newspaper*, Feb. 2, 1861, 176. The task was rendered impossible in the Southern version.

60. "Columbia's Sewing-Machine," *Punch*, Oct. 1, 1864, 137; "Columbia's Nightmare," *Fun*, Sept. 10, 1864, 269. *Frank Leslie's Budget of Fun* rebutted the conclusion of the former cartoon with "Columbia's Sewing Done." "First Visit, January 1, 1864—(From *Punch*) Mrs. Britannia.—'Ah, my Dear Columbia, it's all very well; but I'm afraid you'll find it difficult to join that neatly.'" "Second Visit, January 1, 1865.—(Not from *Punch*) Columbia.—'You see, my good old woman, I've succeeded not only in rejoining the dear old map, but also in eradicating the British stain of slavery from it.'" Humors of War, folder 1, AAS. Although the American magazine took someliberty with the correct date of the *Punch* cartoon (Jan. 1, 1864), the date in the caption from *Frank Leslie's Budget of Fun* correctly places that image in early 1865.

61. The magazine source and exact date of this image is unknown. It is cartoon 174 in the Nineteenth-Century Political Cartoon Scrapbook of Civil War caricature in the Special Collections Library at Gettysburg College.

62. "Mr. Lincoln's Great National Joke," *Funniest of Phun*, July 1864, 15. Actually, this cartoon had appeared earlier in the *New York Illustrated News*, Apr. 2, 1864, 364.

63. "To Whom It May Concern," *Collected Works*, 7:451.

64. "Niagara Doves," *Fun*, Aug. 13, 1864, 219.

65. Horace Greeley, *The American Conflict* (Hartford, Conn.: O. D. Case, 1866), 2:665, 666.

66. "The Big Peace Visit to Jeff," *Phunny Phellow*, Oct. 1864, front page.

67. "Grand Scene from the Last Farce Performed at Albany," *Frank Leslie's Budget of Fun*, June 1864. Humors of War, folder 1, AAS. The same cartoon appeared in *Frank Leslie's Illustrated Newspaper*, June 18, 1864, 208. "Surrounded," *Frank Leslie's Budget of Fun*, July 1864, American Caricatures, folder 3, AAS.

68. "'The Situation,'" *Comic Monthly*, Aug. 1864. The source and date are probable. Because Frank Beard drew the major cartoons for *Comic Monthly* during this period, this magazine is the logical choice. The cartoon may be found in the Nineteenth-Century Political Cartoon Scrapbook.

CHAPTER EIGHT

This chapter first appeared in the *Journal of the Abraham Lincoln Association* 17.1 (1996): 53–87. This slightly revised version appears in this volume courtesy of the *Journal of the Abraham Lincoln Association* and the Board of Trustees at the University of Illinois.

1. Because the *Bubble* was only a brief successor, lasting just two weeks, the major focus of this discussion is upon the *Comic News*. Although the data from the *Bubble* are combined with the *Comic News*, specific citations from the *Bubble* are acknowledged in the notes.

2. Between July 18, 1863 and March 28, 1865, the collective duration of the *Comic News* and the *Bubble*, a comparative content analysis of Civil War prose, illustrations, and poetry in *Punch*, *Fun*, and the *Comic News* (because the *Bubble* was only a brief successor, the statistics from the two periodicals are combined under the *Comic News*) reveals that *Punch* published 50 percent, *Fun* 27 percent, and the *Comic News* 23 percent of the total material. The only category in which *Punch* did not lead was in the percentage of cartoons. *Fun* published 41 percent, *Punch* 35 percent, and the *Comic News* 24 percent of the popular art.

3. *Comic News*, Aug. 22, 1863, 44; Aug. 29, 1863, 52; Sept. 12, 1863, 66.

4. Ibid., Sept. 19, 1863, 79. These dire statements of economic distress were not sustained by the facts. On October 3, 1863,

Lincoln proclaimed a national day of Thanksgiving, in part because of the economic blessings enjoyed by the North. "Needful diversions of wealth and of strength from the fields of peaceful industry to the national defence, have not arrested the plough, the shuttle or the ship; the axe has enlarged the borders of our settlements, and the mines, as well of iron and coal as of the precious metals, have yielded even more abundantly than heretofore." "Proclamation of Thanksgiving," *Collected Works*, 6:496.

5. *Comic News*, Oct. 3, 1863, 91; Oct. 10, 1863, 101.

6. Ibid., Oct. 31, 1863, 125.

7. Ibid., Nov. 21, 1863, 151.

8. Ibid., Aug. 22, 1863, 46.

9. Ibid., Nov. 14, 1863, front page. See Howard Jones, *Union in Peril* (Chapel Hill: Univ. of North Carolina Press, 1992), 146–47.

10. Because art historians are unaware of the existence of the *Comic News*, William M'Connell is credited only for appointments as a cartoonist with *Punch* and the *Illustrated Times*. "His style is always exaggerated and grotesque with slight similarities to 'Phiz' or John Leech but never so well drawn." Simon Houfe, *The Dictionary of British Book Illustrators and Caricaturists, 1800–1914* (Woodbridge, U.K.: Antique Collectors' Club, 1978), 378. "Eventually, thePalmerston ministry clamped down on such shipbuilding activities but not before both physical and diplomatic damage had occured." Jones, *Union in Peril*, 147.

11. *Comic News*, Mar. 5, 1864, 117.

12. Ibid., July 2, 1864, 315.

13. Ibid., Dec. 19, 1863, 182.

14. Following Lincoln's assassination, the issue of Lincoln's so-called manners took on new meaning. "Ralph Waldo Emerson saluted Lincoln as an 'aboriginal man' unspoiled by European culture and tradition. The manners of the living Lincoln had troubled Emerson; with many others, however, he had struggled to overcome that prejudice, and he now embraced him as the inspired leader of the nation. 'Rarely was man so fitted to the event.'" Merrill D. Peterson, *Lincoln in American Memory* (New York: Oxford Univ. Press, 1994), 15.

15. "Not only did the war not greatly impede growth, but it did not even distort the economy unduly." Mark E. Neely Jr., *The Last Best Hope of Earth* (Cambridge, Mass.: Harvard Univ. Press, 1993), 141–42. See also Gary L. Bunker and John Appel, "Shoddy, Anti-Semitism, and the Civil War: The Visual Image," *American Jewish History* 82.1–4 (1994): 43–71; and *Comic News*, Jan. 2, 1864, 4. At this time, Lincoln's actual rhetoric on African Americans included: "How to better the condition of the colored race has long been a study which has attracted my serious and careful attention; hence I think I am clear and decided as to what course I shall pursue in the premises, regarding it a religious duty, as the nation's guardian of these people,

who have so heroically vindicated their manhood on the battlefield, where, in assisting to save the life of the Republic, they have demonstrated in blood their right to the ballot, which is but the humane protection of the flag, they have so fearlessly defended." "To James Wadsworth," *Collected Works*, 7:101.

16. *Comic News*, Sept. 5, 1863, 58.

17. Ibid., Aug. 29, 1863, 52; "Alphabet for Young America," ibid., Jan. 2, 1864, 4; "Are We Not All Brothers?" ibid., Dec. 5, 1863, 165; "The Last (White) Man: Or, a Possibility for America in 1874," ibid., Apr. 16, 1864, 187. The only listing in Houfe's dictionary for a Yorick is spelled *Yorrick*. No first name is given. Simon Houfe asserts that "Yorrick" is a "pseudonym [for an] illustrator of children's books," but does not identify the referent for the pseudonym. Houfe, *Dictionary of British Book Illustrators*, 506. In America, fears of ethnic domination were not confined to African Americans. Comic periodicals whipped up prejudice in cartoons against Jewish, Chinese, and Irish Americans on similar grounds.

18. "The War in America," *Comic News*, July 23, 1864, 29. The correspondent's conclusions are published in ibid., Aug. 27, 1864, 93.

19. Ibid., Sept. 3, 1864, 101.

20. "A General Wish against General Butler, Who's General-Lee Hated," ibid., Aug. 20, 1864, 77; "Old Abe at Home in 1865," ibid., July 23, 1864, 35; "The Great Donkey Show,"ibid., Aug. 13, 1864, 67. No identifying signature of the cartoonist appears on the last cartoon. For Lincoln's general treatment in the domestic press, see Harper, *Lincoln and the Press*, and Mitgang, *Abraham Lincoln*.

21. Houfe, *Dictionary of British Book Illustrators*, 58, 156. None of the biographical sketches of Matt Morgan place him in the employ of the *Comic News*. One sketch erroneously locates him in America as early as 1865 or 1866. See Clara E. Clement and Laurence Hutton, *Artists of the Nineteenth Century and Their Works* (St. Louis: North Point, 1969). William Murrell notes that at the urging of Frank Leslie, Morgan came to America in 1870 after founding and serving as the major cartoonist for the *Tomahawk* in 1867. See Murrell, *History of American Graphic Humor*, 2:53.

22. "Columbia's Nightmare," *Fun*, Sept.17, 1864, 15; "Pull Devil—Pull Baker," *Comic News*, Oct. 8, 1864, 159. The map theme was not new to Civil War caricature, and it was a natural device to symbolize the tensions toward or away from the concept of union. It was used as early as 1860 in Lincoln's first quest for the presidency. The lithograph "Dividing the National Map" was probably drawn by F. Welcker. It showed Lincoln, Breckinridge, Bell, and Douglas either putting stress on the national map or trying to repair it. Bernard F. Reilly Jr., *American Political Prints, 1776–1876* (Boston: G. K. Hall, 1991), 436. Morgan's use of the map theme may have beeninfluenced by a Currier and Ives litho-

graph entitled *The True Issue; or, "That's What's the Matter"* (535). In that pro-democratic print, Lincoln and Jefferson Davis struggle over the "Map of the United States" as McClellan, the diplomatic mediator, tries to forcefully restrain the two leaders with his hands while exercising his persuasive powers with the exclamation "The Union must be preserved at all hazards!"

23. "Sporting Intelligence, Richmond (America) Meeting, Latest Betting—The Richmond Cup," *Comic News*, Sept. 24, 1864, 144; "America and Its Turmoils," ibid., Oct. 15, 1864, 167.

24. See J. G. Randall and Richard N. Current, *Lincoln the President: Last Full Measure* (Urbana: Univ. of Illinois Press, 1991), 71–72; "Advice Gratis," *Comic News*, Oct. 29, 1864, 189.

25. "Exit Abe," *Comic News*, Nov. 12, 1864, 209. By November 12, Lincoln had already been reelected, but the time lag between continents accounted for the belated prediction. "Mrs. North and Her Attorney," *Punch*, Sept. 24, 1864, 127.

26. "The Vampire," *Comic News*, Nov. 26, 1864, 221.

27. "American Intelligence," ibid., Nov. 19, 1864, 207.

28. "The Northern Harmer," ibid., Dec. 6, 1864, 237.

29. "In for His Second Innings," ibid., Dec. 6, 1864, 240. This was not the first time Morgan used this image. Two years earlier, in *Fun* on October 11, 1862, he had drawn "The Real President of the U.S." relishing death and mayhem in "Go It, Ye Cripples!"

30. "Elegant American Extracts," *Comic News*, Dec. 6, 1864, 244.

31. See "The Bridge," Henry W. Longfellow, *Longfellow's Complete Poems* (Boston: Houghton Mifflin, 1908), 63.

32. "Elegant American Extracts," *Comic News*, Dec. 6, 1864, 244.

33. "Our Mutual Friend," ibid., Dec. 13, 1864, 251; "The Yankee Nero," ibid., Dec. 27, 1864, 277; Michael Davis, *The Image of Lincoln in the South* (Knoxville: Univ. of Tennessee Press, 1971); Neely, *Fate of Liberty*.

34. Patricia L. Faust, ed., *Encyclopedia of the Civil War* (New York: HarperPerennial, 1991), 264.

35. "The Wreck of the *Florida*," *Comic News*, Jan. 3, 1864, 7.

36. "A Valentine for Abe," ibid., Feb. 21, 1865, 75. For prints related to Lincoln's proposed hanging, see "The Fate of the Rail Splitter," October 1861, in Weitenkampf, *Political Caricature*, 130. See also, "Jeff Davis, on His Own Platform; or, The Last Act of Secession," "Jeff Davis on the Right Platform," and "The Last and Best Portrait of Jeff Davis," all in ibid., 129, 151.

37. "The Yankee Eagle and the Lion," *Comic News*, Mar. 7, 1865, 95.

38. "Abe's Future," *Bubble*, Mar. 28, 1865, 19.

39. "Britannia Sympathizes with Columbia," *Punch*, May 6, 1865, 183; "Attained," *Fun*, May 6, 1865, 75; "Emancipation," *Fun*, May 13, 1865, 85.

40. Matt Morgan, *The American War* (London: Chatto and Windus, 1874).

41. Omitted, for example, was "The Real President of the U.S.," in which the image of death and misery urges the continuation of annihilation and maiming: "Go It, Ye Cripples!" *Fun*, Oct. 11, 1862, 45. When the success of Lincoln's Emancipation Proclamation is acknowledged in the commentary of one cartoon, the meaning casts a more favorable interpretation on the image, "The Penny Jupiter," ibid., Oct. 18, 1862, 45. For Morgan's words, see *The American War*, commentary on concluding cartoon "Attained"; see also *Fun*, May 6, 1865, 75.

CHAPTER NINE

1. "Portraits of the Prominent Aspirants for the Presidency," *New York Illustrated News*, Feb. 27, 1864, 276.

2. "The Ghost," *Phunny Phellow*, Jan. 1864, 13.

3. "Well Now, I Never Thought You Would [Fill] That [Congressional] Chair," *Phunny Phellow*, Jan. 1863, 8; "Presidential Prospects," *Harper's Weekly*, Jan. 2, 1864, 2.

4. "Presidential Prospects," *Harper's Weekly*, Jan. 2, 1864, 5. In January, Lincoln conferred with political advisors about the probability that Gen. John C. Frémont or Secretary Chase might run on a third-party ticket. Miers and Powell, *Lincoln Day by Day*, 233. There was also considerable lobbying to secure U. S. Grant as a candidate for the presidency: "It is understood that theCongressional caucus of the opponents of the administration is considering the policy of ascertaining if General Grant will consent to stand as a candidate for the Presidency against Mr. Lincoln." "General Grant," *Harper's Weekly*, Feb. 20, 1864, 114.

5. "The Sowers," *Fun*, Oct. 17, 1863, 45.

6. "Abraham Caesar," *Frank Leslie's Budget of Fun*, Nov. 1863, 3.

7. "Perhaps Not," *Yankee Notions*, Nov. 1863, 337. As a rule, William Seward was not linked with the opposition, but his candidacy in 1860 and proven ability as secretary of state naturally generated its share of speculation.

8. "The Question," *Harper's Weekly*, Mar. 12, 1864, 162. One week earlier, an editorial carefully scrutinized and rebutted the arguments in the Pomeroy Circular. "The President," ibid., Mar. 5, 1864, 146.

9. "Government Stables," *Yankee Notions*, Mar. 1864, 81.

10. "National Joker," *Funniest of Phun*, June 1864, front page.

11. "Mr. Chase," *Harper's Weekly*, Mar. 26, 1864, 194. The words "mutual embarrassment" came from Lincoln's letter of acceptance of Chase's resignation. "To Salmon P. Chase," *Collected Works*, 7:419. For a thorough analysis of Chase's political aspiration for the presidency, see "Chase Is Willing," in Randall and Current, *Lincoln the President*, 88–110. See also, "Mike, Remove the Salmon," *Harper's Weekly*, July 16, 1864, 464.

12. "General Fremont," *Harper's Weekly*, Mar. 26, 1864, 194; "The National Convention," ibid., Apr. 9, 1864, 226.

13. "An Independent Landlord," *Merryman's Monthly*, Mar. 1864, 78.

14. "Presidential Cobblers and Wire-Pullers Measuring and Estimating Lincoln's Shoes," *New York Illustrated News*, Mar. 5, 1864, 297. In June 1864, Frank Bellew began editing the comic illustrated periodical *Funniest of Phun*. Corollary evidence that gives credence to Bellew's political apprehensions about Lincoln also derives from Bellew's negative critique of Lincoln's amnesty and reconstruction policy. "Mr. Lincoln's Great National Joke," ibid., Apr. 2, 1864, 364. That Frank Bellew also drew substantial favorable imagery of Lincoln is incontrovertible. In fact, whenFrémont dropped out of the race in September 1864, Bellew jumped on the Lincoln bandwagon for *Harper's Weekly*. In terms of political ideology, Lincoln was much closer to Frémont than General McClellan and the Peace Democrats, so Bellew was willing to support Lincoln, although he was ambivalent. There is, of course, another possibility. Bellew may have submerged his own political feelings for the opportunity to edit another magazine. However, if he was any kind of political animal, the incongruity of that choice militates against this explanation.

15. "The Rival Bill Posters," *Comic Monthly*, Apr. 1864, 26–27.

16. "What a Good Old Gentleman Said to His Faithful Butler," *Merryman's Monthly*, Apr. 1864, 97 (front page).

17. "Old Abe's Prophecy About the Next Presidency," *Nick Nax*, Apr. 1864, 367.

18. "One of Old Abe's Best," ibid., May 1864, 24. For an evaluation of the credibility of such stories attributed to Lincoln, see P. M. Zall, ed., *Abe Lincoln Laughing* (Knoxville: Univ. of Tennessee Press, 1995).

19. "May the Best Man Win!" *Phunny Phellow*, Apr. 1864, 8–9.

20. "Old and New Copperheads," *Harper's Weekly*, Apr. 16, 1864, 243; "The Spirit of the Campaign," ibid., Apr. 30, 1864, 274.

21. "The Bayonet and the Ballot," *Frank Leslie's Budget of Fun*, May 1864, 10.

22. "Humiliating, But What He Must Come to at Last," *Yankee Notions*, May 1864, front page.

23. "The Next Presidency—A Marvelous Prophecy," ibid., May 1864, 145.

24. "The Cake [Is] in Danger," *Frank Leslie's Budget of Fun*, July 1864. Humors of War, folder 1, AAS. Also included in the Nineteenth-Century Political Cartoon Scrapbook.

25. *New York Illustrierte Zeitung*, May 1864, 424–25; "The Journalistic Barnum with His Great Blowing Elephant," *Funni-*

est of *Phun*, June 1864, 8–9. This illustration may also have appeared in the *New York Illustrated News*, but the file I saw for May was incomplete.

26. "J. G. B. Or a Contented Politician Illustrated," *Funniest of Phun*, June 1864, 16.

27. "Union for Union," *Harper's Weekly*, May 7, 1864, 290.

28. Ibid.

29. Ibid.; "To a Jackson Democrat," ibid., May 21, 1864, 322.

30. "House-Clearing at Washington," *Frank Leslie's Budget of Fun*, June 1864, 8–9; "S——d, the Bootblack, Gives an Opinion," *Phunny Phellow*, June 1864, 4.

31. "The Hardest Shell Yet," *Frank Leslie's Illustrated Newspaper*, July 2, 1864, 240. The same illustration appeared in *Frank Leslie's Budget of Fun* in the July or August issue. Separate copies of the cartoon are identified as July and August 1864, respectively, in Humors of War, folder 1, AAS.

32. "The Baltimore Convention," *Harper's Weekly*, June 11, 1864, 370.

33. "President Lincoln and His Secretaries," ibid., 373; "The Latest Portrait of the President," ibid., 370. For circulation figures of *Harper's Weekly* during the Civil War, see Mott, *A History of American Magazines*, 2: 475–76.

34. "The Latest Portrait of the President, *Harper's Weekly*, June 11, 1864, 370.

35. *Collected Works*, 4:531; *Frank Leslie's Illustrated Newspaper*, Oct. 26, 1861, 368.

36. "The Cleveland Convention," *Harper's Weekly*, June 18, 1864, 386; "Just So," ibid., June 18, 1864, 400.

37. Three editorials on the current political situation all expressed concern: "The Union Nominations," "Fremont," and "Political Epithets," *Harper's Weekly*, June 25, 1864, 402. See also "The Chicago Convention," ibid., July 2, 1864, 418.

38. "That's What's the Trouble with John C.," ibid., July 2, 1864, 432.

39. Some Republicans, like Horace Greeley, also wanted a more vigorous peace policy, and allies of General Frémont criticized Lincoln for the suppression of civil liberties.

40. *Funniest of Phun* did not promote Frémont over Lincoln until its July issue. The *New York Illustrated News* endorsed Frémont's candidacy toward the end of June.

41. "Reply to Delegation from the National Union League," *Collected Works*, 7:384.

42. "Old Abe's Last Joke," *New York Illustrated News*, June 25, 1864, 560. After Frémont's nomination, virtually all the cartoons against Lincoln on Frémont's behalf were unsigned in both the *New York Illustrated News* and *Funniest of Phun*. It is probable that Frank Bellew was responsible for most of these images.

43. "Political Expediency," ibid., July 2, 1864, 562. The author has not been able to identify the specific editorial from which this quotation was taken. "Proclamation Concerning Reconstruction," *Collected Works*, 7:433.

44. "A Severe Task," *New York Illustrated News*, June 25, 1864, 560. For Seward's straightforward explanation to the Senate, see "To the Senate," *Collected Works*, 7:370.

45. "The Popular Prejudice and Judicial Blindness of the People on the U.S. Constitution, or, the Constitution as People Have Been Accustomed to See It," *New York Illustrated News*, July 2, 1864, 569.

46. "The Position of the 'Radical Democracy,'" *Harper's Weekly*, July 23, 1864, 466. Although this list of accomplishments was substantially correct, black soldiers did not receive wages equal to those of their white counterparts.

47. "A Firework for the Fourth of July," *New York Illustrated News*, July 9, 1864, 584–85. One week later, the same illustration appeared in its sister magazine, the German version— *New York Illustrierte Zeitung*.

48. "Humble or Slavery Pie," *New York Illustrated News*, Aug. 6, 1864, 652.

49. "To You, Reader," *Funniest of Phun*, June 1864, 2.

50. "Leading, Following, Rebelling," ibid., July 1864, 8–9.

51. "Abraham the Last," ibid., Aug. 1864, front page. As noted earlier, it is probable that these unsigned cartoons were the work of Frank Bellew. On Seward, see "By the People, For the People: Lincoln in Graphic Art, 1860–1865," *Lincoln Lore* (Aug. 1980): 4.

52. "The Herod of the Nineteenth Century," *Funniest of Phun*, Sept. 1864, front page, 2.

53. Ibid., 12.

54. "The National Joker," ibid., 16; A Presidential Candidate Simmering Down," ibid., 16.

55. "The Position of the 'Radical Democracy,'" *Harper's Weekly*, July 23, 1864, 466.

56. "Abraham and Columbia," *Frank Leslie's Budget of Fun*, Sept. 1864, 7.

57. "The Wade and Davis Manifest," *Harper's Weekly*, Aug. 20, 1864, 530.

58. For a more complex, astute analysis of this historic transformation in American politics, see Randall and Current, *Lincoln the President*, 198–231.

CHAPTER TEN

1. "Memorandum Concerning His Probable Failure of Reelection," *Collected Works*, 7:514.

2. In *Funniest of Phun*, virile opposition to Lincoln among

illustrators continued into September 1864 and was contemplated for its October issue. "The Shoddy Lincolnites and Liberty Betrayers will get a scorching that will singe out all their Pin Feathers and knock away all their underpinning of base and hypocritical pretensions to serve the dear people with a vengeance. . . . So we say again, look out for the *Funniest* No. 5 in October." "Hurrah for the *Funniest* No. 5," *Funniest of Phun*, Sept. 1864, 16. However, Frémont withdrew from the campaign on Sept. 22, 1864, so *Funniest of Phun* revised its October issue, and editor Frank Bellew shifted his loyalty in cartoon content to Lincoln. Even so, *Funniest of Phun* was more anti-McClellan than pro-Lincoln; because there was no Radical Republican candidate to support, the periodical had no other choice. For an example of anti-McClellan imagery, see "The Sham Democracy and their Ambiguous Leader, Mac, in their great car juggernaut on their way to the infernal regions," *Funniest of Phun*, Sept. 1864, 8–9.

3. Although H. L. Stephens was one of the most able and prolific Lincoln cartoonists, he is deleted from this list because his major contribution to the legacy of political caricature occurred before 1864.

4. In the 1864 election, Thomas Nast's comic drawings of Lincoln appeared in *Phunny Phellow*.

5. "Don't You Wish You May Get It?" *Phunny Phellow*, May 1864, 8–9.

6. "An Old Story Newly Applied," *Harper's Weekly*, July 9, 1864, 448.

7. "The Chicago Convention," ibid., Sept. 3, 1864, 562. Two other editorials, "Compromise or War" and "Fine Feathers Do Not Make Fine Birds," reproved the Democrats for their allegedly unpatriotic stance. Ibid., 562–63.

8. Ibid., 572.

9. Ibid., 562; "Maj. Gen. George B. McClellan Whitewashing the Chicago Platform," *Phunny Phellow*, 1864, Nineteenth-Century Political Cartoon Scrapbook.

10. "The Chicago Convention," *Harper's Weekly*, Sept. 3, 1864, 573.

11. "The Three Voices," *Fun*, Sept. 24, 1864, 12.

12. "Mrs. North and Her Attorney," *Punch*, Sept. 24, 1864, 127. When the *Comic News* caricatured Lincoln as the devil, it affirmed the unanimous verdict of England's comic press that Lincoln must not be reelected. "Pull Devil—Pull Baker," *Comic News*, Oct. 8, 1864, 159. "The Presidential Campaign in America, Great McClellan meeting in Union Square," *Illustrated London News*, Oct. 1, 1864, 345. McClellan was also prominently featured two weeks later: "Presidential electioneering in N.Y. Torchlight Procession of the McClellan party," *Illustrated London News*, Oct. 15, 1864, 389. "Casual Conversations," *Fun*, Oct. 8, 1864, 39.

13. "Friends of the Enemy," *Harper's Weekly*, Sept. 10, 1864, 578–79. Richmond's *Whig* and *Examiner* also explicitly supported the Democratic Party. "The Chicago Convention," ibid., Sept. 10, 1864, 579.

14. "This Reminds Me of a Little Joke," ibid., Sept. 17, 1864, 608.

15. "The Political Blondin," *Frank Leslie's Budget of Fun*, Sept. 17, 1864, 8–9.

16. Ibid.

17. "Union for Victory, and Victory for Union," *Harper's Weekly*, Sept. 10, 1864, 578.

18. "The Effect of the News from Sherman," ibid., Sept. 17, 1864, 594.

19. "The Blessings of Victory," ibid., Sept. 24, 1864, 616–17.

20. "General Bombshells, the True Peace Candidate; or, the War Path the True One," *Frank Leslie's Budget of Fun*, Nov. 1864, 8–9. For the origin of this phrase, see Boyd B. Stutler, "We are Coming Father Abraham," *Lincoln Herald* 53.2 (Summer 1951): 2–13; "Lincoln's Peace Commissioners to Jeff," *Phunny Phellow*, Nov. 1864, front page.

21. "Rally, Round the Flag, Boys," *Harper's Weekly*, Oct. 1, 1864, 632–33.

22. "Rally, Round the Flag, Boys" ibid., Oct. 1, 1864, front page.

23. "Rally, Round the Flag, Boys," ibid., Oct. 1, 1864, 632–33.

24. "Campaign Pictures," ibid., Oct. 1, 1864, 627.

25. "Campaign Pictures," ibid., Oct. 8, 1864, 643.

26. "Comic Picture Gallery," *The Little Joker*, Oct. 1864, 2.

27. "How the Soldiers Vote," ibid., Oct. 1864, 3.

28. "Politics Makes Strange Bedfellows," *Harper's Weekly*, Sept. 24, 1864, 624; "Politics Makes Strange Bedfellows—The Sequel," ibid., Oct. 1, 1864, 640.

29. "Mighty Particular," *Frank Leslie's Illustrated Newspaper*, Oct. 1, 1864, 32.

30. "The Chicago Candidate," *Harper's Weekly*, Oct. 1, 1864, 626.

31. "The Presidential Race," *Comic Monthly*, Oct. 1864, 8–9; "Union Along the Whole Line," *Harper's Weekly*, Oct. 8, 1864, 642.

32. "Acrobatic Novelties," *Frank Leslie's Illustrated Newspaper*, Oct. 29, 1864, 96; "Marvelous Equestrian Performance on Two Animals," *Harper's Weekly*, Oct. 8, 1864, 656.

33. "The Chicago Platform," *Harper's Weekly*, Oct. 15, 1864, 664–65.

34. Ibid., 658.

35. "Major General Little Mac," *Frank Leslie's Illustrated Newspaper*, Oct. 22, 1864, 80.

36. "The Copperhead Plan for Subjugating the South," *Harper's Weekly*, Oct. 22, 1864, 688.

37. "The Forlorn Hope—The Ship Secession in the Breakers," ibid., Oct. 29, 1864, 697.

38. "The Wreck of Secession," ibid., Oct. 29, 1864, 691.

39. "On the Wrong Track, ibid., Oct. 29, 1864, 704; "Dangerous Traveling," *Merryman's Monthly*, Nov. 1864, 304–5.

40. "Abraham, Wait on this Gentleman to the Door," *Merryman's Monthly*, Nov. 1864, front page.

41. "A British Bantling," *Harper's Weekly*, Oct. 15, 1864, 672. The editorial staff of *Harper's Weekly* also discussed the stance of the *London Times*. "The British Lion Cheers for Chicago," *Harper's Weekly*, Oct. 15, 1864, 658.

42. "Hail to the Chief Who in Triumph Advances," *Frank Leslie's Illustrated Newspaper*, Nov. 12, 1864, 128; "Don't Swap Horses," *Harper's Weekly*, Nov. 12, 1864, 736.

43. "Exit Abe," *Comic News*, Nov. 12, 1864, 209; "The American Brothers," *Punch*, Nov. 5, 1864, 189.

44. "Our Campaign Biographies," *Frank Leslie's Budget of Fun*, Nov. 1864, 14.

45. Ibid.

46. "The issue of *Harper's [Weekly]* dated November 12th did not carry the election results as that number came from the press in advance of its date which was before election day." "The Presidential Election—1864," *Lincoln Lore* (Aug. 1972): 1.

47. "The Eighth of November," *Harper's Weekly*, Nov. 12, 1864, 722.

48. "Election Day," *Harper's Weekly*, Nov. 12, 1864, 723.

49. "How the Copperheads Obtain Their Votes," ibid., Nov. 12, 1864, 725.

50. "The Conspirators in Consultation," *Frank Leslie's Budget of Fun*, Nov. 1864. The cartoon is number 374 in the Nineteenth-Century Political Cartoon Scrapbook.

51. "Response to a Serenade," *Collected Works*, 8:96, 100–101.

52. "The Election," *Harper's Weekly*, Nov. 19, 1864, 738.

53. "The Presidential Election," *Frank Leslie's Illustrated Newspaper*, Nov. 26, 1864, 148.

54. "The Election," *Harper's Weekly*, Nov. 19, 1864, 738; "Abraham Lincoln," *Frank Leslie's Illustrated Newspaper*, Feb. 25, 1865, front page.

55. "Abraham Lincoln," *ibid.*

56. "Long Abraham Lincoln a Little Longer," *Harper's Weekly*, Nov. 26, 1864, 768.

57. "The Two Platforms—Columbia Makes Her Choice," *Frank Leslie's Budget of Fun*, Dec. 1864, front page.

58. "A Parcel for the White House; or, the Presidential Vote," ibid., Dec. 1864, 8. Also on the same page, Uncle Sam has painted a bearded, aged McClellan "in the role of President" of the United States. When John Bull asks Uncle Sam "haven't you made him too old?" Uncle Sam wryly replies, "Not a bit. He'll be fully as old as that before he is President!"

59. "The Giant Majority Carrying Abe Lincoln Safely through Troubled Waters to the White House," ibid., Dec. 1864, 9. The dual contribution of battlefield prowess and the soldiers' vote was not lost on Lincoln. To Henry W. Hoffman, Lincoln confided that from one group of soldiers in Maryland he had received 1,160 ballots from a total of 1,428. In response to this news, Hoffman telegraphed the president with this astute observation: "The soldiers are quite as dangerous to Rebels in the rear as in front." "To Henry W. Hoffman," *Collected Works*, 8:100.

60. "Poor McRobinson Crusoe!" *Yankee Notions*, Dec. 1864, front page.

61. "The Good Uncle and the Naughty Boy," *Frank Leslie's Budget of Fun*, Dec. 1864, 16.

62. "The Winter of Their Discontent," ibid., Jan. 1865, 16.

63. "Jeff Davis's November Nightmare," *Frank Leslie's Illustrated Newspaper*, Dec. 3, 1864, 176.

64. "The Peace-War Eagle Brought to Grief," *Phunny Phellow*, Dec. 1864. The cartoon can be found in the Nineteenth-Century Political Cartoon Scrapbook.

65. "Election Day," *Phunny Phellow*, probably Dec. 1864. The cartoon can be found in the Nineteenth-Century Political Cartoon Scrapbook. For Nast and his artistic colleagues, the satisfaction of contributing to the successful campaign of the president of the United States was a heady experience, but Nast enjoyed a singular professional distinction. In December, George W. Curtis of *Harper's Weekly*, a prominent member of the National Union convention, personally introduced Nast to the man he helped elect: Abraham Lincoln. Miers and Powell, *Lincoln Day by Day*, 301.

66. "The Gloved Hero of Emancipation Waiting for the Indispensable Necessity," *Funniest of Phun*, Feb. 1865, 8–9.

67. "In for His Second Innings," *Comic News*, Dec. 6, 1864, 240; "The Federal Phfinix," *Punch*, Dec. 3, 1864, 229.

68. "The Federal Phfinix," ibid., Dec. 3, 1864, 228.

69. "Lincoln's Re-Election," *Fun*, Dec. 3, 1864, 120.

CHAPTER ELEVEN

1. "United We Stand," *Harper's Weekly*, Dec. 3, 1864, 776–77.

2. "Christmas in Dixie," *Merryman's Monthly*, Dec. 1864, 336–37.

3. "Santa Claus Lincoln," *Comic Monthly* (probable source), Dec. 1864 (probable date). Because Frank Beard drew the major cartoons for *Comic Monthly*, it is the logical source. The

Christmas context suggests December 1864 as the date. The print is in possession of the Lincoln Museum, Fort Wayne, Indiana, and bears the number 432.

4. "Lincoln's Christmas Box to Jeff Davis," *Phunny Phellow* (probable source), Dec. 1864 (probable date). The print is number 361 in the Nineteenth-Century Political Cartoon Scrapbook.

5. "North and South," *Frank Leslie's Illustrated Newspaper*, Dec. 24, 1864, 221.

6. "The Union Christmas Dinner," *Harper's Weekly*, Dec. 31, 1864, 840–41.

7. "Our Mutual Friend," *Comic News*, Dec. 13, 1864, 251; "To William S. Rosecrans," *Collected Works*, 8:116.

8. "Peace," *Harper's Weekly*, Dec. 3, 1864, 770.

9. Ibid.

10. "A Self-Appointed Envoy," *Frank Leslie's Illustrated Newspaper*, Jan. 21, 1865, 288.

11. "This Is the Only Net to Catch That Bird With," *Comic Monthly* (probable source), Feb. 1865 (probable date). The print is located in the McLellan Lincoln Collection of the Brown University Library.

12. "The Whirring of Doves," *Harper's Weekly*, Jan. 28, 1865, 50.

13. "Peace-Making," ibid., Feb. 4, 1865, 66. A similar anxious tone was conveyed in the following week's editorial. "Peace Again," ibid., Feb. 11, 1865, 82. "The Latest Aspect of the Peace Question," ibid., Feb. 11, 1865, 83.

14. "To the House of Representatives," *Collected Works*, 8:279.

15. "The Peace Commission," *Harper's Weekly*, Feb. 18, 1865, 112, 101. In the spirit of his earlier initiative to compensate slaveholders for emancipation, Lincoln proposed to offer the South one final incentive to end the war: generous payment for its slaves, contingent upon total submission to the Union. However, this proposal was unanimously disapproved by Lincoln's cabinet. See "To the Senate and House of Representatives," *Collected Works*, 8:260–61.

16. "The Peace Palaver and Its Result," *Frank Leslie's Illustrated Newspaper*, Feb. 25, 1865, 354. It is worthy to note that the main article in this issue (cited in the last chapter) thoroughly denigrated Lincoln's capacity for leadership. Ibid., 353–54.

17. "The President and His Critics," *Harper's Weekly*, Feb. 25, 1865, 114.

18. "Great Union Ball—An Invitation," *Frank Leslie's Budget of Fun*, Jan. 1865, 8–9.

19. "What's the Use of a Butler That Can't Open My Port?" ibid., Mar. 1865, 3; "General Butler," *Harper's Weekly*, Jan. 28, 1865, 50.

20. Randall and Current, *Lincoln the President*, 281–82.

21. "To the Yankee Braggarts," *Punch*, Jan. 21, 1865, 25.

22. "The Threatening Notice," ibid., Feb. 18, 1865, 67; "The Yankee Eagle and the Lion," *Comic News*, Mar. 7, 1865, 95.

23. "Old Mr. Secesh Prefers Annihilation to Salvation in the Union Boat," *Frank Leslie's Budget of Fun*, Mar. 1865, 9. William Newman also exploited this theme elsewhere. He proposed that Jefferson Davis would prefer to be a lackey to John Bull or Napoleon III than to reenter the Union with the rebellious states. "A Dependence upon England and France," *Frank Leslie's Illustrated Newspaper*, Feb. 18, 1865, 352.

24. "The Grand Peace Overture to 'Our Wayward Sisters,'" *Phunny Phellow*, Mar. 1865, 16; "The National Philharmonic Society," *Yankee Notions*, Mar. 1865, 80–81.

25. "The Narrow Path," *Comic Monthly*, Mar. 1865, 8–9.

26. Although this tribute was published after Lincoln's inauguration, it is obvious from the language that the editorial was written beforehand. "The Fourth of March," *Harper's Weekly*, Mar. 11, 1865, 146.

27. "President Lincoln Taking the Oath at His Second Inauguration," ibid., Mar. 18, 1865, 161 (front page); "Second Inaugural Address," *Collected Works*, 8:333.

28. For grand prints of the inauguration, see "Second Inauguration as President of the United States," *Frank Leslie's Illustrated Newspaper*, Mar. 18, 1865, 408–9; "President Lincoln's Inauguration at the Capitol," *Harper's Weekly*, Mar. 18, 1865, 168–69.

29. "A Diplomatic Reunion at Washington," *Nick Nax*, Apr. 1865, 190; "The Tallest Ruler on the Globe," *Frank Leslie's Budget of Fun*, Apr. 1865.

30. "Amnesty," *Harper's Weekly*, Apr. 8, 1865, 210.

31. For representations in graphic form of Lincoln's entry into Richmond, see "President Lincoln Riding through Richmond, April 4, Amid the Enthusiastic Cheers of the Inhabitants," *Frank Leslie's Illustrated Newspaper*, Apr. 22, 1865, 65. In the caption, the special artist who created the print is identified as Joseph Becker, but the print is signed "AB," Albert Berghaus. Thomas Nast's version appeared much later. "President Lincoln Entering Richmond," *Harper's Weekly*, Feb. 24, 1866, 120–21.

32. "Last Public Address," *Collected Works*, 8:399–400.

33. "From Our Special War Correspondent," *Harper's Weekly*, Apr. 15, 1865, 240.

34. "Abraham Lincoln," ibid., Apr. 22, 1865, 243.

35. "Scene at the Death-Bed of the President," *National Police Gazette*, Apr. 22, 1865, front page; "Assassination of President Lincoln," ibid., Apr. 22, 1865, page unknown. The following week the *National Police Gazette*'s artist Risdon added one more scene to illustrate conveyance of the president from Ford's Theater to the Peterson House. "Conveying the President," ibid., Apr. 29, 1865, page unknown. These prints are in Special

Collections at the University of Chicago's Regenstein Library. Because this study focuses exclusively on Lincoln's life, it ignores, for the most part, images of his death and funeral.

36. "Attained," *Fun*, May 6, 1865, 75; "Britannia Sympathizes with Columbia," *Punch*, May 6, 1865, 183.

37. "Abraham Lincoln," *Punch*, May 6, 1865, 182.

38. These verses represent just a sample of the complete poetic tribute. Parenthetically, Lincoln accomplished in death what he could not do in life. His passing temporarily created a stronger bond between the Old and New Worlds.

39. For a comparison of the *Harper's Weekly* eulogy, see "Abraham Lincoln," *Harper's Weekly*, Apr. 29, 1865, 258–59. Edmund C. Stedman, "Abraham Lincoln," *Frank Leslie's Illustrated Newspaper*, Apr. 29, 1865, 81–82.

40. "We Mourn Our Country's Loss," *Phunny Phellow*, June 1865, 8–9; "Our Country Mourns Her Favorite Son," *Yankee Notions*, June 1865, 177. The *Yankee Notions* artistic tribute was drawn by J. H. Howard. In August, one final-belated print honored Lincoln. "The Martyr President," ibid., Aug. 1865, 247.

41. "After the War," *Frank Leslie's Budget of Fun*, May 1865, 8–9.

42. "The Proposed 'First Step to Peace,'" *Frank Leslie's Budget of Fun*, May 1865, 16.

43. "The Truest Mourners," *Harper's Weekly*, May 6, 1865, 274.

44. "Address Delivered at the Dedication of the Cemetery at Gettysburg," *Collected Works*, 7:23.

Bibliographical Essay

This essay identifies the principal rare and traditional archival sources and holdings known and used by the author to extract and depict Lincoln's image in periodicals. For this research, the word "rare" has two connotations: rarely used in Lincoln scholarship and generally less accessible than the traditional sources. Heretofore, the "rare" sources—including the *Comic Monthly, Comic News \ Bubble, Frank Leslie's Budget of Fun, Funniest of Phun, Illustrated London News, The Little Joker, Merryman's Monthly, Momus,* the *New York Illustrated News, Nick Nax, Phunny Phellow, Southern Illustrated News, Southern Punch,* and *Yankee Notions*—have never been fully exploited by visual Lincoln scholarship. Even the traditional sources, *Frank Leslie's Illustrated Newspaper, Harper's Weekly, Punch, Fun,* and *Vanity Fair,* though generally far more accessible in microfilm or print in sundry archives, have not been subjected to a systematic and rigorous examination in relationship to their periodical contemporaries. These rare and traditional magazines constitute the central focus of the essay.

To be sure, there are other illustrated periodicals that received relatively short shrift in this research. For example, illustrated periodicals for which I found no Lincoln illustrations (*Jolly Joker*), could not locate (the *Raleigh Illustrated Mercury* and the *Illustrated Mercury*), were characterized by insignificant visual images (*Bugle Horn of Liberty*), or had only an isolated illustration (*Frank Leslie's Chimney Corner*), or publications with duplicate illustrations translated into a second language (*New York Illustrierte Zeitung*) or just a few illustrations of the assassination (*New York Police Gazette*) are not treated in this essay (though a few of these magazines were cited in the text). They simply failed to meet the litmus test of significance.

Although research at major Lincoln collections such as the Library of Congress, University of Chicago, Indiana University, The Lincoln Museum at Fort Wayne, the Illinois State Historical Society, Brown University, the Lincoln Memorial University, and the Huntington Library were beneficial, I did not assume that these fine archives necessarily housed the primary sources for the research. Instead, Frank L. Mott's classic *A History of American Magazines* and David Sloane's (editor) *American Humor Magazines and Comic Periodicals* guided the investigation with the usual assistance of the Union List of Serials. In addition, special rare periodical or cartoon collections were invaluable resources. For example, the Meine Collection in the rare book room at the University of Illinois at Urbana-Champaign, the Samuel B. Woodward and William L. Smith Collections at the American Antiquarian Society, the C. Fiske Harris Collection on the American Civil War and Slavery in Special Collections at the Providence Public Library, the Nineteenth-Century Political Cartoon Scrapbook in Special Collections at Gettysburg College, and the Richard Samuel West / Periodyssey private collection of political caricature were seminal tools in the discovery process. Finally, advertisements in *Frank Leslie's Illustrated Newspaper* provided crucial clues to the sources and dates of loose, unidentified cartoons from *Frank Leslie's Budget of Fun.* For example, an advertisement in *Frank Leslie's Illustrated Newspaper* for April 13, 1861, disclosed the identity of five separate Lincoln cartoons for the April 15 issue of *Budget of Fun* that I discovered without the benefit of ever finding the original issue: "The 'Ins' and the 'Outs' are depicted to the life, and the hungry mice and the well fed ones are amusingly portrayed, from a private sketch by our special artist" [1."The 'Ins' and the 'Outs'"]; "The excellent manner in which Old Abe thanks his foreign voters is likewise drawn, and the nationalities are faithfully given" [2. "To the Victors Belong the Spoils"]; "Old Botherham's Honor at receiving a lucrative Foreign Appointment is an admirable illustration of his unselfish patriotism" [3. "Old Abe and His Electors"]; "Lincoln's juggling trick of swallowing his sword is another of the Budget hits" [4. "Great and Astonishing Trick of Old Abe, the Western Juggler"]; "But the grand cartoon is the budget's suggestion of how he should give up Fort Sumter" [5. "The Generous Rivals"]. A list of artists who drew for *Frank Leslie's Budget of Fun* and whose names appeared in *Frank Leslie's Illustrated Newspaper* advertisements also gave clues to the identity of certain artists for unsigned illustrations.

A caution is in order: this is not an exhaustive bibliography of holdings. That is, if a complete set of holdings was found at one or multiple institutions, the research did not pursue other leads for that publication. Also, where the holdings were incomplete, some overlap often existed among various repositories. Moreover, some materials were found in diverse collections at the same institution. For example, the American Antiquarian Society possessed, among other items, some whole issues from *Budget of Fun*, *Comic Monthly*, *Funniest of Phun*, and *Phunny Phellow*, but it also owned numerous separate illustrations from magazine sources, chiefly *Frank Leslie's Budget of Fun*, in the Samuel B. Woodward and William L. Smith Cartoon Collections. Parenthetically, my own modest Lincoln collection obviated the quest for certain magazine volumes, issues, and illustrations from *Comic Monthly*, *Frank Leslie's Budget of Fun*, *Frank Leslie's Illustrated Newspaper*, *Funniest of Phun*, *Harper's Weekly*, *Illustrated London News*, *New York Illustrated News*, *Phunny Phellow*, *Punch*, and *Vanity Fair*.

One major potential heuristic benefit of this essay is to encourage collectors, scholars, print and ephemera dealers, and institutional archives to provide information that might fill in gaps in this research. To the extent that missing pieces from the puzzle are found, a more vivid portrait of Lincoln and his era are bound to emerge. In addition, this essay and research offers another set of tools to explore several other veins of Civil War iconography that await innovative scholarship. This includes a candid evaluation of the questionable scholarly thesis that Lincoln and Civil War caricature in America is badly flawed. In addition, research on specific rare periodicals may illuminate media history, the political climate, and the artists who plied their craft. For example, comprehensive studies that depend on these esoteric sources are needed for the caricature of Frank Bellew, Frank Beard, W. H. Davenport, J. H. Howard, John McLenan, E. F. Mullen, Thomas Nast, William Newman, Will-iam North, O. Morse, H. L. Stephens, and others. Furthermore, there is a genuine need for research to identify the artists for a legion of unsigned prints on stylistic or other subtle grounds. This may require a team of experts, but the challenge begs an astute scholarly response.

To identify the primary source material, this essay notes the origin and periodicity of the periodicals (e.g., daily, weekly, monthly, bimonthly) of publication; the volumes, numbers, and/or years of publication; the temporal duration of the publication; and the completeness of the file for the Lincoln era under investigation (especially May 1860–May 1865). If the file is incomplete, the essay delineates what issues, in whole or in part, are missing or at least unknown to the author, identifies (where possible) a few representative artists who illustrated Lincoln in the publication, and spells out the archival sources consulted. The designation "missing" denotes that the author could not find any remnant of the issue. Even if an isolated print from an issue survives, the issue, to that extent, is considered "known." Whenever a loose print cannot be definitely confirmed as to date, source, or both, but there are plausible reasons for tentatively linking it to a particular source and/or date on other grounds (e.g., context, process of elimination, penciled date on print), the basis for the plausible information is cited. Because dates penciled on prints have not always been found to be reliable, further confirmation has always been sought. Of course, when context, process of elimination, and penciled date converge, the plausibility increases. Sometimes the identification of an artist is also based on circumstantial evidence. In such cases, I have tried to specify the rationale. Only artists whose signed or, in some instances, unsigned Lincoln work was considered "incontrovertible" are listed among the representative artists for a specific periodical. In a few cases, Richard Samuel West, a collector, dealer (Periodyssey), scholar, and expert on antiquarian periodicals, confirmed that no Lincoln content existed for a specific issue that I had not seen. Those issues were no longer considered missing.

PERIODICALS

Comic Monthly

New York, monthly; vols. 1–23, 1859–81; incomplete. Representative Lincoln artists: Frank Beard, Frank Bellew, W. H. Davenport, J. H. Howard.

Missing: Aug. 1861; Jan. 1863; May 1863; Oct. 1863; Dec. 1863; Jan.–Mar. 1864; May–June 1864; July–Sept. 1864 (a plausible but unconfirmed print for August is cited in the volume); Nov.–Dec.

1864 (a plausible but unconfirmed print for December is cited in the volume); Jan. 1865.

Sources Consulted: American Antiquarian Society, Worcester, Massachusetts; Author's Collection, Orem, Utah; Special Collections, Gettysburg College, Gettysburg, Pennsylvania; Library of Congress, Washington, D.C.; New-York Historical Society, New York City; New York Public Library, New York City; Special Collections, Providence Public Library, Providence, Rhode Island; Special Collections, University of Chicago, Chicago, Illinois; Special Collections, University of Illinois, Urbana-Champaign; Richard Samuel West\Periodyssey Private Collection, Northampton, Massachusetts.

Comic News/Bubble

London, weekly; vols. 1–2, July 18, 1863–Mar. 28, 1865; complete. Representative Lincoln artists: Matt Morgan, William M'Connell.

Sources Consulted: Western Reserve Historical Society, Cleveland, Ohio; Brown University, Providence, Rhode Island, is also purported to have a set.

Frank Leslie's Budget of Fun

New York, monthly (plus ten additional semi-monthly issues published in 1860–61); nos. 1–243, Jan. 1859–June 1878; incomplete. Representative Lincoln artists: Frank Bellew, A. Crane, William Newman, William North, J. H. Howard, John McLenan, and H. L. Stephens.

Missing: Oct. 1, 1860 (a plausible but unconfirmed date for print cited in volume); Nov. 1, 1860 (a description of this issue appears in the advertisement section of *Frank Leslie's Illustrated Newspaper*); Dec. 1, 1860; May 15, 1861 (there is some ambiguity with regard to the May 1 and May 15 issues; the advertisement in *Frank Leslie's Illustrated Newspaper* for April 30, 1861 confirms the content for May 1, no. 37, *Frank Leslie's Budget of Fun*, but the same advertisement is virtually identical for no. 38); July 1861; Dec. 1861; Jan. 1862; July–Oct. 1862 (*Frank Leslie's Illustrated Newspaper* contains advertisements for the content of the September and October 1862 issues); Mar. 1863 (a plausible but unconfirmed date for two prints cited in volume); Apr. 1863; Feb. 1865.

Sources Consulted: American Antiquarian Society; Author's Collection; Special Collections, Brown University, Providence, Rhode Island; Special Collections, Buffalo and Erie County Library, Buffalo, New York; Illinois State Historical Society, Springfield; Library of Congress; New-York Historical Society; New York Public Library; Special Collections, Providence Public Library; Richard Samuel West\Periodyssey Private Collection; Special Collections, University of Chicago; Special Collections, University of Illinois.

Frank Leslie's Illustrated Newspaper

New York, weekly; Dec. 15, 1855–June 24, 1922; complete. Representative Lincoln artists: Frank Bellew, Albert Berghaus, J. H. Howard, Henry Lovie, John McLenan, William Newman.

Sources Consulted: American Antiquarian Society; Author's Collection; Harold B. Lee Library, Brigham Young University, Provo, Utah; Library of Congress; New York Public Library; University of Chicago Library.

Fun

London, weekly; vols. 1–8, Sept. 21, 1861–May 13, 1865; complete. Representative Lincoln artists: Matt Morgan, F. Wilfred Lawson

Sources Consulted: Harold B. Lee Library, Brigham Young University; Library of Congress; University of Minnesota, Minneapolis.

Funniest of Phun (also listed as *Funniest of Awl* and the *Phunniest Sort of Phun*)

New York, monthly or bimonthly; nos. 1–30, June 1864–May 1867 (Civil War–period issues are nos. 1–8 [June–Oct. 1864, nos. 1–5; Dec. 1864, no. 6; Feb. 1865, no. 7; Apr. 1865, no. 8]); incomplete. Representative Lincoln artist: Frank Bellew.

Missing: Dec. 1864; Apr. 1865.

Sources Consulted: American Antiquarian Society; Author's Collection; New-York Historical Society; Richard Samuel West/ Periodyssey Private Collection.

Harper's Weekly

New York, weekly; 1857–1916; complete. Representative Lincoln artists: Frank Bellew, H. D., J. D., Theodore R. Davis, Hamilton, J. H. Howard, Theodore Jones, John McLenan, Thomas Nast, M. Nevin, William Newman, H. L. Stephens, A. R. Waud

Sources Consulted: Author's Collection; Harold B. Lee Library, Brigham Young University.

Illustrated London News

London, weekly; 1842–, vols. 1+; complete. Representative Lincoln artists: F. V., C. D. Shanley of New York.

    Sources Consulted: Author's Collection; Library of Congress.

Little Joker

New York, monthly; vols. 1–2, nos. 1–24, Jan. 1863–Dec. 1864; incomplete. Representative Lincoln artist: Frank Bellew.

    Missing: Vol. 1, Jan.–Dec. 1863.

    Source Consulted: American Antiquarian Society.

Merryman's Monthly

New York, monthly; vols. 1–15, 1863–77; Civil War vols. 1–3, Apr. 1863–July 1865; incomplete. Representative Lincoln artists: Frank Beard, Frank Bellew, J. H. Howard, William Newman, H. L. Stephens.

    Missing: June 1863; June 1864.

    Sources Consulted: New-York Historical Society; New York Public Library.

Momus

New York, daily (irregular), 28 Apr.–24 May; weekly (overlapped daily edition, irregular), May 5–June 30, 1860 and July 21, 1860, nos. 1–10, vol. 1 (includes both daily and weekly editions); complete. Representative Lincoln artists: Frank Bellew, William North.

    Source Consulted: Library of Congress.

New York Illustrated News

New York, weekly; vols. 1–10, nos. 1–250, Nov. 19, 1859–Aug. 13, 1864; complete. Representative Lincoln artists: Frank Bellew, John P. Davis, A. Lumley, Thomas Nast, M. Nevin, C .C. Pyne, A. R. Waud.

    Sources Consulted: Author's Collection; the Lincoln Museum at Fort Wayne, Indiana; Newberry Library, Chicago; New York State Library, Albany; University of Chicago; Wisconsin Historical Society, Madison.

Nick Nax

New York, monthly; vols. 1–20, May 1856–Dec. 1875; incomplete. Representative Lincoln artists: Frank Bellew, W. H. Davenport.

    Missing: July–Sept. 1861; Jan.–Apr. 1862.

    Sources Consulted: American Antiquarian Society; Library of Congress; New-York Historical Society; New York Public Library; Richard Samuel West/Periodyssey Private Collection; Western Reserve Historical Society.

Phunny Phellow

New York, monthly; Oct. 1859–1876; incomplete. Representative Lincoln artists: Frank Bellew, T. Gunn, O. Morse, Thomas Nast, J. A. Read.

    Missing: Oct.–Nov. 1863; Feb.–Mar. 1864; July–Sept. 1864; Dec. 1864; Jan.–Feb. 1865 (a plausible but unconfirmed date for a print cited in the volume); Apr. 1865.

    Sources Consulted: American Antiquarian Society; Special Collections, Brown University; Special Collections, Library of Congress; New-York Historical Society; Special Collections, Providence Public Library; Special Collections, University of Chicago; Special Collections, University of Illinois.

Punch

London, weekly; vol. 1+, July 17, 1841–; Lincoln presidency era, vols. 38–48, Jan. 1860–June 3, 1865; complete. Representative Lincoln artist: John Tenniel.

    Sources Consulted: Author's Collection; Harold B. Lee Library, Brigham Young University.

Southern Illustrated News

Richmond, weekly; vols. 1–4, Sept. 13, 1862–Mar. 25, 1865? (vol. 1, nos. 1–42, Sept. 13, 1862–June 27, 1863; vol. 2, nos. 1–25, July 4, 1863–Dec. 26, 1863; vol. 3, nos. 1–30, Jan. 2, 1864–Oct. 29, 1864; vol. 4, at least numbers 1–9—[the last issue I have seen is no. 9, Mar. 25, 1865]); incomplete. Representative Lincoln artists: A. Hurdle; W. B. Campbell was listed as an engraver, and "Casey" also drew cartoons for the publication.

    Missing: At least, nos. 1–7, vol. 4, Nov. 1864–Feb. 1865.

    Sources Consulted: Boston Atheneum, Boston, Massachusetts; Huntington Library, San Marino, California; Library of Congress; Western Reserve Historical Society.

Southern Punch

Richmond, weekly; vols. 1–3, 15 Aug. 1863–early 1865 (vol. 1, nos. 1–25, Aug. 15, 1863–Feb. 6, 1864; vol. 2, nos. 1–25, Feb. 13, 1864–Oct. 2, 1864; vol. 3, at least numbers 1–9 [nos. 1–7 missing; no. 8, Mar. 13, 1865; no. 9, Mar. 27, 1865]); incomplete. Representative Lincoln artists: W. B. Campbell, Van.

Missing: At least nos. 1–7, vol. 3, Oct. 9, 1864–end of Feb. 1865.

Sources Consulted: Boston Atheneum; Huntington Library; Library of Congress; University of Illinois.

Vanity Fair

New York, weekly (except for two monthly numbers, Jan. and Feb. 1863); vols. 1–7, Dec. 1859–July 4, 1863; complete. Representative Lincoln artists: J. H. Howard, J. McLenan, E. F. Mullen, H. L. Stephens.

Sources Consulted: Author's Collection; Harold B. Lee Library, Brigham Young University; Library of Congress.

Yankee Notions

New York, monthly; vols. 1–22, Jan. 1852–Dec. 1875; complete. Representative Lincoln artists: A. D. Coppin, W. H. Davenport, J. H. Howard, Thomas Worth.

Source Consulted: Library of Congress.

Index

"Great Original Wide-Awake, The" (*Budget of Fun*), 61, *62*

"Great Swimming Match . . . on the Fourth of November" (*Budget of Fun*), 46–47, *48*

"Great Union Ball—An Invitation" (*Budget of Fun*), *333*

Greeley, Horace: and 1860 election, 53, 55, 61; and 1864 campaign, 255; criticism of, 112–13, *113*, 146, 154–55; criticism of Lincoln by, 10–11, 148, 291; and divisiveness among Republicans, 36–40, 273; and emancipation, 154–55, 162–68, 176–77; influence on Lincoln, 65, 70–71, 74, 77, 85, 94, 106, 140–41, 166–67, 176–77; and peace, 22, 144, 220–22, 329–30

"Gulliver Abe, in the White House" (*Budget of Fun*), 77–79, *78*, 85

Gunn, Thomas Butler, 45

Halleck, Henry W., 28, 130–33, 139, 189

Halpine, Charles, 210

Hamlin, Hannibal, 71

Hampton Roads Peace Conference, 331–33

"Hard Case—Vallandigham's Reception, A" (*Budget of Fun*), 146, *147*

Harper's Weekly, 3–4, 25–26, 28, 30, 110, 142, 204, 210, 287, 360n48; and 1864 elections, 252, 254–55, 257, 272, 274, 309; on 1860 presidential campaign, 31, 33; as advocate for Lincoln, 5, 12, 112, 149, 168, 192, 268, 287, 289–90, 338–40; after Lincoln's assassination, 345–46, 348–49; and Copperheads, 146, 262, 342; on draft riots, 197–98; on emancipation, 153, 158, 162, 168–69, 177, 361n23; on Greeley, 112, 162; influence of, 2, 290, 307–8, 323; on Lincoln, 20–21, 210, 276, 351; on Lincoln as president-elect, 90–91, 95–96; on Lincoln's humor, 18, 130; Lincoln's image in, 10, 24; on Lincoln's reelection, 290, 310, 339; on McClellan, 114, 293–94, 300, 305; on military leaders, 216, 334; on peace, 291, 310, 328, 330–31

Hay, John, 270

"Herod of the Nineteenth Century, The" (*Funniest of Phun*), 280–82, *281*

"Hint to Father Abraham, A" (*Phunny Phellow*), 146–48, *148*

"His New Facial" (*New York Illustrated News*), 97

Holzer, Harold, 4

"Honest Abe and the Little Boy in Search of His Mother" (*Phunny Phellow*), 48–49, *49*

"Honest Old Abe Marching Forth to the White House" (*Wide Awake Pictorial*), 54

Hooker, Joseph, 133–34, 138, 140–41, 225

"House-Clearing at Washington" (*Budget of Fun*), *269*

"How Abe Lincoln Escaped the Fire-Eaters of the South" (*Budget of Fun*), 87, *90*

"How the Copperheads Obtain Their Votes" (*Harper's Weekly*), 308

Howard, J. H., 90, 144, 264–65; and 1864 election, 315, 323; caricatures by, 3, 6; positive images of Lincoln by, 149, 196; on presidential campaigns, 31, 53, 254

"Humane but Officious Hunter, A" (*Budget of Fun*), 158, *159*

"Humble or Slavery Pie" (*New York Illustrated News*), *277*

"Humiliating, but What He Must Come to at Last" (*Yankee Notions*), *264*, 264–65

Humor, Lincoln's, 16–20, 77, 95–96, 186, 261; appreciation of, 254, 352n10; criticism of, 130, 282–83, 352n12

"Humors of the Presidential Canvass, The" (*Comic Monthly*), 42, 42–43, 353n23

"Hungry Government School in Lincolniana" (*Southern Punch*), 355n9

Hunter, David, 15, 157–58, 183, 361n29

Hunter, R. M. T., 330

"Hurt You, Uncle Bill?" (*Budget of Fun*), 101, *102*

"I Wish I Was in Dixie" (*Southern Illustrated News*), *214*, 215

"Ice Party, or Letting Things Slide, An" (*Budget of Fun*), *132*

Icon, Lincoln as, 30

Illustrated London News, 5, 293, 305

Illustrated press, 11, 142–43, 146–48, 177, 292, 295, 353n7; emancipation in, 151–85; influence of, 193, 323; Lincoln in, 8, 23–30, 148–49, 214–15, 289–90, 299; on Lincoln's assassination, 345–46; Northern optimism in, 324–27; plagiarism among, 359n41; popularity of, 2–4, 353n1; *vs.* separately published prints, 299, 302, 351n6. *See also* Comic press; English press; News magazines; Union press; specific titles and topics

Illustrations: artistry of, 32, 265; of Lincoln, 85, 96, 345–46, 378n32; popularity of, 1–

2; prominence in magazines, 3, 31

"I'm Sorry to Have to Drop You, Sambo" (*Frank Leslie's Illustrated Newspaper*), *152*

"In for His Second Innings" (*Comic News*), 240, *241*, 319–20

Inaugurations, Lincoln's, 24–26, 96–97, 184–85, 335, 339–41

"Incidents in the Career of President Lincoln" (*Comic News*), 92–94, *94*

"Ingratitude of the Republic-ans, The" (*Budget of Fun*), 71, *72*

"'Ins' and the 'Outs,' The" (*Budget of Fun*), 74–75, *75*

"Inside Track, The" (*Vanity Fair*), 71, *73*, 85

Integrity: Chase's, 253–54; Lincoln's, 20, 101, 255, 271, 284; of Lincoln's cabinet, 75–76

Intervention, foreign, 124–25, 142–44, 199–200. *See also* England

Irish, the, 4, 196–97, 300

Jackson, Thomas J. "Stonewall," 28, 111, 120, 125, 186

Jaques, James F., 222

"Jeff Davis's November Nightmare" (*Frank Leslie's Illustrated Newspaper*), *318*, 318–19

John Bull, critical portrayals of, 27

"John Bull-ied!" (*Southern Illustrated News*), 206, *207*

Johnson, Andrew, 273

Johnston, Albert Sidney, 120

Joint Committee on the Conduct of the War, 28

Jones, Theodore, 303

Journal of Commerce, 153

"Journalistic Barnum with His Great Blowing Elephant, The" (*Funniest of Phun*), 266–68, *267*

Kearsarge, uss, 228–29

Laird shipyards, 206–9, 227

"Last Act of the Drama, The" (*Budget of Fun*), 117, *119*

"Last Call, The" (*Yankee Notions*), *199*

"Last Rail Split by 'Honest Old Abe,' The" (*Momus*), *35*, 35–36

"Last (White) Man" (*Comic News*), 232

"Late Triangular Duel, The" (*Vanity Fair*), 164–65

"Latest from America, The" (*Punch*), 120–24, *123*

From Rail-Splitter to Icon

was designed & composed in 12/15 Monotype Fournier

by Will Underwood at The Kent State University Press

on a Power Macintosh G3 using PageMaker;

printed by sheet-fed offset lithography on 70-pound Fortune

enamel matte stock (an acid-free paper), Smyth sewn in signatures,

cased in to 98-point binder's boards using Arrestox B cloth

and Multicolor endpapers, and wrapped with dust jackets

printed in three colors on 100-pound enamel gloss stock finished

with polypropylene matte film lamination

by Thomson-Shore, Inc.;

and published by

The Kent State University Press

KENT, OHIO 44242